Away From My Desk

Away From My Desk

A Round-the-World Detour From the Rat Race, the Tech Wreck, and the Traffic Jam of Life in America

Rif K. Haffar

with photographs by Tracy L. Cigarski

Ameera Publishing
Seattle, Washington, USA

Cover and interior design and layout by Lee Lewis, Words+Design, 888-883-8347

Fonts used: ITC Viner Hand, Adobe Garamond, Myriad

Ameera Publishing
P. O. Box 30161
Seattle, WA 98103-0161
info@ameerapublishing.com

Publisher's Cataloging-in-Publication Data

Haffar, Rif K.
    Away from my desk : a round-the-world detour from the
rat race, the tech wreck, and the traffic jam of life in
America / Rif K. Haffar
    p. cm.
    Includes bibliographical references and index.
    LCCN 2001119834
    ISBN 0-9715451-1-1
    ISBN 0-9715451-0-3 (hardcover)

    1. Haffar, Rif K.--Journeys. 2. Motorcycling.
3. Voyages around the world. I. Title.

G440.H34 2002   910.4'1
            QBI02-701118

■   dedication   ■

For my parents, without whom I would have been impossible

And for Tracy The Lionhearted

acknowledgements

I am grateful to and for my brother Omar, who is always there for me, and who helped in countless ways to make the trip and this book a reality.

Our families, in Pennsylvania, Colorado and Beirut, were champions of the adventure as well. They gave us moral and physical support when we needed it most.

We spent some of the finest moments on the road in the company of friends and relatives in faraway places. All were supremely hospitable. Others among our friends provided valuable advice and contacts. In particular the Bakrs in Provence; Phil Blanton and Susan Tone in Oregon; Danny da Cruz in London; Robin and John in California; the Ghazzawis in Switzerland; Gida and Fernando in Argentina; the Haffars in Oman; the Hibris and Janice Mugrditchian in Caracas; the Jabburs in New York; the Lees in Virginia; the Millses in Mallorca; the Tamers in Abu Dhabi and the Thekkethalas in India and New Jersey.

contents

introduction

Life was good.

I had a great job with a telecommunications company that was about to go public, an apartment in Manhattan, and a girlfriend willing to shuttle back and forth between New York and Washington DC. I was a hard-working corporate citizen during the week, but the weekends were a carefree succession of fun stuff. We went to Broadway shows; we motorcycled up and down the East Coast; we went to movies and good restaurants and theaters. We had it made.

Then everything changed.

The company hired a new CEO. He brought his own VP of Marketing with him, so I was given a nice severance package and asked to go away.

Three months later, Tracy and I find ourselves crouching in fresh mud behind a moss-covered Douglas fir, running low on ammo, wondering how much longer before this round of fighting ends. We're understandably anxious. The enemy has found and surrounded us. A move in any direction and we'll be hit. That right there is the magical magnetism of Paintball. It presents the thrill of battle without the real possibility of death. Pain maybe, death no. The stated object of the game is to capture the opposing team's flag. The real object is to shoot as many of the dirty rat bastards as possible. The weapons are gas-powered rifles that can hold two hundred paintballs at a time. A marble-sized plastic pellet filled with colored gel can get your attention when it slams into any part of your anatomy at 285 mph. And at this particular moment too many of these cruel projectiles scream past as we make ourselves small and hope for rescue. The players are as motley an assortment of yayhoos as you would want to come across. Several children, including my nephews Tarek and Malek, go fearlessly into the fray, scrambling from ditch to tree to burned-out 1978 Chevy truck. A few take far too much pleasure from the demise of an opponent, shrieking out blood-curdling epithets into the woods: "Weenie," "Four-Eyes," "Girly-Boy," as the casualty holds up his gun and shuffles ignominiously out of the battle enclosure. The resident mascot, a lumbering, overweight, phlegmatic Saint Bernard we call Heidi, watches with fat, sleepy eyes.

From the moment my job disappeared, I began planning for our unlikely sabbatical. I had always wanted to see the whole world and this seemed the time to do it. The details didn't much matter. Now, three months later, we're as ready as we're going to get. We've shipped our motorbike to Lisbon; we've been inoculated against everything; we've sold or given away all our stuff; and we have a very rough route planned. We're spending a final couple of days in Seattle with my brother Omar, making last-minute arrangements before flying to Portugal and kicking off a round-the-world motorcycle tour that we expect will take a year. This book is a diary account of the trip.

On the way home from Paintball, we take a windshield tour of Seattle. Capitol Hill has demographics that are in stark contrast to those in the woods. The sidewalks of Broadway are busy with translucently white-skinned, black-clad, pierced and tattooed, longhaired or skin-headed young people. They call them Goths, a reference to the ancient tribe of barbarians that started out on the banks of the Danube and drifted all the way to Spain, pillaging as it went. One guy, in black from head to toe, mousy limp hair down to his shoulder blades, strides in front of our car at a traffic light. A pentagram is tattooed on his scalp. Seattle is socially liberal; fertile ground for Goths and Punks and Neo-Nazis and Cross-Dressers and Survivalists and Born-Again Hippies and Bikers for Buddha. Name the fringe, you'll find it here. The city is also a major business center, home to giants like Boeing and Microsoft. It mixes demographics and hums with character. People come and go, shopping, eating, working, cultivating an edgy left-wing point of view. Seattle contains a grand array of Originals, Ones-of-a-Kind, and Just-Plain-Freaks. It's a good place from which to kick off a round-the-world tour. While very much an American city, it is also, like San Francisco and New York and Washington DC, an international city. Leaving from here, we'll be less likely to gasp and shield our eyes the first time we see a European.

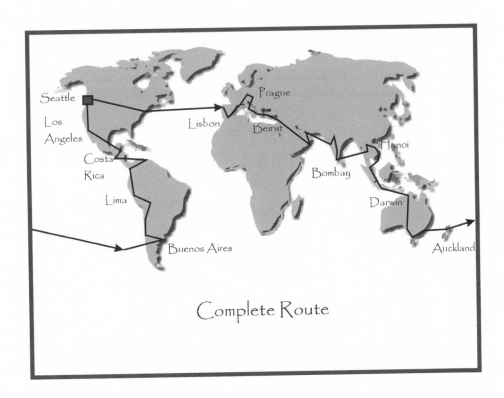

Complete Route

What childishness is it that while there's breath of life
in our bodies, we are determined to rush
to see the sun the other way around?

— Elizabeth Bishop (1911–1979), U.S. poet

■ europe ■

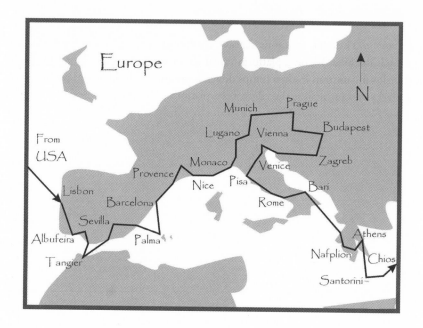

Europe's the mayonnaise, but America supplies the good old lobster.

— D. H. Lawrence (1885–1930), British author.

Lisbon, Portugal, September 8

Our motorbike is already here. We had shipped it from Virginia a couple of weeks ago and I spend our first morning in Lisbon at the airport, recovering it. The bike is brought out within twenty minutes of my paying the tax and signing the forms, and I am invited into the warehouse to ride it off the pallet. As far as I can tell there are six different forklifts operating in here. The drivers are all burly, tough guys with tattooed forearms and broken noses. They all speed and occasionally expectorate. These observations register ominously as I enter the big room and approach the bike. It's on a platform raised about a meter off the floor. One of the men helps me unstrap it, then jumps down, remounts his forklift, and pushes a narrow steel ramp up against the edge of the platform. He waves me down as he leans back in his seat and looks on bemusedly. The steel ramp is maybe twenty centimeters across, barely wide enough for the rear tire. It slopes away from the platform and extends nearly to the base of a concrete wall. There is just enough space between the end of the ramp and the wall for one forklift and a downed motorcyclist. The other drivers pay me no heed and fly past, coming and going, at great speed. So I think to myself: "I could die here." In the four or five meters I must navigate to get the bike on solid ground, I stand a good chance of falling off the ramp, running into the wall at the end of it, being broad-sided by a speeding forklift or skidding on the greasy warehouse floor. Any of these scenarios would be a lousy start to a round-the-world motorcycle journey and would guarantee a page in warehouseman folklore. I take my time, try to relax, and carefully ease the four hundred kilogram Honda ST1100 down the ramp, going fast enough to keep my balance and slow enough to stop in time when I reach the floor. And so, heart racing, I ride victoriously into the mid-morning Portuguese sunshine. Within five minutes I am in gridlock along with 1.5 million of the 1.6 million people who live in Lisbon. The remaining one hundred thousand are smoking in the lobby of our hotel.

■

If Barcelona had a kid brother who was shorter, uglier, less swift, and somewhat inattentive to matters of personal hygiene, that brother would be Lisbon. The city is similar to Barcelona not just in its layout, but also in its climate, culture and spirit. That's a very good thing. The backbone of Lisbon's center is the Avenida da Liberdad. In Barcelona, its equivalent is Las Ramblas. On either side of the Avenida, three quaint old neighborhoods and several pedestrian malls accommodate most of the city's tourist activity. These are the Alfama, the Bairro Alto, and the Baixa. They are the heart of Lisbon.

The Alfama is built on the hillsides surrounding the Castelo São Jorge. It is a confounding maze of narrow streets lined with wall-against-wall little houses. Doorways are often open to small crowded rooms in which families cook, or read, or sleep, or otherwise live life in these cramped but cozy spaces. Children play in the streets and on the endless steps that carve up the hillside. Bougainvilleas and grape vines shroud the whitewashed walls of many of the houses. Aromas come and go as you come and go. Sometimes that's a blessing.

Although you can walk up from the Baixa to the Castelo São Jorge, it's also possible to take a tram to the top of the hill. These electric conveyors of yesteryear break down regularly. We start to get on one just as the driver locks the brakes and jumps out to reengage the electrical contact which had slipped off the cable. Children of inattentive parentage ride these trams for free. They throw themselves at the back of the thing during the slow uphill slogs and grab onto anything they can grip. This could be and often is someone's conspiratorial arm. The police are never far from these budding criminals, however. We watch as one crisply uniformed Lisbon cop lectures two adolescent boys. They listen, eyes downcast, convincingly contrite—and then get back on the tail of the tram and go on to wherever they were going when they were apprehended.

The Alfama and the Baixa barrios are very much like the historic Gothic center in Barcelona. There's always a crowd in these places, so it's fun to hang around and people-watch. While we're at a café in the Baixa, two men approach at different times and offer to sell us drugs. We disregard the first and he moves on without a fuss. The second is very engaging and has a good sense of humor, so I ask if he has any Tylenol. He chuckles, shakes his head, and goes off to proposition other tourists.

The Bairro Alto (high quarter) faces the Alfama from the west hills across the Avenida da Liberdad. The better shops and cleaner restaurants are up here. We intend to find some *fado* to listen to. As we understand it, this is a bluesy song along the lines of flamenco but without the dancing, and darker, with considerably longer faces and intense pained grimaces. There has been much in the city's history to justify such somber art. It's been occupied at one time or another by every dominant European power. In 1521 the city suffered an earthquake that destroyed nearly two thousand houses and buildings. Then, in 1755, Lisbon was almost completely annihilated by another quake, followed by tidal waves in the Tagus River and a fire that burned for four days and leveled whatever had remained standing. Thirty thousand people died. Considering that the world's population has increased sixfold since then, that's equivalent to 180,000 today. Voltaire was so moved by this catastrophe that he wrote a long and deeply depressing poem about it: "Poem on the Lisbon Disaster." He, at the time, lived in Geneva. This earthquake was felt throughout Europe, and it's possible that he was quite literally moved. In any case, he argues in this work—and I simplify grotesquely—that life is a bitch. *Fado* makes that same point, but with guitar accompaniment.

Portuguese is ideally suited for *fado*. It's a Romance language, contains many Spanish words, but sounds Russian. There are so many *sh* (as in shrimp) and *g* (as in rouge) sounds that the overall effect is of someone speaking too soon after oral surgery. Everything gets much more complicated on account of the eleven distinct vowel sounds in the language. Each of these, to further gum matters up, can be passed through the nose. Now the overall effect is of recent oral surgery *and* a world-class sinus inflammation. Portuguese is not a musical language, but it's a passionate one. You could say that about the people as well. Your typical Lisboan is happy to be alive but all too aware of impending disaster. We keep this in mind as we contemplate riding our bike through town.

■

Motorcycling in Portugal is dodgy. We leave Lisbon in the middle of a busy Monday morning and the traffic in town is a churning mess of diesel and danger, but ours is the great satisfaction of knowing that we've successfully packed everything on the bike. It took jettisoning the Samsonite roller, the duffel bag, a couple of books, three shirts, and a complete First Gear rain suit. As we roll away from the Jorge V Hotel, a rich mixture of excitement and dread runs through us. We're adrenalized to the point of quivering. This is Day One. Can we do it? Can we go around the world on our motorbike? And for now, can we make it to the next light without becoming *fado* material?

It doesn't take long for us to get comfortable. The bike is overloaded but only feels that way when we're stopped. Once we reach the outskirts of Lisbon, we're on tree-lined country roads that undulate over and through lovely hills and fields. Traffic is tolerable and, for a few minutes at a time, entirely absent. The arched canopy of foliage overhead is like a cathedral vault.

Sintra was believed by many, including the late great Lord Byron–he did some of his writing here—to be one of the most beautiful places on earth. Mind you, this was back in 1808. Sintra is still beautiful, particularly in contrast to the urban clutter of Lisbon, but the adulation is somewhat overdone. The town itself is small, quaint, stuffed with souvenir shops and, this time of year, German and English tourists. People come to these hills for fresh air and pastoral escape. This is why Portuguese royalty had summer residences here. These are tourist attractions now and we follow the signs to the headliners: The Palacio da Pena and the Castelo dos Mouros, an eighth century Moorish castle. Castles like this one seem to crown every hillock in every town up and down

Palacio da Pena

the Iberian Peninsula. The Arabs built them during their five-hundred-year occupation. They always offer the best view of the area, as you might expect. This is the case here, and the view from Castelo dos Mouros is of red-roofed villages among the wooded hills below and, beyond them, of the sea. The Palacio da Pena, on the other hand, is another thing altogether. This monstrosity sits multi-turreted and gaudy on top of a rock plateau overlooking the green valleys surrounding Sintra. It is an exuberant pastiche of Renaissance, Baroque, Moorish and Gothic styles; something straight out of a fairytale in design no-nos. We are awed and amused in equal parts. The palace's last royal occupant was Queen Amelia, and the building has been left as it was in 1910. One shudders to think what more could have been done.

■

Passing through Lisbon on the way south is again painfully difficult. Traffic is just too hectic. Local drivers combine the temper of the Italians with the machismo of the Colombians. And that's just the women! The whole thing makes very little sense until you accept that there is a particular philosophy at work here: sympathetic fatalism. This is the notion that it's okay to travel via automobile or motorbike to the Next World, as long as you take another motorist with you.

All this changes when we reach the suburbs. The countryside between Lisbon and the Algarve is mostly good-looking farmland. They grow grain here, and raise cattle. We see cows and pigs and goats and smell them, too. It's all wonderfully fresh, in a dungy kind of way. The A2 is the main highway south, but it ends halfway to the Algarve and funnels us onto two-lane roads for the remainder of the journey. Every now and then a whitewashed village with red terra cotta roofs peeks at us from across the rolling hills. With about fifty kilometers left to reach the town of Albufeira, we stop at a café in the village of Santana da Serra, and order a plate of *chouricos*, Portuguese sausages. The young man who serves us our coffees—here they call them *bicas*—speaks English and congratulates us on our choice of Albufeira for an overnight stay. He says it's a great town, the best of the Algarve, with nice beaches and lots of nightclubs, but that we had better keep an eye on the motorbike. He says they steal them in these parts. We tell him that we have an alarm on the bike. He says, "Not enough." We tell him that we have a lockable cover for the bike. He chortles.

We arrive in Albufeira at dusk. The Atlantic is a welcome sight. It's much more humid here than inland, but there is a pleasant sea breeze to mitigate the heat. We park the bike alongside a curb, step off and kiss the ground. We've survived Day One. Three hundred and sixty-four or so to go.

The little, swarthy old lady is at her ground floor window, leaning on her folded arms, hanging well out over the sidewalk, head cocked in our direction. She stares at us, one eyebrow raised, a sneer holding up the left side of her mouth, making her mustache appear darker on that side. I'm intrigued and approach her cautiously. I say, "Boa noite" and "Inglês?" She says, "Não." I say, "Español?" She says, "Não." "Français?" "Não." Somehow, we establish that she has a room to rent.

Maria da Luz Calvario lives on the busiest and noisiest street in Albufeira, perhaps in the universe. Her own room is toward the back of the house. The one she shows us faces the front, not more than two meters from the street. She seems very concerned about our comfort, however, and repeatedly assures us that the area is very tranquil. The room is stuffier than the inside of a warm *chourico*. I twirl my finger at the ceiling and ask if there is a fan we could use. Maria ignores this, reaches up gently from her elevation of four-feet-no-inches, taps me lightly on the cheek and smiles. She then goes to the window and demonstrates how the shutters work. To communicate the promise of cooling breezes through the slats she leans her face against the blinds and blows. Maria then walks with us back to the bathroom. It's adjacent to the ridiculously overgrown garden. There is a canary in a rusty cage on the wall. The bathroom itself is a museum of fungal works-in-progress. It doesn't matter. By now Maria has spun us so thoroughly that the very best we can do is agree to stay only two nights.

Albufeira, which is Arabic for "little hamlet full of incontinent canines and apathetic owners," is widely considered the St. Tropez of the Algarve. As we walk through the little streets in the moonlight, battalions of Northern Caucasians occupy plastic café chairs, sipping tropical-looking multi-color drinks with paper parasols through meter-long straws. One street has chairs lined up on both sidewalks. It feels like some sort of initiation gauntlet as we march past the Long-Straw Sippers. These people are all here for the sun. It's Albufeira's chief attraction. On "Gauntlet" street, we could be looking into the windows of a rotisserie. Once-white humans repose pink and red. I want to shout out: "Stop! Get SPF 50!" but I know that they can't hear me above the pan-flute music coming from the Peruvians in the town square. This is the very same music that can be heard in any shopping mall in the world. I wasn't paying attention when Andean pan-flute bands came to be so popular but they are, and it's a good thing. They lend conviviality to a place, and Albufeira is convivial. Sun, sea, semi-nude tourists, umbrella drinks, and a pan-flute ensemble; how can you not feel convivial?

Back at Maria's, we are happy to see that the bike is unmolested. We had parked it on the sidewalk underneath the window of our room so I can keep an eye on it. It's a convenient spot. We just passed our luggage through the window. Maria did not give us a key to the house, but earlier demonstrated a highly sophisticated security entry protocol. It seems that only we know how to put our hand through the open window in the front door and pull back the latch. She assures us that this is possible only in the "good morning" and the "good afternoon," and that in the "good evening" she is *encerrada*, and nobody gets in. As we walk into the dark foyer, we glimpse her watching TV in the back room. Leaning a little forward in her chair she waves at us and smiles. I wonder if she owns a gun.

We shower somewhat reluctantly; uncertain whether we will end up cleaner than when we started. As we slink by her door our polite "Boa noite, Señora Maria," falls on hairy half-deaf ears. By now Maria, richer for our escudos, has long since started snoring rapaciously in her room.

Sevilla, Spain, September 13

As we ride into town at 1 p.m. on a Wednesday, we're struck by the heat, the pollution, the traffic and the clutter of this city on the Rio Guadalquivir. Magically, following an afternoon nap in a nice hotel, we catch ourselves rhapsodizing about it as we stroll through the center of the Old City. Sevilla is an almost impossibly charming place. Most of what's here to see is on the north bank of the river, so we hit-or-miss our way there with the help of several pedestrian good Samaritans and an occasional peek at a map. Just like everywhere else in Spain and Portugal, we find the average José Public to be friendly, eager to help, and genuinely interested in making a meaningful connection in the brief time needed to get us thoroughly disoriented.

Our hotel is called the Dona Maria and it is right across the square from the Sevilla Cathedral, the largest Gothic construction in the world. Its builders were explicit in hoping that "those who come after us will take us for madmen." Christopher Columbus' tomb is here, as are paintings by Murillo and El Greco. It's open a limited number of hours and charges admission. I guess when you build the world's largest anything, it takes a while to pay off the loans. There's a service going on in one of the chapels. Entry is blocked; it's a private event. We're tempted to crash the piety, but move on peacefully.

The area around the cathedral is dotted with beautiful Moorish palaces, ancient *murallas* (walls), gardens, and fountains. Now that we've showered and

Sevilla Palace Courtyard

stowed the bike, we're happy to hop into a buggy and let someone else do the driving. His name is Manuel. The other horse and buggy drivers call him Manolo, Manolito, or Gordito (little fat man). He has been driving a horse and buggy in Sevilla for *mucho tiempo*, and seems not especially interested in discussing it. The horse, Weewee (I swear), seems well taken care of and happy to be here. They carry us through the historic center with deft confidence. A few times I'm sure Manolito nods off, but Weewee knows the drill, and keeps up a steady stream of trivia about this *infante* or that *duque*. It may have been Manolo talking, but Weewee's lips were moving.

We take a stroll in the Barrio de Santa Cruz. It seems they have one of these in every cute Spanish city. We were bewitched by the one overlooking Alicante, and this *barrio* immediately behind the hotel is just as full of character. As we round the corner we find a modest restaurant, Meson Don Rodrigo, offering a complete dinner for 975 pesetas per person, or roughly five dollars. The place is clean and nicely decorated, the waiters are presentable and friendly, so we pop in to see what five bucks buys you in Andalusia. We get fresh bread; our choice of gazpacho or aspara-gus salad (the waiter calls it Spartacus salad); and our choice of paella, pork chop, or fish filet. After dinner we stroll through the *barrio* and are delighted with the place. The narrow cobbled streets are lit with elegant wrought-iron lamps and the glow from inside open doorways. We love it here. Tomorrow we hope to further test our impressions of Sevilla with a walk during daylight through the Parque Maria Luisa and another visit to Barrio Santa Cruz. We may visit Manuel and Weewee as well. Or we may Weewee first, then visit Manuel.

■

King Juan Carlos I's official Sevilla residence is Alcazár. Now in our second day here, we drift into a sort of sleepwalk through the place. You can only see so many paintings, so many gardens, so much stone filigreed as if it were wax. So we tear our-selves away from the gorgeous ceilings of the palace and walk west into the dustier part of the city, and through the popular (in the proletariat sense) flea market. People, many of whom look to be not from Spain, spread tattered sheets in the dirt and display for sale any trinket or piece of junk they can lay hands on, waiting for The Bigger Fool. One man offers a couple of mildewed prints in termite-riddled frames, a carburetor, several florist vases with the crushed white foam and bits of stem still in them, and a yellow women's suit. We hang around in places like this because we want to experience cultures fully, in their present, and not just through their historic monuments. It makes for fascinating contrasts: the old and the new; the sublime and the bizarre; the opulent and the cheap. It's contrapuntal tourism.

Veronica the travel agent could not possibly be more pleasant. She has a sweet little voice; she is accommodating and gentle; she is eager to help, but she has an urgency deficit. We sit in the two chairs across from her desk and eyeball every poster, every guide, every aspect of this cluttered office. The line behind us builds. The time goes. We pass from fidgety to drowsy. The sun sneaks through a gap between the wall and the shutters and cooks my left shoulder. Veronica will not be rushed. She cradles the phone in her neck for a while then deliberately removes it, shifts it to the other hand, and reinstalls it into the other side of her neck. By the time she has booked us on a ferry to Morocco, half the people waiting their turn are asleep. This is doing business in Spain. There is no point at all in rushing things. Especially in summer; especially in Andalusia.

Tangier, Morocco, September 16

This city is rough.

As we ride off the ferry into the port of Tangier, this is not yet evident. The Port Police and Customs guys are presentable, busy and cordial. They are surround-ed by a group of men whose sole function seems to be collecting gratuities from visitors in return for waving their arms about to attract official ambivalence. It's a hell of a way to make a living. The two guys who perform this essential service for Tracy and me wind up having an argument over the pesetas that I give to the one with the longer arms. At one point a well-dressed and articulate fellow asks how long we have been waiting. When I say "twenty minutes" he is unhappy and grabs an official who quickly produces our finished documents. *Le Responsable* explains that there has been an error in the paperwork and that this passage normally takes no longer than three to five minutes. I believe him. As unappetizing as Tangier turns out to be, the last thing it needs is to hassle arriving tourists who may, if they are not immediately repulsed by the utter degeneration of the place and turn right around and go home, actually stay and spend a couple of bucks.

Tangier has been beautiful. It is now filthy. The city is laid out like many Mediterranean neighbors. Large port, sandy crescent beach, hotels and apartment buildings all along the waterfront. Nearby hills, built up haphazardly. Balconies. Palm trees. Tiled corniche promenade. Street vendors. Something, though, has gone terribly wrong here. Everything is falling apart and showing signs of despair. Some hotels that command spectacular views of the sea are shut down, including Hotel Rif. Some of those that survive are pitiable. Where there is paint left in Tangier, it is peeling off. Roads are full of potholes and debris from dead machines and sheared-off traffic-policeman platforms. You can imagine a day, long ago, when white-gloved gendarmes directed traffic from these perches in the middle of intersections. All this does not make the place nearly as unpleasant as do the cosmopolitan characters prowling the sidewalks. We're panhandled in four languages before we've gone twenty meters from the hotel. The predominant feeling we have as we walk through the city is uneasiness.

Then there's Medina. In Arabic, *medina* means "city," or "town." These days the term is also used to refer to the original or ancient center of a city. The alleys winding through Tangier's *medina* can be quaint. On occasion, when the thicket of odors-at-large is free from the very "personal," you can detect and enjoy the passage of thyme, and mint, and hashish. And there is plenty of that latter weed for sale. Several men, all in the obligatory squat, propping up grimy walls, offer it to us on various occasions. These guys are the real bad news here. They're creepy evil men with bad intent, and there are enough of them about to scare us off.

There are traditional tourist traps as well as some dark, dank holes in the walls of Medina. One shop could not have been larger than a medium-sized fridge. Its doorway is low and just large enough to allow limbo-style entry and exit. The old crumpled bastard inside has not limboed in a very, very long time. It's possible he's been in there since before the walls were built around him. We stand there and wonder what exactly it is he sells. There are crusty sooty scales at the entrance of the hole, but no light inside, so we can barely make out the shape of the man. In contrast, we very occasionally pass doorways that open onto somewhat cluttered but clean and cozy homes. The people who live in these places have managed to hold off the creep of urban poverty and its attendant ugliness just at their doorstep.

Deep inside Medina, we stumble across Le Detroit. This is a restaurant near the gates of the ancient *casbah*, the Moorish fortress. One other couple is here. We sit across the room from them, on cushioned benches that run the length of the hall's walls. It's here, for the first time since arriving in Tangier, that we glimpse the city's erstwhile elegance. They give us *couscous* and sweet tea served hot in tall glasses stuffed with fresh mint leaves. Our host, a middle-aged woman, is trilingual and happy to talk to us about her city. She says it has declined and that Morocco is better represented by its southern cities, like Marrakech and Agadir. "The people of Tangier," she adds, "deserve better."

■

Our favorite acquaintances in Tangier are Antar and Shabshoub. They're rough, a bit unclean, and wholly uneducated, but as camels go, they're first-rate. As for manners, they have at least as much as a few choice Tangerines we had the displeasure of meeting in the street. Antar and Shabshoub, furthermore, never utter the words: "*Amigo, bienvenido, mercado?*" We each take a turn riding Antar. Shabshoub is only five months old and has not yet begun his professional career. Mustafa the camel-man leads Antar along, Tracy giggling uncontrollably on top. I walk alongside and ask how the tourism trade is. He takes a very deep breath and begins to say something but stops, cocks his head in a

Tracy on Antar

"what-can-you-do" sort of way and says, "*Inshallah,*" Arabic for "God willing."

Granada, Spain, September 17

If Tangier had not been such bad news, we may never have decided to go to Granada. Now here we are, on the ferry, crossing the Strait of Gibraltar two days earlier than planned, en route back to Spain. Tangier's skyline, dominated by the minaret of the Great Mosque of Mohammed V, is how we'd like to remember this city.

This ferry ride is a lot less fun than the one we took going south. For starters, the ship itself is one rogue wave from capsizing. On top of that, we are two hours late leaving Tangier. These two hours are not wasted idling in port. They are spent piling onto this rust-bucket a monumentally motley multitude of folks, hundreds of whom spend the two-and-a-half hour journey sitting on the floor of one of the car decks! We might well be unwitting witnesses to a massive white—well, beige—slavery operation. We sleep sitting up for an hour or so then walk out on deck and watch as Africa disappears and Europe closes in.

The E15 leads east from Algeciras. Along the way we stop in Marbella for a snack. This town has long been a destination resort for wealthy glitterati from around the world, but there is scandal and controversy underneath the glitz. The town's mayor, a colorful and meteoric guy, recently unveiled a bust of General Franco in the town hall. His opponents say that he runs the city much like Franco ran Spain from 1939 to 1975—dictatorially. He has been accused of sleight of hand involving vast sums of money, and of encouraging a certain class of tourist; numerous high-profile ex-strongmen or drug lords are reputed to hang out here. We keep our eyes peeled throughout lunch and later, as we stroll on the beach, but not a single nefarious kingpin of any kind shows up.

We circumnavigate Málaga and head north toward Loja, then east to Granada. As soon as we break away from the coastal highway, the air lightens and the landscape stretches out and the world is a simpler, gentler place. We see more Renaults and Peugeots. The BMWs stopped in Marbella. Olive trees dot much of the land here, arranged in rows like so many street-lamps. It's gusty on the highway so we get pushed around a little bit. The road rises and falls over small hills but climbs gradually until we're at seven hundred meters by the time we reach Granada. It's Sunday afternoon and no one's out. The streets are quiet. We've decided to rough it and stay at a hostel on this stop, so we follow the signs to Hostal Atenás in the center of town. There's no way to explain how this happens, but by the time we check into our very modest but reasonably clean and odor-free room, we agree that we're going to like Granada. It's likely we're a tiny bit on the rebound following Tangier, but even allowing for that, this place has it all. The weather is just about perfect: sunny, clear, dry, warm. The people are darn well-dressed, and all have bathed. The buildings have character. The rivers run, the poplars whisper everywhere, there are no mutilated beggars in the street, and most traffic lights turn green just as we come up to them.

Intoxicated with warm fuzziness, we shower, change, and head out to dinner. Hostal Atenás is on Gran Via de Colón, a busy central thoroughfare with shops and banks and restaurants. It's reminiscent of the Gran Via in Madrid but without the ETA (Basque Separatist Front) car bombs. We walk east toward the Plaza de Isabella Católica and the nearby Plaza Nueva. These two are the hubs of tourist activity, and from them you can get to any important point of interest on foot, within twenty minutes. Isabella Católica, incidentally, is one of the most remarkable monarchs to have ruled Spain. She and her husband, Ferdinand of Aragón, are credited with kicking off the Spanish Inquisition in 1478, winning Spain back from the Moors in 1492, and sending Christopher Columbus off to conquer the New World. These were not people on whose black list you wanted to be.

Just a few blocks from the hotel, and before we reach the squares, we find a delightful restaurant, the Via Colón (go figure). The mixed grill and salads are perfect and fortify us for a walk up the hill from Plaza Nueva along the Paséo del Tristes.

This cobbled path overlooks the banks of the little river which, on the free map I got from the Caixa Currency Exchange, has no name and disappears at Monument #33, the Iglesia de Santa Ana. On the other side of this river is La Alhambra, which of course means *The The Red One*, a reference to the red sandstone from which the place is built. The extra *the* in the previous sentence is not a typo. *Al* at the beginning of Spanish words is a vestige of Arabic, from when the Moors were in charge here. It means "the." I heard a man on the bus

Alhambra Courtyard

today refer to it as "the La Alhambra." *The The The* Red One. He was wearing a Dallas Cowboys cap and had possibly the largest feet I've ever seen, so I chose not to enlighten him.

Alhambra is made up of Alcazaba fortress, Generalife gardens, and the Nazaries palace. They are together the most extensive Moorish complex we've seen. The view from on top of this plateau is marvelous. We stand and look out over the fortifications of Torre de Vela and wonder what it must have been like to come up here on a clear day a few hundred years ago, adjust your turban, and scan the valley below and the Sierra Nevadas in the distance. Despite the light smog and the houses and the rooftop water cisterns and the solar panels and the laundry lines, it's beautiful to this day. The top attraction in Alhambra is the Palacio Nazaries. This voluptuous gem was the center of court life in the last hundred or so years of Arab influence in Spain, when they had been pushed back from Sevilla and Córdoba and retained only Granada and points south. Yusuf I and his son Mohammad V are credited with its construction and refinement. The reflecting pool in the Court of the Myrtles is said to have inspired the design of the Taj Mahal. It is built at an imperceptible incline so that the water very slightly overflows the north lip of the pool and covers the bases of the columns at that end. They then appear to be floating. The place is enchanting. You can just imagine how Boabdil, the palace's last sultan, must have felt as he signed the surrender papers. His mother, it is believed, was on hand and said: "Do not weep like a girl at losing something you couldn't defend like a man." Nice gal.

Albacete, Spain, September 19

We ride down from the hills of Granada into the plain of La Mancha, and the storm that we've outrun all day finally catches us. So we pull into the very first place offering shelter, Hostal Los Cazadores. The Hostal manager is a lanky man in his early sixties, and has a certain scruffiness about him that fishermen cannot avoid and poets cultivate. His name is Jesus and he receives us with characteristic Spanish warmth. We cannot help but think of Don Quixote, Cervantes' famous delusional knight, as Jesus waves his skinny arms about in grand welcome.

The Los Cazadores neighborhood is rural. There are no monuments here. There is no cathedral across the street, and no *piscineta* on the roof in which we can have a cooling swim. There is no tree-lined Avenida de la Constitución one block away and no Mediterranean coast. This is farming country; Albacete is where the trains stop to pick up grain and take it to Madrid and Barcelona. From our miniature aluminum window we can see two lethargic horses and an ostrich compound. The ostriches run around like ostriches with their heads cut off until the storm hits, and then they roll up into feather dusters and all fall down. Around us are dry, barren fields that must sometime grow grain. In the distance we can see the beautiful Sierra de Alcaraz (the cherries, in Arabic) and Sierra de Segura. These mountains kept our right for the two hundred kilometers between Ubeida and Albacete. Back inside room 106 we have just the basics. The bed is large enough for two non-operatic people. The dresser is made to look like it has drawers, but in fact is just a prop: nothing opens. There are two nightstands, one on each side of the bed. These have real drawers which fall out if extracted enough to actually put something in them. That's it. Everything is made of compressed wood, the kind that spontaneously combusts. Still, the room is moderately clean. There's even a cellophane sash on the commode, assuring us in florid Spanish that no one has used it for Number One or Number Two. There is also a TV in the room, and it's interactive. You can have a picture if you ingest the antenna and stand by the window. The room rate is four thousand pesetas, or just about twenty dollars. It'll do, and we pass out from the exertion of the day.

We descend at dinnertime; showered, fresh, and hungry. Jesus is expecting us. He has changed into a black waiter's coat and presents us with English menus. We order and sit back to watch a European Football League match between Barcelona and Manchester United. The three of us wait for the cook to do the magic that he does. There are no other guests in the "Capacidad 300" room, unless you count the flies. These also are behemoths, undoubtedly from the same litter as the ones in our room. A day of motorcycle riding can make a person stupid. I don't know how else to explain ordering hunter soup, artichoke hearts with diced Serrano ham, green salads, grilled veal steak and beef sirloin. We help all this down with bread, olive oil, vinegar, and bottled water. We avoid only the French fries. They look used.

The football match is interrupted by news of a car-bomb in San Sebastian. We would have loved to visit that city in the Northeast, and Pamplona, and even Bilbao, but there is too much stuff detonating in that neighborhood. Talks between the government and ETA just seem to aggravate the latter group. Regrettably, the more annoyed they get the more things go kablooey, so we've decided to wait for a ceasefire. What we have seen of Spain, however, has been remarkable and enjoyable. Roads in the country are generally in great condition. Even secondary roads are always paved, well-cambered, and clearly lined. Drivers, as long as you don't even think of getting in their way, are courteous and, darn it, good. They observe the rules of the road. Not so much the rules the state would like them to observe, but rules nonetheless. The most important of these is: If you're not the fastest, get the hell out of the way. As for natural beauty, this country is gifted and still somewhat undiscovered. The big cities are overrun, of course, as is a good deal of the coast, but the interior is mostly ignored, and not far from the busy tourist destinations are quiet low-profile towns that are at least as beautiful and charming. Albacete is not one of them.

Palma, Mallorca, September 20

By the time our ferry reaches Palma after an eight-hour ferry trip from Valencia, we feel like something the cat coughed up. It's all we can do to reach my sister's apartment in the hills overlooking the Mediterranean. We roll in, say hi, throw up, and go right to bed. We sleep through the day, then through the night, then through all of Thursday. On Friday morning we muster up the strength to go see the doctor, who confirms that we have been poisoned—we figure it's the hunter soup from Los Cazadores—and loads us up with drugs that will at least mitigate the symptoms. On Saturday we start to feel a bit better, and by Sunday we're very nearly back to normal. Thank God that we happened to be with family when this happened. Thank God also for Imodium.

Mallorca is in the Mediterranean, halfway between Barcelona and Algeria. It is the largest of the three Balearic islands but can still be crossed by car, from any coast to any coast, in no more than an hour. The climate is temperate. The terrain is richly varied. There are steep mountain ranges running the length of the West Coast and the northeast corner. There is farmland in the interior, coastal citrus groves, and volcanic outcrops at many of the capes, most notably Formentor in the North. Bougainvillea and wisteria and jasmine grow everywhere. Palma is the only real city here, but the island is widely populated and it's fun to drive around and explore the many quaint towns on and off the coast. The beaches run the gamut of sandy, rocky, pebbly, and are generally nipply, clean and safe. The island's road system is very well developed, so getting around is no problem unless it's during a Europe-wide petrol crisis such as we're enjoying at the moment. Castillos abound, as do magnificent modern villas built by the low-profile filthy rich.

There is a rustic *barrio antiguo* in Palma, which morphs into a trendy entertainment district after-hours. It's quite safe, even if you can buy recreational drugs here in several languages. Natty cosmopolitan people can be seen in the alleys through the dinner hour until midnight or so, after which the neighborhood is given up to the less genteel elements. During the day, Palma is a hive of suicidal mopedists criss-crossing through traffic en route to real jobs. Business happens. It's a commercial center with a busy port and airport. The locals accept the perennial tourist onslaught with grace and profit. Mallorca is a continent squeezed onto a rock in the sea, and offers almost everything you could possibly want. Perhaps the ideal place to live if you can handle rock fever. My sister Dana, her husband David and their kids moved here a couple of years ago. Now I can be a good brother and uncle by spending time on a Mediterranean island. Tracy and I have been looking forward to this part of our trip and we set aside a week for the Palma stay. We spend most of it in bed.

Montpellier, France, September 28

There are moments in life that cry out for metaphor. Imagine being a member of the French Resistance during World War Two. You're nabbed by the Germans. Soon your goose will be cooked, but for now they drag you to a nearby farmhouse for grilling. You're seated in a rickety wooden chair with hands tied behind your back. There is a solitary naked bulb hanging over your head. The room is otherwise dark. The nice peasant family that lives here huddles in the corner, watching fearfully. Let this be a lesson to them. A German officer stands in front of you, feet planted firmly, uniform starched, boots shiny. He's bald, monocled, small-headed. Don't laugh, it could happen. This man has many residual childhood issues. We just know this. He bends so that his eye and monocle are level with your own eyes, and blinks a couple of times. Sweat beads up on his enormous forehead. He asks you where your Free French buddies are hiding. You tell him to go pound salt, which of course in French sounds something like: *vattfaighfouttgh*. This really gets his goat and he slaps you hard across the face, then again, this time with the back of his hand. He doesn't stop. On and on. First the open-palm slap from right to left (he's right-handed), then the return trip with the back of his hand. Each time his monocle jumps a bit and catches the light. Goes on like this for a couple of hours…

This is how it feels to go between Perpignan and Montpellier on a motorcycle. The wind is brutal. In fact, this area is known as the *Region du Vent*, or the Wind Region, and there are power generation windmills on some of the hillsides, just like around San Francisco Bay. Farther along we pass a sign declaring *45,000 Ans. Homme de Mouthoumet*. We were traveling at speed, so I can vouch neither for the number of years nor for the name of the town. The gist is that bones from a male human who existed tens of thousands of years ago were found somewhere in this neighborhood. By the time we reach Montpellier, we feel approximately that old.

We've done about five hundred kilometers today, one of our longer rides so far. We are tired down to our socks, but have made no arrangements for a place to stay and must ride aimlessly around Montpellier looking for a hotel. We follow one sign that leads us to the historic quarter and Hotel du Parc. We ride into their courtyard, park the bike, and by now can barely see straight. Luckily, they still have *one* room. This is a two-star hotel and the rate is 350 francs a day, or about fifty dollars. The room is clean, the folks at the reception are delightful, and Christoffe " *'elps us weez ough bagz.*" They expect a storm tonight so we cover the bike. By now we're starving. Christoffe suggests we walk up the hill to the *Centre Historique*, where we will find many restaurants. He gives us a photocopy of a map that must have been originally drawn on a single grain of rice. I can only make out three words on it, scribbled in black marker: *Region du Vent.*

As we peruse the menu at Le Magret, we are choosy not because we feel delicate, but because we don't want to play musical commodes again, ever. We order the Salade du Chef, the Filet de Boeuf, and the Grillade Maison. We've already taken the edge off our hunger with a *ficelle* that we picked up at a bakery on our way up the hill. Dinner is very good. The waiters are attentive and know what they are doing. The average level of cleanliness and presentability in French restaurants is above that in Spain. They're also tidier here. I think we will start a highly unscientific rating system. Our justice will be swift and beyond appeal. If we think Portugal is uglier than Spain, we'll say so. If we think France has better food, we'll say that. This will be the world's most subjective appraisal. It could and probably will be entirely misleading, but will provide us with a place to ventilate our biases.

Overnight the sky opens up and dumps its fury hard on the South of France. So hard, in fact, that the burglar alarm on our motorbike goes off a couple of dozen times just from the force of the wind and rain. It's one of those outstandingly annoying *wee-wee-wah-wah-wah* alarms. We're sure our neighbors heard it as well and that we will not be greeted warmly at breakfast. In the morning the rain eases but does not stop. I take the alarm off the bike and bring it inside, but the works are wet now and the thing goes off spontaneously every few minutes. Our fellow hotel guests are, naturally, further delighted by this.

We could stay in Montpellier one more night, but are anxious to get to St. Rémy and see our friends the Bakrs. And anyway, we have no idea if tomorrow will be less rainy. Today's forecast in the Midi Libre newspaper shows a happy little yellow sun peeking from behind benign fluffy white clouds. So we take advantage of a break in the deluge and load up the bike. Just as we're about to throw our legs over the saddle, a monsoonal cloudburst arrives and begins to wash away Provence. We take refuge in the hotel lobby and wait for a while. The flood moves on so we get on the bike and head out. Traffic is a calamity waiting to happen. The road is flooded and the rain is heavy now. Trucks blast by us and throw up sheets of ugly water. Everybody has their headlights on and is driving slower than normal, but it's not much help. One guy on a bike overtakes us, but his posture suggests desperation. Up ahead, a big nasty cloud that looks like it's carved from charcoal is moving steadily at us, or maybe we're moving at it. A few minutes later we meet and it's a triple-decker sonofabitch. The rain whips us and everything around us. We're going 40 km/h and still having trouble seeing anything. Our jeans, boots, and gloves are wet like they've been in a tub. We ride under a bridge and spot the biker who passed us earlier, parked by the side of the road, on his feet. It's getting very hazardous now so we decide to take the first possible exit. We've only gone twenty-five kilometers from Montpellier, and it's been an hour.

An hour later we've covered twenty-five more kilometers and are looking for the road to St. Rémy, which the map tells us is a turn to the east on Route D999. It hasn't stopped raining and we can't find the damn D999, but we do pass a motel. A motel! Just north of Nîmes, France. This looks like something you might see in seed-ier sections of the Florida Keys. A characterless block building on whose roof an over-sized sign reads: MOTEL. Hopelessly drenched, cold now, disoriented, tired and hungry, we pull a U-turn and head for it. At this juncture, it has for us the allure of a Ritz Carlton.

After a change of clothes and an impromptu lunch of fruit pastilles, we strike out again. The motel manager gave us directions and we know exactly where to go. Within minutes we're drenched again, but knowing the way is emboldening, so we press on. Two hours later, after going through Beaucaire and Tarascon, we reach the charming town of St Rémy-de-Provence, where Vincent van Gogh checked himself into an asylum for ear-mutilators after that unfortunate incident in 1889. This ride has been an ordeal, but even in the rain, we appreciate the pastoral beauty of the road into town, lined with plane trees that arch gracefully above us.

Sam is home when we arrive. We must be a pitiable sight as we slosh off the bike and dribble over to the back porch where we abandon boots and gloves and jackets. While he puts on the kettle and makes a welcome cup of black tea, we show-er and change. This house is comfortable and open and spacious. Sam designed it when they moved here from London eleven years ago. He has given us an upstairs room with an attached bathroom. French doors open onto the balcony and a view of the valley. By the time Lucy and the kids get home, we're good as new.

■

We wake up the next morning to a glorious, sunny, clear-skied Provence day. The air is fresh, birds twitter, the breeze hums through the pines, and yesterday's del-uge is a distant and preposterous memory. After a breakfast of strong coffee, cereal and yogurt, we all drive to Maussane, just ten minutes away, to do the day's food shopping. While Sam and Tracy and the kids sit at an outdoor café and order coffee for us, Lucy and I walk to the *boulangerie* and pick up one *baguette* and one *epi*. By the time we get back to the café, a block away, we've made a substantial dent in the *epi*, which is fresh from the oven and warm; light crunchy crust, soft center, exqui-site in every way. Then we all walk down the street to the produce market and gath-er from the bins around the place the ingredients for tonight's dinner. Meals in

France, whether no more than a loaf of fresh bread or an extravagant feast, are important, seductive, addictive, deeply rewarding affairs. Lucy and Sam are wonderful cooks, and just happen to live in the garden of France. Everything they turn out of their kitchen is wholesome, hearty, full of the aromas and flavors of food that is not long from the earth. There is a microwave in the house that looks unwanted and forlorn.

Top of the World

In the afternoon Sam takes us for a walk in the hills around the house. Small trails run through the underbrush. The hillside is crowded with lavender, rosemary, thyme, bay trees, and fennel. If you carry a little olive oil and salt with you, you can build a serious salad on very short notice anywhere in this countryside. From the top of the hill we can see the old castle at Les Baux. As we stand there catching our breath and marveling at the view, my mobile phone rings. It's my sister Dana, calling from Mallorca to see how we are. I'm happy to tell her that we're on top of the world.

Provence, France, October 2

Today Lucy is driving us around the environs of St. Rémy. We start with a visit to the Cornille olive mill in Maussane. It's no big deal around here. Olive mills are a franc-a-dozen. However, coming as we do from the U.S., this impresses us as though it were an audience with Napoleon Bonaparte. Many locals, including Sam and Lucy, have olive trees. After picking their crop, they bring it here for pressing. The charming old building has a weigh-trough outside. From there the olives are dumped into a stone mill where they are crushed, pits and all, and made into a paste. Then the paste is spread on circular hemp discs about the diameter of a truck tire. These have holes in the center, are stacked in piles of four or five, and slipped over a spindle, sort of like records on a record player. (Record players are ancient sound production devices now obsolete and found exclusively at garage sales.) The discs are compressed and the paste yields a mix of oil and water, which is later separated in a centrifuge. Further proof that oil and water do in fact mix, but only when pressed. We tour the small facility and see milling equipment, storage tanks, and a couple of men hand-bottling a batch of oil. It's all very basic and rustic and French and makes you want to belt out the Marseillaise.

From here we drive to Eygalieres. En route we pass a field in which there is a flock of ewes with their freshly minted lambs stumbling around them. Some still have their umbilical cords. We park the car and slog through the thick grass for a closer look. I'm busy snapping pictures when I back up and plant one foot into a knee-deep canal, landing on the other bank on my ass. Lucy and Tracy show their

Provence Lambs

deep concern with a shameless eruption of snorting laughter. An indignant rooster scatters as we walk past him back to the car. There is a light odor of chicken-shit in the air. Across the street burly farmers, one in overalls, are absent-mindedly loading feed. Ewes and lambs blink at each other contentedly. Plane trees shade the southern side of a barn. All around are olive trees bearing fruit. We drive away certain there must be a God, that He is good, and that He is French.

■

Provence is a patch of Eden bordered by the Rhône River in the west, Orange in the north, the Mediterranean in the south, and Italy in the east. Right in the middle of this region is a cluster of towns and villages called Bouches-du-Rhône, nestled in the foothills and valleys formed by the Alpilles Range. The jewel of these is Les Baux-de-Provence. After lunch at home and a nice nap, Lucy drops us off here for a look. A thousand years ago Les Baux was the stronghold and headquarters of a gang of tough guys who claimed to be descended from the Magi king, Balthazar. To make that point, they tattooed stars of Bethlehem on their arms. Dark Ages Hell's Angels.

Les Baux is a French approximation of Alhambra. Built on a massif that is part of the Alpilles, it's perched one thousand meters high and surrounded by sheer vertical drops. They say that its big shots used to make people walk a gangplank off the edge if they didn't pay protection money. This is one of the most visited sites in France. You can see for miles from up here. And be seen. The entire massif is lit up at night and visible from thirty kilometers away. The chateau and fortifications have original siege machines on display, including a functional battering ram. A Japanese tour group mounts the platform around it and instinctively begins swinging the enormous timber in perfect metronomic teamwork. I can think only *Tora Tora Tora.* Farther along is the Saracen Tower, at the opposite end of the compound from the restrooms. From here Saracens defended the inner reaches of the Chateau. It is high and provides good cover. As I pee into the valley below, I am overwhelmed with the realization that Saracens all these many years ago may have stood on this very same spot and themselves peed into the valley below.

We're starting to understand the Provence "thing." It's not about going to Avignon, or Arles, or St. Rémy. It's really much more about going to *all* these places. Although there are many similarities between the towns, there are enough distinctions that you can only form a complete impression of the region by tooling around and spending a little time in each. What's more, the weather is now cooperating. Although there was a light rain yesterday, today we have lovely sunny skies and about sixty-five degrees Fahrenheit. The *mistral* is blowing and shaking the trees, but we'll take this over rain any day. I'll qualify that: This northerly can reach speeds of 130 km/h. In those cases, we'll take the rain. They say that, as recently as the eighteenth century, crimes of passion were forgiven if they occurred during a *mistral*, sort of a pre-Twinkies "Twinkies Defense."

The trip from St. Rémy to Aix-en-Provence is a quick forty-five minutes on the Autoroute. They have a great road system in France and the toll roads, including the A7 and A8, are excellent. This is how they get away with the speed limits they have. The little sign shows 130 km/h for dry pavement, and 110 km/h for wet. Most people whiz along at 160 km/h. For the metrically challenged, 160 km/h is roughly 100 mph, the speed at which many modern aircraft can no longer abort takeoff. It's a bit frightening, particularly since the French have this nasty predilection for making a slashing return into our lane as soon as they have half-completed overtaking us.

Aix is much busier than I expected. Traffic is heavy but, just at the edge of town, is a Honda motorcycle dealership. We stop to look for rainsuits. Ten minutes later we are proud owners of brand new full-length rainsuits and, dammit, a parking ticket for 230 francs. I actually get back while the young, crisp *gendarme* is still in the process of writing out the citation. My very best *Je-suis-un-idiot-Américain-en-vacances* performance gets me nothing but a polite *desolé*. We leave Officier Dirty Rat Bastard and drive toward the center of town. There we find our way to the Cours Mirabeau, named after the revolutionary and statesman. This is a broad boulevard lined with old plane trees. On one side run several adjacent restaurants and cafés boasting many years of service. *Les Deux Garçons,* for example, has been here since 1798. We decide to go for something a little more contemporary and walk into the *Café du Cours*, founded in 1802. Mirabeau the man was barely ten years dead when these restaurants dished up their first *soufflé*.

■

Aix was fun, but nothing ever happened there that can hold a candle to what happened in Avignon. For a short while at the end of the fourteenth century, the Catholic papacy moved here. There were actually two popes, one in Avignon and one in Rome. Two popes: It's not such a preposterous idea. One pope has to spread himself very thin to cover the whole world. Think how many frequent flyer miles John Paul II has accumulated. Back then, though, the idea of having two popes went over like a lead cardinal. Thus the Great Western Schism. In any case, while the papacy was in Avignon, the pope lived in the Palais des Papes on top of a hill overlooking the old city. This *palais* is seriously fortified. It's more like a citadel than a pope's residence, but there was very good reason for this. Much too often, hordes of heathen, Saracens and such, would surround Avignon and threaten to make a mess of the place. In all cases the pope on duty took the sensible course and paid off the marauders-to-be. They could easily have repelled the aggressors with molten lead or boiling oil instead of ransom, but I suppose that would have laid waste to the whole "other cheek" thing.

Marseilles, France, October 8

"Vive Le…"

That's all there is. We speculate that the graffiti vandal-artist who smudged this on the apartment block wall in Marseilles was either interrupted or politically agnostic. It's also possible he's a new arrival from North Africa and just warming up.

We're here for the day, and our first stop in Marseilles is at the Vieux Port. The harbor is a rectangle, four hundred meters long by one hundred meters wide. It opens to the west on the Mediterranean. Nowadays only fishing and pleasure boats dock here. On each side of the harbor is a promenade with wide sidewalks, pre-fifties apartment blocks and outdoor cafés. The high tourist season is history and the hundreds of tables and chairs sit empty. A *mistral* is winding up and building strength, but for now it's merely a page-turning breeze. The day is pleasantly warm, so we sit at a sunny table in one of the cafés on the Quay du Port and order coffee. From here we have a view of the Quay de Rive Neuve across the harbor and beyond it the hill rising to the south. On top of that is Notre Dame de la Garde. To our right we see Fort St. Jean and Fort St. Nicolas, guarding the mouth of the harbor, one on each shore. And to our left the famous Rue de la Canebiere makes its gradual ascent toward the church of St. Vincent de Paul.

Reading up on Marseilles and enjoying our coffee, we are soon assaulted by a man and his clarinet. He spotlights his efforts, luckily, on the adjacent café, which has a larger crowd. He is not entirely unaware of us, and occasionally lifts and dips his instrument in our direction, undoubtedly to say: "I see you and will be by shortly for money." Less subtle is a black man in a blue dress who drifts up behind me and offers us a limited and uninspiring selection of junk. His inventory includes one authentic faux-leather one-leg-shorter-than-the-rest horse, several Pokémon necklaces, a few sunglasses, and three or four reversible belts. I decline his offer, but he is on his toes and asks if I could use a pair of sunglasses. As I sit squinting at him in the bright noon sun, I realize he has me cornered like a gnu in a *National Geographic* "Carnivores of Africa" special. I accept my defeat graciously and buy the least offensive pair for seventy francs. They're flimsy and worthless, but he moves on.

All coffeed up, we start up the hill toward Notre Dame de la Garde, looking back occasionally at the Vieux Port. This is not a fancy neighborhood, and you're as likely to come across a hole-in-the-wall grocery as you are a drab apartment block like the one where we saw the ambivalent graffiti. After about twenty minutes we arrive at the foot of the Escalier Notre Dame. This staircase takes us up through an older neighborhood and expanses of Aleppo pine, all the way to the gates of Notre Dame de la Garde. The church is in the Romano-Byzantine style, incorporating domes and columns and spires in an Asia Minor kind of way. We spend a few contemplative minutes inside then exit onto the wide patio that surrounds it. By now the *mistral* has become a howling, biting, many-headed screamer. We have to wrestle with the revolving door to force our way out to something like an antechamber, then outside. Once in the open, we are caught and pushed around like human sails. Someone screams. They've lost their hat and it's flying away at good speed.

Our next destination is Rue de la Canebiere, named after the hemp that was grown here and used for making rope and nets and other fishy stuff. We wind our way through the streets of Marseilles like we live here. It might be possible to think us native, except for the passport pouches we both have strapped to our waists and

the matching fleece jackets, round-the-neck wallets, and the map book in my back pocket. Ethnically speaking, however, we fit right in. All along the Rue de Rome, which crosses Canebiere, we are hard-pressed to see anyone who is not Algerian or Tunisian. And on Canebiere itself, there are a dozen *shawarma* shops in as many blocks. Every now and then someone will *salaam aleykum* me, tentatively, searching for any sign of comprehension, poised to pounce. I've already given today's quota of mad money to the man in the blue dress, and I look ahead icily as we mingle with the crowd.

Rif Overlooking Marseilles

We kill the couple of hours until dinnertime in the neighborhoods around the Vieux Port. The Cathedral la Majeure, a nearly gaudy basilica north of the harbor, closes at six. We arrive with a couple of minutes to spare and say a quick prayer for good bouillabaisse. Then we drift up the hill into some of the low-income quarters that surround the Vieux Port. The *mistral* continues to make this a dusty trip, but for at least one local kid, it's a festival. Turning a corner from one narrow street into another, we see him in the distance, maybe six years old, all alone. He has a stick to which he has tied a blue plastic bag, and is flying this makeshift, imaginary spacecraft up and down the alley, happy as can be.

Back on Quay du Port, we stop at Restaurant Oscar. It's one of the smaller places on the quay but cozy and clean. They offer a full menu and feature the bouillabaisse, for which they have won the culinary equivalent of an Olympic gold medal. We are greeted warmly by the man at the door and shown to a quiet table in a corner away from the bar and the kitchen. There is a French couple at the table next to ours. They order the bouillabaisse. We do too. On our other side is another French family, this one including two small children. I'm a bit dismayed when I notice that the man has an unlit cigar in his hand, and occasionally slides it across his nostrils as if to say "any minute now." I'm sure he can't possibly be thinking of lighting the thing in this tiny restaurant. Turns out I'm wrong. He uses his dinner knife to decapitate the tip, then lights up and makes a big acrid cloud in no time at all. The host comes up and says something discreetly to the inconsiderate boar. This does not work, evidently, because Cigar Man says something back that makes the maitre d' very upset. The latter recoils and announces, in an edgy quivering voice, "*Cigaghghghe, Non!*" Well, this launches Mrs. Cigar Man into a torrent of abuse. She insists that she and her husband and their spawn would rather leave than be told what to do. We all approve. They leave, a happy ending by any measure. The bouillabaisse is delicious. After we're shown the fish, it is taken for filleting. Now we are served the broth, which is best taken with the baguette toast, spicy spread and Gruyere. Then, boned and filleted, the fish is brought out. A little of the broth is added to it, and *voila!* another exquisite Provence meal.

We follow our coffee with a little moonlit stroll along the harbor toward the Canebiere. It's cold now and the streets are deserted. We're surprised to see the man in the blue dress still working. He's pitching to the only people seated outside one of the cafés. We admire his tenacity. Then we realize that his targets are Cigar Man and his wife. Marseilles' most annoying visitors have found each other. Poetic justice.

St. Tropez, France, October 9

For as long as I can remember, the mention of St. Tropez has conjured up images of glittering excess, class, money, beautiful people. Truth is, there isn't all that much to St. Tropez. It's a little fishing village that anchors the west end of the Côte d'Azur. It really is quite small. The port promenade is maybe two hundred meters long. The old town is a handful of narrow streets, one church (no lifeguard on duty), a couple of decaying towers, and lots of shops. The main square, Place des Lices, is modest, much like any other main square you might find in Provence. In fact, it is quite similar to that in St. Rémy. There are no grand hotels here, no modern office blocks. It retains its Provençal village charm. After we've completed our reconnaissance ride, we pull into the courtyard of a two-star hotel called Le Cagnard. It's a couple of blocks away from Place des Lices and attracts us mostly because there's off-street parking. The young lady at the front desk is welcoming and helpful. Anyone who thinks that the French are rude has not spent much time in this part of France. Everyone here is friendly, polite, cheerful even. Not once in our two weeks in Provence and the Côte d'Azur have we been received with anything less than genuine cordiality. It's all we can do to stop ourselves from reaching out and kissing the waiters and hotel staff and shop clerks when they *bonjour* and *bien sur* and *a bientôt* us.

It's the off-season, so St. Tropez is relaxed and tranquil. We take the hotel clerk's advice and begin our tour with a walk up to the highest point in town. The citadel here is now a maritime museum. It closes at 5 p.m. We arrive at 4:30 p.m. and see no sense in it, so instead walk around the perimeter and find wonderful views of the Gulf of St. Tropez, the town itself, and possibly the most remarkable cemetery I have ever seen. Once around the citadel, we start our walk down toward the beach on the other side of town. This is Plage des Graniers, and it's deserted. You can imagine that it would be a bustling, fun, breast-infested place in mid-summer, but now it's quiet and lifeless. We continue our walk along the waterfront and soon find ourselves at the gate to the cemetery we saw from the hill. It's right on the sea, no more than a few meters above the waves. Some of the headstones are built on the very edge of rocks overlooking the water. If a view matters when we are laid down to eternal rest, I'll take this one. The neighbors are upscale, as you might think. Roger Vadim is buried here. Quite apart from his brilliant film directing career, he is famous for having been married to Brigitte Bardot *and* Jane Fonda. That's how clever you have to be if you want to stay at the Cimetière Marin.

■

The Côte d'Azur is maybe one hundred kilometers long from St. Tropez to Nice. Our map shows many seaside villages with familiar names: Ste. Maxime, St. Raphael, Cannes, Antibes, Juan-les-Pins, Cap-Ferrat. We start an easy, slow, east-bound excursion on National Route 98, which hugs the Côte d'Azur between Ste. Maxime and Nice. Each of the towns we go through has an old fishing port, a corniche of sorts, and hillsides covered with red-roofed vacation villas. Since the high season is over, traffic is benign. At the start of our ride the day is chilly, but bit by bit the skies clear and it gets warmer. We follow no particular plan as we reach these places, now stopping for a look, now passing right through or driving into the hills above the town. We are struck by how similar this region is to southern California. The Mediterranean certainly has a gentler feel than the Pacific, but these hamlets on the coast could just as easily be Laguna Beach. In Ste. Maxime we're drawn to the high hills overlooking the town, and follow the corkscrew roads as high up as we can before coming down the other side to the coast. Then comes Cannes. As we ride down the palm tree-lined corniche, it's clear that this is a playground for the rich and the famous. Even though the season is over, streets are crowded and restaurants are full. We pull in and park among the many motorbikes at one roundabout and, mostly because we're too tired to look for anything else, go into Café Roma right on Promenade de la Croisette. As far as we can tell, there are no movie stars in this crowd. The foursome closest to us is from Virginia. Only one man in the room has a gold chain nestled in a hairy chest visible in the shirt that is open halfway down. Only one woman has a necklaced poodle on her lap. The waiter is not at all snooty and does not survey us with disdain. These are just plain folks so we relax, have some soup, and pretend we're movie stars.

Across the Promenade de la Croisette is the Palais des Festivals, where, each year in May, the Cannes Film Festival happens. This is the most prestigious international motion-picture showcase in the world. Mind you, this has not always been the case. The real grand-daddy of motion-picture festivals is in Venice, and takes place in September. Benito Mussolini's propaganda apparatus started this thing about the same time Italy was preparing to conquer Ethiopia, in the early 1930s. Its fascist heritage and focus on artistic merit rather than commercial glitz have relegated the Venice festival to second fiddle. Cannes, on the other hand, continues to attract tens of thousands to its annual bash. Vadim was here as well, back in 1968, and presented *Metzengerstein*. Jane Fonda was in it. Bardot was here also, in a film called *William Wilson*, directed by Louis Malle. We wonder if they might have all run into each other at Café Roma.

Nice, France, October 11

Nice has been called "La Grande Dame" of the Côte d'Azur. Well, nobody calls anything "Grande Dame" any more. It's a phrase that went out with flapper hats. Coincidentally, we're staying at the Hotel Albert I, which dates from that era. Albert was king of Belgium during and following World War One. The hotel has an unmistakable *Belle Époque* nostalgia, if not mustiness. My grandfather used to vacation in Nice, sometime back in the forties and fifties. He may have stayed here, and you can imagine that it must at some point have been very elegant. Not anymore. The Albert I is in serious need of an overhaul. However, say what you will about its state of decay, you just can't beat its location. We exit the hotel, turn right, and are immediately on the Promenade des Anglais. If we turn left we're on the original corniche, the Quay des Etats Unis. Behind the hotel is the city's main square, Place Massena, from which radiate many pedestrian-only streets packed with restaurants, shops, and tourist points-of-interest.

Nice is full of contradictions. On the Avenue Centrale it's loud and busy and obnoxious, not to mention just plain noxious. Yet on top of the rocky hill to the east of town, where the dukes of Savoie once built their castle, there are magnificent gardens where the air is fresh and the mood serene. The walk along the broad Promenade des Anglais, particularly at dusk, is easy and relaxing. Lamps line the broad boulevard and the view of the Baie des Anges is sumptuous. Take one of the staircases down to the pebble beach, however, and you will encounter, as we do this afternoon, all manner of human and animal refuse. We see a drowned rat, a hypodermic needle, broken glass, plastic bags and heaps of dog droppings; all this in the few meters it takes us to reach and climb the very next set of stairs off the beach. Give the walk on the beach a miss. You'll be glad you did.

The Musée Massena is closed for *travaux*, but the gardens are pretty and peaceful so we have a little detour through them. Two elegant, elderly, immaculately put-together women, wide-brimmed hats and all, are having a visit on a shaded bench, appropriately oblivious of their dogs, a Yorkshire Terrier and a mutt, who are humping for all they're worth right there under the heroic gaze of Massena's bust. Marshal André Massena was one of Napoleon's men, and played an important role in the history of eighteenth and nineteenth century France. Quite apart from having his name on hotels and museums and sculptures, Massena has been immortalized in dishes such as the delectable Tournedos Massena. This gets us thinking about food, so we turn back and head for the pedestrian-only district near the hotel, where we find a restaurant called Le Love. It's a bit early for the French, so we get the entire staff's attention. The meal is adequate but not repeatable. Afterwards we walk along the Rue de Massena—here he is again— and stop briefly to join clots of people watching street performers. One shirtless man lies

Nice Panorama

face down on a small but convincing hill of broken glass while two volunteers stand on his back. It's all too sordid following a steak dinner, so we move on and can't report the outcome. Farther along, outside the well-lit Palais de Justice, we encounter five young people, well-dressed, seemingly upstanding, in the middle of an elaborate drug deal. It seems various currencies are involved, and there is some disagreement about the prevailing exchange rates.

Our second day in Nice looks like more rain, but we put on caps, grab an umbrella, and go walking anyway. They say there is an elevator up to *Le Chateau*, but we take the stairs. It's a half-hour huff to the top, and the view is well worth the exertion. There's not much left of the chateau, but from here we can see all of Nice. The corniche, the expanse of red roofs, the city's climb into the surrounding hills, all seen from a distance that hides all faults. There is a cascading waterfall here that can be seen from the Old City below. We find it and walk through the spray. Two hours ago we were wishing it would stop raining. Now it has and we're warm from the walk up the hill. The descent is much easier, but we come across a couple of unsavory goons who remind us that down below is a big city and not, as it may have been in the 1800s, a quiet Mediterranean resort where Berlioz composed his King Lear overture. The two men, drunk we figure, look us up and down then decide to leave us alone.

Monaco, October 12

The Corniche de la Riviera starts in Nice and goes to Menton. Our interest is in Monaco, roughly in the middle of it. Along the way we take a long detour through St-Jean-Cap-Ferrat. Anybody missing some money? It's here. There are properties on this tiny peninsula that might cost more to maintain than a small country. We see dogs in hats out for walks with their wealthy masters. One man is apparently using gold jewelry for jogging weights. Although we're drifting along at not much more than 30 km/h, we catch only glimpses of the grand homes. They are all behind forbidding walls and opulent gates. We're on the "tour" road. It takes us clear through and around the neighborhood, leading non-negotiably to the exit. This is not the sort of place where strangers are especially welcome. In fifteen minutes we ride down a steep road into Monaco.

This little country, in Europe larger only than the Vatican, is what happens when a whole lot of francs find themselves in one very small spot. It is impeccable. Every house, every shop, every man, woman and child has been scrubbed and painted and dressed for company. Monaco is made up of four parts: Monaco-Ville, Monte Carlo, La Condamine, and Fontvielle. The last is an industrial suburb, so we skip it. La Condamine is the area adjacent to the old harbor, which today—every day, we'll bet—is stuffed with yachts. We arrive here and find a quiet inconspicuous place to park the bike, next to a church. Monaco-Ville itself is a rock on which reside Prince Rainier III and a small community of people who are under constant observation to ensure that they live up to the royal standard. There's no other possible explanation. No rust exists here. Everything is painted fresh. Not a single geranium in the millions of window boxes is in anything but exquisite condition. The guards at the Palais Princier are so crisp they occasionally crack under their own weight. The fourteenth century cannons in the courtyard are cleaner than most surgical wards in Portugal. And finally, there's Monte Carlo, the capital of Monaco and official seat of all things decadent but legal. All four of these neighborhoods, and the thirty-two thousand people that live in them, are squeezed into an area smaller than two square kilometers. If you squeezed hard you could put most of Monaco inside the World's Largest Mall in Edmonton, Alberta. Monaco is one of the few countries in the world that you can traverse in less time than it takes to make a good bouillabaisse.

We begin our tour of the country with a coffee and baguette at a small coffee shop on Rue Princesse Caroline. All the royal kids have streets named after them, naturally. We're the only customers this morning, but the place is all abuzz on account of two wayward pigeons that flew in and are now perched and pooping prolifically on the ample Baroque frieze. Though mindful of the danger, we are busy contemplating the principality's map.

After breakfast we climb to the Palais Princier. We are caught jay-walking by a Monaco *gendarme* who gives us the *we-don't-do-that-here* look. It involves a raised eyebrow. I hold my hand out, palm up, as if to say: *The rain made me do it.* He wags a white-gloved finger at me. There is only one way to respond to a finger-wagging and that is abject contrition, so we take the long way and begin our ascent of the Escalier Princier, which leads to Valhalla Grimaldi. We find ourselves in a clearing, cobbled with very clean cobbles, entirely encircled by buildings that look like wedding cakes, and sectioned off with heavy lengths of Middle Ages iron chains. We make our way to the entrance of the Palais and buy tickets. There is a brood of almost-handsome young women in smart uniforms, standing stiffly at the entrance. They are the royal tour guides (RTGs).

When you've seen one royal palace, you've seen them all. This place, like its analogs, is packed with portraits of dead antecedents in the royal line. It overflows with royal gold and crystal and other pricey fineries. In all this opulence, the royal throne is uncharacteristically modest. It could easily be mistaken for a mere royal armchair. I think that the royal decorator is aware of this and has therefore cordoned off the area immediately surrounding the throne with some royal super-fancy velvet rope. After the tour is over the RTG slips out the door with us to cop a smoke.

When we walk into the Casino de Monte Carlo, every security man in the place scrambles. Our rainsuits, Kevlar jackets and helmet bags, all gray and black, are not typical gambler wear. We are summarily asked to go to the cloakroom and take all that stuff off before entering the gaming salons. It takes twenty minutes for us to undress, by which time we've become close friends of the coat-check lady and the security guard sent to make sure we're not hiding a nuclear sub under our coats. Unfortunately, we've also made a mess of the shiny floor and elegant dark wood countertops. Nevertheless, everyone is very accommodating. Down to our jeans and overalls now, we stride into the main salon, expecting to find the rich and the famous and the impoverished ex-royalty tenting over their Camparis, red-eyed and intense. Instead we find three lightly-attended roulette tables. The players could be dentists and bus-drivers. This is not the place that King Farouk of Egypt retired to back in the 1950s. If he were to see this, he would roll over in his grave, if he had room. (Farouk was a portly fellow. They say that *The Swine*, as he was affectionately known, preceded his gambling soirees with obscene meals of ten pheasants and dozens of oysters, washed down with champagne.) We down a couple of Cokes in the time it takes us to lose a hundred bucks. Cheap thrills.

It's still raining, but we are back in our waterproof riding gear and ready to roll. The road down to the harbor is closed by the police. Someone lost control of their car and skidded down the steep hill into oncoming traffic. No serious injuries, but a reminder to us to be very careful in this weather as we negotiate the twisty roads along the coast. After seeing the accident we decide to sacrifice the view for the relative safety of not having oncoming traffic, and start the corkscrew climb up the side of the mountain toward the freeway. From here on, the road is either a tunnel or a bridge. It is strung through these mountains like a circus high wire. We cross into Italy and continue the climb. The hills are everywhere. Villages grow out of the groins of valleys and each house is on its own hillock. Everything is green and lush. Once in a while we glimpse the Ligurian Sea. We are rising and it's getting colder and wetter. This scene would be spectacular on a sunny day. Today it's a bit frightening.

Milano, Italy, October 13

The last time I visited Milano was in 1977, a couple of days before Christmas. I was on a bus en route from Athens to London. We stopped here for the night and were given the option of sleeping on board if we couldn't afford a hotel. This was no flush group, and half of us stayed on the bus. Around 2 a.m., a few guys and I decided to go hunt down some cigarettes. We left the bus and started prowling the streets around the central train station. Half an hour into this futile excursion, as we came up to a deserted intersection, three cars—including one marked *Polizia*—screamed up to the curb and stopped, surrounding us. This was a time of severe political tension in Italy. Leftists and rightists were doing an ugly dance of reciprocal terrorism. Under the circumstances, our little party of cigarette hunters might have seemed sinister. Truth is, we were scared dumb. One of the plain-clothed men spoke some French and asked to see our passports. We obliged and I explained that we were en route to London and that our bus was at the nearby piazza and that we were just looking for some smokes and that it would be very nice indeed if he and his friends did not kill and dispose of us. He was very tense, made it clear that we were silly foreign idiots, and directed us to return immediately to the bus and stay the hell put. This time in Milano, I am determined not to be scared half to death.

Besides, much of the ride up here from Nice has been wet and slick and scary enough. After checking into the Hotel d'Este and parking the bike inconspicuously by the side-entrance of a taxidermist, we muster what little energy we have left and wander down the street to a little pizzeria called La Oca Giuliva. The food is just what we want: hot, hearty, wholesome, Italian. The waiter is like a fat, doting old uncle. He doesn't ask for our order, he gives it to us. "You will have the such-and-such." We succumb. We eat. Happy to be in Italy, warm now and somewhat recovered from the ride, we call it a night.

■

The Duomo of Milano is humongously big. The exact dimensions escape me, but I estimate it to be about the size of Idaho. Birds that drift up into the rafters get beak-bleeds. They're still counting, but as of last Friday there were 135 spires and 2245 white marble statues in and on the place. It took five hundred years to build and is the largest Late Gothic Cathedral in the universe. This church has room for absolution of many sinners simultaneously. All along the outer aisles—this place is so big it has five naves—confessionals are arranged like phone booths at a busy airport. Each has a plaque with the name of its resident *padre*. They're all empty now, but then it is lunch hour.

There are boatloads of art in here. Oil paintings, large enough to make several nice tents out of, hang in the countless chapels dedicated to everyone ever beatified. Those of us who can be critical of organized religion must nevertheless remember that without its patronage we would have very little in the way of Western art. The Duomo is itself a work of art. Monumental stained glass windows depict, in hundreds of panels, just about every Bible story from both Testaments. The floor is inlaid marble. Apart from the sheer magnificence and scale of the cathedral, Tracy and I are fascinated by the statue, in the south transept, of Santo Bartolomeo. This unfortunate fellow earned his martyrdom by allowing himself to be skinned alive. The statue depicts him post-flaying, standing up, carrying his skin like a wet suit, looking, well, rather uncomfortable. This story competes with a second version according to which he was beheaded. Regardless, the short hair on my forearms stands up. There is a service going on in the crypt, which lies underneath the altar in the basement, and can be seen through windows that open on the main floor. I guess you can still pray in here, but only if you stay out of the way of the tourists.

Now back outside, we buy some roasted chestnuts and walk around the piazza. There are so many tourists here in the summer that the pigeons get fat. Not today. I crumble a chestnut in my hand and attract a good flock of the crappy creatures, even though there are other people, many smaller than me, doing the same thing. After a few minutes of this I very badly need to wash my arm so we move along looking for a place to buy a coffee and use the facilities. On the north side of the Piazza del Duomo is the Galleria Vittorio Emanuele II. It's a covered marketplace, built from glass and iron and similarly dangerous materials that were in vogue in the nineteenth century. It occurs to me that any one of these panes, falling as it would the distance of some fifty meters, could

Pigeon Attack!

slice through a human person like a guillotine through mozzarella. The building's architect, while we're on the subject of sudden death, met his maker a few days before the building was completed. He fell off the roof.

Fortunately, as we mosey along today I am distracted from this morbidity by the itching that has developed on my pigeon arm. We walk through the Galleria and, utterly without premeditation, find ourselves in the Piazza della Scala. Via Giuseppe Verdi runs along its north wall and is unremarkable. A place with the history of La Scala ought to have a prominent billboard outside that tells its story, and maybe also a big neon sign—World's Largest Opera House—or at least someone in a period costume ringing a bell. The opera house was opened in 1778 with a work of Antonio Salieri. This is the Salieri more often remembered as the man who may have poisoned Mozart.

■

The drive north through Milano confirms that this is a sprawling city of ordinary people who deserve no credit for its reputation as one of the world's premier fashion design centers. We go for miles and see houses and factories and roads and nothing much worth stopping for. Then, as we leave the city and follow the secondary highway to Como, the terrain becomes gradually more rural and alpine. By the time we spot Lake Como, the scene has become magnificently picturesque.

We reach the Swiss border and pull into a services area just before the police kiosks. Switzerland is not part of the European Union, so there's an honest-to-goodness border here, with customs and everything. Some cars are just waved through. We are pulled to one side and asked to show our passports and the highway toll sticker we had just bought for twenty-five dollars. This is how cleverly organized the Swiss are. Instead of stopping you at tollbooths every few kilometers, they merely charge you a flat fee for the privilege of using their national highways. Our sticker is good for three months. From here it's a quick half-hour to the center of Lugano, but what a half-hour it is. Suddenly massive hills sprout out everywhere around us. Tunnels follow tunnels as we again find ourselves piercing hillsides and rounding tight-rope viaducts over plunging ravines. And the rain has stopped. Bonanza.

Now we ride into Lugano and are dazzled. The town sits on its lake and sparkles. Our first impression of Switzerland is that this is a country in which everything is organized and precise. It's cliché, but true. From the time we crossed the border earlier today until now, we've seen an elevated degree of specificity in everything. Here they don't just tell you how far it is to the next tunnel, they also tell you how long the tunnel is. All along the center dividing rail on the major highways, little kilometer markers are placed every one-tenth of a kilometer! The on-ramps to the freeway are long and gradual and clearly marked, compared to Italy, where you get a few meters to slip into the speedball traffic or else kiss your fenders goodbye. Here in Lugano the sense of order is ubiquitous. The squares are clean and tidy. There are no delivery trucks and motorbikes parked every which way in the pedestrian areas. Traffic is heavy but moves along nicely. The people strolling around the center of town are all wearing sensible shoes. There is absolutely no dog shit anywhere. We buy the *Herald Tribune* and stop in a little café on the waterfront for coffee. Everybody here speaks English, Italian, German, and perhaps French. Everyone is polite and obliging. There is not a great deal of sweating going on; it's just not Swiss.

Lugano, Switzerland, October 13

A prodigious shower has broken over Lugano and cleared the city center of all pedestrians. My friend Farid rolls up in his Mercedes and, fine gentleman that he is, suggests that Tracy ride in the car while I follow on the bike. "No big deal," he says, "the house is only five minutes away." As I start out under the torrential downpour, I hear a sickening, shearing noise, metal meeting metal, and the bike jerk-stops cold. Immediately I realize that, in the rush to get going, I had not taken the steel cable and combination lock off the front wheel. Now the cable has become jammed between the axle and the rim. Fortunately, the lock is still accessible, so I remove it, but the cable is stuck for good. Somehow I manage to pull it away from the wheel and attach it to the front mudguard. All this under buckets of rain, in the dark, with a brisk wind blowing in off Lake Lugano. Now tense and wet and nervous, I follow the Mercedes taillights into the night. The Swiss reserve all their rogue energy for driving. They like to go fast. Farid, Lebanese by blood and Swiss by conviction, carries a double dose of the speeding gene. I manage to keep up with him most of the time, but it takes every ounce of strength, every scintilla of skill, every prayer I know, to not hydroplane into the damp darkness outside my headlights. We finally arrive. I'm not sure how long the ride was. "Five minutes" it wasn't.

Lugano is the largest town in Switzerland's Ticino canton, itself one of twenty-six such largely autonomous states in the country. People here think of themselves in very ethno-regional terms. Sure they're Swiss, but it's an important distinction that they're from Ticino. And well it should be. Everything about this region is distinct. They speak Italian. They tend to have bread and eggs and cheese and such for breakfast, instead of sausages and beer. There are no big cities dominating the region, as in the Geneva and Zürich and Bern cantons. It's more casual than in the north. In many ways, this is as much an extension of Italy as part of Switzerland. In fact, Lugano itself lies in the southern part of Ticino, which forms an area about thirty kilometers long and ten kilometers wide, surrounded almost entirely by Italy. Lake Lugano, which runs roughly east-west across this part of the canton, reaches from one border to the other, with both its extremes in Italy.

After a quick shower and change of clothes we pile back into the car and drive into the hills. It's too dark and misty to see anything. Tracy and I huddle in the back while Farid and his wife Ekaterina are in the front, promising us an unforgettable dinner. Eventually we reach a small village that looks like it has been overlooked by the past fifty years. Here, hidden among the modest houses, is a restaurant with a sign and everything. There seems very little point in committing the name to memory, since it would take a miracle for us to find it again. In any case, here we are, and several other friends of Farid's and Kat's are there already, sitting at a long table in a semi-private room. Turns out this is a very special October event in these parts: We are here for a dinner of venison. The late deer is presented in medallions with various pastas and a thick, delicious brown mushroom sauce. The room is warm as a wood fire crackles in the fireplace and the windows get all fogged up. We are soon in the lap of conviviality. Our new friends all live in Lugano or nearby, and waste no time touting the area's great outdoors, its food, its wine, its enviable standard of living. Someone proudly remarks that the area enjoys 2,100 hours of sunshine a year, more than anywhere else in the country. We think it's the Pinot Noir talking.

■

The next day Tracy and I decide to go off on a little day trip to Locarno. The roads here are excellent. They have to be. Half the time they're in the clouds. We are as well today, piercing them on the way up the mountain and then again on the way down. We arrive in Locarno expecting to enjoy a stroll along the banks of Lago Maggiore, but no dice. All the rain has flooded the lake, and now the promenade is

Locarno Deluge

underwater. The lake has actually made its way up several streets and waterlogged a whole bunch of Swiss basements. Police are out in force; streets are cordoned off; children are in thigh-high rubber waders playing in new ponds, and a few people are rowing boats down the road.

"The spirit of Locarno" is not a drink. It is, rather, an atmosphere that prevailed following the Locarno Treaties, which were signed here in 1925. Europe's major powers had reached agreement for mutual defense. Everybody felt pretty good about that until Germany changed its mind in 1936. Switzerland has always been a good place to sign play-nice agreements. Its neutrality has stood since 1515. In 1863 the Red Cross was founded here, in Geneva, and that organization took the Swiss flag as a model for its own. Then in 1920, also in Geneva, the League of Nations was formed. That particular organization did not survive but its progeny, the United Nations, has. And let's not forget the Geneva Convention. Geneva Conventions, to be precise. There have been four: 1864, 1868, 1929, and 1949. The agreements reached at these monumental gatherings are possibly the closest mankind has ever come to acting as one. Where would we all be without Switzerland?

People here have a socially liberal, fiscally conservative, environmentally correct posture. They thrive on the beauty of the regions in which they live, in the arms of the Alps. They hunt, they fish, they eat game. Stuffiness is not for them, but that is not to say they are not sophisticated. Family here is paramount. And food. And fast, reliable German cars. You have to admire this ethic. For one thing, it makes sense. For another, everyone in Switzerland is armed! This country has not confused neutrality with powerlessness. Every man is a member of the national defense force, keeps his weapon at home and is not afraid to use it. This earned Switzerland the nickname of *The Little Porcupine*, and was enough to convince Germany to not invade it during the World Wars. Cynics argue that *The Little Bank* would have been a more appropriate nickname, and that other, more Machiavellian reasons were behind the Germans' uncharacteristic restraint.

Zürich, Switzerland, October 16

It's still raining.

The ride from Lugano to the Gotthard Tunnel is miserable. More rain, lots of traffic, and as we rise into the Alps it's getting colder. In spite of the weather, though, we can see enough of the Alps to occasionally shout *wow!* into the bike intercom. There is a service area just south of the tunnel so we stop and have a nice warm lasagna to fortify us for the rest of the trip. After a hot tea and some chocolate, we mount up and head off, only to spend half an hour in the rain waiting at the south entrance for a broken down truck to be moved out of the road. Once inside the tunnel, the roadway is dry and the temperature rises to thirty degrees or more Celsius. It's like being in the barrel of a hair dryer. So much so that my gloves, which were wet when we entered the tunnel, are now very nearly dry. The Gotthard Tunnel handles most of the traffic through the Swiss Alps since the Mont Blanc tunnel was closed down by fire last year. It occurs to me to let someone know that it's hot in here.

Fifteen kilometers later we emerge from the north mouth of the tunnel and there is no rain. The sun is out and it's several degrees warmer. Cows graze lazily in alpine meadows; German-Swiss folks walk between their houses and their barns in short-sleeved shirts, shouldering kegs of beer, yodeling, followed by their big shaggy dogs. We have to pull over. For one thing, we're now heavily overdressed. For another, Tracy insists she wants to take a picture of a cow. She finds these cows here particularly cute, cuter than our cows in the States, so we pull into a little farming community and down a gravel driveway where we park the bike and bask in the warmth and dryness. Several very attractive cows are intrigued by us and approach the fence with decidedly quizzical expressions. We snap a couple of pictures. The cows lose interest and meander away from the fence, back to their meadow. Some of the peaks looking way down on us are under snow. Not the sort of place you want to be stuck without a taxi, but it sure is spectacularly beautiful around these Alps.

It's abundantly clear that this part of the country differs from Ticino. Road signs are now in German. This is a tiny bit problematic because neither of us knows the language. Our vocabulary consists of phrases memorized in fourth grade and during reruns of *Hogan's Heroes*. We manage to find our way into the center of Luzern, park the bike illegally alongside the convention center, and start out to explore the city. Our stroll through Luzern turns into a free-grazing sort of thing. We begin by picking up three hundred grams of roasted chestnuts at the foot of

Seebrücke. This bridge (*brücke*) is the easternmost crossing over the Reuss River as it flows away from Lake Luzern. Every city we've visited in Switzerland so far has its eponymous lake. Must be a real embarrassment to not have one. Then, across the river, we pick up a pretzel in the Kapellplatz and munch on it while we cross back over the river via the covered Kapellbrücke. Now we have the long stroll along the Banhofstrasse to the Apreuerbrücke but manage it with the help of a bag of cookies. And so on. By the time we get back on the bike to head up the highway to Zürich, we've eaten our own weight in Swiss-German junk food. Luzern, though, has that everything-will-be-okay-so-go-ahead-and-pig-out feeling, which we learn is part of the fabric of all things Teutonic. The short visit is memorable anyway, for the covered bridges, the swans in the river, the well-preserved Gothic and Baroque buildings, and the chestnuts.

Now we're hustling to get to Zürich before dark so we can find a hotel. Zürich is Switzerland's largest city, and you can tell. This is a far cry from Luzern or Lugano. We get to the train station, climb a curb, leave the bike near a lamppost, and start our haphazard discovery of the city. Like Luzern, Zürich straddles a river, in this case the Limmat, which of course flows into Lake (you guessed it) Zürich. The old quarter butts up to the lake and goes for a few blocks on each side of the river. The where-it's-all-happening street in Zürich is the Bahnhof Strasse. It runs north-south from the train station to the lake. After a few blocks of bumping into people, we cut away from the Bahnhof and make our way slowly through the maze of small streets surrounding it. There aren't many hotels around here, and the first one we get to is booked solid. Not only that, the desk clerk lets us know that Zürich is full, and that we're better off asking the Tourist Information Center at the train station for help finding a place for the night. This is a bit alarming because it's cold out, and getting late.

Zürich's old town is full of restaurants, shops, and galleries. The things we do notice are sometimes not in guidebooks. For example, after touring this section of town for a few hours we realize that something *trés* avant-garde is happening in the under-appreciated art of window dressing. It's an odd thing to notice, perhaps, but we look into dozens of shop windows, from upholsterers to haircutters, art galleries, auto transmission repair garages, and nurseries, and they all share a thoroughly modern, neo-minimalist, edgy thing. Zürich, we come to learn, in spite of being the world's largest gold market and fourth largest stock market, is undergoing something of a cultural revolution. "Staid" is out, "fresh" is in. We also observe that many of the city's residents are pierced. The younger population, especially. In one block, each and every individual we pass has a ring, a stud, a post, a disc or some other hardware run right through some part of their person. One man has large circular earrings in his ear lobes. Not "through," but "in," like in the Amazon. We do not report this frivolously. We believe it says something, something good, about a place. It suggests that the society at large is tolerant, that it honors diversity, and that we will not be regarded as freaks just because we're dressed that way.

Our room at the Hotel Poly is adequate, not more. The shower works and, even though it's the phone-receiver type, has a long enough cord to be useful. The hotel is on the east side of the Limmat, near the University of Zürich. It's a quiet neighborhood, but then you could say that about all of Switzerland. We take a leisurely walk down the hill toward the river and tour the city on foot. The skyline is dominated by Gothic spires from the many churches. The high point of our tour, literally as well as figuratively, is the top of one of the towers of the Grossmünster Cathedral. Huldrych Zwingli, leader of the Reformation in Zürich, preached here until he died in 1531. That's nearly five hundred years ago, and there's something about that that gives us the willies. Nevertheless, we pay our four Swiss francs each to the young man reading his Bible at a lonely table in the back of the church and hike up the spiral staircase. At one point the stone stairs give way to wooden ones, then scaffolding. We keep climbing. Just like in the church, there is not a living soul up here. Or so

Gothic Zurich

we think, until we get to a landing that I'm sure is in the ionosphere, and run into a woman standing there catching her breath. By now we are of course being very silly and laughing up a real hee-haw, thinking we're alone. Church Lady is unamused. We say *"Güten morgen,"* which helps very little because by now it's afternoon and we all know how precise the Swiss are.

Fussen, Germany, October 18

We ride from Zürich to Fussen in one afternoon. Back in June, when I started planning this trip, I read about the Romantische Strasse. This highway runs from Fussen in the south, just across from the border with Austria, to Würzburg in the north, 350 kilometers away and halfway between Nürnberg and Stuttgart. It's not one road, but several. They link up to form a wonderful course through medieval villages strung like beads a short driving distance from each other. Each has its claim to fame, its own unique tourist hook, but all share well-preserved medieval houses, churches, and castles. Our interest is not just in these stopping points, but also in the road between them.

We decide to stay at the Kurhaus Hotel on Sebastian Strasse. The room is small, but warm and clean. Breakfast is included, and the first time we take advantage of it, we encounter a middle-aged German couple in the booth adjacent to us, having the traditional *weisswurst*. It's a calf liver and bacon sausage, white like an intestine, stuffed with chopped parsley and onions. You can see the green bits through the translucent skin, and that of course makes it look mildewed. This is the quintessential Munich breakfast. Tradition dictates that it must be consumed before noon. It's served with sweet mustard. You cut it, stick the cut end into the mustard, put it in your mouth, then squirt the sausage out of the skin and chew. Wash down with beer. Puke. Repeat.

Fussen is a marketing triumph. There are a few Gothic buildings here and a small pedestrian mall, but the town has ensconced itself as the gateway and service center to the Neuschwanstein and Hohenschwangua castles, a few kilometers away along the Romantische Strasse. Neuschwanstein was commissioned by wacky Mad King Ludwig II of Bavaria. That Ludwig II was loopy is open to question. He was certainly mercurial and fickle in matters of foreign policy. Still, politics do make strange bedfellows and the fact that he changed teams every few years could be considered brilliant statesmanship. It was he who brought Bavaria into the fold of the German Empire in 1871, and it was he who, when the composer was still a young man, supported Richard Wagner. As we stand and look at Neuschwanstein, however, we find ourselves wondering if the man wasn't, if not crazy, at least hyper. The palace kept him and several architects occupied for two decades, and was still unfinished when he committed suicide in 1886. He was forty-one. Mind you, this was not the *only* royal palace, just the most famous. It is an orgy of spires and towers and ramparts and, what's more, happens to be in the Alps overlooking the Pöllat River gorge. The scene is magical, but when we stop for a look at the nearby Hohenschwangua Castle, where Ludwig II grew up and where Wagner often stayed on visits, the Neuschwanstein is no longer so preposterous. It was his twenty-seven-inch color TV to his parents' eleven-inch black-and-white. What's nuts about that?

From here we ride north on the Romantische Strasse. For miles on end we're in pastoral scene after postcard pastoral scene. There are no big factories stinking up the air here. It's unspoiled German meadowland. There are fat cows about, munching on fat grass. The villages along the way are small and quaint. Each has a main church, and the mass schedule is posted on hopeful signs by the road into town. Our next stop is Landsberg. It's one of the bigger bergs on the Romantische Strasse, but not many tourists stop. We're interested only in a coffee and find a small café at the town square (actually oblong). It's slow. Tracy and I are the only non-locals in the joint, but we become popular quickly as I sing along to "Raindrops Keep Falling on My Head." Seventy-five or so years ago, Landsberg had a somewhat less good-natured guest: Adolf Hitler was here. He was imprisoned at the local jail after his Beer Hall Putsch had failed to overthrow the government. It was in the Landsberg pokey that he wrote part of *Mein Kampf.* The city was occupied by the good guys after World War Two, and many Nazis were hanged for their crimes during the war. It's been quiet since.

Now we take a planned detour and head for Munich. We will rejoin this delightful road in a couple of days, at Augsburg. We're astonished at just how little we know of the language and how difficult it is to pick up, unlike Italian. So we amuse ourselves with the ignorant and petty diversion of making fun of words that sound funny. *Ausfahrt* is a favorite. This is of course shamefully childish, but we like it. As we ride around Munich looking for the center, we speculate that Germans might be happier if their language were less abstruse. Apart from the fact that it contains a few additional letters or variations on those in the English alphabet, German punishes the aspiring student with a sort of compulsive conjoining of words that in English stand happily on their own. For example, "boiled potatoes" in English translates to *salzkartoffeln*. It can't be plainly evident to the novice that this mouthful is actually made up of two words and that the latter half is potatoes. And so on. *Petersillenkartoffeln* means "parsley potatoes." You can see the problem. By the time I've finished the chore of reading a word, I have to start over and review the letters I've already forgotten. We're not ordering parsley potatoes.

Munich, Germany, October 19

It's raining in Munich. This has become such a predictable state of affairs that we now always wear our rain gear when we ride. It's late afternoon and traffic is nearly as unpleasant as *weisswurst*. One guy in a 325i BMW zips in and out of his lane, getting nowhere fast, before finally slamming into the rear of the line of cars. His heroics complicate an already ugly snarl, so we leave the main road and look for an alternative route to downtown. Of course we get lost. This time I am not at all timid about stopping and asking for directions. I not only learn how to get downtown, but also that *einbahnstrasse* means "one way."

We soon ride waterlogged but victorious into the center of Old Munich, the lovely and enchanting Marienplatz. As we come around the corner from St. Peter's Church, the Old Town Hall appears directly in front of us. It's still raining, but now we don't mind so much. We go around the block and this time pull up to the south wall of St. Peter's where we park the bike, counting on divine supervision while we're away. Even in the light rain, Marienplatz is buzzing. We like this. It always makes us happy to see people out and about, humanizing a city. Just like we did a few weeks ago in Granada, we get an inexplicable feeling we will like Munich. We haven't eaten since breakfast in Fussen, so stroll through the streets around Marienplatz, looking for somewhere to have a late lunch.

Not far from there, on Sparkassestrasse, is the renowned (we come to learn) Scholastichaus Haxn Bauer Restaurant. Their menu has the following introductory paragraph, fortunately translated into English: "We are proud to say that we are the biggest *haxn* restaurant in the world." Let me be plain, *haxn* are pig knuckles. They call it a knuckle, but judging by the size of the thing, it's either the knee, or the elbow, or these pigs were on growth hormone. To us they looked like chickens on a rotisserie in the window, so we crossed the street and walked in. I'm certain that I cannot do this delicacy justice merely by describing it here. I will add, however, that

Marienplatz

this eatery has been serving pig joints since 1368. To put that in perspective, it's exactly 632 years from when we walked in and sat down to lunch. They have utensils here that predate the Gutenberg Bible, which was printed in nearby Mainz in 1455. Consider also that when Johannes Gutenberg was born, this restaurant had already gone through two generations of bus-boys. That's how old this place is. We find the food heartily delicious and finish the meal off with apple fritters flambéed right at the table. Our waiter is the youngest and least experienced among the staff of seasoned old gents in the place, and he very nearly flambées Tracy with the dessert.

In the grand scheme of things, we are approaching the end of our northerly route. From here we finish the Romantische Strasse, pop over to Prague then begin going south again, hopefully through Budapest and Vienna, then through the rest of Austria and back to Italy. In the meantime, something altogether unexpected is happening. The longer we're away from living in one place and carrying on a particular routine, the harder it becomes to imagine such a thing. This itinerant way of life, two nights here, three there, is endlessly fascinating. We get tired, naturally, but the long breaks with Dana in Mallorca and the Bakrs in Provence recharged us for the time being. I expect that by the time we get to Beirut in mid-December, we will be ready for a couple of weeks of rest.

Our hotel is The Condor, fifteen minutes' walk from Marienplatz, just around the corner from the main train station, Hauptbanhof. Our neighborhood is Nouveau Seedy. Every nationality is represented. There are restaurants serving most cuisines, but especially Middle Eastern. We are very much at home here, and not the least bit troubled that the police travel in threes. Our stay is nearly without incident. The second night at the hotel, very late, the occupants of the two rooms on each side of ours come back from a night of drinking and proceed to have a loud party. They figure out a way to open the gates on the balcony and annex ours, thus creating a "beer garden" in which they can be rowdy and obnoxious. I ask them nicely to keep it down. An unsteady voice replies in a thick accent, "Okay, vee vill keep it dawn, hahahahahahaha." When they don't, I call the front desk and ask that they either quiet our neighbors down or give us back our money. The desk clerk, whom I later meet and discover is a retired Turkish wrestler, is on our floor pronto and nearly breaks down the door to one of the culprits' rooms. It was quiet very soon after that.

We learn from this experience that being in Munich and not being a drinker is a sad thing. The brew is fundamental to life in these parts. Had we been more in the swing, we might have found our neighbors' incursion a welcome opportunity to party, rather than an imposition. Something similar to this little episode took place in Munich in 1923. Remember the Beer Hall Putsch? At that time, Adolf Hitler and six hundred armed friends, spoilsports like us, broke up a perfectly happy beer bash, captured the head of the provincial government, and attempted to take over Germany. We know already that he wound up jailed in Landsberg, proof that *Das Leben besteht nicht nur aus Vergnügen* (Life is not all beer and skittles).

The city center of Munich is monumentally lovely. Gothic, Renaissance, and Baroque buildings are numerous and well-preserved. They function as churches, or theatres, or as in the Marienplatz, a town hall. We discover the city on foot, walking from one square to the next, stopping for coffee often, enjoying the colorful mix of characters here with us. There is a man playing the accordion. He is surrounded by a thick throng of rapt listeners. When he concludes a piece, the crowd erupts in wild applause and demands encores. You won't see accordionists receiving encores in many other places in this world. The accordion is a German invention. We attribute its popularity to national pride rather than musicality.

We visit many of the great buildings, even if peripherally, and are impressed all over again by the wealth of Western art brought about by Christianity. The Frauenkirche in the middle of Old Town is a remarkable example of Gothic ecclesiastical architecture. The church's tall twin towers are a Munich landmark. One of the towers is open, so we climb a bit, then have no choice but to take the elevator the rest of the way up. The volunteer elevator operator explains that there is no alternative access to stairs going the rest of the way up or down the tower because the structure is five hundred years old and therefore very frail. We wonder how it can support an elevator if it can't support humans. We also wonder what the hell to do in case of fire. Then we wonder if the people who built this thing used to have lunch at the Haxn Bauer Restaurant.

◼

The Isar River originates in the Alps then runs south-north, through Munich, before flowing into the Danube. We walk the length of Maximillianstrasse then cross the river on the Maximillian Bridge. Behind us in the distance is Max Joséph Platz. Ahead of us, on the east bank, is the Maximillianeum, an imposing late Baroque building from which you could throw a rock into the river if you had a pretty strong arm. The Bavarian parliament meets here. Now we turn south and stroll through the park, also named after King Maximillian, which stretches for the entire length of the city on this side of the river. It's chilly and damp. Whereas Marienplatz and the Condor neighborhoods are swarming with folks, it is very quiet here. Most of the time we are entirely alone. Occasionally someone walks by, always at the end of a leash. We turn back toward the city and cross the Ludwig Bridge. Now we're in a neighborhood that is a bit removed from the tourist center. Truth is we're a bit lost, but enjoy seeing this unrehearsed part of Munich. Later in the day, following a big *haxn* lunch (again!), we take the metro to the opulent Nymphenburg Palace in the northwest corner of the city. The palace is closed, the *haxn* kicks in, and we end up taking a nap in the palace gardens.

No account of Munich is complete without mention of Oktoberfest. This sudsiest of all fairs is a two hundred-year-old tradition of merrymaking that takes place in late September. The whole thing started with the wedding in 1810 of the future king of Bavaria, Ludwig I. He had such a good time during the wedding that he decided to keep the party going for a few days. This was a happy time in Bavaria. Ludwig I would eventually become king, from 1825 to 1848, but his heart was never in it. He abdicated to Maximillian II who, while we're at it, would beget wacky Ludwig II. Nowadays Oktoberfest can attract more than seven million visitors to the city. Between five and seven million liters of beer, thousands of kilos of sausage, and cartfuls of antacid are consumed in the two-week period. We just missed it.

■

Augsburg, about an hour's ride from Munich, was once Europe's wealthiest city. To be honest, we find this assertion somewhat suspect. It seems that every city we ever visit claims to have had that distinction at one time or another. Who's going to go back and verify? These days it's famous for being the birthplace of Leopold Mozart, Willi Messerschmitt, and Bertolt Brecht. These three—musician and father of Wolfgang; aircraft designer; and playwright—are all dead now, but personify the incredible range of German ingenuity. You cannot but sense, as you travel through this country, that its people have given the world a great deal more than they're given credit for.

We stop for tea and cakes at the very German Ebers on the main square in the center of town. No question that we are a spectacle. It takes five minutes to unzip, unvelcro, and otherwise undo ourselves before we sit down. And even when that's done, we are not the typical couple that goes through here. The patrons at Ebers are openly curious. A silver-haired lady of maybe ninety sits hunched over a salad at a table next to ours. She has a pack of cigarettes on the table, even though we're in the *nicht rauscher* section. Every time I glance in her direction, her gaze is fixed solidly on us. Maybe she's trying to stare us down so she can smoke. I smile but get no reaction. Maybe she's blind, I wonder. Our ignorance of the language severely limits our ability to break the ice. Sure, we can say *hallo, bitte, eine kleine nacht musik* as well as *einbahnstrasse*, but what do you do after that?

The tea hits the spot. We warm right up and continue our ride on the Romantische Strasse. It's lovely, no rain today, and the road is dry. Mostly farmland, it's quiet, pastoral and we are having a great time riding. We make a couple of brief stops in *Hänsel und Gretel* villages, then press on to Rothenburg ob der Tauber. This is a town that has been held in very near mint Gothic condition. The medieval ramparts are nearly intact. Inside these walls the town, surprisingly large, is much as it was six hundred years ago. We find a nice hotel at the southern gate. They have their own little parking lot, so for the first time in a long time we park legally. After settling in we stroll through the village. There is quite a crop of tourists here, many American. Cameras everywhere. As we walk up toward the town's *Marktplatz*, two couples amble along together behind us, arm in arm, singing lovely German songs in four-part harmony. We're munching on the local specialty: a pastry ball that's dipped in whatever flavor strikes one's fancy. Ours is chocolate. A car comes along occasionally, thumping across the cobblestones, but there is an overall sense of calm and serenity, like we're suspended in an unreal world, a time of lamplighters and fairy tales. A person could go out of their minds here in three days flat.

Sedate as the village is these days, it has had its share of drama and crisis, most recently near the end of World War Two. It had become a refuge for German soldiers in retreat. The Allies bombed the *weisswurst* out of the place, destroying hundreds of homes as well as a substantial section of the ramparts. A U.S. general overseeing that particular advance was aware of the cultural and historic value of the town so interceded and prevented further bombing. Now, as we walk all the way around the covered wooden battlements, we see plaques acknowledging donations made by people from all over the world to restore the wall. It's a quiet evening and we're often up here all alone. The sun sets and

Rothenburg Ramparts

a chill catches us underdressed. We look down on the roofs of the darkening old city and feel a medieval melancholy set in. It takes us no time at all to get back to the hotel, find a table by the fireplace, and chase the chill and the gloom away over a supper of *sauerbraten* and *wiener schnitzel.*

Prague, Czech Republic, October 23

There is a precipitous drop in the quality of everything when you cross from Germany into the Czech Republic. The roads, the signs, the cars, the air, the buildings, the terrain all suffer. Now, instead of being unceremoniously passed by BMW 720s and Audi A8s, we have to look out for circa-1980 Skoda Estelles barely breaking 30 km/h, lest we wind up in their back seat. The freeway ends abruptly ten kilometers west of Pilsen, this town famous for nothing but its beer. It starts up again fifteen kilometers east of the city, but not until we have taken a most interesting detour through the suburbs. We pass two very cold and unappetizing hookers at the gates of what looks like a paper mill; several other industrial complexes spewing pugnacious fumes into the already yellow-brown air; and pitiably neglected apart-

Waldstein Hotel

ment blocks almost entirely curtained with clotheslines and laundry. Now as we drive through Pilsen itself, we see the sky only through a web of electrical tram cables. The trams themselves look ancient. People in their cars whip their heads around to gape at us. Whereas in most of Western Europe, children in the back of their family cars took no notice, preoccupied as they are with their busy little electronic lives, here they practically go through the windows in excitement to see such a sight as us. We enjoy the undeserved notoriety and wave a lot. As soon as the freeway picks up again, things begin to gradually improve. By the time we arrive in Prague, we have practically forgotten about the country's western region, as the country itself seems to have done.

Prague is like no other city. The entire center, made up of the Old Town, the New Town, the Little Quarter, and the Prague Castle, is stunning. Gem after gem, wonder after wonder, to the point where another exquisite building in perfect condition from five hundred years ago can be passed by with nothing more than a perfunctory glance. This is astounding. Munich is grand, but largely rebuilt after the war. Paris, London, Madrid, nothing comes close. It is possible that somewhere there is as large and well-preserved and beautiful a collection of buildings and statues, but I haven't seen it. Even our hotel, a lowly three-star, is adjacent to the Waldstein palace, merely four hundred years old. No question that Prague is striking, but it's also old. Nothing wrong with that, except that to live and work here, and be around five hundred-year-old buildings all the time, could be weird. It's marvelous to visit, but we're feeling mustier by the minute.

If Old Prague has a heart, it's the Charles Bridge. This is one of several that connect the east and west banks of the Vltava. The stone span was completed about six hundred years ago. It bows gently across the river, supported on sixteen arches. Since the seventeenth century, fifteen statues stand on each side of the bridge, raised on stone pedestals, hulking like black ghosts over the stream of humanity coming and going. Our own comings and goings in Prague take us across this bridge three or four times a day. It is now restricted to pedestrian traffic, and there's a whole lot of that. Artists and craftsmen can have a spot to the side if they acquire a permit. If you stand somewhere in the middle of the bridge and do a slow clockwise revolution, you will see at least the following, in order: the Rudolfinum, the church of St. Nicholas, the church of St. Francis of Assisi, the church of Our Lady Before Tyn, the Old Town Hall Tower, the Powder Gate, the National Museum, the National Theatre, the Michna Palace, the Church of Our Lady Victorious, the West Bridge Towers, and the jewel of the city: Prague Castle. At night, these buildings, with their fantastical towers and spires, are floodlit. So if you repeat the pirouette after dark,

you will wonder if you've died and gone to fifteenth century purgatory. Also, you will probably collide with one
of the many hawkers of everything from roses to theater
tickets to junk.

Tonight we're at the church of St. Francis of Assisi
to hear an organ concert. We really had no idea what was
on, but most churches in the heart of Old Town have
music nightly. Walk to any of them before 8 p.m. and
you have a good chance of catching some decent music.
Tonight's performance is, to be kind, meteorically bad.
The organ, we are told by the man pitching the tickets,
dates from 1702, and is made of the same fine stuff as the
one at St. Paul's in London. We raise our eyebrows in
grave admiration. The organist, up in one of the aisle gal-

Charles Bridge

leries, dates from not much later than the organ. We see only his hump and the very
top of his head above the balustrade as he sits down at the machine. The program is
promising and includes some Bach cantatas, as well as a few Handel and Mozart
arias. The bass and the mezzo-soprano alternate in the gallery with the organist. Our
butts fall asleep on the wood bench. Bless them all for trying, but the organ, King
of Instruments that it is, will not be ignored. And for most of the evening, this one
sounds like a very complicated traffic jam. The pedals clatter from three hundred
years of being stepped on. (You would too.) Organ Man's hit-rate is poor. Every
other note is close to what it was intended to be, but not close enough. The music
is not all that is assaulting our sensibilities tonight. This church needs a new decorator. There are far too many chubby cherubs hovering unconvincingly on stunted
wings; too many golden rays of ecclesiastical sunshine vectoring this way and that;
too many statues in white virginal flowing robes, having too many passions. There
is entirely too much of everything here. The effect is kitschy. Although it is difficult
to worship among all the clutter, we nevertheless pray ardently for the pain to stop,
and it eventually does, but not before Organ Man strikes his final pulverizing blow
with J.K. Kuchar's "Fantasia for Organ." Czech, please!

There are cities in the world, like Prague, where just hanging around is entertainment enough. Wenceslas Square is a good place for that. The National Museum,
dark-stoned and somewhat spooky, stands at one end of the square. We sit in its
shadow at McDonalds and munch on burgers while contemplating the city's history and the Prague Spring. Russian tanks held strategic positions here after they
invaded the country in 1968. That marked the end of a hopeful season in Prague;
eight months of "reform" that went over in Russia like a fart in church. Leonid
Brezhnev was not amused and sent in the Warsaw Pact troops on August 20. That
put an end to that until 1989, when communism was defeated in a non-violent public uprising that came to be known as the Velvet Revolution. All this is very distant
as I hunt down and suck out the last drops of my chocolate shake.

■

The Czech police force uses a highly sophisticated new radar: It detects money. In our case, it determined that we were attempting to leave the country with some Czech crowns still on us, something wholly unacceptable. Magically, it notifies the officers who pull us over on the E59 going south between Stonarov and Zeletava. This is actually a bit scary because there is no one else around. In fact, the last two villages we drive through manifest sparse evidence of life. We see exactly one bicyclist in each. The houses are shuttered. There is no livestock anywhere, and no shops. Now I see a uniformed man standing in the middle of the narrow road running through this village. He is holding up a short stick to which is attached a circular red sign about the size of a tea saucer. I slow to a stop as I reach him. Now he motions to his colleague, who is still in the car by the side of the road. This second policeman approaches us and salutes, accidentally tapping his cap and knocking it askew. He informs me that we were locked onto by the radar "away back," and that we were going "fast fast." I could disagree and argue my innocence but have a pretty good idea what this transaction is about, so to save time and trouble, I ask how much I owe the Czech government. "Minimum two thousand crown," he says. I turn out my pockets and come up with 350 crowns, which I offer him apologetically. I say that I'm sorry but can't come up with any more money. He says, "Minimum one thousand five hundred crown." I rifle through my waist-pouch and pull out the Hungarian forints we bought in Prague. He grimaces. "Only crown, minimum one thousand crown." This goes on for a few minutes, the two crooks conferring sternly, the "minimum" gradually descending, until we finally agree on the sum of three hundred crowns, a little under eight dollars. I thank him for his "help" and walk back to the bike. Tracy is now pissed off because she's gathered the drift of the visit, and erupts in a voice loud enough to be heard in Manchuria, "what the *hell!*" She overlooks the fact that she is wearing earplugs and has a helmet on, and that what may to her seem quiet is in fact loud to other humans and deafening to dogs. The officers perk up like pointers on a Cornish hen, but I avoid eye contact, jump on the bike and blow the hell out of there. We spend the forty-five minutes to the border discussing the difference between U.S. traffic court and rural Czech prisons.

JR's Restaurant and Casino is our final stop in the Czech Republic. Here we are, in the belly of Europe, land of palaces and Gothic magnificence and dynasties predating soap. Yet by the side of the road is a large building dedicated to the American television show *Dallas*. They serve Sue Ellen cheeseburgers, and J.R. steaks, and more. However, in patently European style, they also serve dogs. Not hot dogs, just dogs. It is remarkable that this country, until ten years ago solidly behind the Iron Curtain, can have come so far. Not good, necessarily, but certainly remarkable.

Vienna, Austria, October 28

If you look good in a powdered wig and knee-stockings, you will have no trouble at all getting work in Vienna. We see want ads like this:

> *Wanted: Man or Woman willing to dress in eighteenth century outfits and parade in front of tourists from all around the world. Must know how to say "Eine Kleine Nacht Musik" in English, Italian, French, and Japanese. No experience of any kind necessary. A pleasant disposition desirable but not required. Facial hair, particularly large black mustaches, out of the question. People darker than weisswurst need not apply. We categorically do not accept Czechs.*

We park the bike on the street for a change, and walk around the Staatsoper (State Opera) looking for the Tourist Information Office which our guidebook assures us is hereabouts. No dice, so we descend into the U-Bahn for a look. It's here that we first see the many eighteenth century people walking around, going to work like nothing was at all odd about the way they're dressed. I suppose it's petty and narrow-minded of us to be so tickled by something so epidermal, but *damn* it's hard to see this and not wonder just how far a person has to go to earn a living. I want to throw a speech urging insurrection. I want to take them all away from all this. I want to ask if their scalps itch.

The lady in the powdered wig at the Tourist Information Office, which is nicely hidden and poorly marked in the darkness behind the Staatsoper, uses the word "hotel" loosely. The International Haus is not really a hotel, but a pension. So, even though it is a four-star, these stars do not weigh as much nor shine as bright as real hotel stars. They're more like jelly doughnuts. Still, four jelly doughnuts are better than a kick in the face. At least the place seems secure. We know this because we're in the street, in the rain, and can't get in. Finally someone crackles over the intercom, "Second floor please" and buzzes us in. In Europe the second floor is up on the fifth somewhere, but there is an elevator. As we slosh off it we are impressed by the automatic doors that open in our way and reveal a hallway of red crushed carpeting and white faux-enamel (Formica) walls. This is how I would decorate a whorehouse, if I had one.

Vienna makes life easy for visitors. Most everything of historic or artistic value is contained within the series of wide boulevards which ring the city and are together known as the *Ringstrasse*. This ring took the place of the ramparts that encircled the old inner city. We ride tram Number One all the way around and see many of the neo-classical buildings that epitomize Viennese architecture. I wish I knew more about that, but it's not a straightforward

North Hofburg Gate

thing. Anyone can learn the basic characteristics of architectural epochs. It's not so tough to tell the difference between a Romanesque and a Baroque Church. Renaissance style is very different from, say, Gothic. Many of these buildings, however, start out life as one thing and end up something altogether different. St. Stephen's Cathedral, for example, was built in the thirteenth century. It looks High Gothic, so you might guess it was built later, like in the fifteenth century, but you'd be wrong. Then there's war, and fire, and flood, and other acts of man and God, which can wipe a place off the face of the earth. In some cases this can be a blessing in disguise. The original 1869 Staatsoper in Vienna was so roundly criticized that one of the two responsible architects, caving in under the pressure of public vilification, killed himself. The second architect had a stroke and died a few months later. In 1945, long after anyone cared, the Allies bombed the place nearly all the way to Constantinople. The new building is a big hit.

Mozart is big business in Vienna. You cannot walk down any street anywhere in this town without seeing someone making a living off the man's name. We have Mozart chocolates, Mozart houses, Mozart cafés, Mozart concert halls, Mozart marionettes and at least one Mozart museum. There's even a Mozart wiener stand at the intersection of Sellengasse and Graben. Tonight we're at the Musikveriensaal, where the Vienna Philharmonic normally lives, to hear some, yup, Mozart. This is a beautifully ornate hall located on the outside of the Vienna Ring, not far from the Operstaadt. The inside of the place is exuberantly decorative Vienna Art Nouveau. The balcony that follows the perimeter of the building is held up by thirty-two columns carved into gilded semi-nude female figures. What's not to like? Tonight's orchestra—not the Philharmonic—is a happy orchestra. The audience is frisky. The event is casual, almost burlesque. The First Violin is on the very verge of bursting out in laughter for most of the performance. One couple two rows in front of us carry on a conversation only while the musicians are actually playing, but no one "shshshshshs" them. A lady in a magenta coat, in the seat behind mine, takes a flash picture on every downbeat. The program is a Mozart's Greatest Hits sort of thing, with arias from *Don Giovanni* and *The Magic Flute*. They perform an entire horn concerto. The French horn is an instrument that tends to accumulate spit. We've all seen players clean their pipes in the course of a concert, but a horn concerto summons up a prodigious amount of saliva. At nearly every opportunity, the poor man amputates some section of his horn and spends the time until his next note running hankies through it. When the piece is finally over, we erupt into applause as much for his heroic defense of spitlessness as for his musicality.

■

It needs to be said that there is a serious pigeon problem here. I can't recall seeing anything like this in the U.S. It seems that every time I return to Europe, more of it is under wire mesh. How this will solve the problem is beyond me. Shoot them,

I say. Pigeons are not a threatened species. Hell, they're not even offended. Bring in a few of the guys we played Paintball with in Seattle. They'll exterminate the problem in no time. Then we can see the world's architectural patrimony without the omnipresent protective hairnet.

Still, this is Vienna, and my thoughts are only briefly with pigeons. On our second day now, we are going to see *Lucia di Lammermoor*, at the Staatsoper. Not seeing an opera in Vienna is like not having the runs in Delhi—unthinkable. So we go. We're already very familiar with *Lucia di Lammermoor*, having seen it not long ago in Barcelona at the Liceu. However, it's the hall we're here to see, and what a place it is! We're a few minutes early and stroll around enjoying the building. This is not as much about looking at things like columns and paintings and sculptures and frescoes and such. It is rather very much about moving in the space, through arches, alongside colonnades, all around interior balconies. As we do this, the opulence seeps into us. Here we are in jeans, turtlenecks, drab fleece cardigans, and black weathered motorcycle boots, and yet we feel elegant and prosperous and cultured. Some of the attendees might disagree, and a few look us up and down with unmasked mortification. The performance is top-notch. We applaud often and enthusiastically. Every important aria is gorgeous. Lucia's "Mad Scene," in spite of all its corny melodrama, is electrifying. After all, you don't go to the opera for reality. This is certainly very much the case when Ashford, mortally wounded, goes on singing strong for twenty minutes before the curtain finally drops.

Vienna can stand a second, longer visit, like Prague. It's a walker's city, full of sumptuous architecture and art, straddling a river, brimming with music. You can also visit, as we did, places like Mozart's home. Actually, this is one of *eighteen* apartments he occupied at one time or another in the city, before dying despised and destitute. The official story is that he died of typhoid fever. Vastly more interesting is the possibility that he was offed by Antonio Salieri. In either case, given his posthumous success, Mozart is one man for whom reincarnation would have been good news.

Budapest, Hungary, October 30

I still labor under impressions that I formed twenty years ago about Hungary. Back then it was dark, socked away behind the Iron Curtain. Very little information was available about it that wasn't state-baked propaganda. I stopped listening. Things got interesting in 1989, when the country demoted its communists and began to claw its way back into Europe and the rest of the world, but by then I was already too accustomed to not paying attention. As a result, much of what I see here surprises me. We find the border hassle-free. They take a look at our passports, at the bike's license plate, and wave us through. The countryside is lovely and quiet, just like everywhere else we've been. It's vast, but flat and easy to get through. It would be unfair to compare this to our first impression of the Czech Republic because in that case we detoured off the freeway, whereas here we are on good roads in fine weather and have all the time in the world to get where we're going. As we roll across these countries of Europe overland, it's easy to imagine armies marching through them. When you read that the Germans took a country in two weeks, you think that's really something, when in fact there's nothing to take but the big cities. Everything in between is farmland. You can drive across Hungary in half a day. Take Budapest and you're done.

We ride into Budapest and quickly find our way to the Tourist Information Office at the Eastern Railway Station. Soon we're on our way back across the Danube to Buda, where our hotel, the Victoria, sits down the hill from Matthias Church. We like it here. After Vienna, it's already obviously less pretentious. Hungarian men would not think of hanging out in powdered wigs and stockings. Certainly not without first getting thoroughly smashed.

Most people find it mildly surprising to learn that Budapest is actually made up of Buda and Pest. That's right. Buda is on the west bank of the Danube. Pest is on the east bank. Buda is hilly and leafy and home to the big castle. Pest is a maze of winding streets and cobbled old squares. The Inner City of Pest is a semicircle, bordered to the west by the Danube, and ringed to the east by boulevards that arc between Chain Bridge to the north and Freedom Bridge to the south. We stroll through town and find our way to Gerbeaud on Vorosmarty Square. This historic café, something of an institution, is today out of chocolate, vanilla and strawberry ice cream. Almost every item pictured luxuriously on their menu is thus rendered academic. So we order one of their specialties: *somloi galuska*, a Hungarian-style chocolate ballast. It's delicious and rich, which is good because the coffee is terrible. That's a sad thing. You can't get a good cup of coffee in Budapest. I don't know why that is and am too listless to think about it.

One of the things that drew us to Budapest was the reputation of its thermal baths. A friend in the U.S. who spent some time here in the past tells us that Budapest is his favorite European capital for this reason alone. We march down the west bank of the Danube to the most famous of all, the baths at Hotel Gellért. The building itself, like most notable Budapest monuments, was put up about a hundred years ago, and combines neo-Classical and Hungarian Art Nouveau styles. The over-all effect is crusty. Whether or not it's beautiful is entirely open to debate but some-one spent a great deal of time and money making columns and scrolls and friezes and frescoes and reliefs. The baths are a big business for the hotel. The ticket counters at the front are staffed with nice folks who nevertheless have very little patience for questions. This makes me their worst nightmare. It doesn't help that the price list is longer than a Chinese menu. To move things along we buy the Everything ticket. The process is a bit confusing, but there are just enough Hungarian English-speakers who speak just enough Hungarian English to get us to the point where our clothes are hanging in a locked cabin, and we are in our bathing suits in a large tub of warm water with assorted human dumplings. Everyone is required to wear a bathing cap. Most of us have to use the disposable blue ones offered by the hotel. If you could survey the scene from up high, we would look like blueberries in lime Jell-O. This is all very chummy and somewhat relaxing, but frankly, I don't see the big deal. It's a beautiful place and everything, but without the smell of sulfur, this whole exercise is just a bath with people we don't know and would not ordinarily consider undressing for or with. That's when we realize that there is more to it. At the far end of the pool, on each side, are small entrances to the gender-segregated men's and women's thermal baths, and it is in here that they put the "thermal" in thermal baths.

I make an exploratory foray into the men's section, while Tracy checks out the women's. We meet up back by the co-ed pool. I've learned that there are two thermal pools in there, Turkish style, as well as massage, sauna and steam facilities. She, in the meantime, has discovered a similar setup on her side of the building, and also that it is traumatizing to be surrounded by large, naked Eastern European women. She's afraid that they can smell fear and is ready to call the whole thing off, but gamely goes back in, towel clutched close.

Back in 1995 I visited a Turkish *hammam* in Damascus with a local buddy of mine. Following the soaking portion of that visit, I was ex-foliated by a man with a rough burlap mitt. It's considered a high point of the whole "baths" thing, but I made a mental note never to let that happen again. Here at the Gellért, they offer something called the soap massage, and it sounds painless. I walk into a room furnished with tables that look something like trampolines. The fabric stretched across the metal frames is a sort of plastic mesh. On top of that is a white sheet. Two fat men in their fifties, wearing towels, are poised to massage. The Damascus experience comes to mind but I note that no one here is wearing a mitt. So I give my eight-dollar token to the kinder looking man and lie down. He hoses me down, then massages my legs and upper body with soap. It's like a carwash. At the end I feel quite relaxed, but am equally grateful that I am no longer being given a bath by a man.

In countries where the language is out of reach, like here in Hungary, we feel most at home when we are at a concert. Tonight we are at the Music Academy for an all-Bach choral program. The main foyer is dark. This is a vestige of the communist years: not enough light-bulbs. Still, if you look closely you see remarkable examples of the art and architecture of that fuzzy *fin-de-siècle* era. The hall is ornate and embellished and overdone. On the whole the building is Impoverished Bourgeois. One day long ago, for a brief time, when everything here worked and was cleaned regularly, this was an opulent and extravagant place. Now it tantalizes you with its past and potential. All this becomes utterly irrelevant when the people of Budapest take their seats and the orchestra and choir begin the concert. There is simplicity here, a genuine modesty that you could not find in Vienna or Prague. You could put on airs, but would find yourself in a very small minority. The music is exquisite. The soloists, a bass and a soprano, are accomplished and intense. The orchestra is tight. The choir is rich and crisp.

On the way back to the hotel we buy two apples, two pears, one large bottle of Evian, and one bar of Cadbury Milk Chocolate; $2.25. Money's a funny thing. In Vienna we paid about a hundred dollars a night for an adequate room in a four-jelly-doughnut pension. In Budapest, seventy dollars a night gets us a wonderful four-star hotel room with a spectacular view of the Danube and Pest. In Vienna a cup of coffee costs about three dollars. This would cover four cups of bad coffee and a healthy tip in Budapest. Our tickets to the Mozart Laughathon at Musikveriensaal in Vienna were forty-five dollars each. Here we pay five dollars apiece to see virtuosi musicians and a brilliant choir. In relative terms, our cash goes much farther in places like Prague and Budapest than in Vienna and Monaco. So what if they don't have enough light bulbs?

■

We're glad we decided to stay three nights in Budapest, and are doing what we can to see as much of the city as possible before we hit the road to Zagreb. At the Deak Ter subway station we are stopped again by the fare enforcement police. We have an all-day pass, so there's no problem. Last night, mind you, it was a different story. Here at this very same station, we were busted when neither of the tickets we had was valid. The first, which we thought was a round-trip fare, turns out to be one-way. The second was for the following day. The man who stops us is bent on extracting the on-the-spot fine, 1,300 forints, or about four dollars each. We think this stinks because we are innocent of any premeditated wrong-doing. It's a matter of principle, of course, and not the four dollars. Well, eight dollars. So I start an argument that takes the better part of fifteen minutes. I speak no Hungarian, except for *goulash*, but am unable to use the word constructively in a sentence, certainly not under these circumstances. He speaks no English, except for one word: *meester*, and uses it often as he communicates that he wants me to pay the 1,300 forints now. He's being a jerk about it so I want to make him rue the moment he laid his beady little eyes on me. Unfortunately, there is a circumstance that complicates things somewhat: He is solidly in the right. Tracy and I are well and truly not holding a valid ticket. Technically speaking, then, the sonofabitch has us cornered, even if I claim the moral high ground. If I were him, I insist as his eyes glaze over and frustrated sighs escape in succession from his flatulent uniform, I would let us run upstairs and buy two tickets for the regular fare of ninety-six forints each. Also, I would floss more often. "*Meester*," he starts again, holding up the expired ticket and pointing a fat finger at the English instructions on the back. I am adamant and pouty. Finally he breaks the impasse by calling over the two regular police officers who have been watching us from a safe distance and occasionally shaking their heads to each other as if to say: "It's always something with these damned Americans." I do not want to be hauled off to a Hungarian prison, not even for an orientation visit, so I pull the money out of my pocket. Still, in a final act of insubordination and civil agitation, I say to the man as I walk away, "You really ought to be ashamed of yourself, *meester*." I think I won; he seemed shaken.

Budapest is a grand old city. It's sprawling, and has many boulevards reminiscent of those in Paris, leading to large monumental squares. Traffic is thick and pollution is unpleasant. We escape to the very large City Park, Vasroliget, and are spared the fumes somewhat. High on our list of things to do is lunch at Gundel's Restaurant, or its cheaper brother, Bagolyvar. Among the attractions in the park is

Budapest Nap

the Vajdahunyad Castle, a weird smorgasbord of architectural styles along the lines of the Palacio da Pena in Portugal. It's a silly thing, particularly when we have fresh in our memories exquisite examples of these styles in the palaces of Bavaria, Bohemia, and Vienna. Also at the park is the Museum of Fine Arts. We pay the five hundred forint admission fee because we have to pee. Two small steps inside the Eighteenth Century Room, we are stopped by one of the uniformed guards who outnumber visitors eight-to-one. He wants us to turn in the backpack in which we have such valuables as our super-duper ultra-spendy Sony Digital Camera. "Hell no," we say, and withdraw all the way to Heroes Square, where deranged twenty-first century boys do skateboard tricks on the Unknown Soldier's shrine. We find Gundel's, but it intimidates us. There are people in there wearing cuff links, for crying out loud. So we shuffle along to Bagolyvar and have a wonderfully hearty lunch of mushroom soup and mushroom-stuffed tenderloin over fettuccine.

Zagreb, Croatia, November 2

We're riding in the rain again, en route to Zagreb. The freeway out of Budapest ends and becomes a country road for a hundred kilometers before the Croatian border, and it's a slow, messy ride. Trucks, tractors, mule-drawn wagons, they all use this road. This feels like that miserable ride between Nîmes and St. Rémy, when we were soaked to the bone. We're much better off now. It's only our hands and feet that are wet, but it's also a much longer haul. We have 350 kilometers to cover today, and there are very few places to stop. We pull into one roadside café and splash in for a cup of coffee. There is a gang of young men in there who look guilty and desperate, like they've just finished tying up the pope in the basement. They're all drinking something that looks like urine. We gulp down our coffees and march back out into the weather. Following long kilometers of open farmland, we start riding up into some mountains. The temperature drops and the rain gets bigger. Huge trucks come barreling around sharp turns. Through their splashing windshield wipers, the drivers all resemble Lucifer.

Everything changes at the border. The shabby yayhoos on the Hungarian side spend ten minutes watching us idle on the bike before one of them comes along to raise the barrier that's in our way. No "goodbye," no "have a good trip." Now on the Croatian side, crisply uniformed border police are all business. They check the passports and wave us through. And here, rolled out in front of us like a welcome carpet, is a beautiful, spanking-new freeway. It starts at the border, so there is no traffic coming from anywhere else. We are all alone. It has stopped raining. The sun peeks through every once in a while. Now as we make a gentle long turn in the road we find ourselves driving on glass. The sun is low in the sky straight ahead of us and makes the still-wet road glisten. It's weird to be in Croatia. This country wasn't a country until 1991, when it broke away from Yugoslavia. Someone had to go around and change all the signs. I think about the four-year war with Serbia. I think of poor St. Gellért, martyred in the name of Hungary when he was rolled down Castle Hill in a barrel. I think of the countless young and old who died at one time or another defending or giving birth to a nation. I think how nice it will be to find a hotel in Zagreb and get a hot shower.

We notice something is creepy as soon as we leave the freeway and start going through inhabited areas of Croatia. The countryside is beautiful, but no one's around. Shops are closed. Even some gas stations are shut. Here in Zagreb, the city center is practically deserted, yet there are police duos at most corners. We're not sure what to make of this. Zagreb is apparently home to one million people, so it's no small town. We learn this the hard way as we attempt to find the Center. It's signposted, but not quite enough to get you there. So we follow a trail of *Centar* arrows and then, as though this is some kind of twisted game, no more clues. We become lost. And to make matters worse, imagine if all the subways in London or New York were above ground. That's the situation here, and it makes it impossible to get around because trams and nasty slippery tracks are everywhere. Every street in Zagreb is one-way only. To get anywhere you must make great big circles and then sneak up on where you're going. It may actually be in the block immediately adjacent to the one you're on, but good luck getting there without taking a nice, long circumnavigation. Eventually, tracking as best we could the direction in which people appear to be gravitating, we find ourselves on the edge of a pedestrian section of town. I jump the bike up on the curb, park it alongside a recycling dome, and we walk away looking for a Tourist Information Office.

After not much more than fifteen minutes, we stumble upon the Dubrovnik Hotel, which is so close to the city's center that it is completely encircled in pedestrian-only streets, making it absolutely unreachable by motorbike. We discover this only after we've checked in and left my passport with the front desk. Now we're back on the bike, riding around for a half-hour in crazy downtown Zagreb, dodging trams and police officers. We cannot make it back to the Dubrovnik, so we abandon the search and pull right up on the curb in front of another hotel, the Astoria, where we check in again. This hotel is a bag lady to the Dubrovnik's super model. It's ugly, it's falling apart, and it's on a busy street. There is a Chinese restaurant on the ground floor, for Pete's sakes. In Zagreb!

The center of Zagreb is Ban Josip Jelacic square, just down the hill from the cathedral and around the corner from the open-air market, the best shopping, and the train station. We start our walking tour there. By now it's evening, and there is a huge crowd walking past the cathedral to a crematorium farther up on the hill. They're very orderly. No one makes trouble here. We walk up the hill as well. We're looking for the Dubrovnik again, because I need to retrieve my passport. There's a policeman up here helping manage the crowd, which really doesn't need any management at all. I ask if he speaks English and he says "*Leetle.*" So we say we're looking for a hotel. He's very amused by this and says "Hotel California?" This is funny, because

Zagreb Art

that's the title of a song by The Eagles. He himself is amused, which fact encourages us because so far Croats have seemed far too serious a bunch. So we ask about the crowd. "It's, ekh, Day of Death," he says gravely. This frightens us for a brief while, but we figure out that it's the equivalent of All Saints' Day. Except that here, everybody buys flowers and candles and goes to the cemetery. *Everybody.*

After picking up the passport we have dinner at Piccolo Mondo, right on Ban Josip square. This is probably one of the top restaurants in Zagreb. It certainly has a prime location. The service and food are very good, and the place makes for a great spot from which to watch people. On the whole, though, there really isn't much to watch. Zagreb is not hip. Still, as we stroll through the old part of the city, particularly along Tkalciceva Street, we can see that the young are trying to differentiate. There is occasional green hair here, and pierced noses, and other evidence of generational revolution, but Zagreb is slow. Compared to, say, Prague, it's a shabby snore-machine. We're happy to have seen it, and to have spent a day walking around and seeing the sights, such as they are, but would not plan a second vacation around it.

Venice, Italy, November 4

We leave Trieste as it is, adding very little to its already substantial misery, and outrun the rain storm which is heaping it down on this rough and tough city. Within twenty minutes we're in sunshine on the coastal ss14. Outside Trieste, this

Venice Canal

becomes a corniche with dramatic unobstructed views of the Adriatic. Then around Giorgio de Nogaro we merge onto the A4 Autostrada. It's flat and straight and dry and all's well with the world. After yesterday's exhausting fight to get from Zagreb to Trieste, this is a real treat, but we're worried about what to do when we get to Venice. Everything we've read says that if you arrive by car, or in our case a motorcycle, you must park it at the terminus and then take a water-taxi or bus or gondola to the hotel. However, as we round the cul-de-sac at the end of the road from the mainland, we see a hotel that seemingly defies this rule. So we ride up on the sidewalk, as usual, and here we are at the Santa Chiara Hotel, billed in its own brochure as the Only Hotel in Venice Accessible by Car! Do not lose this name! The Santa Chiara has its own parking; clean, nicely furnished rooms; an Internet station in the lounge; and an exit right onto the Grand Canal.

We are very near the train station, at the extreme northeast corner of the island. Holy Roman Empire! What a maze Venice is. We start down alleyways that dead-end into canals. Bridges go up and over and put us right back where we were ten minutes ago. We will not look at the map. This is so much fun we want to skip rather than walk. Every turn leads us to another thing of beauty! Wonderful villas in Venetian Gothic, decorative and believable only here. I don't think it's possible to completely prepare someone for Venice. If you've been, you know. If not, how do you begin to imagine a place in which streets and canals are interchangeable; dead-ends are everywhere; there are no cars, no mopeds (can this be heaven?), not even bicycles. Why? Because you can't go very far without running into stairs. There are no Attention Deficit Disordered skateboarding adolescents here! It's quiet and blissfully serene. We walk down deserted streets only a couple of blocks from piazzas where thousands throng and shop and loll. Now we're trying hard to outrun the nun to the Number 51 bus which we think will take us back to Piazzale Roma. This isn't really a bus. It's a boat. Everything in Venice is something else. Streets are canals. Bridges are markets. The moon is a pizza pie.

It's nearly three in the afternoon and we're getting very hungry, going as we are only on Trieste croissants and the electricity in the air of Venice. We've walked through Santa Croce and Dorsoduro, and crossed the Ponte dell'Academia over the Grand Canal into the San Marco neighborhood. Now we're winding our way through quaint little streets, crossing limpid canals, taking it all in, when we arrive at the Campo San Stefano. A "*campo*" is a square. At the east end there are two cafés. We sit at the one with the blue table-cloths. A couple of other couples are here. It's about twenty degrees Celsius. The sun is halfway down the western sky and shining brightly into this delightful spot. There is a statue of San Stefano in the middle of the square. This was Christianity's first martyr, stoned to death at the dawn of the first millennium. This in no way spoils our mood. Here's a well from 1754. A group of young Africans have spread large collections of Yves Saint Laurent and Louis Vuitton knock-offs across the square from where we are. There aren't many people here. Everybody seems languid. There's no rush to buy, or sell, or eat. Our waiter must count on this, because he is almost quintessentially inept. He takes our order once, then again after trying to retain it through a conversation with another table. Now he's back to confirm that I'm having the spaghetti. We don't mind. The salads are fresh and crisp and cool and clean and Italian. How can people who live in a country with food like this, and language like this, and climate, and the pope on their side, not be chronically giddy to be alive? As I suction the last delicious drop of espresso out of the adorable hand-painted ceramic cup, the sun winks and slips behind the Palazzo Loredan at the west end of the square.

Speaking of language, we were speculating today on the subtle influence that language can have on one's concept of the world. Does anyone think that it's possible to have *joie de vivre* in Czech? Is *la dolce vita* even remotely conceivable in, say, Swedish? Give me a break! We're destined or doomed, as the case may be, to living our language. That's why Venetians can afford to be smug; they have the world's most beautiful language in which to gloat. I know enough Italian to make out simple exchanges, and am perpetually surprised at how luscious they can sound. Try this: *Bisogna smontare la scatola del cambio.* If you pronounce it right, as an Italian might, it sounds deeply romantic, poetic, heroic, sexy even. It means: The clutch will have to be disassembled.

Now we're at Piazza San Marco and dazzled. We've seen many churches in the past eight weeks, but nothing's taken our breath away like this. We enter the piazza from the west end, and are immediately overwhelmed with the façade of St. Mark's Basilica. The large semi-circular window in the central arch catches and reflects the sun, golden now in these last minutes of the day. The wildly colorful mosaics in the half-domes of the four smaller arches are, well, wildly colorful. The five domes, many spires and minarets betray the church's multicultural parentage. It was started over a thousand years ago but built through several centuries. Many of its most remarkable features were "borrowed" during the Crusades from their original homes. The famous Golden Horses on top of the central arch were brought here from Constantinople by Doge Enrico Dandolo. They sat on the terrace for five hundred years. Then Napoleon came along and schlepped them off to Paris. A few years later, in 1815, they were brought back to Venice. The things on the terrace today are copies. The originals are in the basilica museum. Consider that these were made by a Greek three or four centuries before Christ. Christ, what a story!

All this is very nearly too much for us to take standing up. So we sit down at the Caffe Lavena and order a cappuccino and a tea. They have a small orchestra playing Vivaldi, Pergolesi and Neil Diamond. There are three other large cafés like this one around the square. They are distinguishable by the different color of their tables and chairs. If you get hold of an aerial photo of the Piazza San Marco, we'll be in the yellow chairs. There's a distinguished chap in a tux strolling around being host. He's charming and hospitable and makes us feel right at home, but he's absent-minded, like our waiter at the Piazza San Stefano, and has to come back and ask again what we want. Then he delegates the work of actually delivering the stuff to a younger man with one large eyebrow that travels clear from one of his ears to the other. What a wonderful thing it is, to be sitting here in this spectacular place, contentedly sipping our warm drinks as the orchestra plays and the sun drifts away. There's a nice crowd, but not a mob. The requisite pigeons are here. We're leafing slothfully through a photo guide of the city. Maybe we'll take a bus-boat back to the hotel. Maybe we'll walk. Maybe we'll just sit here and let our eyelids drop for a sneak snooze. Maybe we'll dream in Italian.

■

Tracy and I carry a weather curse. Everywhere we go we bring rain and floods. Yesterday Venice sparkled under a bright sun and clear blue skies. Locals and tourists went about happily in short-sleeve shirts. The harbors and canals were calm and

Acqua Alta!

friendly. Today we woke up to a driving rain that has stayed with us all day long. The Piazza San Marco is under a meter of water. Hapless tourists caught unprepared slosh about trying to find some high ground while their umbrellas are shredded and inverted. Most canals have gone over their banks. Teams of municipal workers hustle to put up catwalks. On the north side of Piazza San Marco, we're part of an increasingly nervous crowd that waits for two men to erect the next section of viaduct so we can get the hell out of there. Bus-boat schedules are turned on their heads. Many stops are taken off the usual routes because they are inundated. Boats that are still running are packed. What a difference a day and a curse make!

We nevertheless consider this a gift of sorts. Now we see first-hand what all the ubiquitous *Acqua Alta* signs mean. Apparently, this is not an unusual phenomenon in Venice. The water comes up every year, many times, particularly during the winter months and sea-storms. Shopkeepers are prepared. They install knee-high boards in front of their storefronts which keep out water but not customers. Following the devastating flood of 1966, there was some question about the city's survival. It's not difficult to imagine, as we watch the water rise today, how this place could quickly become uninhabitable. Not as a result of some sort of cataclysmic event, but rather by a slow paralyzing creep of sea. I would not invest in real estate here.

■

Now it's 7:30 p.m. and Venice is spooky. The hustle and bustle of the city is gone. The canals are dark and deserted except for the occasional bus-boat and police or ambulance, flashing blue lights, working overtime. When we get to Rialto both sides of the bridge are under water. There are catwalks in place for us to get out of the bus stop shelter, but no way to get to the concert at the church without wading through knee-high water. We've come this far and are not going to let that stop us. So we follow every dry trail we can, then climb over to the other side of the bridge, and there, a testament to human industry, is a kiosk with two men selling rubber boots and light-weight plastic cloaks. We leave them several thousand lire and splash away merrily in our new rain gear.

Chiesa San Bartolomeo is a modest church dating back to the second half of the seventeenth century. We join a damp little group huddled at the entrance. Soon they let us in to take our seats and it becomes clear that the audience might not outnumber the orchestra tonight. The concert begins and we settle in for a little Baroque-induced snooze. This, the snoozing I mean, is an art. It takes years to perfect and can be perilous. What if you rip one of those lugubrious snores? What if your grip relaxes and your reading glasses go crashing onto the marble floor in the echo-prone nave? What if your head falls back and your hairpiece lands in your neighbor's lap? All this is academic because tonight's young cellist has no intention of letting any of us doze. He is on fire, nearly orgasmic during the Vivaldi cello concerto. When his eyes are not sealed with passion, they are fixed on us, making sure we're all ears, all awake, all witnessing his paroxysm.

Verona, Italy, November 10

Italy is fattening. Our staple diet is pizza. They have wonderful names for it here. There are the standard *Margherita* and *Primavera*, but then you have your ultra-exotics, like the *Cappriciosa*, which comes with artichoke hearts and Parma ham. Or the *Giocosa*, this one served with three kinds of ham. Is there a *Bellicosa*, with beans? For in-between-meals snacks we generally find a *gelateria* and slip down a few scoops of ice cream. We then wash these down with double *machiatti*. This is exactly the routine tonight at Spizzico, a fast-food place at the start of Via Mazzani. So we're traveling through Italy hopped up sky-high on carbohydrates, caffeine, and sugar. This has the effect of gradually turning us into human time-bombs. No wonder I'm having road rage.

Earlier today we rode from Venice to Verona. From the moment we merge onto the A4 and go northeast, we play a dangerous game of run-the-motorcycle-off-the-road with the legions of trucks that use this road. There is a nearly uninterrupted line of these behemoths for the whole of our hundred-kilometer trip. By the time we get to Padova we're up to here with it. Some sorry Luigi in a blue Fiat makes the mistake of squeezing into our lane and then cutting dangerously close in front of us. He picked the wrong guy on the wrong day to mess with. I catch him at the light, ride right up to his window and give him a serious fist-shaking scare. This is not at all like me. I'm losing some of my customary equanimity, and must remember to not chase down motorists who piss me off. Tracy is no help at all in these situations. She's usually rummaging in her purse for pepper spray and brass knuckles.

■

The Adige River cuts an S-shape through Verona, and most of the historic buildings and places of interest are in the belly of that S. Several bridges span the river, and we start our exploring at the Old Castle, or Castelvecchio. This is a straight-ahead castle of the sort you or I might build if we were being stalked. The man who ordered it apparently had every reason to be concerned. His people nick-named him *Cani Rabidus*, or Rabid Dog. Yikes. In any case, this charmer, whose real name is Cangrande II della Scala, got the Castelvecchio started in 1354. Just about that time, and while he was on a trip out of town, his half-brother Fregnano stages

Verona Gargoyles

a coup, claiming that Cangrande was dead. Now Fregnano enjoys being top salami, but his glee is short-lived. As soon as Cangrande gets wind of the mischief, he gathers an army at Vicenza, comes back to Verona, and kicks royal Italian ass at Campo Marzo. Trying to escape by swimming across the Adige, because he knows he's in hot water with Rabid Dog, Fregnano drowns. We stood in the middle of the Scaliger Bridge today and contemplated the scene. I'm a pretty good swimmer, but estimate that if I were to try to cross this fast angry bull-dog of a torrent and did not get pulled down to the bottom, I would be a few hundred meters downstream before I was done. Imagine trying to pull that off with a suit of armor on. There's more. Another brother, Cansignorio, who evidently also had a healthy dislike for Cangrande, kills him one night in 1359 near the Church of St. Euphemia. We learn that a medieval instrument, sharp or blunt (the only available choices at the time), was involved. Now Cansignorio is king. All these guys are members of the della Scala clan. They ran things in Verona until they ran out of brothers in 1400.

Happily, the news gets a little less bloody as we continue today's tour deeper into the belly of Verona at Piazza delle Erbe. This is the old market square, and still serves that function today, albeit as a quaint appendage to Via Mazzani, where the serious shopping takes place. Piazza delle Erbe—literally, Herb Square—is in the middle of a number of important buildings. Among these is the church of Santa Maria Antica. This small Gothic church was sort of appropriated by our old friends the della Scalas, and they have their sepulchers stuck in and on it everywhere you look. You couldn't swing a dead cat in here without hitting one of theirs. The stone and marble coffins are creepy, and in this setting, creepier still. Just around the corner is Piazza dei Signori, which contains several statues of Italy's notable guys (no gals, I'm afraid). Dante stands in the middle of the piazza. At the moment there is a pigeon on his head. Today lunch is at Vesuvio 3, near the Lamberti Tower. Pizza. Gelato. Macchiato.

"I Hate You Forever. Sally." Only this inscription, among several million left at the top of the Lamberti bell tower by lovers from the world over, fails to exemplify the spirit of Verona: the City of Love. Our climb up the tower is a leap of faith, considering mounting evidence that Italians are nearly as good at building towers as they are at choosing sides in World Wars. For about twenty minutes we're the only people up here, enjoying the view and reading love messages. Then a young man shows up, toting every tourist accessory imaginable: books; camera and case; large bottle of mineral water; several Nike products; fanny-pack with multiple zippered compartments, and a baseball cap that reads U.S.A. We figure he's American. I guess he could have been something else, but when I say "Hiyadoin?" he says "Hiyadoin" back.

On the way back to the hotel, we find ourselves at Juliet's House. There's a brisk business responding to letters written by the lovelorn to Juliet, and Verona has the entrepreneurs to milk that particular cow. So, lest we be regarded as unromantic or worse, illiterate, Tracy and I visit the courtyard of Juliet's House, and we look up at Juliet's Balcony, and we take a picture with Juliet's Statue. It's cast in bronze, but is especially shiny in the region of the right breast, where I understand it's become ritual to rub for good luck. I rub and feel quite certain that I will get lucky. Romeo is under-represented at this shrine to a figment. Not a lot of letters have been coming in for him. Thousands of messages have been written with great care, in all colors, by pilgrims from near and far. These are messages of love. The walls of the courtyard are blanketed with graffiti, like at the Lamberti Tower. Not the kind you might see at train stations or on underpass walls. Here it's smaller and cuter, more like *graffiteeny*.

As the day winds down, we walk to the Piazza San Zeno for a look at the church and its famous doors, decorated with forty-eight bronze panels depicting biblical scenes. Later, while exploring the neighborhood, we find ourselves in front of Punto Snai, an off-track betting operation. For no purpose other than to figure out what this thing is all about, we walk in. It's 9 p.m. on a Thursday night, nearly the end of the gambling day. We learn that we can wager on just one more horse race, taking place in a few minutes somewhere in Germany. I foist a fifty-thousand lire bill, about twenty-three dollars, on one of the two guys manning the computer terminals, and in my best Italian announce my intent to put the whole calzone on horse number nine, Sweety. That done, we take a seat in a couple of the plastic garden furniture chairs provided by the establishment and watch as Sweety, odds-on favorite to win, comes in dead last. Dinner is at the original Vesuvio near Piazza San Zeno. Pizza. Gelato. Macchiato.

Florence, Italy, November 11

What is the right wine with French fries? Well, the two truckers at this Autogrill rest stop en route to Florence have made a bold choice, going with a '99 Gewürztraminer. In Italy, no less. We watch these geezers intently. After polishing off this bottle of wine and their lunch, they will be pouring themselves back into their trucks and barreling on down the road, our road. They are dangerous enough without the wine. Both are unsteady. One has an eye that wanders freely. He has to stab at his plate several times before actually spearing anything. The other, smaller man, seems more alert but must use his one good arm for everything. Just like during our trip from Venice to Verona, there are masses of trucks taking up the road, but today the weather is horrendous, and whereas on dry pavement we can zip and swing and shoot away from them, today we are very vulnerable and must hold a straight line in our lane. It's scary being on wet, twisty mountain roads in thick fog along with tired, tipsy, near-sighted truckers who are snoozy from a big lunch.

We ride into Florence in the rain. This is getting old. It seems that most of our arrivals are wet, but we are happy as hell to be off the freeway. Florence is a zoo. The streets are small and crammed with small Italian cars and loud Italian mopeds. After only a tiny bit of getting lost, we find the Duomo and park the bike, illegally. The only way to park anything legally in Florence is to put it in a garage, unless it's a moped, in which case you can lean it against all the other Vespas stacked neatly in endless domino lines on most streets. From here we visit different hotels, two of which are recommended in our guidebook. They're all bad. This is a case of too many tourists chasing too few rooms, like in Vienna. Hotels that are assigned three stars—real stars and not jelly doughnuts—are second-floor pits that have been sub-divided into contortionist irregularities. Showers are stuck above latrines. This is wickedly opportunistic, it's flagrantly parasitic, it's supply and demand! *Note to self: buy a hotel in Florence.*

Anyway, after looking at five of these cash cows on Corso Cavour, we give up and get on the bike again. Incidentally, there is a Corso Cavour in many Italian cities. Camillo Cavour was chief architect of Italy's unification in 1870. Riding aim-lessly around Florence, looking for a hotel with a ground floor (is that too much to ask?), we accidentally find our way to Piazza Santissima Annunziata and get a room at Le Due Fontane. This is an excellent location. Close to the Duomo and all the other monuments, it is nevertheless far enough away to be relatively quiet. The square is for pedestrians only. Our room is spacious and only a bit scruffy. The show-er is fine. The floor is tiled, and that means we can walk around barefoot. You take your pleasures where you find them.

We've been here less than two hours and are attending mass in the Duomo, or Santa Maria del Fiore. It's the only way we can see the place after it's closed to tourists. We did not plan this. It's just that we walked in the side door and the guard said it was closed except for mass. Tracy was all for it, and I was happy to fake it. God forgive me. At least I'm discreet and take my seat quietly and respectfully. One woman is spread out on her back in one of the pews across the aisle from us, doing a video of the dome frescoes as she whispers her voice-over. This is no ordinary Duomo. We've seen other Duomos, and this is a major Duomo. Bada bing. Our first look at it left us shaking our heads, partly because we were trying to clear them from too much carbon monoxide, but also because this is an amazing structure. What a contrast to the severity of Gothic architecture and art! It must have been exciting to live and build churches during the Renaissance. You can almost hear Florence's notary instruct the architect Arnolfo di Cambio: "Hey Arnie, go ahead and have *fun* with it."

Waking up in a new city is always a bit disorienting, but this morning we're perky as bunnies. We have an important agenda. Last night, on the way back from mass and dinner, we spotted a self-service laundromat just around the corner from the hotel. So now we're sitting here in shorts, freezing our asses off, watching *all* our clothes spin happily in lather. Not only that, there's an old-fashioned barber just down the street from the hotel. I need the grooming badly. I'm tempted to do a facial hair design thing like a lot of Italian men do. It's basically an approach that regards the face much as one would an ornamental garden. Facial hair can be trimmed to create interesting designs. We've seen some wildly creative work. One man had shaved his entire beard off except for a pencil-thin line that starts at one corner of his mouth and goes not in the traditional direction, inward along his upper lip, but out, toward his ear. Then, halfway up his cheek, this line turns sharply south until it arrives at his jaw, which it follows to his chin and then traces the symmetrical counterpart on the other side of his face, terminating at the opposite corner of his mouth. He looks like an Etch-a-Sketch. You want to shake him and have the little metal filings settle back to the bottom of his face so you can do something sensible with them.

Here we are in Florence, for crying out loud, and we're excited about laundry and haircuts. This says something. It says that Florence is overrated. I'm sorry, I blaspheme. This is a very popular town with huge armies of discriminating fans, but I'm ranking it somewhere near Zagreb for user-friendliness. There are two reasons for my harsh condemnation of the Birthplace of the Renaissance: It is impossibly congested and it is unspeakably polluted! The narrow sidewalks are clogged and pedestrian traffic is often at a standstill. Everywhere we go there's a mob. There are lines to the Duomo, the Academia, the Baptistery, the Uffizi, and all the public toilets. Here we are in the dead of autumn, the low season, and still the place is packed. Florence is certainly one of the world's richest cities in works of Western art and architecture. You want to see a masterpiece of Italian Renaissance sculpture? Fine, that'll be two hours of queuing, forty-eight lung-hacks, seven pushes into the wall, and a dozen body odor assaults. I'd rather pick up a fat full-color illustrated treasury of art.

To recover from this fit of indignation, we take a walk over the Ponte Vecchio. This bridge has the distinction of being the only one in Florence that did not get blown up by the Allies during World War Two. It is lined on both sides with jewelry stores, and is reminiscent of the Rialto Bridge in Venice, where we bought rubber boots during the flood we brought on that city.

■

The church of San Miniato al Monte is on top of a hill on the southeast side of Florence, overlooking the city. Around this church is a pine forest whose floor is covered in a delicate mantle of something that looks like clover. It's everywhere, that new-growth green that is jam-packed with chlorophyll. Carefully, gently, we wind our way through this little forest, making sure to stay in the narrow trail through the undergrowth. When we've gone clear round the high retaining wall, we arrive at the bottom of the stairs leading up to the church. San Miniato has the same green and white marble skin as the Duomo but is older, having been built in the eleventh century, more than two hundred years earlier. The skin was added sometime between the twelfth and thirteenth centuries. Come up on a quiet day in mid-winter, when there are no people here, and walk back to the sacristy. It'll be dark in the church. You can get some lights turned on by feeding coins into electronic control panels, but don't bother. Part of the special appeal is seeing it in the gentle natural light that filters through the stained glass windows and the gaps in the doors. Once you arrive in the sacristy, sit in one of the half-dozen carved wood choir high-backs all in a row against the wall. And just be. It's so quiet in here that you can actually hear yourself think. I don't mean this figuratively. Try it. Plug your ears and close your eyes in a very quiet place and listen. What do you hear? It's like a muted electrical buzz, isn't it? My theory, take it if you like, is that you're hearing your synapses firing and your blood running. You're hearing yourself think. (All this assumes strict gastric calm.) The crypt here is the resting place of many of the church's finest dearly departed. Some headstones are simple: ELIZABETTA GABELLOTTI. This one has no date, no epitaph, no news at all. Others are quite gabby:

Florence from San miniato

MARCO CARLO SANTILLI
Semplice Nei Mozi Della Vita
Cattolico Per Convinzione Profunda
Senza Fasto Soccorito Dei Poveri
Che Non Dementico Nel Suo Testimento
Mori Celibe De Anni 74
Nel Gennaio 1862

I took this down because I wondered why anyone would want all eternity to know that they died celibate at seventy-four. Then I looked it up and discovered that *celibe* means unmarried, not necessarily unscrewed.

Florence could use more church concerts, like Prague and Venice. We can only find two. One is at the Santa Maria de Ricci (Santa Maria for rich people?). It involves an organ, and we will not attend another one of these without having tested the organist first. The second is almost too good to be true. The Orpheus Chamber Orchestra is at the Teatro della Pergola, which is a five-minute walk from the hotel. We score tickets. Fourth row center. The Schoenberg is predictably painful, and so is the Webern. As a reward for sitting through these challenging atonal train wrecks, we are coddled and stroked and made to love life all over again by the Mozart and the Beethoven. Our walk back to the hotel is lovely. It's warmer than it's been in a few days and there's a moon out. The streets are still damp from an earlier drizzle. We've had some wonderful moments like these in Florence. The piazzas, all of them, are exquisite outdoor galleries. The people, by and large, are warm and accommodating. There's more: Not far from San Miniato, at Santa Croce Church, Niccoló Machiavelli is buried. Not one of the world's nicest guys, he is nevertheless an important native Florentine. He was born here in 1469 and died, also here, in 1527. He is of course remembered primarily for *The Prince*, a discourse on political power: how to get it, how to keep it, and how to inconvenience as many folks in the process as possible. Few people are aware that Niccoló had two sisters, Margherita and Primavera, named after pizzas.

Pisa, Italy, November 14

Now we're in Pisa. People here are super-vigilant, we learn as we are told by a whole mess of them that we are parked illegally. Super-vigilant people tend to be snitches as well, so we move the bike to a semi-legal spot. There doesn't seem to be much to Pisa other than the Piazza del Miracoli. On the ride into the center we see just traffic and a somewhat shabby working town. The three buildings that define Pisa are the Duomo, the Baptistery, and the Tower. The Leaning Tower of Pisa was begun by Bonanno in 1174. It is said that the architect designed the tower intentionally to lean, as it does. We doubt it. If I were commissioned to build a tower and it came out like this, back in the days when they put people to messy death by attaching their limbs to draught animals with diametrically opposed directions of motion, I too might have made that claim. I might have gone further to proclaim it a miracle, the work of a deity, a genuine glorification of whoever it is that's writing the check for the Tower.

The Italian government, realizing as it must that without Pisa the entire northwest part of the country would become famous for, er, the Green Grocer of Lucca, has leapt into action with a number of initiatives to restore the Tower. Architects and engineers from everywhere have submitted plans. Realize, however, that straightening the thing is not an option. Would you travel to see the Once Leaning Tower of Pisa? So instead, they propose to spend many tons of lire to arrest its leaning, while fortifying its foundation so that it does not suddenly collapse and become Pile of Stones, Once Leaning Tower of Pisa. Look, this is a cute, small tower that hit the big time because of a congenital disorder. Something like a bearded circus lady. If you happen to be in the general area, by all means go see it.

After the obligatory photos, we find a pizzeria just off the piazza and have our pizza at the piazza in Pisa. We are the only customers for a little while, but then a busload of American women trundle in and arrange themselves at two tables. The staff should be happy for the business, but seems concerned. Soon it becomes clear why; they've played this game before. First, one of the ladies makes it clear that they want separate checks. Given how many of them there are in the group, this could be as complex as U.S. presidential election recounts. Then, and this is verbatim, the following gem: "Do you have a showcase so we can see these dishes before we order?" The young lady waiting on them looks like someone just gave her a spinal. She gapes unbelieving at the oracle behind the question. The maitre d'—that is, the man who smokes the cigarettes while everyone else works—comes over to the table and says, simply, but emphatically: *non!* I don't know why he felt compelled to use French at this moment, but he did. Maybe he was aghast that anyone could possibly need a "showcase" for spaghetti, or pizza, or penne. It's not like this is a four-star restaurant.

This trivial drama gets us talking about "The Ugly American." There was a time not long ago when the American tourist was considered rough, inconsiderate, and culturally rigid. If this were ever really the case, it no longer is. With very few exceptions, we've observed our compatriots behaving splendidly. Americans tend to spend freely, tip well, pick up after themselves, and make every effort to communicate with the local population in its own language. What's more, we handily outnumber other national tourist contingents. Europe would be a very lonely place without us.

From Pisa we go south on the ss1 to Livorno. Soon we're on a coastal highway. The sea is to our right. This is what we intended, our only plan being to take a couple of days to reach Rome, and to do it unhurriedly. After we get through Livorno, there is very little traffic. And that's when we come up on the Hotel Universal. This is a villa that sits right on the ss1 and has an unobstructed view of the sea. It's windy here. High winds. From our window we can see a small fleet of wind-surfers—

board-heads, as they call themselves—out on the water. They're very good, racing out toward Spain and then back to shore, flying off the surface of the water when they catch a wave just right. I tried this sport in Cyprus many years ago. There was barely a breeze that day. As a result, I spent an hour wrestling with the damn sail trying to stay upright, but losing the fight and winding up in the drink time and again. Now when I see these guys making it look so easy, I'm very impressed. Unless it's following pizza, gelato, and macchiato, in which case I become really excitable and want to take shots at them with an air rifle.

Rome, Italy, November 15

Traffic in Rome is just as we expected, frenetic. We enter the city from the northwest and are immediately sucked into a heaving clot of machinery. Mopeds far outnumber anything else. At one point, as we idle at a light waiting for green, we count thirteen clustered immediately around us like obnoxious, hyperactive little possums. On a motorbike, you don't have the luxury of looking at the map as you do in a car, so we just go with the flow, sensing the momentum to the center, hoping for the best. So it's with surprise, pleasure, and a sense of reward that we look up, after making a turn in the thick of a wave of honking and smoking, and see Saint Peter's Square and Basilica at the end of the road. We're at the base of Via della Conciliazione, which runs for a mile and would take us right up to the central doors of the basilica, except for the concrete barriers. There is blunt contradiction between the magnificent four hundred-year-old building crowned with Michelangelo's dome and its frenzied, urban neighborhood.

We're staying at Pensione Silla, not far from the Vatican. The proprietor and his wife agreed to let me put the bike in the building's courtyard, thus immediately rising in my estimation to the level of Giuseppe Verdi. If you have some trouble empathizing with me on this, imagine traveling with a young child and not being

able to put them up in the same hotel. Of course a Honda ST1100 is not a child. It's quieter. Our room is on the first floor of a four-story building. It always smells like cake here because there is a *pasticceria* on the ground floor. From our window overlooking the cluttered courtyard, we see laundry drying outside windows, mopeds parked below, hanging plants, green shutters open or closed, and on the roof a forest of antennas. We're getting to know the neighbors, if not by name and per-

Pensione Silla Courtyard

sonally, at least by the color of their undies and sound of their voices. This morning there is a woman going on about something or other. I think we heard her yesterday afternoon as well, while we were still in Civitavecchia! She owns one of those

voices that tears through life like a chainsaw at a harp recital. It's not that she's shouting. No, she merely opens her mouth and allows the accumulated angst of all of Italy
to pour out in shrill arpeggios on the heads of her husband and children and neighbors. The neighborhood would not be the same without her. It wouldn't be nearly
as Italian.

■

There is so much to see in Rome! Or perhaps it's more accurate to say that
there is so much of Rome to see. We strike out from the Pensione Silla daily, always
in the direction of the inner city, and walk and walk and walk. Piazza del Popolo,
Via Corso, the Campidoglio, Piazza Navona, the Pantheon, Fontana di Trevi,
Fontana Tritone and Via Veneto, and on and on and on. Each of these is a thrill, and
there are dozens more. The overwhelming feeling we have as we make our way from
one exquisite monument to the next, is of great anticipation. When we arrive we're
dazzled and elated and buzz around with all the other tourists, marveling at
mankind's patrimony. Then we move on and the cycle repeats itself until we're overstimulated like puppies at a sausage factory. We've walked miles since arriving here
and have barely scratched the surface. By the time we get to Ancient Rome it looks
even more ancient than earlier in the day. Granted, it's dark now, and fewer people
are about, but we prefer those monuments that are still in Rome's daily life. So, we
will not be going back to the Coliseum and the Forum. We will read about them,
perhaps, and look at some nice pictures later. Instead, we'll spend our time at Piazza
di Spagna, sitting on the Spanish Steps. These are a thing of soaring grace. Or we'll
hang out at the Pantheon, my favorite building in Rome. Ordered by Roman
Emperor Hadrian, it has stood for nearly two thousand years and looks substantially the same today as it did in 128 AD. It's a simple, elegant structure; a domed cylin-
der fronted by a colonnaded portico. The interior is illuminated by a single window,
called an oculus, in the center of the dome. Tonight, while Tracy and I enjoy a late-
night macchiato and gelato in the Pantheon piazza, I call my brother in Seattle. I tell
him how wonderful it is in Rome, how warm, how dry, how incredibly beautiful the
Pantheon is in the moonlight. Across the square by one of the other cafés, some guys
play old Italian songs on an accordion and violin. Omar is at his office. It's mid-
morning in Seattle but he says that the fog makes it feel like evening. He's happy for
us; I can tell by the quiver in his voice when he calls me an indolent gadabout.

Mind you, there are other things about Rome that endear it to me; things that
are not at all monumental. For example, there don't seem to be as many pigeons
here! Where have all the pigeons gone? Florence? Then there's the modern art of the
city. Here and there in front of shops and alongside metro stations we see wild and
wacky sculptures; noses, ears, half-casts of nudes. You can miss Modern Rome if
you're not careful, and that would be a shame, because there is a great deal to see.
And how about the chestnuts here? They are by far the very best I have ever had.

They are the largest and best-looking. They are arranged by their vendors in the most fetching displays. I am happiest when strolling through a city like Rome in autumn with warm chestnuts. Well, warm nuts in general.

■

Rome Chestnuts

The smell of cake that we first found appetizing and homey at our *pensione* is now getting a bit much. We could close the window that looks out on the courtyard, but it's our only one, and then we'd have nowhere to hang our laundry. They take baked goods seriously in Rome. Last night, along the Nuova Via Appia, we walked by a large bakery that specializes in replicas of Rome's monuments. *Belli come Roma, buoni come pane*, "beautiful like Rome, tasty like bread." They had on display shrink-wrapped Coliseums, Pantheons, and Campidoglios, as well as one very approximate Vittoriano. So, here we are in the room on Sunday morning, getting ready to go out, watching mass at Saint Peter's on TV and smelling cake. The pope is delivering the Readings. What incredible fortitude. I don't know how old he is these days, but he is clearly frail and his Parkinson's is very evident. Tracy asks me if it's possible for a pope to "retire." I don't know, but doubt it. The square is packed. It's raining. We are happy to be in the room as we watch the mass and the masses getting drenched. There is some sort of corresponding military event as well, and thousands of troops from all over Italy are here for the service. We've seen some of these guys in the neighborhood in the past couple of days. They wear the most amazing hats. Tassels, feathers, rings, tails, puffs, pom-poms, chains, little bags, olive branches, buttons; no adornment is too outlandish to be worn in an Italian military hat.

We gather ourselves up and, in spite of the miserable weather, join the thousands departing St. Peter's and walk in the rain to Trastevere. Now that we're up closer to them, we remark that the men wearing the decorated hats look tougher in person. The oldest church in Rome is Saint Mary's in Trastevere, which literally means "within Tevere." That's because the area is mostly inside a bend in the *Tevere*, or Tiber River. It's a very different place from what we've seen so far in Rome. Sort of a *Rive Gauche*. The streets are narrow and cobbled; the houses are small and seem fragile; there are people living out of suitcases in one or two of the parks here. The average tourist in Trastevere is younger, more likely to be backpacking. We're here because we found out yesterday that there is a cinema called Pasquino that shows movies in the original language. What with all the culture we've had lately, we miss seeing a good old commercially slick American movie. We get our tickets and spend a couple of hours strolling around the neighborhood, starting with a visit to the church. It's old, quiet, smells good. Two bums are having lunch in the atrium.

They're foreign bums. I think we've established beyond question that the bums we see in Rome—and there aren't many—are of foreign extraction. Germans, Americans, maybe a couple of Dutchmen. Italians can't be bums because their mothers would kill them. This neighborhood is considered by some to be "the heart" of the city. That may be going a bit far. Perhaps the spleen.

The Vatican, Vatican City, November 19

Anybody remember the name of the pope immediately preceding John Paul II? He's the one who got his one-way ticket to heaven within thirty-four days of hitting the big time as Papa. Karol Wojtyla must have been a tad jumpy when the bishops named him successor. I mean, when you get that close to the top, you have to take events like the premature death of a preceding pope as a pretty heavy hint; nothing at this level is coincidental. The guy who really had a lot of guts was Theodorus II. He was pope for a few years back in 897, but only following the untimely deaths, in order of disappearance, of Formosus, Bonifatus VI, Stephanus VII, and Romanus. These four expired in rapid succession in the course of 896–897. If I were Theodorus II, I would have called in secular. "Sorry guys, but I want to be a dancer. I do appreciate the votes; don't think I'm not grateful, but why don't you go ahead and let Father Doobius have the hat. He wants the job and, after all, has a shorter commute."

The history of St. Peter's Basilica is rich and fascinating. The place took 176 years to build. Anyone who's anyone in Italian art and architecture has had a hand in it. Michelangelo, Bernini, Bramante, Raphael, Sangallo, and the list goes on. The Vatican Treasury is where they keep all the stuff that people would nick if it were left

St. Peter's Basilica

out in the open. Everything in here is gold-plated, even the plates. There are papal vestments on display that weigh more than I do. We see chalices possibly worth more than entire churches in other parts of the world. In fact, if they were to sell off all the goodies in here, I'm quite certain they'd pull in enough to make *Roman Catholicism II, The Sequel.*

The tour of the Vatican exhausts us and this without even having stopped at the Sistine Chapel. So we call it a day and head home. On the way we stop at Caffe San Pietro on Via del Conciliazone and have a coffee and some gelato, in order to fuel the ten minute walk back to the hotel. I'm happy to say that only ten or so days into our stay in the country, I have reached a level of linguistic proficiency that guarantees, at least, restaurant survival. In Italian, with only light gesticulation, I can:

- Order a *caffe doppio macchiato*
- Buy a bottle of water, *senza gas*
- Ask where the bathroom is

■

It's a good thing we didn't try to do the Vatican museums on the same day as the Basilica. The Sistine Chapel is at the end of a very long corridor. In order to arrive at Michelangelo's masterpiece, you must walk for about four hundred kilometers through a gauntlet of other art. Here you will see maps, tapestries, sculpture, gold and other metal work, and a lot of closets that line the corridor nearly from end to end. What's in there? More art? Papal shoes? We don't know, but plod along with the faithful and the curious, overdosed on art stuff we don't completely understand. We find ourselves here out of our depth. I've studied art, some art, and must confess to being utterly submerged. By the time we get to the Sistine Chapel, we're overstimulated and exhausted. Lucky for us there is space on one of the wooden benches that line the chapel. So we take it and lean back to marvel at the ceiling.

We'll, it's not technically the ceiling. A good deal of Michelangelo's painting actually runs down the wall. "The Last Judgment" is entirely on the west wall of the chapel. And of course there are wall-panel masterpieces of Renaissance painting by Botticelli, Perugino, Ghirlandaio, and others. The real credit for this place, however, belongs to Julius II, the guy who "ordered" Michelangelo to paint the ceiling. "Mick," he said, "get up there and don't come down until that ceiling is painted." If you've been here, you know that it defies description. However, we make a few observations that are a departure from the customary adulation heaped on it. Here they are, then, our observations about the Sistine Chapel:

- The chapel floor is a really busy marble inlay and deserves its artistic obscurity.
- The ventilation system is broken.
- By the time the Renaissance rolled around, fig leaves were optional.
- We think Michelangelo had an irreverent sense of humor. Next time you're here, look at the panel depicting the "Creation of the Sun and the Moon." There is a figure hovering in flight in the left side of the scene, facing away with its robes down, doing what can only be described as "mooning" us.
- The capacity of the Sistine Chapel is three million people, if today is representative.
- The signs "No Photography Allowed," do not apply to the thin French man on my left.
- Pee before you start down the Endless Corridor.
- If you lean back far enough, you will topple.

71

As for the pope immediately preceding John Paul II, well, he was John Paul I.

■

I had the bike serviced by my new best friend Virgilio. He runs the cleanest motorcycle shop in the area and wants about fifty thousand more lire to do the work. I'm happy to pay the premium and have taken a great deal of time making out a list, in Italian, instructing him on what I want done. I'm very proud of my list. Here it is:

Cambiare (replace):
Olio e filtro di motore
L'olio dei freni
L'olio dei cambio
Pneumatico posteriore
Filtro d'aria

Controllare (check):
Candele
Carburatore
Acqua di raffreddamento
Lubrificazione
Pasticche dei freni

As anyone could plainly see, this is an extensive list. I think Virgilio appreciated the effort I had gone to, because when I turned the list over, he quickly stuffed it into his rear overalls pocket for safekeeping. This was at nine a.m. Well, actually it was at 9:30. Our appointment was at 9:00, but Virgilio was detained. Instead, at the appointed hour, another man arrived and opened the shop. I'll call him Stinky. He tells me that he's expecting Virgilio *pronto* and goes about preparing the shop. Then, when he's rolled out the half-dozen bikes that had been inside, he shuffles to the bar across the street and throws down a couple of shots of something to take away the morning chill.

Italians are a wonderfully animated people, and that endears them to me immediately. It does not require a real emergency for an Italian to get adrenalized. Just raise a political issue. Any issue. U.S. presidential elections. Hunger in Somalia. Immigration from Albania. Deforestation of the Amazon. Any one of these, and of course, soccer, is guaranteed to get pulses thumping and hands gesticulating. It's an endearing quality because, unlike the English, the Germans, and certainly the Swiss, you feel that an Italian immediately invests in you. They go to the trouble of becoming excited, or upset, or delighted, even if they barely know you. Virgilio and Stinky are like that.

■

Now that we're ready to leave, it's raining she-wolves in Rome. There was thunder and lightning most of the night and it hasn't stopped. We're sitting in the room at Pensione Silla, packed, hot in our rain gear, paralyzed by the storm. The bike is under its cover in the courtyard. I want to go move it into the building lobby and do my pre-ride check, but the rain will not let up even long enough for me to do that. This morning we are trying to get to the coast because we do not want to tackle the Rome-Napoli expressway in the rain. When we finally get going, it takes us an hour just to get from the *pensione* to the ring road. No question, this is the very worst traffic we've seen. We start down the ss601 through Lido di Ostia and play a cat-and-mouse game with the storm for fifty kilometers, all the way to Anzio. This fishing village is a household name in the U.S. because of the drawn-out battle that took place here near the end of World War Two. Less known, however, is the fact that Roman Emperor Nero was born here in 37 A.D. History is littered with murder and mayhem, but few personalities can claim, as Nero can, to have killed not just his mother and his wife, but also eventually himself.

Lunch is grilled fresh fish at a harbor restaurant. It's fine, but a far cry from dinner last night at the Originale Alfredo on Piazza Augusto Imperatore in Rome. This is the birthplace of fettucine Alfredo, and a culinary shrine in a league of its own. Alfredo's is too fancy a joint for our wardrobe, and under normal circumstances we might have walked by and made faces at the *glitterati* inside. We were there last night, among the *glitterati*, because my mother said so. When in Rome a few years ago, she had dinner there, met Alfredo III and they became fast friends. Since then, others sent to Alfredo's by Mom have returned bearing gifts. We were disappointed that he was not there Monday, but it was a nice change to eat with silverware. The service was professional and tip-top. Our waiter was happy to see us, but not too much. The portions were adequate, but not over-generous. Two men, one with an accordion, the other with a violin, made a tour of the tables, playing where they were wanted. The lights were dim, but not too dim. This was a place that knows its place. It's no exaggeration to say that Tracy's and my boots are the roughest things Alfredo's has seen since Mussolini.

We started the day on the Tyrrhenian Coast of Italy, lunching on grilled fish and reminiscences of Nero. Now we're ending it on the Adriatic Coast, at Bari, waiting to board our ferry for Greece. We have very little time to explore the town, but make the trivial yet amusing discovery that its ancient name was Barium. There's a metal by that name. Also an enema.

Olympia, Greece, November 25

It's twenty-five degrees Celsius; the air is perfectly still; it's clear; a day so beautiful that the islands we've sailed by all look like Eden. Tracy and I each took one Dramamine just as we set off last night at 8 p.m. Then, a few hours later, I took a second one before going to bed. We slept through the docking at Igoumenitsa, which happened at 6 a.m. I tried to say Igoumenitsa three times fast and got a cramp in my epiglottis. I'm still groggy, but beginning to appreciate the beauty of combining drugs with travel. Soon we'll be docking at Patras and we still don't know whether to go south to Olympia, north to Delphi, or east to Corinth. It's great to be footloose. It's also great to be arriving in a country where each point of the compass promises wonder.

Patras is a bigger town than I expected. Several large ferries are in the harbor, and there's traffic in and out through the bar. We load up the bike and spill out of the boat onto the dock. The customs booth is occupied by two men reading newspapers, so we slow respectfully, then remember that Greece is in the European Union and wave cavalierly as we squirt by. There's a new national road that connects Patras with the southern parts of the peninsula. It's just one lane each way, but in good shape. Drivers here compensate for the limited number of lanes by driving along the very edge of the road, allowing faster vehicles to get by. That's good for us, but bad for critters. We go through Paralia, Lapas, Gastouni, and Amaliada, then turn east just before Pyrgos. Although the road is fine and the drivers are courteous, the surface is occasionally pot-holed. These are major league ruts. In a car they'll bruise your kidneys. On a motorbike they'll trim branches off your family tree. Also, signs are inadequate, at best. Some are no longer legible. Some are confusing. We do learn, however, that if you have any trouble with your bougainvillea, stick a Greek road sign next to it and it will grow like runaway morning glory.

We reach Olympia in the early afternoon and have the town to ourselves. Most hotels are closed for the season. Most restaurants as well. We're hungry, and the young lady at the Visitor Information Center recommends Praxiteles, a *taverna* up the hill. I wonder at first why a restaurant would take its name from gum disease. Later I learn that Praxiteles was a great sculptor back in 300 B.C., responsible for the statue of Hermes that was recovered during excavations at the nearby archeological site. We're happy, regardless of its cognates and etymology, that Praxiteles is open. As we eat, Mr. Praxiteles and one of his boys are loading up the outside tables and chairs on a truck. Tomorrow they'll be closed for the season. After lunch we walk through town to Hotel Ilis. They will be closing tomorrow also but have a room for tonight. Ladies are on every floor cleaning and packing and shuttering things up.

So far we suspect a conspiracy to make us fall in love with Greece and the Greeks. Everyone, without exception, is being helpful, hospitable, kind even. The language is no problem. Everybody seems to know at least enough English to help us. Back in 1976, I spent a few months here recovering from a bout of the Lebanese civil war. I picked up enough Greek then to manage in my job as a slave on a construction site. I'm surprised at how much of it is resurfacing. Words that I had forgotten suddenly make themselves available. This is like getting a little present every time it happens. A gift from my own memory. The result is not elegant, but the people we've come across so far are happy to see us, and do not allow my demolition of their language to bother them.

The archeological site in Olympia is a half-hour walk from the hotel, and contains constructions that have been around longer than dirt. We're way back in antiquity now. The Temple of Hera is 2,600 years old. The Temple of Zeus is a little younger. It used to house a statue of the eponymous god that stood twelve meters high and was considered one of the Seven Wonders of the World. The remains of the stadium are nearly three thousand years old. *Three thousand years!* I go into a crouch on the marble starting line in the first Olympic stadium and feel an urge to run the length of the field, then realize it's actually an urge merely to visualize myself running, and not to actually run. It helps to enjoy places like this if you know a little about Greek mythology, and I do, very little. Among the deliciously sordid stories is the one about Leto, who apparently took refuge on the island of Delos to escape the wrath of Hera, Zeus' wife. Turns out that Leto's twin kids, Apollo and Artemis, were the result of an unauthorized merger between her and Zeus. The ancient Greeks were a pragmatic people. They afforded even their gods the opportunity to fool around.

Temple of Hera

The highway across the peninsula, from Olympia to the East Coast, is reminiscent of some of our rides in southern Spain and France. A little like Provence. Every once in a while we come across a herd of goats, or sheep, or cattle. More often than not they are on or very near the road. There are olive groves covering much of the land, but it has that arid feel of Mediterranean hillsides. After riding for a while, we pull into the village of Zacharos. We find a small café and agree to the proprietor's recommendation of frappé coffees. They're vile, but refreshingly so. Soon a young man at the bar joins us. Yanni looks like the fruit of an unnatural union between a squid and a hippo: Rotund, jowly, white as ligament, with iridescent skin and fat wrists. He's from the neighboring village of Tholo (pop. 67), and friendly as hell. He offers us cigarettes. Here in Greece, offering cigarettes to perfect strangers is still considered a nice thing to do. From Yanni we learn that you can buy a nice house in the area for about $30,000. Spend another $5,000 on it and you've got a little palace. A couple of other men join us, and they also offer us cigarettes. We're having a very nice time, and feel quite at home with the guys, but sense that we must either start smoking or leave.

The drivers we pass on these Greek roads are courteous and calm. No Lucifers. When they overtake us, they do so considerately. When we approach to overtake them, they move over to the side of the road and slow down. There are long sections of very winding mountain roads. Up for a while, down for a while. Then again. I am very happy that we're not doing this in the rain. Some of these curves are steep incline hairpins, difficult enough to manage with a heavy bike when the road is dry. However, because there is so little traffic, much of the stress is eliminated, and we can take our time. At one point we stop to verify our direction with a lone goat herder on a windblown plateau. He smiles big and communicates with us entirely in German, because he thinks we are. We don't want to disappoint, so *danke* him and roll on. A couple of hours later we reach Nafplion and check in at the King Othon hotel.

Nafplion, Greece, November 26

Just like Olympia, Nafplion is nearly deserted. We stroll through the empty streets and alleyways until we find ourselves at the base of the famous staircase to Palamidi. Depending on which guide book you read, they say there are 800, 999, or 1000 steps up to the fortress. We are unafraid and, as we make the trek up, perform our own count. Here are the official certified results:

589 steps to the first real archway
916 steps to the ticket booth
968 steps to the highest point of the first castle
1,128 steps to the highest bastion in the upper castle
2,590,087 steps to the restrooms

Palamidi is a huge compound made up of five fortresses, crowning the hills overlooking Nafplion. The Venetians, back when they ran things around here, built it to defend the neighborhood. They spent three years and lots of loot putting the place together. As we walk around we wonder if that could possibly be true. It's huge. You'd think ten years at least to build it. Seen from below, it completely dominates the skyline and seems impenetrable. In any case, no sooner had they finished the thing in 1715, than the Turks showed up and took it.

We're interested in Palamidi not just because of the fortresses, but equally because it overlooks everything. As we walk up the stairs, we stop every hundred or so to take a picture, marvel at the view, and catch our breath. Once in the structure, we stroll around and poke our heads into the many dark, dank dungeons that were used as prison cells. Kolokotronis, a hero of the country's war for independence, was held here for a while. It could not have been very comfortable. There's also the charming little St. Andrew's Church on the grounds, old and cluttered and not at all opulent, but very quiet. We think of San Miniato in Florence, and how utterly cloistered we felt there. Thunderstorms gather over the Mediterranean, and I secretly hope they arrive soon so we can wait them out in the church.

The Peloponnese peninsula is still largely unspoiled, despite heavy tourist traffic to the many archeological sites. Things may have turned out differently had Nafplion remained the capital of Greece, as it was from 1828 and 1834. This crowned the country's war of independence from Turkey, a bloody conflict that began in the Peloponnese and lasted nearly ten years. Athens became capital in 1834, an event without which we might not have been able to enjoy our long, quiet, grilled fish lunches at Savouras. This is one of several restaurants on the seawall overlooking the Mediterranean. These guys know their fish. Yesterday they grilled three red mullets for us, and now I'm hand-picking a cod from the ice drawer. Grilled with a little salt and oregano and nothing else, this is pure beautiful food. Both days we sit and eat for nearly two hours, slowly, luxuriously.

■

The ride from Nafplion to Epidauros is wide fields of red earth and olive trees; blue skies that make your heart feel bigger and stronger; eucalyptus trees lining the road and scenting the air and, all the while, easy hills and gentle slopes. Once in a while the road leads through a village, but otherwise we're out here on our own. The people we see are locals. Goat herders, women tilling vegetable gardens, and the occasional kid riding an old tractor. We are not pressed to arrive.

The amphitheater at Epidauros has been here for twenty-four centuries. Again we get that feeling of transience that we experienced at Olympia. It's more than a little unsettling to sit in a theater where at one time fourteen thousand people a night,

all now dead, had a nice evening of entertainment. The fabled acoustics deserve their fame. For a few minutes we have the place all to ourselves. Tracy is in the stands. I deliver a short speech from the small marble circle at the center of the theater. She can hear me even when I whisper. They hold a festival of ancient Greek drama here every summer. I can think only that it must be damn uncomfortable to sit on these stone seats through a performance. Also, if you were to lose your footing near the top of the stands, you too could become something of a Greek tragedy.

Epidauros Amphitheater

We're riding through Corinth en route to Athens. The road skirts the Saronic Gulf. Occasionally, the sea comes into view as we make a turn or come over a hill. Shimmering, grand, and from here seemingly pristine. We sneak up on Corinth from the southeast, through Isthmia. There is nothing much of interest to us in modern Corinth. An earthquake destroyed the city in 1858, and the new city is just that, historically speaking. Ancient Corinth, on the other hand, must have been a fascinating and dodgy place to be. The city-state was allied with Sparta against Athens in the Peloponnesian War in 404 B.C. They won; not enough for Corinth. Ten years later it switched sides, formed an alliance with Athens, and beat Sparta in the Corinthian War. Understandably, there is a wealth of archeological treasure in these parts. And what a nice little surprise it is to ride over and across the old canal, carved into the rock between the Saronic Gulf and the Gulf of Corinth. "Carved" may give the wrong impression. It looks carved, but it was actually exploded out of the rock back in the late 1800s by the French. This must have been a fun assignment: "Jean Luc, Alphonse, go to Corinth and blow up six kilometers of rock between the two gulfs." We park the bike, dodge the souvenir peddlers, buy souvlaki sandwiches from one of the eateries alongside the canal, and eat standing up, surveying the scene, wondering why it is that the Greeks and the Turks just can't get along.

Athens, Greece, November 28

You will find Athens a better place if you're a tourist instead of a refugee. Back in 1976, my family and I were here for a few months to get away from the civil war in Lebanon. Granted, we weren't destitute and living in tents, but we were refugees nonetheless and sightseeing was not a priority. I have no photos from that visit, or any other evidence that I had a good time. I don't think I did. It was a difficult time. Coming back under these vastly improved circumstances is something of a redemption. Our first residence in Athens in 1976 was the Ilisia Hotel, very close to the center of town and a stone's throw from the Athens Hilton. So now as we ride into the city looking for a place to stay, I instinctively find my way back to the Ilisia. It's still here. They have a room that looks out on busy Michalakopoulou Street. We take it. This is déjà vu all over again.

It's a nice afternoon in Athens. Warm, dry, occasionally sunny. So we waste very little time settling in and then head out for a look around and dinner. This stroll from the Ilisia Hotel to Syntagma (Constitution) Square is familiar. The only notable change is the new Metro, which has a stop on Vassilissis Sophias. Otherwise, I'm in a weird time warp. This stretch of road is lined with beautiful buildings, most of which are embassies. They have not changed since I was last here. To our left is the large National Garden, to our right the Kolonaki area, an upscale district of Athens where boutiques and everything expensive can be found. Syntagma Square is also much as I remember it. The Parliament Building has been here for more than a hundred years. It's a modest building compared to its analogs in other European capitals, but elegant in its simplicity. The Tomb of the Unknown Soldier is here. A changing of the guard is in progress. It's one of those occasions in life that demand gravity in the face of excruciatingly comical costumes. The evolution of these out-fits would make an interesting study, but for now we can merely speculate about the peculiar circumstances that brought together kilts, red clogs, pom-poms, white panty hose and caps with waist-length tassels. We very carefully hide our amuse-ment. Greeks are a brave and indestructible people with a long history of national heroism. Any one of them could hurt us.

We keep walking and find Plaka. This is old Athens; a dense area of narrow streets and old buildings, which runs right up to the east wall of the Acropolis. Back in the seventies, Plaka at night was a big party. Restaurants set up their tables and clubs played bouzouki music outdoors. It was a nightly Mardi Gras. Then the gov-ernment, in what can only be described as anti-fun Puritanism, outlawed amplified music in the neighborhood. Now Plaka is a much more sedate place. No more drug deals, no more drunks sleeping in the street. Fortunately we, also since the seventies, have become anti-fun, so find this place delightful. After walking around for a while we happen across a wall of vines, overlooking the remains of the Diogenes Temple. Greek philosophers are a tough bunch to keep track of, because they are so numer-ous and have names that are nearly always impossible to pronounce. I've always remembered Diogenes because he has a short name that rhymes with Dirty Knees. Also because he was a member of my favorite Greek school, the Cynics, who held that action speaks louder than words, and that virtue is attained by freedom from passion and dependence. They were early Buddhists, if you like, and would have dis-approved of our next indulgence, a delicious dinner at Diogenes Restaurant, which commands the best spot near the temple ruins. For a main course, we take the roos-ter souvlaki and the pork Athenian style. We've been staying clear of beef. That's because cows are turning up nuts all over Europe. Just this morning there were two stories in the *Herald Tribune* on the subject. At least two cows in Germany have been found to be carrying mad cow disease, and farmers there are royally pissed off. Everyone blames the English for starting the whole thing. Everyone blames the French for being less than forthright about the degree of exposure in their country. In any case, we're off cow for now.

Most people here speak some English. This is good because my level of apti-tude in Greek was characterized by one waiter as "speaking *khoriatiki.*" *Khoriatiki* is the traditional, trademark Greek salad and contains cucumbers, tomatoes, feta cheese, black olives and olive oil. Greek is a curious language; so familiar, yet so remote. The greatest danger in attempting it is mispronouncing words which con-tain letters we recognize. That's because, though they look exactly the same, they *sound* completely different. Take, for example, the word *mepa*. If you fail to pro-nounce the "p" as an "r," you will be saying *nose hair*, instead of *day*. Here's another one: *exite* can mean *you have*, if you pronounce the "x" as you should, or *more lotion please* if you pronounce it like in *saxophone*. If this sounds complicated and confus-ing, imagine Greek Braille.

■

The Acropolis is almost deserted today. A handful of people are scattered around the site taking photos quickly and ducking into the museum to get out of the rain. We, however, water-resistant as we are, take our time, stomping around in our boots and blueberry-colored raincoats from Rome. *Acropolis* is Greek for "high city," just as *acrophobia* is "high fear." The term, however, has come to mean this particular high city on this hill in the middle of Athens. The compound contains a number of temples and other classical buildings, including the Parthenon. This fifth century B.C. temple to the goddess Athena was in much better shape as recently as

The Parthenon

the seventeenth century than it is today. Sadly, in 1687, during yet another Turkish-Venetian war, Francesco Morosini bombarded the Acropolis. At that time, the Turks occupied Athens. A missile fell inside the Parthenon, where the Turks stored ammunition, and a good deal of it and the statues inside it turned into rubble. There's more. The Venetians prevailed and General Captain Morosini later tried to remove statues from the west pediment of the temple. They fell to the ground and were smashed. Fortunately, enough of the place has

been preserved to give a very good impression of its original shape. Many of the sculptures that decorated the temples are now in the museum, and we follow the few other visitors in there for a look.

After the Acropolis tour, we go on through Plaka, and finally stop for lunch in the Mitropolis Square. There's a tiny but elegant church here. We see many of these small churches in Greece. Maybe we just haven't looked hard enough, but the Great Big Cathedral Overlooking Everything does not seem as important here as it is to the Catholic world. There's no Duomo here. There's no St. Peter's, or Frauenkirche, or Grossmünster. And if there is, it isn't where all the chestnut vendors do their roasting. For lunch we split a salad and a club sandwich at the Mitropolo. Although at first we were a bit self-conscious about it, we've found that waiters go out of their way to make the sharing experience a convenient one. They bring extra plates and sometimes they divide the portions in the kitchen. We think they find it sweet. Except in Austria, where sharing food is considered unnecessarily intimate.

There is a rocky hill in the middle of Athens called Lykavittos. The way up is a winding path of broad steps, lined with pines, eucalyptus, and yuccas. I think we passed maybe five other people during the entire climb, and three thousand stray, mangy, smelly cats with milk mustaches. At the top of this outcrop in the city's sprawl there is the pretty little church of St. George. This place is so small it might fit in one of the many super-sized solid gold tiaras we saw at the Vatican Treasury.

The church is cared for by an old woman dressed in rags, a scarf, and ill-fitting men's shoes. She gets a few coins here and there from the faithful and the compassionate. Here also, there are very few people. The weather and the off-season are working in our favor. It's a stormy day. The sky is very busy, dramatic. As the sun falls, it reaches a razor-thin clear spot between the bottoms of the clouds and the tops of the mountains. The result is a magnificently intense shard of red fire, something like a filament in a light bulb, which lasts for a few minutes against the gray, then shrinks to a pinprick before it's gone. All the while the clouds rush over us, dark, threatening, sometimes wet. It gets cold when the sun sets, so we go to the café under the church for a coffee. From here we watch as the lights of the city gradually come on. If you come to Athens and can do only two things, go to the Acropolis, then Lykavittos.

It's our last day in Athens, and we're having high tea at the venerable Hotel Grande Bretagne on Syntagma Square. We were a little concerned that our sandals and jeans might be inappropriate for the place and the ritual. Then we agreed that sandals are a long-standing Greek tradition. All the gods wore them. Look at the urns! So here we are, sipping oolong and orange pekoe, and nibbling on cucumber sandwiches and little personal fruit tarts. Three or four tables are occupied. Everyone is very hushed. If they're conversing, you can only tell from the nodding or head-shaking. The room is opulent; we have palms; we have marble. We have mirrors, and fake statues, and gold paint, and dark wood armchairs. We have tablecloths and silverware and china. Our waitress is the very climax of propriety. She smiles only halfway. It's as though allowing the smile to reach the edges of her mouth might somehow shatter the scones. Her uniform is perfect. There is much starch. She couldn't bend at the waist if she wanted to. Not that she wants to. At high tea, it's all in the knees. She bends hers and lowers her entire stilted torso just far enough to deposit our tea and crumpets. Underneath the table we're wiggling our exposed toes in gleeful insurrection.

Santorini, Greece, December 3

It's 5 a.m. as we approach Santorini's port of Athinios, after an overnight cruise from Athens. There's another ferry in the small harbor and we pull up alongside it. We're actually in the caldera of a dormant (*please God!*) volcano, which in 1550 B.C. let loose and destroyed much of the area. Looking straight up we see some lights on the rim of the caldera, which towers a good three hundred meters above us. The port is tiny. There are a few people on the dock. A half-dozen naked bulbs and two huge floodlights provide all the illumination. One row of stubby buildings lines the far side of the street that runs the length of the port. We're ready to get off this tub.

Sailing at night is spooky, no matter how well-charted the waters are. And anyway, it gets a little tiring to be on a boat for a long time when you can't sleep. Also, it's never far from our minds, as passengers of the *Aris Express*, that the man who ran this ferry company threw himself from his office window in Piraeus three days ago. Minoan Flying Dolphins also owned Samina, the ferry that sank off Paros not long ago and took eighty-one people down with it. The company's now-defunct managing director had been in the middle of a storm of controversy, and the story is front page news every day. The captain and first mate are in custody, which is a good thing because that means they're not on the *Aris*.

We ride off the boat and follow the few cars and trucks that are left after our stops in Naxos, Paros, and Ios. It's still absolutely pitch dark as we climb the steep switch-backed gravelly-in-spots road up from the port to the rim of the caldera, where the capital of Santorini is built. Fira is about ten kilometers from the port, so we're there in no time, even though we're taking it slow and easy, enjoying the night ride and the solitude. Santorini is the southernmost of the Cyclades Islands, halfway between Athens and Crete. It's an indescribably beautiful place. Imagine sitting on the rim of a volcanic crater now filled with sea. From here the view is astonishingly grand, but one or two good shakes of Mother Earth and all of Fira might crumble into the sea like a mountain of sugar cubes. In the middle of the lagoon is a small island, Nea Kameni, which is the cone of the volcano and occasionally produces puffs of steam. On the other side of the lagoon is the island of Thirasia, inhabited, but just barely. The north slope of Santorini is a gentle descent to black sand beaches and the sea. This is not a very big island, maybe twenty kilometers long and six or seven at its widest.

We're staying at the Hotel Panorama, one of the three or so still operating. It's fifty dollars a night. This same room goes for twice that during the high season, and even then would be worth it because the view is tremendous. We are on the sheer slope, overlooking the roofs and terraces of lower houses and buildings, and then the deep blue sea. You can't seriously hurt yourself jumping from most balconies here, because you will travel only a couple of meters then land in someone's patio. In summer, you'll most likely land on an English person. The room itself is a little on the small side and a little on the dusty side, like most rooms we've stayed in. On the other hand, it has a bed that does not pitch, and there are no nautical bolts clanking against the yardarm, so we have ourselves a lovely little nap.

The sun in the southwestern sky peeks through our balcony door at about 4 p.m. It's tempting to draw the curtains and sleep on, but that would throw our already discombobulated body clocks completely off-sync. So we get up and go out for a walk. The Greeks call this a *volta*, sort of a constitutional that they take before dinner. Our *volta* takes us through narrow alleys that wind and twist and fold back on themselves between the white-washed houses on the cliffs. You actually can't see any cliffs anymore. The whole side of the volcano, about half-way down to the sea, is completely covered in houses and walks and walls. Maybe a strong earthquake will not cause the sugar-cube crumbling I described earlier. Maybe the whole thing will crack and slide off in one piece, like hardened wax off a table top, and just float away to Crete. We stop often to marvel at the view across the lagoon, but also at the typical Cycladic architecture. Whitewash and blue paint are used almost exclusively. One rebel family painted their picket fence a rather bold fuchsia, but that's about as wild as things get. It's all very romantic and soft and serene.

Santorini

The next morning after breakfast we walk down to the Old Port. Someone once counted five hundred steps. These steps are the only way, other than cable cars, of reaching the Old Port. Since donkeys are not allowed on cable cars, they make their way, often with tourists atop them, exclusively by this route. The donkeys are not running today, but incontrovertible evidence of previous journeys is everywhere. You have to look where you step. We can tell that they favor walking along the cliff walls, because that's where the evidence is thickest. Nevertheless, we make our way down the slope's broad steps, dodging shit as we go. It occurs to us that this imitates life.

Santorini can easily be seen in a couple of days, especially if you have wheels, but a week here is better. One day to look at the sights, and the rest of the time to chill. We're back at the port now, and board the *Poseidon Express* for the return journey to Piraeus. This cabin is more comfortable than the one we had on the *Aris*, and it's newer. We have all the comforts here, including a TV. It will not receive any channels, but we appreciate the thought. Our cabin is near the middle of the ship, on the left-hand side, an area seasoned mariners call "the midriff." As we ease away from the island, it's just past 7 p.m., and it's dark. We stand on the backside deck and watch as the half-dozen or so folks who had come to see the ship off drive away up the slope. There's a low stone wall along the road that obscures the cars, but we can see the play of their headlights on the cliff-sides. Soon there's no one there. In the light of the naked bulbs on the dock we can see a lone donkey meandering down the middle of the road to the port.

Chios, Greece, December 5

Piraeus is a port city and fits that stereotype, but beyond the docks, up the hill from the harbor, is a town that in spots sparkles a bit. The main streets are busy with traffic, but side streets are quieter, some even cozy. We've had enough of the docks, with which we have become very familiar, and make for higher ground. As we begin our walk away from the port, we are acquired by a stray dog. Of dozens of people milling about at one intersection, he picks us out and becomes our new pet. We struggle with a name for him, but settle on Pestilence. This poor mutt is a mess. He walks sideways with a pronounced limp. Skin conditions from several bacteriologi- cal universes have made a home of him. He's probably blind in his right eye because things coming from that direction seem to always catch him by surprise. We want to show affection, but will not touch him, for fear we also might become startled by things approaching from our right. Eventually, after a half hour of strolling togeth- er in the busy streets of Piraeus, he leaves us at a sunlit square where three other strays are asleep on the warm marble floor. There is a crying need for dog family planning in this country.

In the meantime, all sorts of stuff is happening back at Piraeus Harbor. Ferries are docking and undocking, big trucks roll along the piers as scooters zip between them. Watchmen watch and the man with the mobile bar is making a killing. This is a guy whose enterprise is a low-sided wooden crate in which he lines up bags of nuts; little pouches of pistachios, almonds, peanuts, and pumpkin seeds. And he sells them for a few drachmas. His Ace, however, is a bottle of Johnny Walker Red Label Scotch Whiskey. His regulars approach in twos and threes. The old man knows their usuals, but the options aren't numerous. It's straight, or it's with a lit- tle water, jealously dispensed from a thermos he keeps under his chair. He rinses out the empty plastic cups and is ready for the next round. Our ferry departs Piraeus at 7 p.m. We are aboard the *Express Teophilo* along with a wild mix of Aegeans, many of whom sleep on the landings between decks while we luxuriate in our cabin. We are not insensitive to the plight of the less fortunate, and sleep badly. The *Teophilo* steams through the night and reaches Chios at 4 a.m., a time filled throughout human history with painful childbirth and violent crime. It's a cold but clear and still Tuesday morning. It's dark, of course, so we can only make out the harbor. Within half an hour, the ferry has spewed out its trucks and cars and motorcycles and gone off to Lesbos. Most of the passengers are locals, and they drift away to their homes and beds. We sit outside the one open café, debating what to do next. It's cold and we're very tired, but we can't sit inside because of the over- powering ambiance.

We're here because we've finally nailed down the fact that you can indeed get a ferry across to Turkey, but only from Chios or Samos. An awful lot of bad water has gone under the bridge between Greece and Turkey, and none of it is forgotten. In fact, it's cultivated. In the atrium at the Athens Hilton there is an olive tree they call the Old Lady. This was transplanted from its original spot in Plaka to its pres- ent place at the Hilton in 1962, and has become the hotel's emblem. In the center of this two hundred-year-old tree, there is an iron cannon ball which landed and lodged in its trunk. It was fired by the Turks during Greece's War of Independence in the early 1800s. The symbolism is rich: cannon ball in olive tree. That's like bar- becuing a dove. The debacle over Cyprus is fresh. And now Greece is making

Turkey's inclusion in the European Union contingent on resolution of the countries' disputes. As a result of all this geopolitical inflammation, we had a very hard time getting a straight answer about ferries from Greece to Turkey. Chios, in particular, was the site of an early massacre during the War of Independence. Thousands were killed by the Turks in 1822. It wasn't a happy time. Nowadays it's very quiet here.

■

The Archeological Museum in Chios is a new facility funded in part by the European Union. Its exhibits are extensive and well-documented. The staff is hospitable and knowledgeable and bored to tears because there's no one here but them and the chickens that sneak under the fence from the coop next door. You could ride a chariot through here and trample Greek curators exclusively. So we get a private tour, a nearly endless one. Each time we announce our intention to leave, the young lady showing us around foists yet another wing on us. An entire "upstairs" full of engraved tablets shows up just when we think we will collapse from excessive antiquity. Up here we read letters, actually stone tablets, from everybody who was anybody. Here's a three hundred kilo memo from Alexander the Great to the people of Chios setting out the terms of their indenture to him. And up against the wall are many versions (drafts?) of a law dictating which parts of animal sacrifices may be given to the gods, and which may not. It seems that folks at one point figured out that eating the meat and sacrificing the bones made more sense than giving up the whole fattened calf. Someone had to stop the trend, or the gods would have wound up receiving nothing but the wax paper.

On the north side of town, there is a neighborhood inside the old Ottoman citadel. It catches us completely by surprise. We had expected to walk through the fortress walls and see a limited display of abandoned structures, like at Palamidi in Nafplion. Instead we're in old narrow streets with vestiges of the Turkish occupation of the island. We come across an old Muslim cemetery. The headstones are shaped tall, narrow, and flat. They're like high tablets on which Koranic verses are engraved. A few are topped with marble turbans or fezzes. They stick out of the ground irregularly, some at angles, moved around by the elements. We think they look like the little plastic plant-care markers you find in flower pots.

Chios Headstones

The formalities at Passport Control and Customs are abbreviated. You pay the tax, you say *yassu*, and you board the boat. It's a small boat, called the *Psara*. In Greek the "ps" is one letter, which looks like a trident. I think it's clever to have one letter for "ps," and would support a move to include it in English. This would make psychiatry and pseudonyms and psychosis far easier for us all to pick up. Two cars and my bike pretty much fill the *Psara*. There are ten passengers all told, and three crew. This is not a roaring route of tourism and trade. As we chug away from Chios, we stand at the rail on the second balcony and look back on Greece. Then we turn and look forward to Turkey.

■ middle east ■

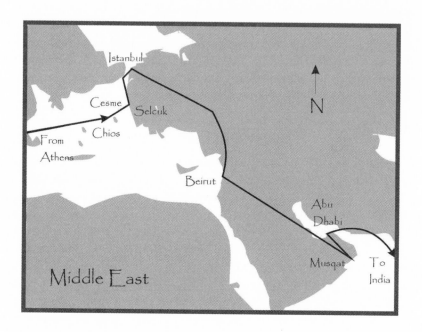

The fathers have eaten sour grapes, and the children's teeth are set on edge.

— Ezekiel 18:2

Selçuk, Turkey, December 7

Getting to Selçuk from Chios is a breeze; less than an hour by ferry. Getting through Turkish customs and passport control is also easy, especially because I do not dispute the exchange rate on the Greek and American money from which I am being gently but firmly separated. This after I had already surrendered all the Turkish money I have. When all is said and done, I estimate that we paid about a hundred dollars in taxes and exchange discrepancies to get into Turkey with the bike. In Turkish money, that is about seventy million liras. That's right, *seventy million.* How much sense does it make to keep printing a currency which is seven hundred thousand to the U.S. dollar? Beats me. On the bright side, however:

- Every Turk is a millionaire
- The average Turkish citizen can out-arithmetic anyone in Europe and Asia
- And if you're out in the woods …

The ride to Selçuk is partly via freeway. This one is practically deserted, like that stretch of road from the Hungarian border to Zagreb. We leave it just past Urla and start making our way south through the Turkish countryside, in the direction of Seferhisar. Traffic is heavy and the going is slow. Trucks, tractors, name it. At one point I gun past a truck carrying three times the weight anyone would consider safe. Three minutes later we come up to a policeman in the middle of the road frantically waving at us to pull over. He already has three cars on the gravel and his partner is in the police car, being cashier. This is reminiscent, naturally, of our encounter with the officers of the law in the Czech Republic. This time we think the guys really do have a spotter earlier up the road calling in culprits on the walkie-talkie. When we overtook the truck, we were cooking, doing 85 km/h in a 50 km/h zone. The fine is two hundred thousand liras per kilometer, so we have to pay seventeen million liras. I offer no resistance at all. There's a long line of unhappy Turks behind me. If I question the fine and create further delay, I could get hurt.

Yesterday while walking in Chios, we met Donald. At first we couldn't make out the person waving to us from inside the grocery store. We're up the block, in the bright sun, and the store is dark inside. By the time we reach the place, he is out by the door, hand outstretched. He's English, medium height, maybe seventy, vigorous and ruddy and apparently very, very happy to see us. We shake hands and exchange introductions. Donald is from Nottingham. He was a flight steward as a young man, then quit to become a coal-miner, like his father and grandfather before him. He shows us his hands to prove it. He lives on Chios with his wife and gives tours in the summer. His colonial-era turned-up mustache is white, except where it's yellowed by nicotine. When he hears that we're going on to Turkey, he invites us to his house to meet his wife and look up friends of his in Selçuk (pronounced Selchuk). Donald is an expert on Aegean Turkey in general and Ephesus in particular. He is full of information about the history of the region, and recommends a place for us to stay.

That is how we come to be sitting up in bed at the Artemis Guest House in Selçuk, Turkey. We have finally brought the temperature in the room up to where we can't see our breath. Earlier, when we checked in, the room was colder than a witch's tit. All things considered, this is as good a place as we could have hoped for. The room we're in is the newest and has more comforts than the others. Donald's friends are happy to hear from him and very welcoming to us.

We've only been at the Artemis a few hours before becoming part of the itinerant yet strangely familial group here. There's a large lounge on the ground floor where meals are served and the TV is located and everyone hangs out because they have no heat in their rooms. It's here, over a homemade dinner of creamed spinach with eggs, boiled cauliflower with tomato sauce, spaghetti and an apple, that we meet Walter and Irene. They're a young Dutch couple on their way to Istanbul for the last few days of a four-month vacation during which they've visited Russia, China, Pakistan, Georgia, and Armenia. These are all places we are not touching on our trip but would like to, so we listen intently as they tell us what they saw. At the next table Adam, a twenty-two year-old Canadian man traveling on his own, is en route to Egypt. He's working here for a few days in lieu of paying rent. Another Canadian, Lawrence, works at the salmon hatchery in White Horse, up in the Yukon. He invites us to "stop by" when in Canada. It would mean a three thousand kilometer detour, but they say there's no better venison anywhere. Then there's a Korean guy—we never got his name—whom we had seen at the IVIS Internet Café on Syntagma Square in Athens. We may have come from different places, and be on our way to different destinations, but one thing we have in common: We are all potential marks for the Carpet Cartel.

Everyone we've met who knows anything at all has warned us about the Australians and New Zealanders selling carpets in Turkey. How did this happen? There is a large contingent of the Down-Under and the Down-Lower-and-Off-to-the-Right gang that has carved out for itself a market in local rugs. It turns out that the owners of the Artemis Guest House are also in the carpet business. When it's time to go to Ephesus, we ask for the complimentary transportation. The car, it seems, is parked just across the street from the family's carpet shop, and would we like an "orientation?" We decline, our intransigence prevails, and we get the free ride to Ephesus in a circa-1970 yellow Chevy.

Our main objective in coming to Selçuk is to visit Ephesus. We want to see this Ionian city, three thousand years old and preserved, they say, about as well as any other antiquity. The country here is fresh, open. There are hills covered with pines and their needles, and dirt trails, and open sky. Hardly anyone else is here, except for the cats that lie on the warm marble toasting their bellies. Ephesus is so old that even its history has a history. Long before we started counting years forward, the city had been invaded by Cyrus the Great *and* Alexander the Great. The Goths came by later and leveled the place. It never really recovered, even if it was rebuilt. The substantial ruins of a number of important buildings survive, however, most notably the Temple of Artemis and the Celsus Library. We take our time walking down the city's ancient stone walks and loitering among the colonnades. It's true that you can picture yourself living in this town when it was still inhabited. There is enough of it left that you don't need to stretch the imagination as you would in, say, Olympia. My favorite building here is the Library. Less monumental, but no less important, are the ancient public latrines of Ephesus. This is one large hall whose walls are lined with stone benches into which remarkably modern-looking holes have been cut. We stop in and even sit down for a while. Here's the truth: It's spooky to walk in Alexander the Great's footsteps, but it is really chilling to occupy the same throne.

Celsus Library

Before leaving Ephesus we drop a mountain of liras on a shoeshine. Then, anxious to not dust it up, we ride to town in a mule-drawn carriage operated by a multi-millionaire.

■

Turkey is a secular state. We've read that ninety-nine percent of the population is Muslim and, now that we've spent a few days here, can confirm that. So, this being Ramadan, the Muslim holy month of fasting, we expect to see most people walking around hungry as heck, but they're not. Everywhere we go folks are drinking tea and smoking cigarettes and munching on this or that snack. Our initial sensitivity about eating in public soon dissolves into an all-devouring hunger of Koranic proportions. We eat *kofta*, and Turkish pizza, and *sujuk* (a Turkish sausage) sandwiches. We drop into unlit pastry stores and sample syrupy shredded wheat desserts sweet enough to give you a cavity in your implants. The greatest impact of Ramadan, however, is on our sleep. In addition to the five regularly scheduled prayer calls, there is a bonus event. Somewhere in the middle of the night, men with drums, tambourines, or other obnoxious percussion instruments walk the streets making as much noise as they can. It's sort of a pre-technology wake-up call. The fact is, these guys are paid by the public. They work on a strictly volunteer, publicly supported, non-commercially endorsed basis. On days when they expect donations, they walk especially slowly and make a great deal of noise, off beat.

From Selçuk we ride north via Izmir to the town of Bergama, where we spend an uneventful night, look in on the amphitheatre ruins, and then ride on to Canakkale. It's only about 240 kilometers, but the road is mostly one-lane, and the going is slow. On top of that, I have a nasty cold, my second in the past three months. We stop for a cup of tea at the charming fishing village of Ayvalik. The sun's out, and where we sit out of the wind, it's warm. We go on and follow the road along the coast past Edremit and Kuchukkuyu. We reach the ferry dock at Canakkale at 3:30 p.m. and get tickets for the 4 p.m. crossing to Eceabat, across the Dardanelles. It's a wild scene here on the docks. Food vendors are selling everything from roasted chestnuts to grilled lamb sandwiches. I haven't had good roasted chestnuts since Rome. These here are possibly the worst.

The ferry ride across the Dardanelles is brief. This waterway is barely one mile wide in places. You could swim across it; Lord Byron did. That was in 1810. The water was probably quite a bit cleaner then. The strait connects the Mediterranean to the Black Sea, so it's strategically important; a real geopolitical crossroads. Ancient hordes have crossed going east and going west on their way to conquering less well-armed hordes. Alexander the Great did it. Now we're doing it. The sun sets as we cross the strait, so by the time we reach Eceabat, there's not a lot of time to find a place to stay. No problem, we have exactly two choices, both bad. One, T.J.'s place, is a hostel about which we heard while in Selçuk. The other, previously Down Under Guest House (what is it with the Aussies here?) is now the Eceabat Hotel. This one is marginally better so we take a room. We're paying thirteen dollars for the night, so it's no Hilton. In fact, I think I want to sleep standing up in my clothes and leave at daybreak, but am comforted by the knowledge that Alexander the Great probably slept in his clothes and left at daybreak as well.

Istanbul, Turkey, December 11

Once we get out of Eceabat and hit the coast road going northeast, toward Istanbul, we are overwhelmed with the scene. To our right, the Dardanelles, a low fog hanging over their waters. A few ships sit in the strait, seemingly motionless. Ahead of us the sun is still low in the sky, climbing behind the Sea of Marmara. To our left low rolling hills are covered with olive trees. It's freezing cold. Maybe not if you're standing in the sun having a cup of tea, but certainly on a bike going 100 km/h. There is no traffic. The road is dewy in spots, but not enough to cause any great concern, so we enjoy the ride immensely for as long as we can, before having to stop and beg for something hot to drink so we can thaw out. Somehow, gratifying for us, we pass through a couple of speed traps like the one that got us outside Çesme, but are not stopped. It's nice to get away with something. We make only one more stop before reaching Istanbul. It's around 2 p.m. Traffic is very bad. Stop and go. Mostly stop.

Istanbul is one of those cities, like New York, Prague and Venice, which has a distinct and unique physical profile. The Agia Sophia Museum, ex-mosque, ex-ex-church, is only one of the landmarks within a *kofta*-throw of our hotel. Nearby are the Sultanahmet Mosque, Topkapi Palace, and a number of other smaller monuments. We're staying at the Saint Sophia Best Western. Our room has a balcony, a

Jacuzzi, reading lamps, a shower that works, heat, and clean sheets. It's perfect and reminds us of the room we had at the Waldstein in Prague. The hotel manager, like most Turks we've met, is wonderfully hospitable. I ask if there's a place I can put the bike. He says "Of course," and points to the hotel entrance. It means riding down four steps of the broad staircase leading from the upper to the lower road on this side of the Agia Sophia, but I have become good at that sort of thing. The bigger concern is making it past the carpet shop on the corner without being ambushed by Mr. *Where-Are-You-From-My-Friend-Would-You-Like-See-Turkish-Carpet?*

Turks are among the friendliest people we've come across so far on our tour. They are unpretentious and sincere and always willing to strike up a conversation. Most often they break the ice with "Where are you from?" Unfortunately, the "Where are you from?" approach is also put to frequent use in Istanbul by people with something to sell. We have yet to leave the hotel without being ambushed by several young men wanting to know where we're from. Some of the guys, particularly the younger ones who haven't yet figured out when a prospect is never going to become a customer, can be aggressive. Mostly, though, it gets to be a predictable though no less pesky annoyance. Now we're adopting a new strategy. When approached, I will speak only Arabic. These guys are prepared for English, German, French, and Spanish. Not Arabic. Also, I will attempt to sell my scarf, the one I bought in Munich for three dollars, to anyone who bugs me. I will ask for thirty dollars. If they shake their heads as a couple of guys did earlier today and walk away muttering "crazy man," I will follow them and call them "my friend."

Ramadan in Istanbul is more fun than wrestling in Jell-O, but only if you don't have to fast. That's the category in which we squarely belong. The ancient Hippodrome alongside the Sultanahmet mosque is converted to a barbecue extravaganza for the entire month. Tens of little restaurants with stubby tables and chairs are put up in temporary but cute fire-traps. They decorate with various folkloric and religious icons, dress Ottoman, slap a few *halal* lambs or parts thereof on some charcoal and *Efendem!* have we got a cook-out! Unless you're vegetarian, in which case you will run screaming from Asia Minor, it is impossible to walk by without eating something. In most cases the food is exquisite. However, a word to the wise: Just because it looks good and smells good does not necessarily mean it will taste good or be chewable by human persons.

Sultanahmet Mosque

Last night we joined the faithful in one eatery and sat patiently together waiting for the *muezzin* to announce *iftar*, the breaking of the fast. When that happened, we were first served a lentil soup worthy of any palate. Then, oh my, the main dish, a chopped and barbecued lamb sandwich came. Holy rubber boot! We could barely gnaw through the gristle and bone and other unattractive bits to get to the other side of the *ekmek*. I finished mine from fear of divine retribution. Tracy is fearless and left half the thing on her plate. This unappetizing event stands alone in our experience of Turkish cuisine.

■

The Cargo Terminal at Atatürk Airport is not plush, unless you've just arrived from an Afghani prison. It's a hive of highly inefficient activity whose eventual purpose is importing and exporting goods. I'm here to send the bike to Bombay. The nice people I'm to work with, Lufthansa agents, have an office about the size of a Triscuit. Four people work in here. Several more visit regularly. Nobody speaks English, or French, or Spanish, or Italian, and certainly not Arabic. With typical Turkish hospitality, however, one of the guys gives up his seat for me. I accept it because by now I've learned that, if offered a chair in Turkey, take it; chances are whatever it is you're hoping to do will take a while. And so begins a long day of waiting and sign-language and last-minute discoveries of disasters relating to critical missing documents.

I hope that my experience at the Atatürk Cargo Terminal can be useful to the next guy attempting to ship a motorbike from Istanbul to Bombay, and for that reason have compiled the following list of helpful hints:

- Never appear rushed. In Turkey, much as in Cairo and Damascus and Beirut, this is interpreted as a code for everyone to further ease their level of interest and activity on your behalf.
- Wear real shoes. Sandals may work in Martha's Vineyard, but here you want to shelter your toes.
- "How are you doing?" if understood at all, will be misunderstood to mean "*What* are you doing?" Although this is often an understandable question here, it is always unwelcome.
- Pee and do the other thing at the hotel. You will be very sorry if you don't.
- Do not attempt to negotiate price. These guys wrote the book on it. Save your breath and get the pain over with.
- If you can help it, *do not* attempt to ship a motorbike from Istanbul to Bombay.

I acquired these nuggets at great emotional cost. Nevertheless, by 3 p.m., five hours after I arrived, the bike is safely stored in Lufthansa's warehouses, and I can go back to town. This is a good thing because all the sights, including Tracy, are in town.

■

The Agia Sophia has had a long history of building and collapse and fire and retrofitting. It started life as a church, then became a mosque, and finally a museum since 1934, thanks to the foresight of Atatürk, founder of the Turkish Republic, who found the only possible way to not piss off the Muslims or the Christians in unequal measure. If you can imagine the scene without the four late-model minarets that were grafted onto the church, you'll find it one of the most beautiful in Europe. On the inside, it's severe and unornamented. When the Muslims took over, a noted calligrapher, Hittat Izzet Efendi, whose work is all over Istanbul, was asked to redecorate. So he inscribed some Koranic verses in the dome. These are gilded, substantial,

exquisite. At this point, I can only surmise that Hittat Efendi was struck on the head by a falling herd of dromedaries, because the rest of what he did here is iffy. Eight large wooden discs, each over seven meters in diameter, are attached to the walls halfway up to the ceiling, and inscribed in stylized gilded calligraphy: Allah, Muhammad, Omar, Abu Bakr, Ali, Hassan, Hussein, and Othman. Subtle they are not. Having said this, it occurs to me that the Mizquita mosque in Cordoba got a whole cathedral jammed into the middle of it when

Agia Sophia

the Spaniards took the town back from the Arabs. So, in the ledgers of who did what to whose holy places, both sides have had their equally disgraceful "duh" moments.

After our visit to Agia Sophia, we run the gauntlet between it and the Sultanahmet, ignoring all the *Where-Are-You-From-My-Friend-Espanol?-Francais?-Have-You-See-Blue-Mosque?* entrepreneurs along the way. Once inside, we stand around quietly for a while and admire the tiling and inlay and mosaic work. As visitors we are kept out of the kneeling-down area of the mosque, where real Muslims are praying. I am tempted to join them, but it's been a long time and I don't remember the words. Praying in Islam is not at all like in Christianity. You are required to actually kneel and put your head to the ground. In some countries, exuberantly pious men advertise their godliness by cultivating on their foreheads a scab resembling a large raisin or a small prune. They plow this disfigurement by rubbing against the prayer rug. It's a distasteful practice that could not possibly have been endorsed by the founders of the religion, not when everybody prays on the same rugs. None of that here in the Sultanahmet. It's impeccable. There are men quietly dusting and cleaning in corners you may never expect anyone to check. It's also a beautiful place. If you look closely, you see tile work and inlay and calligraphy that are highly intricate, even busy. Seen as a whole, however, the interior of the mosque hides this, and glows like an indoor firmament.

We spent today on the Bosphorus. I've always wanted to say that. There's a ferry that starts at the foot of the tram line, from Pier Three, and makes a number of stops in its ninety-minute trip to the village of Anadolu Kavagi, on the Asian side of the strait. A round trip ticket costs 1.8 million liras per person, about $2.50. There is only one boat a day, so we make sure to be at the pier an hour before departure time. While waiting for the ticket counter to open, we take in the sights and smells of the port, not necessarily a first-rate idea near bodies of water where millions of people live and do stuff. The boat trip is relaxing and uneventful. At times we're reminded of Venice. It's a gray day. There are a few notable villas and other structures along the banks, including castles constructed in the fourteenth, fifteenth, and sixteenth centuries while the Ottomans were slowly dismantling the Byzantine Empire. One palace, the Dolmabahce, is particularly interesting. This was the residence of Sultans for a while, and Atatürk as well. He died here. It's not often that one individual can be credited with creating a nation. The consensus here remains that Mustafa Kemal Atatürk did just that. The name Atatürk means "Father of Turkey," and what's more relevant is that he did not take it for himself, but was rather given it by the young country's representative assembly. His singular achievement, if it can be summarized, was taking the helm of the remains of the Ottoman Empire and skippering them into a country at least as European as it is Asian. Here, between Thrace to our left and Anatolia to our right, seems a most appropriate place for this reflection.

Turkish is a language for which I have an intuitive affinity. During the six centuries of Ottoman rule, Arabic incorporated many Turkish words. The reverse is also true. Even though the alphabets are different, there is such a large common vocabulary that I can usually make out billboards, road signs, and other written stuff. The greatest common link is the Koran. Any Turk will understand *al salaamu aleykum*, "Peace be with you," and its reply. Titles thrown around in the Arab world can be useful here as well. *Hajji* is one of my favorites. Most men of advanced years are flattered by this title, usually reserved for those who have completed the Muslim pilgrimage to Mecca. Remarkably, "guys" has the same effect on younger people, male or female, assuming the latter are not under wraps, in which case no form of address is appropriate unless you're contemplating marriage.

■

You just never know what you'll run into when you're out and about in this city. This morning, while on our way to visit the Blue Mosque, we are approached by a stocky man of about thirty, selling something. Tracy is to my left. He nudges up to my right from the street and sticks a packet of women's underwear in my face. In Istanbul during Ramadan, this is very peculiar. I ease him away and we keep walking. He comes up again and this time touches his shoulder to mine a little. I don't know what made me stop in my tracks and look down, but I do. The sonofabitch, in that instant when he bumped me and was waving distractingly sheer women's undergarments in my face, had managed to unzip my belt pouch. One more approach and he would have had my wallet and both our passports. I look up and he's a couple of meters ahead, getting ready to swoop in again, but sees that I'm onto him, and makes a quick escape into a side street as I unleash a delicious torrent of Arabic to help him along. In the process of insulting him and his mother and his sister and all their relatives, I also shout out the word *Polis!* liberally. Down the block he goes, hooks up with a buddy of his, and makes another turn to disappear from sight. I check and double-check my pouch, but everything is still here. Then I notice two police officers walking up the street behind us. I give them the run down and describe the man. They listen intently, and once even recoil in horror at my account, but neither speaks any more English than needed to say "minimum English, maximum Turkish."

Istanbul University

Following this chummy brush with crime, we decide to rein in our adventurous natures and spend the day in the relative safety of the city's museums. Most are conveniently located near the Agia Sophia and our hotel. At the Archeology Museum we see the Alexander Sarcophagus, discovered in Sidon in 1887 by the museum's founder, Osman Hamdi Bey. This dates from the fourth century B.C. but did not belong to Alexander the Great. Historians speculate that it belonged to King Abdalonymous (seriously) of Sidon. The high-relief carvings on all sides of the marble tomb depict battle and hunting scenes from Alexander's life. You might wonder, as I find myself doing, why King Abdalonymous would have ordered this particular pattern, rather than scenes from his own life. Turns out that this king of Sidon had been a poor, inconsequential man, living in obscurity, until Alexander came through Sidon and made him king. It's important to not make too much of these stories. Back then, that is to say Before Christ, the title of "king" was handed out quite without qualifications.

At Topkapi Museum, we while away the rest of the afternoon strolling between the buildings and enjoying the gardens. This complex was home to Ottoman sultans from the fifteenth century on. Inside the Treasury of the Swordbearer and the Apartments of the Sacred Relics, we see Mohammedan relics including hair; clothes; one tooth; graveyard dust; beard; swords; locks and keys to the Kaaba; Korans and stands. For something a little less monumental, you might take a swing by the Circumcision Room. Also at Topkapi, you can have Turkey's worst and most expensive cup of tea while overlooking the Bosphorus. The view is marvelous. The pudding was pretty good.

Beirut, Lebanon, December 20

You can begin to observe the distinguishing behaviors of the Lebanese as soon as your plane lands at Beirut International Airport. Just as the wheels hit the ground, a rabble of passengers gets up from their seats and nonchalantly begins to prepare for getting off. This is accompanied by a round of applause. We see one man, across the aisle from us in a window seat, get up and stride over and across the other two passengers in his row. This guy is larger than a Chevrolet. His shoulders are so broad that when he faces forward in the plane, they touch both overhead luggage compartments. He could cause an eclipse. This is a big dude. If he were to lose his balance and fall on someone, perhaps me, it would hurt me more, much more, than it would hurt him. And he is utterly unmoved by the flight attendant's public address exhortations to sit back down and remain buckled. Nor are the other brigands. For the rest of us, dutifully waiting for the captain to extinguish the Fasten Seatbelt sign, this is the most hazardous part of the journey. We watch as overhead baggage compartments, in which we all have known for years that "objects tend to shift during flight," are flipped open while the plane is still doing 200 km/h. Large bags containing whiskey and cigarettes and cologne and other Lebanese staples are passed over our heads. By the time we reach the gate and the plane stops, half the passengers are standing in the aisle with all their carry-on luggage. I'd laugh but there isn't enough air in here.

This new airport is very nice. It reminds me of the Athens subway, brand new and shiny and looking like it hasn't yet been used much. This time the people-movers are all moving, so the long walk to Passport Control is not as painful as it can be. There are several officers in the kiosks. That's a good thing, and the queue is shrinking steadily. These guys are all crisp and clean-shaven and, well, cool. This is a uniquely Lebanese thing. There is no place else in the world where a passport control officer can look this cool. It has to do with generations of training. By the time Lebanese children are verbal, they have been exposed to every concept of coolness on the planet. They know how Italians do it. They know how the French and the Americans do it. If the English did it, they would know that, too. As a result, Lebanese Cool is second nature to everybody here. It's a melding of fashion, personal grooming, posture, attitude, and various synthetic substances, all working in close harmony. In contrast, we feel patently uncool. In our matching gray riding jacket fleece zip-up cardigans, we look like Archie and Edith Bunker.

The road into town is even better than when I was here last year. The physical infrastructure in Beirut continues to improve. To the people who live here, this is never enough. To me, dropping in as I do once or twice a year, the change is always remarkable. In fact, after its civil war and the Israeli invasion, the mere existence of this country is remarkable. That people never tire of complaining about conditions is not surprising. As long as they're here, they want better everything, and they want it now. Their observations about the sorry condition of the economy are accurate and they have every right to complain. Fortunately, this comes naturally to the Lebanese, and in three languages.

On the evening of the first day of our visit, the whole family comes over to welcome us. Our get-togethers are noisy affairs. We're almost all very animated people. Most Lebanese are. It is in their nature to welcome a stranger, to be generous and compassionate and sincere. They are also among the most complicated, particularly in Beirut. Ethnic and religious diversity have long been touted as one of the distinguishing characteristics, even strengths, of this country. In fact, this diversity is wedded to an equally broad political array, or disarray, and this has played a leading role in the country's conflicts. Years of war, education, travel, conquest and emigration, affluence and loss, violence and grace, have loaded this people with a towering angst. The Lebanese accommodate four languages, six major religions, countless nationalist derivations, and the constant threat of war in one form or another. All this in a country you can drive across in two hours. That can make a person edgy, even jumpy.

■

We're touring Lebanon today in the company of my uncle Fadlo and my cousin Danny, both fine men and world travelers. The guys pick us up at 8:00 and we drive north along the Mediterranean coast highway. This is a major road lined on both sides with office buildings and shops and restaurants. We stop at Casper and Gambini for breakfast. You get that here. Restaurants that might just as well be in New York, or Paris, or Rome clutter up every other corner of Verdun or Ashrafiyeh

neighborhoods. It's not at all surprising that Casper and Gambini serves a great bagel. The food is delicious. The young man serving us speaks three languages. The bathrooms are spotless. The fixtures are new. There is no sense at all that Lebanon needs to catch up to the First World.

Lady of Harisa

After breakfast we continue the ride north toward the port city of Jounieh and hilltop Lady of Harisa. Just before there the Dog River runs a muddy apron into the Mediterranean. It's high with recent rain and run-off, although most of it is used to provide Beirut with drinking water. Along its south bank are numerous inscriptions, carved into the rock by conquering armies over the millennia as they've marched north to Asia Minor or south to Egypt. The oldest dates back to the thirteenth century before Christ. Pharaohs, crusaders, Roman emperors, Turks, as well as French and British colonialists have left their marks. Here you see it in the rock. Around Lebanon you see it in the culture and customs and language. This is the quintessential Melting Pot.

■

On a second day trip, we leave Beirut and head south on the Corniche. Near the American University the sidewalks are the playgrounds of the Lebanese middle class, small as it has become. You're just as likely to hear English as French or Arabic. There are joggers and in-line skaters and razor-boarders and even the occasional power-walker. You pass fancy hotels like the Riviera, rich in reputation for being the gathering place of the beautiful people in the summer. Farther east, in Ayn el Mrayseh, you run into the very posh Phoenicia Hotel, and the Holiday Inn Martinez, and the Vendome Intercontinental. These are all four and five star hotels, and every bit that. However, as you leave this up-scale section of the Corniche and follow the coast south toward the airport, the scene changes. The road is now lined with shantytowns thrown together during and following the war years by refugees from the south of Lebanon. In the early days this was very much a slum. As we drive by on this lovely and warm December mid-morning, we see a thriving and bustling, if somewhat haphazard suburb. The lean-tos along the roadside have evolved into permanent structures. Restaurants, shops, mosques, bakeries, and auto-repair places do a brisk business. You can buy things here for half what you would pay elsewhere in Beirut. Back before the war, this road passed some of the city's best beach clubs. The Côte d'Azur and the St. Simon were my stomping grounds. The little beach chalets here are now homes for families of refugees. Many people lost their property in the flood of humanity from the south. It's not fair, but tell that to the folks who live here.

We continue on the main road south and turn inland just past the village of Damour. We're quickly in the Chouf Mountains. This is the southern section of the Mount Lebanon range, a beautiful area, alternating between craggy brushy hills and terraced orchards. They grow olives here, and apples, and other fruits. Just like the land to the north of Beirut, this mountain chain is bitten into by a number of rivers and ravines running from the sea inland. It's tough country with tough people. They would have to be. Some of the ugliest and bloodiest fighting of the Lebanese civil war happened here. The traditional rivalry between the dominant Druze and the Maronites has bloodied these hills for a long time. You wouldn't know it today. Druze men in their white skull caps and baggy *shirwals* stroll unhurriedly along the side of the road. We roll into the Maronite village of Deir el Qamar and park at the town square. At one end there's a mosque. At the other end of the square there's a shabby little café with plastic furniture out in the sunshine. It's a beautiful day. There's a woman outside the café making thyme pizzas, *manakeesh*, on a traditional dome-shaped *saj* oven.

When we cross the square to take a closer look at the mosque, we are joined by a smallish man with Keds sneakers on and a rough approximation of a suit. He just appears and falls in step with us. He has the keys to the mosque, and opens the doors for us to take a look inside. From here we walk together through the square to the back street which leads up the hill to the old synagogue, now a library. Along the way we see three old stonemasons chipping and shaping and placing fascia on an old house.

The rest of our stay in the country is uneventful, just how we like it. For me, under these circumstances, it's difficult to get enough of Lebanon. We're spoiled here, and surrounded by family and friends. People who live and work in Lebanon, however, are tired of the continuing stresses: political, economic, social, and environmental. Many say they would leave if they could. This is nothing new. The Lebanese have been leaving Lebanon since Phoenician times. There are 3.5 million Lebanese inside the country, but something like eleven million outside. Yet we keep coming back.

Muscat, Oman, January 4

Our plane lands in Oman Airport at midnight. This is a very different crowd from any we've flown with recently. The vast majority is from India. There is a smattering of Omanis, some in traditional dress. The airport is quite what you might expect: one long, two-story building with Arab-style arches running the whole front of it. Since we checked no luggage, we are the first to exit customs and emerge to a

sea of Indians and other subcontinent folks, waiting for their loved ones. Fortunately, my cousin Marwan is the tallest person in Oman, so I see him right away, waving to me from behind the crowd. He and his wife Rula and their daughter Bana are here to meet us. Driving from the airport to Muscat at night is very pleasant. Not a lot of traffic, and the road passes a number of lovely Arabesque buildings, including several embassies and ministries. There are strict codes here on construction, and builders must maintain the Arab architec-

Muscat Green Mosque

tural element and certain acceptable colors. Everything is white with blue or green trim. Our room at Marwan's is on the top floor, with a great wide balcony from which we can see the Gulf of Oman in the distance and the swimming pool right below. Unlike Beirut, Muscat is very quiet. The country is thirty-three times the size of Lebanon and contains only 2.2 million people. They'd have to all get together in this neighborhood to make a Beirut-caliber racket.

We sleep well and don't get going until noon. Oman is stunning. Rugged, jagged, stark, dry, it looks terribly inhospitable in a beautifully dramatic kind of way, like Arizona and perhaps bumpier. It's possible here to imagine how the world looked before man. We're on our way to the Waheeba Desert. I guess we're going "camping." Somewhere out there, in the sands of this desert to the west, we will be spending the night. It takes us three hours to get to the rendezvous spot. A young Omani fellow from the tour company is waiting for us at the Qabel Rest Area. We follow him into the desert. This is not exactly virgin territory. Many other cars have made the trip before us, wearing a nice, wide, flattish road into the sand. Once in a while we hit a rough spot. All things considered, however, this is about as wild as we like our camping to be, and are pleased to see these rudimentary signs of human habitation. Camp is a few huts built from bamboo. There are no doors. Each has a couple of cots in it. A few meters away there are four smaller huts containing seatless porcelain commodes. And in the middle of camp are two large canvas tents and a large lean-to, the kitchen. We arrive, claim our huts, and strike out over the adjoining dunes like kids who've just been let out of detention. We'd scamper over the dunes but you can't really scamper when you sink as we do. So we plod, I think, over a couple of them before realizing that we will not reach the highest point. Each dune reveals another, higher one, just beyond. You would not want to be lost here.

Soon we are summoned back to camp for the obligatory camel ride. This is Tracy's and my second such jostling in less than four months. The last time we attempted it was in Tangier. This time our whole group is riding at the same time. Riyad, the guy who runs the camp and owns part of the business, gathers us together by the camels. He and Hamad, one of his helpers, are having an interesting conversation about which camel to mount first. One of the beasts—I'll call him Widowmaker—is acting up, snarling, snorting and generally making quite a fuss. He's pissed off about something. Maybe something he ate. All I know is that no sooner do I, as designated go-first guy, throw my leg over him than Widowmaker springs up off his double-folded gams and nearly throws me. I hold on and manage to maintain surface equanimity, but it's possible that I've bruised my prostate. The others are helped onto their camels and we're strung together in a wobbly caravan, then led out of camp by Saiid. I notice that he's barefoot. This seems peculiar, until it becomes evident that our camel trek will consist of a leisurely stroll down the road we just drove in on. No rough stuff. No racing across the dunes with our robes flowing behind us and our sabers rattling. This is very tame indeed. No complaints here, mind you. Riding a camel is a pain in the ass. It's romantic and reminiscent of something vaguely heroic, but these ugly ruminants are infested with fleas, and the fleas are jumping. In the meantime, I have a pretty good idea that Widowmaker would like nothing much better in his dull life than to throw me. So getting back to camp and dismounting is happy news.

The highlight of the overnight stay in the desert is the fireside chat we have with Riyad and his guys. We sit with our feet on the stone firewall and have a conversation with these young men who have lived in or around the desert their whole lives. Omani Bedouins speak a nearly unintelligible dialect of Arabic. Fortunately they are a people of few words, except for Hamad, who is a chatterbox. These guys remind me of the movie *City Slickers.* They can talk the talk, but don't ask them to navigate the desert by the stars unless you also give them a cellular phone and a four-wheel drive.

After a reasonably good night's sleep in our hut without a door, we spend part of the morning four-wheeling across the dunes with Hamad and stop for coffee at a typical Bedouin dwelling. It's a fenced compound of three huts made from bamboo and panels of woven goat and camel hair. The fence is to keep the goats out. The man of the house is not here but his wife is, and so are her children: Sultan, Nafisah, Hamad, Hameed, Mahmoud, Muhammad, Hamdan, Faysal, Salem, and Khadijah. All have bright eyes and sparkling white teeth and skin the color of molasses. The young boys come and sit with us in the *majless* tent, their sitting room, and serve bitter coffee in small ceramic cups. Bedouins are nomadic tribes that inhabit the deserts of the Arabian Peninsula, the Sinai, and

Waheeba Bedouins

portions of North Africa. Some scholars argue that they are the "original" Arabs, and that they went north to the Mediterranean in search of richer pastures before turning toward the Sinai and Egypt. Nowadays their numbers have dwindled and their lifestyle has been corrupted by technology and commerce. Whereas I'd like to believe that the man of the tent we are visiting is out herding his camels and goats, it is more likely that he is in town or on an oil drilling installation, drawing a paycheck.

Musandam, Oman, January 8

The flight to Khasab leaves Muscat at 6:30 a.m. Muscat is the Garden of Eden compared to this place. Ironically, though I'm sure unintentionally so, *khasab* is Arabic for "fertility." From the plane, you can see that there is nothing here that is not made from stone. We are met at the airport by a tall, large-framed, blond woman. In the midst of all the locals and other Asians here, she looks like a telecommunications tower. She's Claudia, our assigned guide from the tour company. We all troop out to the large bus waiting for us, with Abboudeh, a local Omani, at the wheel. From here we're driven the short couple of miles to the Hotel Khasab, one of two such establishments in the town. Two-meter high walls surround everything here. It's to keep the goats out. Claudia explains that these living garbage compactors do have homes, but are fed in the morning and set loose to scavenge for the rest of the day. They return home at suppertime. In the meantime, they can be seen roaming the dry, wide streets of Khasab, yanking at anything they can reach.

Claudia gives us an hour to freshen up, then picks us up and takes us for a tour of the town. There are a couple of things to see here, including a fort and some boulders on the edge of town that feature ancient pictographs. We understand how some people might find these interesting, but we don't, so Claudia rearranges the

Musandam Kingfish

itinerary and takes us right to the headliner: Khasab's port. This place bubbles over with Asian intrigue. Those who know will point out that the harbor is made up of three sections. The first and least interesting is the official port. Nothing much happens here. Once in a long while a boat comes from the Emirates or Muscat and delivers goods. To its west lies the small fishing harbor. This is moderately more interesting. A couple of dhows and several small power boats are docked here. One boat is unloading a catch of small sharks

and kingfish. On the other side of the wooden pier from the fishing harbor, is the smuggling harbor. That's what it is and that's what they call it. Tens of lightweight fiberglass powerboats race in and right up to the beach, where they unload goats and sheep from Iran, then load up U.S. cigarettes and electronics and automobile parts. Their return trip across the Strait of Hormuz takes a couple of hours. Claudia explains that these guys are not breaking any laws here in Oman, but that they are outlaws in Iran. I suppose that the locals declare and pay taxes on all incoming and outgoing goods, but that the Iranians do not on the other side of the strait. Whatever the case, ferrying livestock across these waters seems to me a decidedly limiting career path. On one side you have the Iranians, notoriously anti-fun. On the other you have the pirates who occasionally poach these entrepreneurs. We stand and watch the operation from the dock. All around us are Omani, Iranian and Indian men in robes. There is compound chemistry in the air. Fish and diesel and livestock and people mingle to produce an exotic perfume. We are very much out of place in our western clothes and with our array of cameras, but Claudia assures us that the locals and the Iranian "visitors" are accustomed to this and will not open fire.

■

It's Day Two in Musandam and we're back at the harbor. Our dhow is docked and ready. The scene around us is just as chaotic as it was yesterday, but we are now seasoned Smuggling Harbor visitors and pay little attention. Our crew consists of Abboudeh, the bus driver; Samsoom, the captain-cook; Mohammad, the old shipmate; and Harry, the guide. Samsoom is somewhere in his thirties. He's wearing a *kuffiyeh* wrapped around his head the way Omanis do it. He's wiry, dark, and warmly hospitable. Mohammad is a leathery old salt who's been out on these waters his whole life. He was born in Iran but has always lived in Oman, so speaks Arabic and a couple of other mysterious regional dialects. Harry is from England. This is a young man who has had entirely too much beer for entirely too long. This morning he looks a little ragged, and speaks in little mini-sentences uncluttered with verbs: "Boat...out...dolphins...maybe..." He closes his eyes and cocks his head as though tipping fuel to the side on which it's most likely to fire a synapse.

We spend the day on the water. The fjords of Musandam are extensive inlets underlooking sheer cliffs rising dramatically from the calm waters of the Arabian Gulf, but there is nothing in them thar hills. No trees, no shrubs, no deer, no goats, no nothing. The metronomic chugging of the motor below decks, and the gentle swaying of the boat eventually get to me. So, after an hour or so, I lie down against one row of cushions in the back of the dhow and commence a series of light naps. It's only when we stop for a swim at 11:00 that I finally get on my feet. The water is clean, cold but not fatally, and calm like a swimming pool. Afterwards, we motor farther into the fjord and anchor in the nook of a quiet, picturesque cove. Samsoom's been busy gutting fish and peeling potatoes on deck all morning. Now he presents the fruits of his labor: fried grouper, biryani, and a vegetable stew he calls *saloneh*. We each also get a serving of hummus and a small salad. We're sitting on deck around the food, cross-legged. It's all wonderfully authentic.

Back in town, we are shepherded into a four-wheel-drive truck for the much-anticipated "Mountain Safari." Abboudeh is at the wheel. We head out of Khasab into the mountains to the East. If you keep going in this direction you will eventually wind up in the United Arab Emirates desert. There is rock on top of rock all around us. It is so dry, so severe, that you wonder how anyone or anything can survive, but we learn that mountain Bedouins live up here. Every once in a while we see one of their dwellings. Abboudeh pulls over and points out a couple of shacks built on the far side of a ravine, against the rock face. The ledge on which they are built is only a couple of meters wide. A few goats hang by their toe-nails to the side of the rock by the shacks. Abboudeh stands at the edge of the precipice and calls out "Sultan!" a couple of times at the top of his voice. Nothing happens. He hollers again. After a while we see the yellow door to one of the shacks ease open. Now we hear a stream of muffled oaths, curses layered upon curses, all inviting the wrath of *Allah* against the infidels disturbing the peace. The author of the diatribe, a bent old man in rags with a white beard, eventually emerges. Sultan, I presume. Abboudeh says he lives out here all on his own. Well, he and his goats.

■

We spend our last evening in Muscat with Marwan and the family, watching a total eclipse of the moon. The Sultanate is the center of this particular eclipse. At 12:21 a.m., the moon is completely in the shadow of the earth. We sit here in the open, sipping tea under a vast dark sky, between the sun and the moon.

Abu Dhabi, United Arab Emirates, January 12

Here's a flash from Abu Dhabi: Americans need a visa to visit, and they can't just get it at the airport without prior application, like in most of the rest of the world. We discover this distressing bit of news when we arrive at Passport Control. I dropped the ball on this one but here we are, passports and luggage in hand, trying to figure out how the hell to get into the country. I learn that, as a service to their American customers, Gulf Air can arrange a temporary visa so we trot back to their counter in the main hall and ask for help. The young woman on duty is in a peach-colored outfit, with matching veil thrown over a tall hat, making her look something like a schooner. She's lambasting someone on the phone when we belly up, but soon gets off and dedicates every ounce of her charm to us. It's immediately clear she hates her job. Tracy's clenching and unclenching her fist and looking hard at the woman. I sense hostility, perhaps even a schooner sinking. Luckily, the woman hands over the precious document and averts trouble.

The United Arab Emirates, or UAE, is something of a fantasy. Education and medical care are free here; there is no poverty, hardly any crime, and *no taxes!* I lived in the Middle East for more than twenty years, and still much of what I see here is surprising. That's because the UAE only made the map when oil and natural reserves were found underneath it about forty years ago. In that time, the country has gone from a subsistence sandlot to an economic powerhouse. For the record, at the rate that the country produces oil and gas today, its proven reserves should last through this century and into the next, so there's no concern about the money running out anytime soon. Abu Dhabi is the wealthiest and most influential of the confederation of seven Gulf States that hang on the northern coast of the Arabian Peninsula. The country's singular achievement, in my view, is managing to stay out of destructive regional conflicts that have allowed most of the rest of the Arab world to slip into political and economic disarray. This place is a well-kept secret.

We're staying with our friends the Tamers. The view from their apartment is of Abu Dhabi harbor and, just beyond, the Arabian Gulf. Somewhere in the distance is Iran. Below us is the Corniche. All along it are modern apartment and office high-rises. I expected a modern city, but the bustle here is surprising. As you drive along the Abu Dhabi Corniche, or any of the other broad streets running through town, you could be in Phoenix or L.A. The men walking around in white shirt-dress *dish-dashehs* are only slightly incongruous with this comparison. The indigenous population is greatly outnumbered by nearly two million foreigners working and living here. And of those, eight hundred thousand are Indian. You can get a quick sense of the mix because only the locals can wear the white robes and headdress typical of the area. We learn to tell the difference between UAE, Kuwaiti, and Saudi robes. It's all in the collar. No collar is UAE. Nehru collar is Kuwait. Shirt collar is Saudi. The ideal environment for this sort of rigorous census is the mall. Just like in Arizona, where summer temperatures make doing anything outside impossible, this area teems with huge shopping centers. We visit the City Center mall in Dubai and have lunch with friends at the Havana Café. Then we go downstairs for coffee and dessert at Starbucks. This used to be a desert not long ago.

■

Today we're at the Intercontinental Hotel Beach. It's a beautiful day, with brilliant sunshine and a warm breeze coming off the Persian Gulf. This is a fancy place. A young man meets us at the entrance, leads us along the boardwalk to a nice spot under a thatch parasol, and lays out vast fluffy white towels for us on the comfortable beach beds. Now another young man comes up for our drinks order. The sand is impeccable, white, fine, and the sea is clean. We stride fearlessly into the surf. I have a feeling that we will soon look back on this with fond nostalgia, perhaps even biting our lips in rue. In a couple of hours we'll board Gulf Air 05 for the three-hour flight to Bombay. No more coddling; no more cozy conversations with lifelong friends; no more vast fluffy towels. We'll be back on the road again, and Bombay will almost certainly be a precipitous drop in the lifestyle to which we've recently become accustomed.

Our last get-together here is a barbecue with the Tamers and their friends. Someone's been fishing and large, caught-today groupers are grilling in their scales on an open charcoal fire. Someone brought a "secret" sauce that contains equal parts fire and garlic. A few of us are smoking water pipes, *shishas*. From here on the patio we can see the pool and beyond that, the harbor. It's a warm, clear night. The fish is exquisite. We take turns grabbing chunks of it with Arabic bread and dosing them with the "secret" sauce. We'll be leaving the Gulf in a couple of hours but it won't be leaving us for a couple of days, at least.

■ asia ■

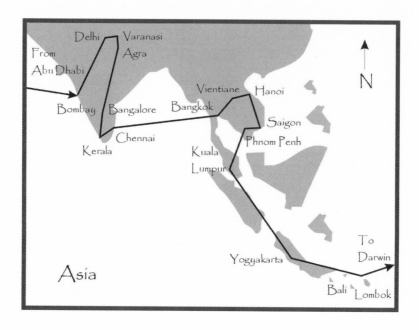

Asia is not going to be civilized after the methods of the West. There is too much Asia and she is too old.

— Rudyard Kipling (1865–1936), British author, poet

Bombay, India, January 13

It's not a happy crowd that joins us on this 1:30 a.m. Gulf Air flight from Abu Dhabi to Bombay. Two fights break out on board. A man and his wife in the row in front of ours start a shouting match with one of the flight attendants over the latter's delay in giving them water for their kid, who wails like a banshee for the first forty-five minutes of the flight. Two guys farther up come close to blows over the front one leaning his seat too far back. Their exchange is in *Bhindi*, that curious mix of English and Hindi that is so typical of Bombay and its movies. They are serious as hell, but I am childishly amused by their accents and inside-out syntax: "Tell me please why you are so far leaning?"

We land on schedule at 5:30 a.m. The usual shoving and bumping and racing ensues. Gulf Air ran out of arrival cards, so the Passport Control hall is jammed with gamy men and women filling them out. The ventilation system here is sadly inadequate. I'm doing our cards when a woman in a sari approaches Tracy and gestures that she needs help filling hers out. She apparently can't write. I notice that she has two thumbs on her right hand, both manicured (this is not a tasteless joke), and figure maybe that's why. As soon as Tracy is done helping her, the lady's husband asks the same favor. He only has one thumb on each of his hands, so I decide they're illiterate. Tracy, fortunately, misses the whole two thumbs thing, or I'm sure she would have lost consciousness. Anywhere else this deformity might be regarded with hushed sympathy. Here, now, as we prepare to exit into apocalyptic Bombay, it's pretty damn creepy.

Shifty men, stinking in their dirty clothes, line the road outside the building in the pre-dawn darkness, hustling for cab rides. There is a look in their eyes that defies light. It's desperate, stupid, hopeless. A couple of guys in uniform are organizing the mess of cars and fares. They point us to one of the same-same little black and yellow taxis all in a jagged row. We squeeze into the beat-up back seat. There is a cloud of mosquitoes waiting for us. The driver is stoned. There's no other explanation for the glazed-over, red-eyed, dull-as-dirt look on his face. We get rolling at 20 km/h, no more. Bombay at 6:30 on this mild January morning is repulsive. Everything I've read and heard makes the disclaimer that it is not possible to prepare for arrival here, that you will inevitably be shocked. It's not true. You can prepare for Bombay. Picture a sea of dark rotting humani-

Dharavi Boy

ty, alive and piled like shit on the side of the road, burning garbage to heat tins full of water. They live in cardboard shacks laid up against each other, joining grime with grime. All around is sickening poverty and unspeakable filth. The air is acrid with effluence from industry, traffic, garbage, animals and people. Open sewers run between the huts. Or maybe that's their water source. Probably not much difference. Even inside the terminal building, it was thick with a gray pungent mist. Out here, in the open, it's exquisitely foul. Picture all this in an unrelenting slum stretching for miles alongside the road leading into town from the airport and you should be not at all surprised when you arrive.

This old heap of a car is on its very last legs. There isn't enough power here to make tea. We chug along in the leftmost lane as marginally faster taxis nose by. The driver doesn't turn on the meter, so we have an uninspiring little haggle about the fare. It's all academic, however, because twenty minutes out we get a flat. It's still dark out. Even dark is dirty in Bombay. This poor bastard is too much for me to take at 20 km/h, let alone sitting still by the side of the road waiting for him to change the tire. We grab our bags and step out into the morning. I start hailing everything that moves and another driver in another heap pulls up. Our first driver is pissed. It's now our new man's turn to be obtuse. We negotiate a split of the fare between the two and continue our ride. Galaxies of silent eyes in cardboard houses watch us from behind their garbage fires. This is one spooky place. As we approach the city, things start looking up. Now the air is tolerable, merely carcinogenic. Except in spots, like when we cross the bridge over Mahim Bay, where you would swear someone had just taken a crap in your lap. By the time we get to the Ritz Hotel—just Ritz, not Ritz Carlton—Tracy is ready to get on the next flight to Beirut. I am less distressed because I know that there is more to Bombay than squalor, but it's clear that this is a place like no other.

Our first walk in Bombay is a sweaty, smelly, jostling, affair. By the time we've had a nap and gotten out on the street, it's past noon. This is one of the better neighborhoods in the city, but that's not saying much. The homeless are everywhere, washing their children in the street, picking through garbage, begging. Amputees are a rupee a dozen. Children not much bigger than cats come up to us with their hand out. Winding up in this scene twenty-four hours after having been at the Intercontinental Beach in Abu Dhabi is a shock. We push on and spend a couple of hours exploring Churchgate, our neighborhood. We take Veer Nariman Road and then turn onto Mahatma Gandhi Road. Bombay University has a few buildings here, as well as an impressive clock tower. We try to get in but the guard says, "Yes no please" and blocks the door. The High Court is here as well. It's a sooty neo-Gothic vestige of colonial influence but still houses courtrooms and judges and lawyers. Now we're at the Prince of Wales Museum. It's a collection of Indian relics and art, organized somewhat poorly on three floors. We enjoy our tour of the place, as much for being off the street as for the sometimes exquisite sculptures of the many gods and goddesses of Hindu mythology.

By the time we get back to the hotel, we're filthy ourselves. We shower and ask room service to bring us tea in an hour. Then we take a little nap. The tea comes and is very good. Dinner is courtesy of our friends in Muscat and Abu Dhabi, who had the foresight and kindness to load us up with dates and dried apricots and chocolate. Our room is spacious and clean. The bed is comfortable and fresh. We watch a little TV and read bits of the guidebook and road atlas we bought earlier. I'm reviewing all the things we have to be thankful for, particularly compared with the people we've come across today, but the list is long, and I fall asleep somewhere after "only one thumb per hand."

■

We sleep fitfully. Sometime during the night, we wake up smelling garbage fires, but we're both asleep when our morning pot of tea is brought up at 8:30 a.m. It's a sunny day out there, but misty and smoggy as well. We're in no rush to leave the room so take our time reading the Sunday *Times* and sipping tea. As I read, a picture of the city's ills takes shape:

- Two million people here do not have access to a toilet.
- Several million do not have drinking water.
- Breathing here is like smoking three packs of cigarettes a day.
- Thousands die here each year from being bitten by stray dogs.

There is compelling evidence that this is, in fact, Hell, but we dress anyway and take a black and yellow taxi to the Gateway to India. Here is a monumental stone arch overlooking Bombay Harbor, which was erected in 1911 to commemorate the visit of King George V of England. For years it marked the spot at which arriving British disembarked onto India. Now it's the departure and arrival point for the swarm of small ferries to and from Elephanta Island. That is why we're here, and we're not alone. The dock is mobbed with weekending locals. Peddlers tout ice cream, oversized gourd-shaped yellow balloons, Polaroid snaps, and open-air peanuts. We buy passage on a "luxury" ferry, which features enclosed seating. It's full. About fifty people, mostly locals, sit quietly and keep to themselves. A number of young couples are on board, off for a Sunday afternoon getaway to Elephanta. The women are all in colorful, pretty saris. Many of them have a gold stud in

Elephanta Cave

the left side of their noses, piercing the nostril. One young woman across the narrow aisle from us has *henna* designs on her hands. She notices Tracy's and mine (acquired at Oman 2000 Fair) and excitedly points them out to her boyfriend.

Bombay Harbor is a repugnant cesspool. For the entire nine kilometers, one hour, from the Gateway of India to the Elephanta dock, the water is a thick brown oily swill. Debris of all sorts bobs on this muck: plastic bags, shit, food, more shit, bits of metal and wood, garbage of every color. It is painful to look at this. Particles the size of sand and the color of, well, shit, are suspended thick as bisque as far as the eye can see. We are lucky to be here in winter. Come summer, this ride to Elephanta must be unbelievably gross. We are amazed that such a large body of water can be so horribly polluted, but already we are becoming somewhat desensitized. Yesterday's overpowering repulsion with Bombay has given way to occasional incredulity. Now we're beginning to notice its people. In spite of all the environmental challenges, there is a gentility and grace here that transcend materiality. This may be oversimplification, but I think that Hinduism plays the critical role of pacifier here, much as Islam does in Cairo. Religion steps into the vacuum created by poverty and lack. I have great respect for those who live here and manage to maintain any equanimity at all, let alone optimism. I couldn't do it.

Once on Elephanta we walk up the stone steps to the rock-carved temple dedicated to Shiva. On each side of the stairway, all the way to the top, vendors have set up tarp-covered stalls and offer trinkets, food, books, and fake jewelry, mostly junk. They are mercifully non-aggressive, however, and accept our polite "Thank

Elephanta Thief

you" as the end of our acquaintance. All around are monkeys and cows and crows. These are exceptionally ugly creatures, one and all. The monkeys are particularly nasty, living off scraps from the tourists and supplementing that by stealing from the food vendors. One flea-bitten specimen, about the size of a small poodle, darts right past us with a bag of popcorn in its hand. It scrambles along the stone wall alongside the stairway and practically flies into the trees, scampering from one branch to a higher one until safely out of

reach. Locals pay about twenty-five cents each to get into the temple compound. We pay ten dollars. I don't begrudge them this. Many are here for religious reasons. We, on the other hand, are gawkers, and deserve to pay for the privilege. And it is that. These sculptures, hewn out of the rock nearly 1,500 years ago, are magnificent. The main cave is about half the size of a soccer pitch. Shiva, in his/her various incarnations, is carved massively out of the walls on each side of the cave. In the very back there is a three-headed Shiva, the climax of the place. There are other caves with more sculptures, so we stroll between them, taking in the picnic atmosphere. Large groups are scattered throughout the grounds, relaxing, playing, eating, chasing away klepto-monkeys.

Back on the mainland, we reward ourselves for our exercise on Elephanta with a nice lunch at the ultra-swank Taj Palace Hotel, just down the street from the Gateway to India. The place is opulent, grand, air-conditioned. Bach wafts through the speakers in the halls; several restaurants offer Indian, Continental, and even Arabic cuisines. There is a spectacular pool in the large central courtyard and atrium—For Residents Only—but we trespass long enough to have a picture. For lunch we order *Pav Bhaji*, a spicy vegetable concoction which is served with leavened dipping bread; Chicken *Biryani*, served today with both a yogurt and vegetable sauce; and a spicy tomato soup. On the side, making my day, are *achar* (mango chutney) and a wicked pickled-lemon hot sauce. It has a distinctive and very powerful smell, marvelous stuff that can char your esophagus if you overdo it.

■

Traffic this morning is unbelievably bad in spots. So I sit in the back of Cool Cab 6125, a Padmini Premier, and contemplate Bombay as we drive through Dharavi, Asia's largest slum and home to one million people. Most of the action happens at traffic lights. A woman with a child in her arms knocks at the cab window. She's in a sari, has silver bracelets and a nose-stud. Her kid is dark to start with but more so for the accumulated filth on him. At another light I watch as a procession of amputees cross the road from one side of the vast slum to the other. They seem nonchalant, strolling, as though on their way to a social. When we rode in on this road a couple of days ago, it was still dark out, so we saw shadows and shapes and little fires. Now, in the bright haze, there is no fuzzing up the dehumanizing conditions. Scum is everywhere. Impotent, poetic slogans are painted on the occasional wall:

To keep Bombay clean
Just do a little bit
Don't urinate on walls
And be sure not to spit

I could spit.

It takes an hour and a half in traffic to reach the Sahar Cargo Complex. The Lufthansa office is here, and so is the bike. The shipping company clerks are immensely efficient. They do the paperwork and hand me the delivery order within twenty minutes. Now I can go to Customs and clear the bike. I am very excited, even if I have to ride in Bombay smog for two hours to get back to the hotel. I march, full of optimism, right into the large inner hall of the Customs building and approach three officers in white uniforms, sitting behind desks, reading newspapers. Must be on break. I explain that my motorbike is here and that I am trying to clear it so I can ride through India. They study me amusedly. The senior member of the triumvirate asks if I've completed the required paperwork. Immediately I realize that this will not be easy. They're thinking, "Poor, naïve, ignorant bastard. Let's torture him."

"How you will be clearing motorcycle without carnet?"

"I don't know. I was hoping you could help me with that."

"Impossible, no?"

"Okay, but what exactly is a carnet?"

"You have a carnet?"

"No. Well, I don't think so. I'm not sure what it is."

"So, no carnet?"

"No."

"How you will clear vehicle, please?"

Indian bureaucrats are polite, but the seemingly impassable conceptual road-block we have to cross together is that I do not know what this "carnet" thing is or where to get it. Honestly. When I finally convince these guys that I am quite that ignorant about this all-important document, they become very helpful, perhaps even sympathetic. They explain to me the purpose of the carnet, and suggest that I visit the West India Automobile Association, where a carnet "might be issued, possibly yes, certainly please, no?"

On the heels of this disheartening exchange, we anticipate the worst and begin to consider alternatives to riding through India. Maybe we'll forward-ship the bike to Bangkok and see India by train and plane. Maybe fly to Delhi while we figure out this "carnet" thing and do our riding when we fly back. One thing is certain: There is now a big hitch in our git-along.

■

Here we are again, in a Cool Cab, sitting in traffic, crawling to the airport for the second day in a row. Our driver is a very pleasant young man, Sridehr, who points out landmarks to us and smiles big. Here's Hajji Ali Mosque. It's accessible by car during low tide. I think we'll pass. Tracy falls asleep. Soon, I too nod off. I couldn't have been out very long, but when I open my eyes, I immediately see that Sridehr is pretty much asleep himself. His eyes, which I can see in the rear-view mirror, are slits. I offer him a stick of gum and say, "You're sleepy too, huh?" He smiles big and does that adorable head-bob that Indians do.

Now at the airport, we find the Deputy Commissioner's office, to whom we were referred by the U.S. Consulate. She hands us over to one of her subordinates, a smiling, polite young man. He immediately asks if we have a carnet. After slapping him up against the filing cabinet, I bring him up to speed and tell him that we just came all the way from Bombay to hear something other than "No carnet, no possible clearing." He is sympathetic. It seems he too is a traveler, and has gone around the world, sort of, on a bicycle. I don't pay a great deal of attention to his story because I'm not in the mood. As we get up to leave, he gets a brainstorm and informs us that there may be an alternative to the carnet. If we can come up with a Bank Letter of Guarantee for four thousand dollars, they will let me bring the bike in. When we ship out of India, we will inform them of the fact, and they will then cancel the guarantee. In the meantime, the money will be frozen. Sounds good to me. At this point, hot bamboo spikes under my fingernails sound good, if I know for sure that I can get the bike and get the hell out of Bombay. Ah, but here now is new information. It seems that this fellow was not aware, until this very moment, when his buddy at the desk next door joined our conversation, that the bike is at the Cargo Terminal, and not in Baggage! So, now we must go to the Cargo Terminal Complex and dance this whole dance all over again with the Commissioner there. This is where I spent several unforgettable hours yesterday. I already made the gentleman's acquaintance, and he also delivered the "No carnet, no possibility" speech. We thank the man and get up to leave. He smiles big, bobs head.

The head-bobbing is emblematic of Indians. I've studied this peculiar motion. It means "Yes." It also means "No." Mostly it means "Maybe yes, maybe no." The notions of fate and fatalism are all wound up into it. Its analog in Islam is *inshallah*, or "God willing." When you ask someone in Cairo to be there the following day at 9 a.m., they don't tell you they can and they don't tell you they can't. They say *inshallah*. This is in Cairo, as the head-bob is here, code for "We'll see if I oversleep." In extreme cases, like if you're dealing with the government, you can expect entire decades of *inshallah*s. In physical terms, the Indian head-bob is a combination of a nod and shake. Considering what it means, this is quite appropriate. But there's still more. I've spent some time discreetly observing people who do it a lot. The key to understanding the motion is in keeping your eye on the head-bobber's nose. You'll see that the tip describes a horizontal figure eight. Try it in the mirror. Make a horizontal figure eight with the tip of your nose. Uncanny, isn't it? There's still more. A horizontal figure eight is the mathematical representation of infinity. Karma, dharma, Nirvana, the continuing cycle of birth, death, and reincarnation, all are in the Indian head-bob. When you get one of these from someone on whom you are depending, go to Plan B.

Bombay exacts a high price for its meager gifts. We are really trying to maintain an open mind, to see the bright side, to enjoy our stay. I'm very sorry to say, nevertheless, that this is not for us. It's not for anyone, really. The very most fundamental elements of life are corrupted. Air, water, earth, and living itself are compromised. You can find tiny islands of beauty and peace, but must cross oceans of despair to get to them, and even then, how tenable can they be when all around is abject horror. Perhaps worst of all, not much here is funny.

■

For a change of pace, we are going on a suburban tour of Greater Bombay. This tour is the work of the Maharashtra Tourism Development Corporation Ltd. (MTDC), which is "A Government of Maharashtra Undertaking." Big words in India are incontrovertibly pleasurable and furthermore ubiquitously communicated with thoroughly ambidextrous jocularity in phenomenally erroneous appliances.

Three men make up the bus crew. They are:

- Speedy Shah, the driver, formerly inmate VH87654 at the Maharashtra Correctional Manor, vehicular homicide.
- Thomas Slippery Mayan, money-launderer and all-round sleight-of-hand artist, also our guide.
- Snuffles Dust bin Abdullah, untouchable, in every sense of the term.

We depart from the MTDC shack on Madame Cama Road, at Nariman Point. Our bus is a circa-1950 death-trap. It idles irregularly and then, every few moments, shudders. One day, it will shudder its last and fall down. Maybe today. The seats are Naugahide into which fifty years' worth of passing humanity has ground itself. So here we are, hurtling along where hurtling is possible, on an itinerary that includes Juhu Beach; Hare Rama Hare Krishna Temple; Sanjay Gandhi National Park and Kanheri Caves; and Lion and Tiger Safari Park.

Juhu Beach is a strip of surprisingly uncluttered sand alongside the main road just northwest of Bombay. We're invited to disembark and enjoy ourselves for twenty minutes. There are two snake-charmers doing their bit on the beach. Each carries

Juhu Snake Charmer

a backpack of sorts into which they place the basket containing their cobras. When they see someone who could be worth a few rupees, they whip out the baskets, place them on the sand, cross-leg themselves, lift the lid very, very carefully, and spend a few awkward moments waking up the snake. One eventually succeeds in getting his cobra to do a brief dance, but only after he has helped it stand and whacked it up the side of the head. Tracy is terribly afraid of snakes, however, so we observe this from Pakistan.

For lunch the bus pulls over to the side of the road once again, and we are informed that there is a restaurant here that is expecting us. Through the window we can easily see that this neighborhood might be a good place for an earthquake, a famine, or perhaps an outbreak of the plague. But lunch? We don't think so, and barricade ourselves on the bus with a South African couple of Indian descent, who are very good at barricading. I eventually step off the bus and walk down the road to buy some bananas and crackers, which we share with our new friends from Durban. They're a little older than me, maybe fifty and clearly in shock. It's their first trip to India.

Between stops, we cling to our seats as Speedy does what can only be characterized as a masterful job of navigating through Bombay's hellish traffic. He is fearless. He knows that his is the biggest wreck around and he's ready to use it. I should remind him that this is not doing much for his karma, and that, only on the basis of his misdeeds today, he has set himself way back in the get-to-Nirvana department, and will probably come back as a tapeworm in his next life. As frightening as the ride is, we are happy to be elevated above the traffic and look down with sympathy on the auto-rickshaws, Padminis, and pedestrians. The road is very bumpy. That, or Speedy's running over people.

We go on, snaking our way through Bombay. Every view is weird. Homeless, discarded people lie in the gutter in front of shops with fancy-sounding English names like Crompton Greaves and Thompson Thompson. If Kafka weren't dead, he'd be here taking notes. Bollywood movie and soap opera billboards are everywhere: *Quest for a Drop of Happiness*. How true. How very, very sad. The ride gets bumpier. So much so that I think it has resolved that kidney stone that's been bothering me. The streets are teeming with men, mostly swarthy, sweaty, rather shabby men. Occasionally we see women in their saris, so incongruously graceful and colorful and clean. Or little girls, in Catholic school uniforms, prim and serious, in the middle of this purgatory. Now we're in yet another crumbling Bombay slum, and stop just short of a lane too narrow for the bus. We're told to follow Slippery to the Hare Rama Hare Krishna Temple. It's the usual horde of barefoot people all along the road to the temple. Once there, we too become barefoot and enter. I am almost totally ignorant in the ways of Hinduism. This makes practically everything I see in this place very amusing. The haircuts, the make-up, the idols and icons, the unfortunate lingering memory of devotees ambushing me in airports. I'm ashamed to admit this because I know that in India alone, more than eight hundred million people take Hinduism very seriously indeed. It can't be good to have eight hundred million people pissed off at you.

All day I have been looking forward to Sanjay Gandhi Natural Reserve. Being in Bombay makes you yearn hungrily for clean air, for wide open spaces, for room enough to scratch your ass without elbowing the guy behind you. Ass-scratching is big at Sanjay Gandhi Natural Reserve. That's because it is home to a small army of extra-bold monkeys of the most unsavory kind. They line the short uphill walk to the official entrance, picking fleas off each other, snarling occasionally, scurrying about like hairy little hoodlums. We are actually already deep in the reserve. The narrow winding dirt road we took made for some particularly terrifying moments. We're here to see the Buddhist Kanheri caves. Monks with time on their hands began carving these out of the rock in 200 or so A.D. Over the following seven hundred years, they expanded the settlement until it became a large monastic community. Then came air-conditioning, so the caves are deserted now except for young Indian couples making out, if you can call it that, and monkeys. Public displays of affection are frowned upon here. Whereas you might see lovers kissing openly in, say, Rome, you can forget about that in India. The extent of acceptability is holding hands and perhaps leaning against each other, but not frontally. The monkeys do not subscribe to these conventions, and are freely exploring each others' various orifices all across the landscape. There's a yellow-brown haze around us. If you subtract the smog, the monkeys, the mosquitoes, and the standing water, Kanheri is really quite a place.

The ride back to town is a blur but I am rewarded with the following sign by the side of the highway:

Help Create
An Accident
Free Mumbai

The nefarious secessionists of Maharashtra at work again, but it's too late. Mumbai is already a serious train-wreck.

The upshot of our failure to negotiate Bombay's Customs is that we will be forward-shipping the bike, probably to Bangkok. Even this, an abject surrender on my part, is not going well. Now Bombay Customs wants to kick off a brand new sequence of asinine red-tape and I can't stop them because they have the bike. Well, we're leaving. If they do actually release it, I understand that getting into and through Thailand, Malaysia, and Singapore should be far less daunting a task. So we are rearranging our visit in India to include Goa, Bangalore, Kerala, Agra, and Varanasi. A little later this morning we'll be meeting with the Thomas Cook Travel people to try and organize this in advance and avoid any further scrapes with anything remotely approaching officialdom in this country. Then, as soon as we can, we will be leaving Bombay and never ever coming back.

In an inexplicable, almost perverse way, I have developed an affection for this city and its people. Perhaps that's because, despite all handicaps, they survive. There is a family that lives on the sidewalk in the next block from the hotel. They are completely in the open. No tarp overhead, no cardboard walls, no nothing. The mother is in her early thirties. She has baby twins. Two other kids, a boy and a girl, are maybe four and six. She goes about her routine as though she were in a nice bungalow and the street was the beach. She cooks, she bathes her children, she does the wash and hangs it up to dry on a line strung between a tree and a post. They take afternoon naps and have dinner together when the father comes home in the evening. They're clean, modestly but neatly dressed, and very well organized. The space they cover is only about three meters squared, but holds everything they need to survive, and it isn't much. I don't know how they got here or where they'll end up. I do know that I have never seen greater courage.

Varanasi, India, January 24

A great thing about Varanasi, or anywhere else for that matter, is that it is not Bombay. That's how we feel as we fall out of bed at 4 a.m. today. Our flight from Bombay leaves on time at 7 a.m. Turns out we make stops in Delhi and Lucknow en route. We don't care. For one thing, we're exhausted, numb. For another, it is wonderfully liberating to leave a place that's held you there in spite of yourself.

Varanasi airport is out in the country, surrounded by fields and farms. There is livestock in the road and shacks alongside it, but none of the ravages that met us when we arrived in Bombay. It's colder here, so the regional dress is different. More wool, lots of scarves, some worn by the men around their heads like they have a toothache. The man from the tour company is waiting for us, sort of. He thought we were on the next flight, but happened to be at the airport with the air-conditioned 1961 Ambassador anyway. We are given the car, a driver, and another man, Mumtaz, who rides along and checks us into the hotel and provides an introduction to the region. We're staying at the Taj Ganges, the best hotel in Varanasi. This is our new India strategy, to stay at the best possible hotel. There is so much pollution and congestion and inconvenience to traveling here, that you need a place where you can recharge at the end of each day before going at it again.

Varanasi, or Benares—everything in India has two names, it's just that there isn't enough ambiguity here—is the one place where to die ensures ascension to Hindu heaven, Nirvana, and a final withdrawal from the endless cycle of birth, death, and rebirth. So, as you might imagine, the city has become a final address for folks who are knocking on heaven's door, something like Palm Beach. If you're sick, if you're getting up there, if you have some reason to suspect that your days on Earth are numbered, then pack a bag and come on down. There are many tens of "retirement" homes in Varanasi that cater to the transit gang. These are funded by donations from wealthy Hindus who are on the way

Varanasi Ghat

out. It's a good and useful system. This way even the poor can have a shot at dying at Varanasi. Jai Deep Srivastava, whose card reads Government Approved Tourist Guide, is our tour guide. He's a handsome young man, somewhere in his twenties, in jeans and a polo shirt. He's soft-spoken, gentle, a bit meek. I question J.D. about this whole thing:

> Me: So, if I understand what you're telling me, then every Hindu who kicks the bucket in Varanasi gets to go straight to Nirvana, and no more lifetimes as a rag-picker or dung beetle or anything else?
>
> Jai Deep (head-bob): Yes, definitely, one hundred and one percent.
>
> Me: But if that's the case, and Nirvana is the ultimate ambition of every Hindu, why are there eighteen million people in Bombay and only three million here? Why doesn't all of India come to Varanasi for lights-out?

Jai Deep: People who do not die here sometimes have their bodies brought to Varanasi for cremation. This is also considered acceptable for admission to Nirvana. Even further, some people bring their decedents' ashes to Varanasi and drop them in the Ganges. This also works. We think.

So the Ganges, holiest of rivers, as it winds through Varanasi is where a lot of dead people wind up. Or wind down. Since Hindus do not believe in burial—no big surprise considering the space constraints here—they either cremate their dead or drop them in the river with some stone luggage. The guide points out that it is not unusual to come across a stray corpse during the popular river cruises. One of these cruises is on our agenda tomorrow morning. Can't wait.

■

I tried *paan* today. This is a favorite Indian street tidbit, and contains the following:

1 betel nut
1 betel leaf
 Lime paste
Pinches of spices and condiments
Tobacco, on request
Opium, on request

The *paan-wallah* (*wallah* means "man") starts with the leaf and spreads some molasses-like lime paste on it. Then he places the betel nut in the middle and covers it with various pinches of powders and shavings and other stuff. He rolls the leaf up and hands it to the customer, who pops it in his mouth. The idea is to chew the little package for a few minutes, let the mixture coat the inside of the mouth, and then spit out the residue. No swallowing, mind you, because they tell me the stuff tastes like Drano. Somehow it all turns a bright red. You know that Indians love this stuff because you can see the red spit-blotches all over the streets and sidewalks. Also, years of use can blacken teeth and cause cancer. I don't know what the hell came over me, but in a moment of swashbuckling brotherhood, I agree to join J.D. and the driver in a *paan*. They have a very serious discussion regarding what should be included in my package, and rule out tobacco. So we belly up to Varanasi's leading *paan-wallah* (actually we belly up to the rear-ends of the last row of addicts in front of us), and J.D. places the order. By the time my *paan* arrives, it has been handled by eight men, at least one of whom

Paan Stand

had just been cleaning his ears with an extra-long pinky nail. It's now too late for squeamishness. I'm in. It's in. The leaf is bitter and very tough, but the stuff inside, that's the real treasure. I've never actually tasted a hairball, but imagine it could not be far from this. Later, I looked up betel. Turns out the nut contains an alkaloid that produces the stimulating effect. There's more: Alkaloids are compounds generally found in plants, which produce variously interesting consequences for the human body. Nicotine is the most famous. Coniine was used to poison Socrates.

■

Varanasi is like no other place on earth. It's a cross between a stable, a race track, a spice bazaar, a crematorium, a nut-house, and a church. They say that the city's population is about two million. No way. I counted that many people taking a leak against one of the many pre-soaked corners around town. I estimate something on the order of eighteen billion. Plus there are ten million water buffalo, three hundred million cows of various denominations, horses, goats, mules, camels, pigs, and many thousand stray dogs. This is to say nothing of the rats and monkeys, interchangeable now in our estimation. Still, things are looking up. Varanasi, for all its congestion and pollution and filth, does not contain the urban ugliness we left behind in Bombay. In fact, for moments, we actually glimpse what might be described as rural poverty. That is to say the absence of material wealth, but not abundance. We see people who don't have much, who live by the dozen in cramped homes, and whose prospects are dim. They seem content, if not outright happy.

We're up at 5 a.m., half an hour before our wake-up call. This always happens when we're excited about the day, and *boy* are we excited today. Jay Deep and Maulana the driver pick us up at 6:00. From here we ride in the comfort of the air-conditioned Hindustan Ambassador 2000 in the direction of the Ganges. Already the streets are difficult to get through, full with people, bicycles and livestock. There are traffic circles here, on top of which men in uniforms slouch sleepily waiting for the day's disorder. It won't be long in coming. We walk with J.D. through the narrow, crowded streets of downtown Varanasi. There's a barricade in front of us at the top of the street and no cars are allowed through. That's because this way leads to the city's busiest Dasawamedh *ghat*, and there are thousands of people here already. *Ghats* are mountain ranges that run the length of the Indian sub-continent's eastern and western coasts. The term is also applied to the wide flights of stairs that descend into rivers and seas around the country. The Varanasi *ghats* have names and are held in differing levels of esteem and sanctity depending on their history and significance. Most are used for bathing and the daily ablutions that the faithful perform. Several are used for cremation. These are delicately called "burning *ghats*."

We walk down the stairs to the water, threading a timid path through holy and not-so-holy men and women. Some are wet from their Ganges bath. Others have not yet taken the plunge. It's cold this morning. Two older women are nonchalantly topless. Their nipples are indifferent to the morning chill. Down by the water, small boats are bobbing alongside the *ghat*. We step across three before landing in the one hired for us by the tour company. It's a rowboat. Before we cast off a young boy appears on board and sells us each a dried leaf shaped like a bowl, containing a small candle, a couple of tiny marigolds, and some other stuff we do not recognize. J.D. explains that this is a tribute to the Gods. We each lower our tribute into the water with our right hand and make a wish. Mine is for a nice thick juicy filet mignon that is one hundred and one percent free of Bovine Spongiform Encephalopathy, but I know not to look at a cow that way in India. We head south, staying close to the river bank. Everywhere people are praying, washing, humming, chanting, performing interesting movement in or by the water. It's some of these movements that make me wonder about the wisdom of actually getting in.

The buildings that rise up behind the *ghats* are colorful, weird, Hindu-looking. The sun is coming up now and painting them all golden. There are monkeys in mischievous mobs traipsing up along the roof-lines. One solitary man in a loin cloth stands in a large open doorway high above the *ghats*, doing chest-presses with a barbell. A young ascetic sits in the lotus position on top of a high pier and chants to the river. Just behind him is a Japanese guy in glasses and a white robe, also sitting in that position, but quietly, eyes fixed on the horizon. That, or he's stoned. This is not a joke. I understand that many people with hallucinogenic tendencies come to Varanasi to participate in a busy drug subculture.

The sun comes up and chases away the chill. Now it's getting really busy at the water's edge. After rowing for a half hour, we arrive at one of the two most popular burning *ghats*. All you can see now are huge piles of firewood, stacked neatly against

Ganges Meditators

walls, ready for the day's customers. I understand that this is a pretty straightforward affair. When there is need for a cremation, the family and friends of the departed hire *Dalits*, members of the untouchables caste, who bring the body to the *ghat*. They carry it on a bamboo stretcher down to the river and give it a good dunk. Depending on the size of the corpse, they buy wood. It's the weight of the wood that determines the cost of the cremation. Also, they must buy fire. I guess it's not done to just strike a match or whip out your Zippo. There is a man, also from the *Dalit* caste, who lives in a big house overlooking the river, and who is the fire source. It's sacred fire. Now that you've bought the wood and the fire, you have merely to find a spot on the *ghat* and build a pyre. This would be the most awkward part of the process for me, because the fires I build always go out and I'm not sure what cremation protocol is. Are you allowed to blow on the fire? Can you stoke?

We leave the cremation *ghat* and walk through Varanasi. This, the Old City, is a maze of dingy, smelly alleyways. They're not much wider than two meters. Shabby little houses and stores line both sides. There are miniature temples everywhere. We can see into many of the houses and spot in nearly each one shrines to several Gods, but mostly Shiva. We peek through a narrow open doorway. There's a small dark room, then another low doorway, then a massive bull sitting in the living room, masticating. No question about it, this is the strangest place I have ever seen.

Agra, India, January 27

Varanasi Airport could easily be mistaken for an insane asylum if not for the planes outside. The soldiers, the passengers, the cling-ons and the grimy vendors mingle in a cramped, dirty, hilariously two-left-footed dance. We see several people going home from Allahabad via this airport. They've been at Kumbh Mela, greatest of all Hindu pilgrimages, and have taken their holy dips. Many wear mementos of the pilgrimage. One couple, from Venice Beach, I would guess, has taken the whole Hindu thing and crossed it with the movies *Saturday Night Fever* and *10*. They both have perfect tans. He's in matching purple and periwinkle linen pants and baggy shirt, with a braided headband holding his brains in. She has corn-rows, like Bo Derek in the movie, and wears a psychedelic ensemble of netting tops and *I Dream of Jeannie* pantaloons, all in carefully coordinated but painfully loud pinks and blues and yellows. She has on a headband as well, but hers has gold thread running through it, giving a sappy halo effect. And three metric tons of face makeup. I estimate that it takes them three days each morning to get ready.

This year's Kumbh Mela is extra special because it's the first of the millennium. The festival normally takes place every twelve years in northern India and attracts millions of worshipers who come here for a sin-cleansing dunk in the Ganges. Hindu legend is that the gods spilled a drop of immortality tonic at the confluence of the Ganges and Yamuna rivers. The spot now promises absolution on an unbelievable scale. This is the largest congregation of humans in the history of the planet, an event that needs not many words to describe it, and here they are: One month; one hundred million pilgrims, seventy-five million of whom bathed in the Ganges; fifteen new pontoon bridges; 210,000 toilets, not counting the five hundred thousand trench-style urinals; six hundred metric tons of rice; 1,600 metric tons of sugar; fourteen shopping complexes; one hundred thousand foreigners, two of whom (from Venice Beach) just don't get it.

■

Taj Mahal: two words that conjure up a vision of opulence, grandeur, and majestic love. Some say it is the most beautiful building in the world. Others believe that a wish made here is destined for fulfillment, but we discount this last bit because we've heard it said about everyplace we've been. The story is touching, nevertheless. Its author is Shah Jahan, one of the last Mughal kings. These are the Muslim central Asians who ruled India for several hundred years until the British came along and offed them. His wife, Mumtaz, died in childbirth. Just before she breathed her last, she made him promise to never marry again and to build a grand monument in her memory. So Shah Jahan honors her wishes. The place took sixteen years to build. Twenty thousand workers lived in and around it during the construction. There is a boat-load of stories about the whole adventure but most are apocryphal, and since this is a rigorously factual account, I will not go there.

The Taj Mahal is an unbelievably beautiful place. White marble, perfect proportion, excruciatingly fine inlay work, and nothing but sky in the background.

Taj Mahal

Once we're inside the building, though, it becomes difficult to see anything because there is no artificial light. What natural light had been intended to enter the place in the original design, is now obstructed by walls erected to prevent visitors from entering the outer corridor surrounding the central vault. We just happen to have one of our minuscule flashlights with us and are able to surreptitiously examine some of the more intricate and detailed inlay. We also see the Shah's and his wife's sarcophagi in the middle of a cut-out marble screen enclosure. This is particularly and dramatically striking in contrast to the usual Indian street scenes outside the walls. In here there are gardens and birds and quiet walks and the obligatory limpid ponds. Most notable is the reflecting pool seen in all the postcards. Lime-green parakeets the size of small parrots streak across the hazy Agra sky, from tree to parapet to fence and beyond. Out there is the real India.

Agra Fort is reminiscent of Alhambra. For starters, it's a similar color, having been constructed from red sandstone. For another, it is similar in layout and content. Twenty-meter high walls ring the compound. They are nearly three kilometers in circumference. Just outside these walls are two moats: a dry one, to hold lions and tigers and other creatures that discourage trespass; and a wet moat, once loaded up with water serpents and crocodiles and who knows how much of this is true. Today it's a swamp. Inside the fort are the usual Muslim gardens and fountains and ponds. Also in here is an apartment of sorts that served as Shah Jahan's prison for the eight years preceding his death. He had been deposed by his son, but the latter put his dad up in style. The Shah's digs are called the Muthammanah, Arabic for *octagon*. From here, you can see the Taj Mahal unobstructed, across the Yamuna river, and can imagine the ex-Shah, sitting here alone, aging, gazing across the river valley at his wife's mausoleum. It's a bit melancholy.

The drive to Fatehpur Sikri is harrowing and quickly deletes any leftover fuzziness we took away from the Taj Mahal. This is the most dangerous ride we've had, ever. Name it, it's in the road. Trucks overloaded with hay and bamboo come at us, horns blaring, going as fast as they can without the wheels coming off. We're doing exactly the same thing. Bicycles and little scooters and auto rickshaws and water buffalo and camel-drawn wagons and dancing bears flash in front of us, skimming by only millimeters away. I'm not sure that to go slower or honk the horn less obnoxiously would be any safer, so I leave Nisar the driver to do what he seems to be very good at doing. It's at least part voodoo, or whatever the Indian analog is. Dozens of times I am absolutely certain that we are going to collide with another vehicle, and brace myself. The night we arrived in Varanasi, we saw a big mess of metal and tires by the side of the road being removed by traffic authority crews. The next day we read in the paper that eleven people bought the farm in that particular crash. Today, as we dodge this truck and that bus, all loaded to bursting with humans, we can see how that can happen. It wouldn't take much, really. One minor bullock-dodging and you could send a small village to its maker. That is the nature of life in India. When we arrive at Fatehpur, I want to drop to the ground and kiss it, but the ground alongside Indian roads is no place to drop, let alone place your lips.

All this is India. The poverty, the inefficiency, the bureaucracy, as well as the wonder. There are millions of Hindu gods, and they all have their hands full. Keep in mind, many have several hands.

Kumarakom, India, January 30

If it's getting to know the Real India that we came here for, then we've done well. The loop we've taken from Bombay to Varanassi to Agra to Bangalore and now to Kerala has included brief stops in Delhi and Lucknow. So we have a sense for the north of the country, as well as for the south and west. The contrast is startling. As soon as we arrive in Kerala, we can tell that things are different here. For starters, the road from the airport going south is more like Route 1 in the Florida Keys. Here it's one lane each way, however, and calls for a stouter heart. In the median, every five hundred meters or so, there is a green sign with Traffic Poetry:

Speed Thrills But Also Kills
Being Rash Can Cause a Crash
Safety Check May Save Your Neck
Chance Takers Are Accident Makers

The likelihood of a head-on collision with a banana truck is increased a hundredfold if you try to read these. We also quickly observe that the Great Squat is not practiced here as it is in the north. I refer to the amazing contortion of which northern Indians are capable, which reduces them to a package no bigger than an ottoman. As you travel throughout that part of the country, you see these ottomans everywhere: by the side of the road, on stoops, in windows, and occasionally by the river, peeing.

We're picked up at Cochin Airport and driven south for nearly one and a half hours. Then we rumble along tiny roads for another fifteen minutes before arriving at a small dock. At first we thought this might be the place and braced ourselves for camping in India. Happily, there is a ferry waiting and it takes us across lovely Lake Vembanad to Coconut Lagoon. The resort can only be reached by boat. This means that the cancer of Indian traffic, that ubiquitous auto-rickshaw, isn't here. On arrival, we are served coconut milk, straight from coconuts that have just been decapitated. We're given tiny bouquets of flowers. Our first host, Tibbi, takes our passports and checks us in. We're escorted to the room, where our luggage has already magically arrived. The rooms are cottages called *tharawads*. These are the tra-

Coconut Lagoon

ditional Keralan wooden houses. Some are originals, dismantled and brought here to this site of an old coconut plantation, where they were reassembled. We have wood-slat ceilings, heavy wood doors, and brown tile floors, as well as a banana tree in our bathroom, which is open-air. It's cleverly designed so that the sink and commode are protected by an over-hanging eave. Handy in a thunderstorm. It would be less than dignified to be struck by lightning while answering the Call. The show-er, on the other hand, is right there under the palms and the sky. We shower in the open, and just step out onto the warm tiles to drip dry in the balmy tropical air. The idea that we are only a few hundred kilome-ters south of Bombay, on the same coast, is preposterous.

From the porch of our bungalow we overlook paradise. There's a canal that runs away from here, through the property, and all alongside it are nose-bleed-high palms and rich colorful bougainvilleas and thick green grass. A number of wood bridges cross over the canal, connecting our strip of bungalows to other strips and to the main hotel grounds, the restaurant, and the reception desk. Birds from the nearby sanctuary swoop in and land in the ponds dotting the place. We see heron, and egret, and various other beautiful birds that we don't recognize. There is absolutely no man-made noise. No cars, no horns. Even the boat that brings people from the other side of the lagoon and takes them back is practically silent. The air is invisible, also nice for a change. The staff is impeccably dressed, polite, charming, happy. A young man, here from Delhi with his wife, says hi and strikes up a con-versation. He says the country needs to lose a nuclear war. I'm startled, but he explains that he means this only figuratively, to illustrate that the mountain of chal-lenges facing the country is daunting. Here, though, we're a long way from any of that.

Pathra sweda is a form of Indian massage. The words are Sanskrit, and loosely translate to "slippery messy oily massage followed by merciless exfoliation." It is one of the many treatments offered here at the Coconut Lagoon Ayurvedic Center. Ayurvedic physicians believe that they can restore and maintain health with treatments based entirely on stuff that grows in the neighborhood. A salad to you may be the cure to someone else's dermatitis. Despite my skepticism, I am always happy to take a massage, no matter what they call it. So Tracy and I sign up for the *Pathra Sweda*. Tracy's masseuses, (two of 'em, they're small), show up and take her away. I stay in the office with one of the doctors, waiting for my masseurs. He has a very unfortunate sinus condition that causes him to snort and suck stuff through his nose repeatedly. It's indelicate, to say the least, and I make light of it by saying that there are herbal treatments for this sort of thing, y'know? The joke, and the hint, are wasted on the good doctor. He continues to suction and grunt while we try to have a conversation about his life and occupation.

We're chatting and snorting when the receptionist rushes in and says that something is wrong with Tracy. I hurry back to the massage room and find her sitting on a stool in the middle of the room with the young ladies standing beside her, steadying her. She's had a fainting spell, but takes just a few minutes to recover fully. We check her blood pressure and it's normal. She feels fine and wants to go on with the treatment, but thinks that the first part of it, during which the head is massaged and pummeled and slapped around a bit, may have caused the problem. I chuckle. Now my own attendants show up and lead me to a room containing two high solid wood benches. They look vaguely like medieval torture racks. There is also a large tank of propane and a small gas range burning under two pots of gurgling, bubbling black liquid. Nobody said anything about boiling oil, but I'm just as concerned about the propane tank. These seem to be going off daily all around India. Every day there is a story in *The Hindu* or the *Times of India* about a propane tank exploding and demolishing entire districts.

I introduce myself to the guys and learn that they are Prashant and the Marquis de Sade (not his real name, but appropriate, as I come to learn). I undress and am given what amounts to a loin cloth thong thing with which to mask my individuality. They ask me to sit on a low wooden stool in the middle of the room. Immediately overhead is a large ceiling fan spinning at warp speed. There are more impending accidents in this room than in a cooking class for three-year-olds. The Marquis, who looks more like an ascetic than a maestro of torment, stands behind me and begins to pummel my head with slaps and knuckle punches. Now I understand why Tracy fainted. She was knocked out! I ask the Marquis to take it easy, and manage to remain conscious. After attempting, lucklessly, to crack my neck by twisting it so I could see my own ass, The Marquis summons Prashant. They ask me to lie face-down on the wooden bench. Then, each on one side, they begin to ladle warm oil with their hands and trickle it up and down my back and legs. The stuff smells pungent. I ask what it is and they say it's medicinal oil mixed with sesame oil. I'm in fact being basted. They then begin to massage my entire body. One on each side. Sliding their hands up and down the length of me in sync. I feel like I'm in the wrong movie. The guys dispense with the painless stuff pretty quickly. Now they each grab a pouch about the size of a baseball. It's made of linen, and contains crushed herbs. They dip their pouches into the hot oil and then whack me with them repeatedly, still one on each side. Now I'm a bongo. When they're done whacking, they start rubbing. I don't know if I'm bruising or exfoliating or just getting to know these guys really well. By the time we're done, I'm done.

■

You never know quite what you're looking at in India. There is so much of it, and so much about it to learn, that you can remain ignorant and naïve even after spending considerable time studying. If there's any truth to the hypothesis that a people's religion is as complex as their culture, and vice versa, then India takes the complexity cake. That brings me to Indian mythology, a subject that gives me a headache of Upanishadic proportions.

At the top of the Hindu mythological heap is Brahman. The whole theological problem of characterizing the Supreme Being is avoided here by describing It as being without attributes. It is the ultimate reality. If Hinduism had stopped there, and thank Shiva it didn't, we might have had just another predictable thou-shalt-thou-shalt-not religion. Instead, the designers of this richly variegated creed went on to accessorize it. The entire Hindu world was pressed into action. Deity after deity was conjured up. Every day more are made. That's a beautiful thing about Hinduism: All faiths are recognized and respected. If none of the available millions of Hindu gods and goddesses float your boat, heck, make your own!

These ruminations come and go as I lounge by the pool at the Taj Village Holiday Resort in Goa. We're here for the last three days of our India tour. If you get the opportunity to go to Goa, don't. *Goa to Kerala!* Goa is like a geriatric hooker. There's not much left here that hasn't been, well, you know. The hotels and the people and even the beaches are tired. We complain and get a better room than the one we are first issued near the Nepalese border. We want, at minimum, to be within walking distance of the pool. We were spoiled by Kerala. The Goans could offer us their eye in a cup and we'd still find plenty to complain about.

Soon India will be a distant memory, but even now, as we criss-cross the country in search of the exit, we feel an unexpected tug of

Tusk Traffic

affection for the place. We know that we have only scratched its surface, and it, ours. What's more, we understand how Indians can be so in love with their country, not in spite of, but perhaps because of its myriad monumental troubles.

Bangkok, Thailand, February 7

Bangkok International is modern, clean, well-organized, complete with every convenience and automated gismo. It is air-conditioned. We could just camp here for a few days. Passport Control has maybe twenty booths. Several are manned. It's only just 5:30 a.m., and the lady who gets us is obviously sleepy. Far from cranky, she is that fuzzy kind of relaxed you are when you wake up happy after a good night's rest. We ask for a fifteen-day visa. She gives us thirty. We thank her; she thanks us. We wave bye-bye; she waves bye-bye. These simple kindnesses loom large following the treatment we had in India's airports. Now, as we approach the Nothing To Declare lane, we are greeted by two officers who also got up on the right side of the bed. I realize that I wrote yesterday's date on my customs declaration, and go to correct it. One of the guys just waves us through. "No problem," he says, smiling. Still within the terminal, we swap a few dollars in a money-changing machine. You feed it dollars, it spits out bahts. Just like that. And there, waiting for us, is the driver from the Hilton. The sign he's holding up reads "Mr. Rif Haffar." He smiles, lets his eyes close, puts his hands together and prays to us. I pray back. Then he says, "Would you like to use the restroom before we go?" We decline what might be the most thoughtful gesture made to us since leaving Kerala. "Not to worry, only fifteen minutes to hotel," he says, and asks us to wait inside one of the terminal exit doors while he brings the car. Five minutes later he pulls up in a forest-green 7-series BMW, with tan leather interior, naturally. The road to Bangkok from the airport is perfect. There is hardly any traffic. What's this? A real freeway? Holy cow! Actually, no Holy cows for a change.

The hotel upgrades us to the executive floor (EF). You can get anything done when you're on the EF. More coffee? No problem. Middle-of-the-night fax to Antarctica? Right away, sir. Sheets too stiff? Here, let me just rub them together for you and work out some of that pesky textile tension. The room is spotless. There are bathrobes and slippers parked right where our feet land when we take our boots off. The A/C works beautifully, both On and Off. There is a fully stocked fridge. Coffee maker. Fresh fruit basket. Bottled water, his and hers. The shower is a triumph of modern engineering. Our towels are snow-white. There are three sheets on the bed: one under us, and two completely enveloping the blanket. We are swaddled in fresh white linens. Two pillows per head. Could Nirvana be a five-star hotel?

Even though it's already 7 a.m., we shower and slip into bed for a little nap. At 11:00 we get our wake-up call. We pull ourselves together, have coffee and fruit while we read the papers in our pajamas, and contemplate the day. After much deliberating, we decide to not overdo, and call Perfect Hair for simultaneous appointments. They can take us right away, so we hurry along to be taken. The salon is in a stubby shopping complex attached to the hotel. On arrival we are each acquired by one of the young ladies in the blue uniforms and shown to the reclining shampoo chairs in the back. This is no ordinary shampoo. In some countries you'd have to marry someone after a shampoo like this. I'm fighting to stay awake as my attendant works out weeks of aggravation that have crept under my scalp. Tracy is in the chair next to mine, getting the same treatment. Now we're escorted to meet the young man who will be doing the styling. After our haircuts, we get another shampoo. Then we all pray to each other. I love that.

The bike is still in Bombay Customs. Lufthansa continues to try to extricate it for me. We just submitted a brand new letter to the Splendid Vice Admiral of Paper Cuts and Consolidated Baksheesh Assessment. He has awarded the Lufthansa guy an audience later today, at which time we hope to have a carefully studied and meticulously documented dispensation in our favor. I'd like to believe that, but suspect we will actually receive a further postponement of any movement whatsoever for no particular reason. In the meantime, customs charges me fifty dollars for each day they have the bike in "storage." I should have seen this coming; none of those Bombay Customs guys ever prayed to me.

We're not sure what to make of these Thais. It's clear that they're up to no good. Everywhere we go they act all friendly and happy and hospitable. They smile when we wave, they do the praying thing; it's enough to make a person very suspicious. So we decide to spend as much time as possible roaming the streets of Bangkok, despite the smog, and finding out where the real Thais are. Our first destination is the oldest of all the city's temples: Wat Pho. A *wat* is a temple. We'll be seeing many of these. In preparation for the visit, we do a quick study of Thai society and architecture, just enough to know what we're looking at. It's much like anywhere else. A typical social unit, the village, contains a temple in the middle, a school nearby or even in the same compound, a market, a public forum, citizens' housing, and a massage parlor. I'm not kidding. Massage is an old and rich tradition in this country. I don't mean "massage," as with fragrant oil of jojoba and fluorescent condoms. No, I mean the non-erectile kind that is practiced in reputable spas and Ayurvedic healing pods. This tells you something about the people of Thailand. They can some-

Wat Pho

times be depressed. They might even fight a war if they have to, but they would really much rather get home and have a rub. So they are a calm people whose priorities lie in precisely the right order. Wat Pho, incidentally, has what is considered the leading center of massage education in the country. There are master masseurs in there giving tourists a sample of the art for two hundred bahts, or five dollars, but it's too warm for that today, so we move on. All the buildings in the compound are made of wood. Most are elevated, on stilts. When it rains here, it rains torrents. The structures are A-frames, pure and simple, but they are pitched steeper than elsewhere, and some have multiple roofs, built into each other like telescoping plastic cups. Then, on each roof corner, the top two and the four at the base are attached *ngao*s. A *ngao* is an extension, usually made of wood, sometimes metal, that sticks up and out at a forty-five degree angle, or sometimes even inward toward the roof, pointing at the sky. You can think of them as building antlers. One antler per corner. These antlers have a graceful, shallow wave to them. They are often painted a bright gold. The effect they give is whimsical, exotic. This simple adornment tells you that Thais are people who appreciate elegance, subtlety, lightness of spirit. Stand Wat Pho against the Grossmünster of Zürich and you'll see what I mean.

Thailand is a constitutional monarchy. Once in a while during the past few centuries, it has been a Constitutional anarchy. Still, the royal tradition has survived. They are on the ninth King Rama in a row and he is revered, even if technically a figurehead. In fact, after being on the throne for fifty or so years, he is enormously powerful. His portraits are everywhere. A very large one in our neighborhood depicts him from the chest up, in a light blue jacket, reading what looks like blueprints. His forehead and cheeks are covered in perspiration. I like that. I think it's important to show a king perspiring. It makes him of the people. It shows he cares enough to break a sweat. Mind you, this king is no youngster. He's somewhere in his early seventies, but robust and busy. Just now while we're here on our unofficial state visit, the Queen of Denmark and her consort are in town spending some time with His Majesty Bhumibol Adulyadej (his real name; Rama IX is just a nickname). They are everywhere, attending dinners, making speeches, blessing ships, and inaugurating schools. At the National Museum, there is a special exhibition celebrating the two countries' historical relationship. It's a sleep aid, so we move on to the zoo for some real entertainment.

The Bangkok Dusit Zoo contains most animals you would expect to find in a zoo, except elephants. That makes sense. Going to the zoo in Thailand to see an elephant is redundant and unnecessary. They're everywhere. Our favorite resident at the zoo is an orangutan we name Slomo. This ape has taken lounging to a level as yet unmatched in the animal kingdom. When he moves, and that's not often, it's with a weariness that makes you want to lie down and take a sympathy nap. He has an expression of unqualified indifference. You can stay if you want, or you can go. He could care less. His eyes are very nearly shut. If he blinks, he heaves a sigh, as though he's just raised a great weight. When we arrive, Slomo is on the floor of his enclosure, on his back, contemplating his nipples and delicately picking his nose. We watch him and talk to him for twenty minutes. Eventually, I think to get rid of us, he climbs up on a post and raises his arms over his head. He holds this pose for five seconds. We applaud. He collapses into a heap of lips and fuzz, and looks down into his lap. It's clear that the show is over, perhaps for the rest of the decade, so we amble on.

It's warm and muggy here, but not intolerable. The temperature in Bangkok hits highs of thirty-five Celsius in April and May, but stays near thirty the rest of the year. It's humid, so we come back from our daily explorations thoroughly marinated. Bangkok is polluted and congested, but not nearly as badly as I believed. It's clean. It's organized. Traffic is heavy, no doubt, particularly during rush hours, but we're avoiding travel that time of day. It's a modern city. They call it Venice of the East because of the canals that radiate out of the Chao Phraya River. We took a kind of gondola for a swing through some of these canals today. Here they call the waterways *khlongs*. Along the way several small boats, some being rowed along by solitary skippers in lampshade hats, come alongside to sell us everything from barbecued chicken to sarongs. The canals are also lined with "floating markets," where you can stop for a potted plant or a pot plant, depending on your proclivities.

We do enjoy Thai food, especially here at the Hilton. Every night, the chef and his sous chefs (which is French for underwear) prepare ten hundred different dishes for the exquisite buffet dinner. Three nights in a row we eat here. At 7 p.m., a small Thai orchestra begins to play in the lobby atrium. That's our signal to purge in preparation for the feasting that lies ahead. The music continues for just a half hour. Actually, the musical program is not one of the Hilton's strongest suits. One night, following the Thai music, they piped in Bach's "Sheep May Safely Graze" continuously throughout our meal. Even Bach can wear thin. Anyway, a song about grazing during a buffet dinner may be a bit off the mark. Thai music, with which I am badly out of step, is troublesome. I can't really describe it musically because it uses a different scale. Also, certainly in the case of the Small Hilton Orchestra, it is made up entirely of metal percussion instruments. I'll go out on a limb and assume that, just because they sound like it, these are not pots and pans.

We have seen enough Thais now to stereotype them. The average Thai person is small, gentle, sweet, calm, devout, clean, friendly, respectful, and not very hairy. Most have tans, or olive complexions that tend to the yellower tones. They are an industrious and energetic people. We have not spotted many just lounging around. So far only two nose-picker sightings. And even then, the perpetrators were busy doing something constructive with their other hand, like frying up some prawns or cobbling a sandal. Age does not slow down a Thai. It just bends him. We see several bent people shuffling about doing work, or shopping, or tending a child. You can wrap all this up into the conclusion that Thai society seems to have struck that perfect note between the "Me" model so prevalent in the U.S. and the "Nobody" model at large in India. There is enough affluence and industry for the ambitious, but also serenity and "family values" for the traditionalists. I wish we had the bike. We would be happy to spend a few weeks riding here.

Certainly not all Thais are nice people. We know this, but now that we have been softened up by the rest of them, we tend to have a much happier predisposition for the not-so-

Thai Boy

friendly Thais. It's a virtuous circle. Unlike the people, Thai language is unapproachable. They have their own alphabet. It looks like a construction of Sanscrit, Alpha-Bits, and socket wrenches. I know one expression: *khawp khung khrap*. This means "thank you." If you're female, you cut the "*khrap*" and say *khawp khung kha*.

Our revised bike-less itinerary includes a comprehensive swing through Southeast Asia. After Thailand, we'll hit Laos, Vietnam, Cambodia, Malaysia, and Indonesia. From Bali we will fly to Darwin. We hope to arrive there around the middle of March. That gives us six weeks to rescue the bike from Bombay Customs. In the meantime, the Burmese and the Thais are having a little border war up north, so we'll be skipping Rangoon.

Ayutthaya, Thailand, February 11

We've rented a Kia Sportage. It's a sport utility vehicle (SUV). It's good to be in a country that supports roaming, so we roam. Take this turn, that turn, we have no fear. Thailand is like certain parts of Spain and Italy. Not the climate, but the roads and the facilities and the pace. We squeeze the one-hour drive to Ayutthaya into three hours of meandering.

We expected a much bigger crowd of tourists here, but in fact have come across only a handful. There are more *wats* per capita in Ayutthaya than anywhere else in the country. It's a good thing we have the Kia because these temples are spread out over too large an area to cover on foot. Some are in the middle of muddy fields along rugged dirt roads. As we drive around, people wave and smile. Going down one lane, following only our instincts, we come across two lone wooden houses built on stilts, one on each side of the road. The first one has a porch, and a throng of young people, teenagers, is gathered there. They shout out "hello!" as we drive by. The next house owns a small herd of water buffalo, and it is now in the road. A young boy who sees us approaching grabs a handful of rocks and zaps two of the animals on the rump to make them move. Another road takes us to a monastery adjacent to the marvelous Wat Maheyong. Monks in orange wraps lead a couple of hundred pilgrims around the temple. Men and women are in separate groups, but all are barefoot and dressed in white sheets. There is some sort of ritual going on, but we can't figure it out. Here we are, in our shorts and T-shirts, stumbling ignorantly around trying not to step on anyone's lotus bud. Despite numerous welcoming gestures from the people there, we feel terribly out of place. It's obvious that we're not into this for the spiritual content. So we're intruding, and beat as dignified a retreat as we can. Once out of the immediate temple, we buttonhole a monk who speaks English. He explains that this is a retreat, and that Buddhists from all over Asia come for a three-week meditation extravaganza. Are we interested? I ask him if there are TVs in the rooms. He chuckles, puts his hands together and prays to me.

Lopburi Stupa

The history of Thailand is conveniently organized into dynasties that bear the name of the country's capital during that time. This is the Bangkok era, and has been since the Burmese sacked Ayutthaya in the eighteenth century. For the four centuries preceding its destruction at the hands of Burma, this was the capital of Thailand. We learn all of this at the Ayutthaya National Museum. Also here is a collection of Thai art that includes Buddha heads; Buddha Subduing Mara; Buddha Repelling Fear; Buddha Meditating; Buddha Walking; and Buddha Preaching. Each of these activities is associated with a very specific Buddha pose. Fear Repelling is where he has his hands out as if to say "Stop! In the name of Love!" Subduing Mara is where Buddha is cross-legged, with one hand open palm up in his lap and the other extended away from himself and palm-down. Incidentally, this is not the pot-bellied Buddha in which tropical drinks are served. Thai Buddhas are thin, almost effeminate. I mean no disrespect. Buddha himself would have appreciated the irony of this situation. Buddha-love has become a potent opiate in Thailand. In a sense, this is counter his teachings. The gist of Buddhism, after all, is avoidance of suffering through elimination of desire. That means, in lay terms, that you wear an orange sheet, shave your head, beg for food, sweep the temple dirt from one side to the other, do whatever you must, but do it all with unruffled equanimity. It doesn't make sense that you would be passionate about Buddha. For my money, Buddhism is the closest thing to a sensible religion, but there are plenty of statues and the world doesn't need more. The tradition of making golden Buddha images is an old one and will be difficult to arrest. The country is littered with pyramid-like cones they call *chedis*, or *stupas*, or *prangs*. These are memorials erected at the expense of individuals or governments who believe that you can buy credit in your Nirvana account by having statues of Buddha hidden in mounds of earth and mortar. Kind of like a frequent flyer program.

And now, I would very much like to dispel some popular myths about elephants:

- Elephants are not clean animals. They appear that way on TV because they have enormous surface area and dirt gets spread pretty thin.

- The end of an elephant's trunk is not dry and fuzzy, like slippers. It's wet, like a dog's nose, but thirty times as excretive.

- An elephant can't reach its ass with its trunk but it can reach its neighbor's, and often does. Therefore, you can never be sure where the elephant trunk you are handing bananas to has been.

- Elephant jockeys, *mahouts*, do not have a special language in which they communicate with their animals. They do have a stick about the length of a walking cane, at the end of which is a sharp steel hook that can pierce titanium. That speaks volumes. It's a talking stick.

- Baby elephants, though cute as hell, are usually surrounded by dung ants. These will bite you if they can, and it hurts like a sonofabitch. This not to mention that they've been biting dung immediately preceding you.

All this apropos of our first-ever elephant ride. Following the visit to the National Museum, we climb into our Sportage and just drive around. We see, in the distance, a whole caravan of elephants, complete with colorful *howdahs* containing white people scratching their legs and a *mahout* sitting in front, carrying a talking stick. We know from our guidebook that there is an elephant park here, but this is much more elaborate than we expected. There are about seventy elephants. Their names, ages, heights, and the names of their handlers are listed on a big sign at the ticket booth. There's a paddock of sorts by the side of the road. At one end, near the souvenir shop and snack stand, there's an elephant shower. When they come back from a walk and unload their passengers, they're led to this area and allowed to rest for a while under a constant, fine spray of water. Just like the produce section at Safeway. When we drive in, half a dozen elephants are standing under the spray. They are separated from the tempting opportunity of stomping on us all by a flimsy metal barrier. Some of the tourists buy baskets of bananas and feed them. Judging by the mountains of poop in the area, there's been a bit too much banana-feeding going on. These elephants need tea and apples. Outside the enclosure, mingling with the crowd, are two babies. Saying "baby elephant" is like saying "minor galaxy." These are big, lumbering animals. If one of them spooks, we are all in trouble.

Elephant Shower

Tracy and I buy the thirty-minute ride. It's five hundred bahts each. That's one thousand bahts total. Twenty-five dollars. I once paid twenty-five dollars for a mesclun salad, so this is one hell of a deal. We are issued our tickets and directed to the mounting platform. It gives you a keen sense of how high an elephant really is when you have to climb up a flight of ten steps just to reach its back. We do. Our elephant is Tongdee. Her handler, Number Fourteen, is a man of few words and he uses them all. They are: camera. When we reach the midpoint of the ride, Number Fourteen parks Tongdee up against a brick wall overlooking a ruined temple, and dismounts. He has to say "camera" several times to get our attention, because we are busy shitting our pants. Here we are, not twenty-four hours from our last Hilton breakfast in bed, left alone on top of a behemoth that we barely know. Turns out there's no need for alarm; Number Fourteen and Tongdee have done this together several thousand times. We relax and take turns riding on the elephant's head and waving the talking stick while Number Fourteen takes our picture. To tell the truth, elephants are a much more comfortable ride than camels. Whereas camels' backs describe a forward sinusoidal wave and cause nearly immediate motion sickness, not to mention a herniated groin, elephants merely wobble.

Hua Hin, Thailand, February 13

If you come to this part of the world, you have to not let lizards bug you. There's a small gray one fused to the wall about an arm's length away from me right now. He hasn't budged in twenty minutes. I keep expecting him to flick his tail and slither away like lizards do, but he just clings to that spot on the wall. Maybe he died. Maybe he's taking a nap. Our ignorance about Thailand is that comprehensive. We are not only in the dark about the culture, the religion, and the language; we don't even know if Thai lizards nap.

Now that our tour has taken us to a couple of dozen temples, we have decided on a change of approach. We're going to check out some Thai beach resorts. We're just looking for a place with a nice pool so we can relax for a couple of days before going to Laos. Most of the famous beaches are in the south. After looking at a couple of places on the way from Cha-am to Hua Hin, we finally settle on the Springfield Resort. The lovely young lady at the reception thinks we're stupid as well as good-looking, because she tries to put us in a suite with two bedrooms, six beds, two baths, two living rooms, and a staircase to an empty second floor. VIP room. We settle for a smaller room that contains only one of everything. This is a nice place with a great pool. The sea is not especially inviting, like in Muscat and Abu Dhabi. Here, there is a film on the surface of the water. Could be oil. Could be natural sea organisms that infest your ears and drive you mad with pain. Either way, we pass, and hang out in the pool instead.

There is a palace on the road to Hua Hin that is unforgettable, an absolute must-see. This morning, while driving south to town, we see a sign for the Phrarachanivet Mrigadayavan Palace, so we follow it. There's a checkpoint, but the young sentry smiles and waves us through. King Rama VI ruled Thailand at the turn of the twentieth century. He is the present king's great-grandfather and the first Thai king to study overseas. He racked up degrees at Sandhurst and Oxford. Then, between running the country and founding Thailand's Boy Scouts, he translated all of Shakespeare's plays and wrote a fair number of his own. He was a poet, as well. Rama VI built this summer palace in the early twenties and spent a good deal of time here conducting affairs of state and relaxing. It is not a "palace" in the way that Versailles is a palace. This is more of a bungalow. It just happens to be one hundred meters long and fifty meters across, built entirely on 120 three-meter-high stilts, and elegant beyond belief. Simplicity defines the building and its contents. There is only one level. Rooms are interconnected by long sky-

Phrarachanivet Mrigadayavan

bridges. The flooring is all dark hardwood. The roof is red tile, and extends down to low-hanging eaves that keep the shade in. We see the king's bedroom, his study, his theatre, and the royal dining room. We also see his wife's rooms. They are furnished now as they were then, simply, gracefully. There are nuances of Japanese design here. We walk all through the corridors, down to the bathing pavilion, a platform at the beach end of one of the long elevated corridors. We learn that when his wife was expecting their first child, the king would have two canvas deck-chairs placed here every afternoon. While they sat looking out over the gulf, as we're doing now, the king would lecture his unborn child on matters of governance, on the rules of king-ship, on love for Thailand and the Thais. The day after his daughter was born, the king, who had been ill, died. We sit here and look out to sea. We have the place to ourselves. Eighty years ago the king of Siam and his wife sat here, sipping tea, chatting.

Vientiane, Laos, February 17

The flight from Bangkok to Vientiane is only an hour long, but the journey takes us forty years back in time. At least. We got our visas in Bangkok, so we pass through Passport Control quickly. The officials are pleasant behind ill-fitting, drab green uniforms, rainbows of ribbons, and red stars. The airport is just north of Vientiane. As we drive in, we see the mighty Mekong to our right. I can't say that name without the word "napalm" popping into my head, and that conjures up violent confrontation. The history of this place is all wrapped into that of its neighbors.

Thailand, Cambodia, China, Vietnam. I don't know where on earth you could have had worse neighbors during the sixties and seventies. Laos has the distinction of being the world's most bombed country. All we've found so far, however, is a gentle and hospitable and good-looking people. They smile, they greet us warmly, they're a lot like Thais. Very occasionally, one or two of the older guys view us with thinly disguised but minor hostility. In the seventies, they were in their thirties, so they remember. We don't mind. You would get about as much flak walking through a mall in Arlington, and no bombs were dropped there.

Our hotel is in the center of the capital, which is easy to distinguish from the rest of Vientiane because it's where the traffic light lives. Ours is the tallest structure in the city, perhaps in the country. Six floors. This is a quiet, dusty, provincial little place. The streets dissolve into sandy edges. They're paved in the middle, but the shoulders would fall back into the Mekong if left alone. You could say that about the whole city. Many streets in Vientiane are red sand, unpaved. There are a few cars here, but most people get around on scooters and bicycles, or on foot. Even then, there just isn't activity as you might expect it to exist in a country's capital city. There have been no traffic jams reported in Vientiane. Ever.

We arrive at the hotel to a wonderful reception. Hell, they have the red carpet rolled out. Laos, red carpet, could be that they mean something different, something more, I don't know, Marxist? We stomp our way importantly into the spacious and well-lit lobby of the Lao Plaza. There are many soldiers around. I'm neither surprised nor disturbed. This is par for the course in a communist country, but it turns out something special is on. There is a Vietnamese military delegation visiting, and they're staying here at the Plaza. Hence the red carpet. We check in. Our room is fine. We have a TV and can receive CNN, CNBC, HBO, MTV, ESPN, and a couple of Thai channels. This is more capitalistic than I anticipated. Still, I find myself scanning the room for bugs, electronic as well as organic. Good news, there are no mosquitoes in the room, but something lives in the carpet, something tiny, maybe no-see-ums, and our feet begin to itch if we walk around barefoot.

Mosquitoes aren't what they used to be. Back when I was a kid, we got bitten all the time. It was no big deal. In Damascus, every summer, small planes would buzz the city and drop several million liters of DDT on the bugs. And on us, because we were almost always playing in the garden, with the bugs. Apart from my chronic inability to keep a job, I am unaffected by the DDT and wish they would start doing it again everywhere. That's because nowadays, unlike during the Cold War, a mosquito bite can be very bad news. The mosquitoes of the sixties and seventies were dreaded only to the extent that they caused itching. If you had Calamine lotion around, there was no reason for alarm. We had bigger things to worry about, like Nikita Khrushchev.

Laos is stuck in that uncomfortable space between what's left of communism and the rising tide of American-style capitalism. You could call it sociopolitical puberty. This is a People's Democratic Republic, but there isn't the kind of oppression we read goes on in Burma, sorry, Myanmar. We are also delighted to see that Lao people have retained, to a great degree, the traditions of their culture. Women dress in the embroidered skirts produced here. Only occasionally do we see young people who have adopted western dress. Still, the creep of pop culture, American in particular, is unmistakable on TV and in the music. Slowly but undeniably, the promise of openness is being seized here, and it's only a matter of time before Laos looks more like Thailand. It's such a small country, with so few people, that its prospects for rapid development are greater than, say, India. That may sound counter-intuitive, but it makes sense because they don't have any of the problems that come from overpopulation. It would take much less foreign investment to jumpstart the Laos economy. The people's natural ease and hospitality are a tremendous asset, as well. We work all this out in our busy heads just minutes after checking in, and take a quick nap to recover.

We've arrived early enough in the day to make something of it, so head out for a little walk around the neighborhood. It's a quiet, laid-back place. There is nothing fancy about Vientiane, more small town than city. Small shops line the street. Most are shabby. It's not always obvious what they sell, either. One place serves food at a small stainless steel counter, but also rents scooters and has a photocopy machine. The staff consists of one woman in her forties, who's also tending somebody's young children. Several shops in this neighborhood rent scooters. We take the 100cc Suzuki Swing. It's bright red and has a basket in front. There are four gears. You shift by stepping down on a pedal. No clutch. Going from

Bikey-Poo

a Honda ST1100 to a Suzuki 100cc is like starting to wear diapers again. You can do it if you have to, but would rather your friends didn't know.

We hop on our bikey-poo, gently, and shoot east. It's great to be on a bike again, even this little tyke. Turns out the Swing can do 90 km/h, or 60 mph. On a bike this size that's red-hot fast. It's rural out here. Along the road there are shacks and lean-tos selling food and hats and pots and pans and, occasionally, live chickens. Most of the traffic around us is mopeds, but not many of these, either. Once in a while we pass through clusters of hovering dragon flies, big ones, like hummingbirds. We're only doing 50 km/h now, so we can dodge the ones that don't try to dodge us. When people pass us, they are always two per bike, minimum. They smile and wave. We're a spectacle here, even though we're on a small scooter just like everyone else. We don't mind.

■

The entire Vientiane mounted police department is parked outside our hotel today. Six Suzuki motorbikes. All white. All fitted with lampposts that stick out of the back and support single red revolving lights. In a high-speed chase you could confuse one of these bikes for a rapidly approaching brothel. The Lao Plaza is a good place to stay if you're interested in staying abreast of the government's development activities. Just during our stay, the hotel has hosted the Defense Minister of Vietnam, and now the Prime Minister of Vanuatu and his rather populous delegation. We were confused on our arrival from the airport, and briefly believed that the red carpet was for us, but it was for the Vietnamese minister. When he left, the carpet was immediately vacuumed and rolled up.

English is not widely spoken in Laos and neither is French. To get yourself understood you must boil your sentences down to their bare bones. For instance, you could say, "Yeah, I'd like two eggs over medium." This will get you a blank look. "Two egg, cook two side," works better. I'm not making fun of the way they speak here. I'll do that later. This is rather to explain that it is unfair to expect locals to understand sentence construction as we know it. Eliminate all unnecessary words, and you'll do better. Yesterday Tracy called and ordered dinner from room service. She closed with "That'll be all." It didn't matter that she repeated this slowly five times. We still got an extra bowl of soup. Then, when she called the reception to ask that someone come and clear our "dinner tray," a room attendant delivered an "ashtray." It's like this. These little misunderstandings are never a problem, since everyone is doing their level best to understand and comply. I test this hypothesis by pulling over on the way back from the Cultural Ethnic Park and trying to rent a 600cc Honda Shadow parked in front of a feed store. The mother behind the counter wants to sell the bike outright. She even has a price in mind: one hundred thousand bahts, or $2,500 American money, and a large calculator on which to flash me the price in three currencies. When her older son comes downstairs, just out of the shower, there's no more of that and he gently invites me to go to hell.

Great Sacred Golden Wat

The annual per capita income in Laos is three hundred dollars or so. They manage on that. Riding around on the Swing 100 today, we can see how. Theirs has to be a simple life, of course, but it doesn't seem inordinately difficult. Housing here is basic. So is transportation. So is food, and clothing, and entertainment. In short, theirs is a world without the clutter of ours. If you can manage that, maybe Laos is an option for you. From a strictly economic point of view, it's unbeatable. If you anticipate living for another thirty years, you can retire immediately and live out your years here for a measly $12,000. It's not polluted, it's not overpopulated, there's no war, no famine, no plague, and the political situation is acceptable. In one hour you could be in Bangkok or Hanoi. In two you could be in Singapore. A few more hours and you could be in Australia, trying to figure out why anyone would want to fire up Barbie.

Laos' most important national monument is the Great Sacred Golden Wat just on the outskirts of town. This is a multi-storied tiered structure that dates from the sixteenth century. It is painted all in gold. Since there is so much of it, eighty-five meters on each side, it is quite a visual extravaganza. Yet all around is dust, and sand, and scooters. There is an almost comical grappling with money going on here. We can get in to see most monuments for one thousand kips per person, about twelve cents. Once inside, however, we see shoddy little books for sale at six dollars a pop. These are government publishing house-issue booklets, the kind whose pages stick together. We add to the surrealism of the scene as Tracy learns to ride the scooter in the shadow of the Great Sacred Golden Wat.

■

A *tuk-tuk*, also called an auto rickshaw, is a three-wheeled vehicle that in most countries is used to transport vegetables, propane tanks, and sometimes sheep. In India and Southeast Asia, it's the most popular mode of communal public transport in the cities. These things are noisy, they stink, and they're only slightly less dangerous than Russian roulette, so we've left them to the other tourists. This morning, though, as we walk back to the Lao Plaza from surrendering our scooter, we are weakened. Two *tuk-tuks* are parked in the block just before the hotel. As usual, the drivers "*Tuk-tuk?*" at us. We say "Thank you" and keep walking, but then I go nuts and offer one of the men five thousand kips if he will let me drive. Surprisingly, he agrees, but asks for ten thousand kips. That's a little over $1.25. It's a deal. We take a long loop through the adjacent

Tuk Tuk

blocks. As we pass by people, especially locals, I accost them with a "*Tuk-tuk?*" Some are amused. Some are annoyed. The man sitting next to me alternates between laughing out loud and yelping in anguish as I grind his gearbox looking for third gear. Tracy is in the back, guffawing. I consider the $1.25 well-spent.

Hanoi, Vietnam, February 20

Vietnam Airlines has grounded its Tupolev Sputnik aircraft. We see a few of them on the ground at Hanoi International. This is comforting, since we'll be flying this airline again to Ho Chi Minh City and then on to Phnom Penh. Hanoi airport itself is unassuming, somewhat scruffy, but not depressing or dirty. A new terminal is under construction. Airport officials, as well as parking officials, wear very large caps with hyper-extended shiny visors. These must be a point of pride. When we get off the bus and walk inside the terminal building, we see that every passport control officer has placed his hat on the counter in front of him, facing us. We're received politely, but there's no gushing here. The man processing our papers is serious, all business. He greets us in and greets us out. It's as good a start to our Vietnam visit as I could have hoped for.

We were never supposed to be here. The original plan was to ride from Bangkok, south through Malaysia and Singapore, before shipping the bike to Indonesia and continuing the trip from there. However, when we lost our fight with Bombay Customs and realized that we would not see the motorbike again for a while, if ever, we figured we might as well take a swing through Southeast Asia. So here we are, and glad for it. We're staying at the Hanoi Hilton. This Hanoi Hilton was completed in 1999, and it's a beautiful, modern, luxurious place. Just down the street is the other "Hanoi Hilton" of Vietnam War fame. The old prison has since been torn down, but there's a museum we will probably visit. For me, the image of American POWs being marched out of here in the seventies is still vivid. Vietnam's tourism slogan is "Vietnam is a country, not a war." Well, okay, but that's going to take some getting used to.

The first motorcycle we get in Hanoi is called Husky. It's a black Harley looka-like cruiser, and has twelve trillion miles on it. I have misgivings about this bike. For one thing, it has no rear-view mirrors. For another, the throttle is somewhat prostatic, and leaves us gasping for power in the middle of intersections. And anyway, rid-

Comrades

ing in Hanoi is a thrill-a-thon of danger, even without these extra challenges. We take it anyway, on a trial basis, and have an inaugural ride through this part of town. But it's just not safe, so we trade it in for a more comfortable Honda with rear-view mirrors and a basket on the front. Traffic in Hanoi is unpleasant, unpredictable, and downright perilous. Fortunately, there aren't that many cars. If you do tangle with anything, it's more likely to be a scooter or bicycle, or even a pedestrian. If you're finicky about rules of the road, riding or driving in Hanoi can seem impossible. There's so much going on. Armies of riders and drivers, some at great speed, enter intersections at the same time. Traffic lights are almost entirely ignored. Somehow, against all odds, they all get across. So far. The key is to never, ever, look anywhere but directly in front of you. Your only responsibility is to not plow into anything that appears in your path. The people behind have to watch out for you. If you hear a horn, don't change direction by even a hair, or you will likely lose skin to a passing maniac. Like this, it works. We park our new bike in the Hilton lot, for now, and head out on foot to get our bearings.

Our initial impressions of Hanoi are ambiguous. This is a big town, with a lot to do and see. It's busy, just like Bangkok. Everything can be and often is done outdoors. Haircuts, lunch, naps, card games, it all goes on in the midst of sidewalk rush. Shops by day are bedrooms by night. Young children are everywhere, being fed or cleaned or otherwise sustained. Not many people here waste time minding appearances. It's life in the open, and it is what it is. It's also now lunchtime, and everybody eats at the same time. Sidewalks are teeming with entrepreneurs selling soup, noodles, or rice. Customers sit on little red plastic stools. They eat quietly, studiously. If I had to make a sweeping generalization about the Vietnamese, this early, I could say that they are an industrious, conservative, serious people. Although not nearly as approachable as Thais or Laos, they are similarly gentle. I think that they are people who would leave you alone if given the choice, but hundreds of years of occupation by the Chinese, followed by French colonization and the war with the U.S., have left them a tad jumpy, and for damn good reason.

There are good moments to be had here, though. Walking around Restored Sword Lake in the evening is one of them. This little lake is at the center of Old Hanoi, and a couple of blocks from our hotel. Sure, we get assailed by postcard peddlers, money changers, and Cyclo drivers. One of the money changers approaches us with the universal greeting: "Doh-lahr?" I say we don't have any doh-lahrs, but can he change Lao kip? He says okay, and offers me one dong per kip. The math is troubling. One dollar is worth 4,500 kips, or 14,500 dong. In other words, one kip is worth nearly three and a half dong. I ask for his calculator and walk him through my math. He smiles and offers me two dong per kip. I counter with two and a half. No deal. So we walk away, but we've had a good time. Fifteen minutes standing in the street in Hanoi trying to do a currency exchange deal worth a grand nine dollars. That's entertainment!

■

Hanoi's most cliché tourist attraction is the Thang Long Water Puppet Theatre. This is equivalent to the "genu-wine" shootout in downtown Jackson Hole, Wyoming. The performance features a series of tableaus from Vietnamese history and myth. Literally hundreds of wooden painted puppets are trotted out during the one hour show, and made to splash around in the large tank of water that's been standing here for a very long time. We see dragons; fish, water buffalo and fowl; people-puppets on horseback or in boats; all brilliantly colorful and hideously festive. Occasionally fireworks or flares are ignited. It can be very dramatic. This art form was developed sometime around the eleventh century by Vietnamese rice farmers. It hasn't changed much since. It really needs to, if only for the sake of the puppeteers—we count ten—who stand in water up to their nipples behind rude green plastic screens and manipulate the puppets underwater with long rods. These poor bastards spend five hours a night standing in this muck. The musicians have it much better.

They're on a platform, out of water. They perform a couple of traditional Vietnamese songs at the opening of the show, then accompany the action on stage. When we go in, we are given folding fans. These are not for making breeze. They're to fight off the bugs that travel miles to be in this poorly ventilated hall with the human puppeteer soup and these tender, tasty whites from overseas. Also, they can be used to slap the singers, who sometimes squeal tinny, nasal, congealed arias. This falsetto, a form of which is also wildly popular in India, reminds us just how different cultural and artistic sensibilities can be. They say it can destroy human tympanic membrane.

■

The weather in Hanoi has been great. Not too hot, and no rain; tourism weather. First thing after a nice breakfast, we mount up and head for the Ho Chi Minh Mausoleum, in the western part of the city. I have really been looking forward to this, but it's rush hour in Hanoi. So, even worse than the usual madness, this is an out-and-out jungle-fire stampede. Every street is clogged, sidewalk to sidewalk.

Family Bike

Every intersection is a mixing bowl. We're like crazy super-accelerated particles, racing randomly through space, missing each other by micrometers. It's a very different experience from commuting by car. There is a powerful sense of community in this. Entire families travel on one bicycle. Dad pedals, while Mom, with perhaps a child in her lap and a bowl of pho bo soup under her arm, sits on the little plate over the rear wheel, legs dangling, skirt flirting with the spokes. A motorcycle can carry five people. They're small. The extent of our relative affluence in the First World is apparent here. People make do with so very little in Vietnam, but there is positive momentum. The country is at peace with all its neighbors. We're at peace with all our neighbors as well, except for the lady to our left on the Honda Wave, who keeps drifting at us while fumbling with her mobile phone.

The Ho Chi Minh Memorial is no place for levity. The perimeter is secured by a small army of very serious young soldiers. You get the feeling they'll arrest you if you chuckle. Traffic patterns, both vehicular and pedestrian, are non-negotiable. Very broad boulevards are blocked, silent, respectful. Everything in the neighborhood is gray and explicitly sign-posted with big red signs that warn against any sort of capitalist mischief. Goof off here and you'll be filling long months of solitude with readings from the Communist Manifesto. You can see the forbidding mausoleum from most directions, but getting to it is another story altogether. We park the bike where we're told to and pay a guy to guard it; motorcycle theft is commonplace in Hanoi. Then we follow stern finger-pointing from the many sentries, around long blocks of barriers, and finally line up to look in on the Father of the Revolution. Except for two months out of the year, when he is in Moscow for repairs, Ho lies in state here, taxidermed. The trip to Moscow is necessary because that's where the world's best embalmers are; they've kept Lenin looking good for seventy-five years following his death. Uncle Ho also gets a new suit on these trips.

We've already surrendered the camera and our new embroidered shoulder-bag. There is a long procession of visitors, held at bay by a small man with a large gun and a brooding, nauseated expression. When the go-ahead arrives from sources unseen, he lets us pass, and we follow another soldier, two by two, down the block and up the stairs into the burial chamber. The building is a charcoal-colored block. It's a modernistic cubic pagoda, high on a tiered pyramid. Six severe pillars hold up the roof on each side of the building. No curves anywhere. All angles. There's a red plastic carpet down. We flock along it, enter the base of the pyramid from a large doorway in its center, make a quick left jog, and climb two flights of stairs to the Big Room. Dead silence. Here, inside a glass sarcophagus, lies the man who led Vietnam to liberation from the French and became the country's first president. The man they call "Uncle Ho." We enter from one cor-

Uncle Ho's Mausoleum

ner of the room, then glide deferentially along three walls before exiting. It's a sixty-second necro-circumnavigation. This man in this room stands for a people's tenacious struggle for independence from foreign dominance. You get the distinct impression in Hanoi that, happy as they are to live their lives as shop-keepers and artisans and farmers, the Vietnamese will fight to the death if they have to. They've done a lot of that.

■

Ho Chi Minh City, Vietnam, February 25

Okay, so it's not the greatest thing in the world to start your day by setting the Omni Saigon Hotel on fire. That was not at all the plan. It just worked out that way. I guess I thought that a toaster at a fancy hotel like this would know when the toast was done, and would expel it. Evidently, that's not the case. Tracy and I are sitting happily munching on our "egg cook two side" when the fire alarm goes. The staff on the executive floor scrambles. We're in the Lounge for Special and Gifted Guests, naturally, but even here there is immediate panic. We soon realize that the alarm was set off by a modest plume of smoke emanating from the toaster on the buffet island in the middle of the room. I rush over to help the young lady who is trying to pull the offending toast—my offending toast—out of the machine. She brushes me back impatiently, flips the toaster so the openings are facing the floor, and whacks it on the butt. The now-incinerated seven-grain heel pops out and slides across the floor to a final resting place at the slippered feet of a pissed-off Japanese man in his bathrobe. He is the only guest who reacted immediately to the fire alarm. You really don't want to lollygag during a hotel fire when you're on the top floor.

We arrived in Ho Chi Minh City last night, from Hanoi, on Vietnam Airlines. That, in my view, is a good day's work. So we take it easy for the balance of the evening and just cool our jets in the room. Even during the brief ride from the airport, we can tell that things are different here from the north of the country. Women dress much less conservatively. So do men; not one comrade hat. We see a young couple on a scooter; he's in jeans and a polo shirt; she's in a miniskirt, sits side-saddle, cross-legged. You wouldn't see this in Hanoi. Buildings here are taller and newer. There is much more neon per capita. My very preliminary guess is that, though they lost the war, the south will win the peace. The relative prosperity you find here is going to be very difficult to resist as more of it reaches Hanoi. That's already happening. Also, something like two-thirds of Vietnam's population is under thirty. That is, they weren't with us during the war years. It's not their beef. They just want to have normal lives and make piles of money. Don't get the impression this is like Bangkok. It's not. More like Zagreb.

Today we wake up to a bright sunny Saigon morning. Incidentally, people still call it that. Ho Chi Minh City is a mouthful, plus we don't know that people living here feel as devoted to Uncle's memory. The Omni offers an hourly shuttle to downtown so we take it, and are dropped off at the Saigon Center. At twenty stories high, this is maybe the tallest building in town. It's clear the French were here not that long ago. We see their style of Colonial-era buildings. There are also broad tree-lined boulevards that are unmistakably French. This could be a very pleasant walking city, albeit somewhat spread out, but today it's over thirty-five Celsius and too damn hot. After an hour of beating the pavement, we're nearly dehydrated, so we catch the shuttle back to the Omni and take a nap. The heat has taken us somewhat by surprise. We wake up refreshed and decide to rent a motorbike. A nice young man delivers it to the hotel. He's brought us a Honda Dream, 100cc of fun and frolic, but no basket and no side mirrors. It's now a lovely late afternoon here. The sun is low enough that the air is considerably cooler. Traffic is far lighter than we expect. So we scooter around the shaded streets, taking our time to gaze at the gracefully aging villas and old government buildings. This time of day Saigon is charming. So are its people. Everybody's happier when the cool of the evening sets in and the day's work is over.

Having a haircut in the open is an underrated pleasure. When we come across a bank of these sidewalk salons, we pull over. Three guys have set up shop. Each has a chair facing the wall, away from the street. On the wall is a small mirror, nipple-high to me, head-level to your typical Vietnamese person. One of the barbers is free, so we ride the bike onto the sidewalk (love that) and park near his chair. A group of young men in tank tops is having a pho bo dinner at a sidewalk kitchen a couple of meters away. Our arrival is big news. My man has a bicycle leaning against his piece

of wall. There is a backpack slung by a nail. It contains his gear: one pair of mechanical clippers, one pair of scissors, two relics with enough teeth between them to make a whole comb, and two cans of hair spray. There's a small blue towel with frayed edges draped over the back of the wooden chair. I don't see any hair on the sidewalk; either it's been a slow day, or he sweeps. This kid is maybe nineteen. He speaks no English. We negotiate a price. He shows me a fifty thousand dong bill, or just over three dollars. I make a sad face and show

Al Fresco Buzz

him a twenty thousand. He nods and smiles. So I give him thirty thousand and we get started. I sit and slide way down in his chair so I can see myself in the mirror. He pulls down a white cover from yet another nail in the wall, and ties it around my neck. Then he waves his clippers in front of me. I nod consent, and fully expect a rough, quick shearing, but this is no half-assed rush job. This young man takes his work very seriously. It may be a two dollar haircut, but it's his profession. I watch him in the mirror. His whole world is now my head. Every sweep of the comb, every squeeze of his clippers is deliberate, important. He squints often and cocks his head. He hovers around me to get varying perspectives of the cut. When we're done, I give him another thirty thousand dong. That makes him very happy, so I take advantage and ask him to sit in his own chair while I clown for the camera and pretend to be the barber. The whole neighborhood is openly amused and undoubtedly certain now that Americans are an eccentric lot.

■

In general, we find people in Saigon to be much more outgoing than their cousins in Hanoi. This is not an indictment of the folks in the north. It's just the way it is and so we feel less hesitant about riding into the suburbs. We hope to eventually escape Saigon's sprawl and see some unspoiled countryside. Here again though, like in Hanoi, we find miles upon miles of urbanized rural slums. The road, which starts out nicely paved and broad in Saigon, degenerates through increasingly gravelly states, finally becoming a dirt path. In spite of the dust, young women wear the traditional *ao dai* dress. This is a pair of silk or satin slacks over which they wear an ankle-length dress with Mandarin-style collar, also silk or satin, that is slit up to the hip. It's very elegant, and completely at odds with the rough world in which they live. Please do not confuse *ao dai* with *Bao Dai*, who happens to have been Vietnam's last emperor. He was removed in 1945 by the Viet Minh. Technically speaking, he abdicated, but the alternative of getting in Ho Chi Minh's way might have seemed foolhardy. In any case, Vietnamese independence from the French, though declared in 1945, took eleven years of war to effectuate. I may seem to digress, but this is Vietnam. Its history is full of conflict, and you can scarcely turn a corner without being reminded of that.

As we ride on, we see that many people wear face masks against the smog and dust. Some have handkerchiefs tied around their heads. Some of the women on motorbikes wear evening gloves that reach above their elbows, presumably to protect from the sun. It's dusty and sooty enough out here that we also decide to get some cover. Tracy spots a roadside shanty selling these riding accessories, so we pull over and buy ourselves masks and caps. This helps, and we can now go even faster, sometimes reaching blinding speeds approaching 30 km/h! We've also inadvertently become less conspicuous. The masks and caps cover up our hair and faces, and make it that much harder to see from miles away that we're what Thais and some Vietnamese call *farangs*, or Westerners. In the Middle East, Westerners are called *al farange*, a term derived from "Franks," the Germanic tribe that eventually became the kingdom of France. We wonder if the word *farangs* has the same roots. We also wonder how it's possible that so many people here ride motorcycles, yet no one's suggested they wear helmets. We wonder about many other things as we wind our way through Southeast Asia, looking forward to the day when we'll be able to order room service and actually get what we thought we asked for. We are undeniably *farangs*. It's crippling to be so out of sync with local language and custom, but we're getting a valuable lesson in ethno-racial sensitivity. Never again, not unless it's something really funny, will we tell jokes in a language that others present do not understand.

■

The Reunification Palace looks today as it did on April 30, 1975, when the government of South Vietnam sat in a large conference room on the second floor and surrendered to the North Vietnamese. The building is reminiscent of the Kennedy Center in Washington, and that monumental style that characterized public buildings of the time. We walk along the broad corridors and peek into roped-off rooms that have a residual air of heaviness. This feels a lot like walking into Ho Chi Minh's tomb. We're somber, without really knowing why.

Even though the country wants to shed its wartime image, it is taking advantage, as it should, of that legacy. There are several museums around town that draw people interested in that history. The Museum of War Crimes, now diplomatically renamed Museum of War Remnants, is one of the most popular. It's downtown, not far from the Reunification Palace. Several rooms surround a courtyard and contain a pictorial chronology of the American War. There are exhibits of weapons. There are wax figures depicting U.S. and Vietnamese soldiers. There are two large jars containing deformed embryos, blamed on Agent Orange. One whole room is dedicated to war photographers who were killed in action. As we stroll quietly through the museum, we become overwhelmed with the images of destruction and death. Now I'm not so sure why we stopped here in the first place. I guess it's to see how the war is remembered by the Vietnamese. There are no surprises. The Americans are depicted as cruel killers in an unjust fight that wasn't even theirs to begin with. We tell everyone that we're Chilean.

Phnom Penh, Cambodia, February 28

Here we are in Phnom Penh. We listened carefully to the flight attendant on Vietnam Airlines when she said that. *Fnom Pingg.* That's how she pronounced it: *Fnom Pingg.* We're staying at the Sofitel Cambodiana. It's on the Tonlit Sap River. Our room, the third since we checked in, overlooks large propane tanks and exhaust stacks, but it's better than the first two they tried to shoe-horn us into. Now, by gum, we're up on the Mekong Club Floor.

Soon after settling in we head out to rent a bike. Phnom Penh is a dusty burg, like Vientiane, but much busier and seemingly also dirtier. Lucky Lucky is a motorcycle rental store on Monivong Boulevard. The owner speaks pretty good English. He asks us in for a chat. His wife makes us green tea. We don't touch it because we don't want to die. She's offended. Not a good start to our negotiations. Still, I take a Suzuki 250 dirt bike for a spin, and like it. The roads in town are dismal, so this is just the bike for it. He wants fifteen dollars a day, since it's a new machine. Sort of new. I offer ten dollars. He says he's never done this, ever, in the past, but will let me have it for twelve dollars. Okay. Now he wants to keep my passport for security. We've had that come up before, but were always able to leave my Virginia driver's license instead. Not this time. The man and his wife are adamant. No passport, no bike. So we leave and walk on up the street.

On the way back to the hotel we pass a motorcycle mechanic's shop. A dozen bikes lean against each other out in the yard. They're mostly 250s, dirt bikes. On the sidewalk, though, is a golden 400cc Suzuki, and it looks pretty damn good to me. The shop owner is an outgoing young Malay whose English is very good. He introduces himself as C.K. "Calvin Klein?" I ask. It's a good start to our conversation but, when I ask about the Suzuki, he says it's just for sale. I suggest he rent it to me for three days and at least earn a couple of bucks from it. He's not in the rental business, but relents when I press him. We

Golden Suzuki Deal

agree on twenty dollars per day. That's a little steep, but I take it for a spin, and now I'm hooked. As we ride away it's getting dark, and we discover that the bike's headlight doesn't work. It's dodge-the-Khmer time.

The National Museum is a couple of blocks from the hotel and contains Khmer masterpieces. Sadly, there's a small problem. We learn about it while perusing today's *Cambodia Daily*. It seems that between one and two million bats got there ahead of us, and have taken up residence in the building's attic. Each day, at dusk, these repugnant flying mammals stream out of the museum and go for a spin around town. The Pasteur Institute of Cambodia has tested some of the bats and determined that they are rabid. Now we don't really feel terribly excited about the museum. Maybe in a day or two we'll forget we read this and go in broad daylight.

Cambodia, like Thailand, is a constitutional monarchy, but it's had a very bloody contemporary history. In 1975, a couple of weeks before Saigon fell to the North Vietnamese, Phnom Penh fell to the Khmer Rouges, the "Red Khmers." From 1975 to 1979, in an effort to impose communism, the Khmer Rouges killed nearly two million Cambodians. They did this in the name of creating a Marxist state. Tough love. In 1978, Vietnam invaded Cambodia and chased the Khmer Rouges to the Thai border. Then followed fourteen or so years of guerilla warring. The Rouges were supported by the Thais, and China, and some indirect U.S. money. Everybody got together and signed a peace accord in 1991. Norodom Sihanouk was reinstalled king again in 1993. The country has been at peace, however, for just three years. This does not inspire great confidence. We have a nice bike and are willing to handle bad roads, but do not have a clear sense of what to expect from the people.

What better way to find out than to jump in the deep end. After breakfast in the Mekong Club Super Duper Lounge-a-rama, we get on the Suzuki and ride north along the Tonlit Sap River. Our eventual destination is Udong, a village roughly forty kilometers out of Phnom Penh and long famous for nothing at all. It's already warm and the sun is sharp. We're riding without helmets. Just caps. Traffic is brisk, mostly small motorbikes. Cars are not numerous here. We see the occasional Land Cruiser and Mercedes. These, we understand, belong to the city's big-shots and ruling apparatchiks, all people with whom you don't want to tangle. Anyway, we're attracting all the attention. It's the bike. This is probably the only golden 400cc Suzuki in Cambodia. It's a good-looking bike and we are coveted all the way to Udong. The road is awful. It's rutted, uneven, narrow, and frequently becomes a red dirt track. This reminds me of a story I read in the paper a couple of days ago. It seems that Hun Sen, the country's prime minister, loaded up his entire cabinet and their staff on buses, and took them for a ride in the outskirts of Phnom Penh in order to give them all a first-hand impression of the deplorable state of the roads. We pass through three police check-points but are not asked to pull over. That's good because I have no papers for the bike. My agreement with C.K. was a handshake.

The suburbs of Phnom Penh are like those of Hanoi and Saigon, urbanized rural slums. The worst of both worlds. Both sides of the road are cluttered with flimsy wooden homes on high stilts. Beyond the ones to our right is the Tonlit Sap River. Along with the diesel and dust, we go in and out of clouds of intense fish stink. So we're not at all disappointed when the road veers west, away from the river. It takes us an hour and a half to get to Udong. This town is just a bigger slum. From the main road, dirt streets run out into the fields. What we see of the countryside we like, but all around us are dirty, crowded, jumbled shanties. Children run naked in the dirt. Piles of people sit on top of motorcycle-drawn roofless carts. Carcasses of pigs and other livestock go by on the back seat of farmers' scooters. Standing water ripples with diving bugs. Cambodia is poor, all right. When we reach the end of Udong, there is yet another police checkpoint. They have a barrier in the middle of the road. I'm nervous about this type of situation. Ten or so men, in two kinds of uniforms, sit or stand in the shade. I reach the

Udong Temple Gate

barricade, slow, and make a U-turn, coming to a stop near the guys on that side of the street. I point to the ground and say "Udong?" A couple of the men nod. Most just gaze at me as if to say, "You really are an idiot, aren't you?" These guys are not shakedown artists. They're just doing their job, hanging out, guarding the shade. When we reach that point in the conversation where they smile less and fidget more, we say "Bye now" and head back to Phnom Penh.

A couple of kilometers later we pull into a shanty café. We're thirsty and dusty. They have Coke and it's cold. God bless America. A bunch of boys are washing a car next door. One of the guys comes over and says hello. He's the car owner and is on the way to Phnom Penh from Battambang up north. He studies at university and speaks good English. As we chat a crowd of locals gathers. A woman offers to sell us something glutinous from a plastic bag full of water, maybe. We politely decline. Another woman comes up with a bunch of three stems of something that looks like a green trumpet. Our young friend explains that these are Lotus pods, and teaches us how to work out the fruit. We hang out with this group for a little while. One by one they build up the courage to get close and say something. The oldest, a skinny, sweaty, shirtless man in his sixties, is the most interested. He has in his arms an adorable little boy, maybe two years old, who looks like he's been rolled around in a tub of mud. The kid has a cherubic face. You can't help but smile. I do. The old man raises a gnarled and filthy hand, gently passes it over the boy's head, and grins with unchecked joy. I wonder if he might have been with the Rouges in the seventies.

■

Now approaching the end of our Asian tour, I think we miss most the freedoms of the West. Freedom of speech, the press, congregation, religion, politics, dress, hairstyle, hypo-allergenic nose-rings. Whatever. Here, especially in countries like Laos, Vietnam, and Cambodia, we sometimes worry about somebody getting fiercely and suddenly indignant about our presence. If that somebody is a civilian, we could suffer a hostile look, an angry word, or even a thrown stone. All this has happened, but if it's a soldier or a policeman or a passport control official, we'd find ourselves in the works of exquisitely corrupt systems. The possibility makes us nervous. While riding to Udong and back yesterday, we gradually overcome this apprehension. Cambodians are generally friendly to us. More like the Thais than the Vietnamese.

Today we're going to the Killing Fields via National Highway 2. National highways in Cambodia are roads on which a tank can advance. They tend to start life in the middle of the capital as paved, broad, congested boulevards. As they leave the city, they enjoy a steady deterioration. They get narrower. Sidewalks give way to drainage ditches and abrupt drop-offs. Soon, long stretches of road are unpaved. Then a little more paved road. Then unpaved again. After leaving the two or three suburban slums closest to town, the road goes to pot. It would be far better if it were completely unpaved. At least that way there would be some predictability. Instead we bump up into crags of broken down blacktop, then slide on a sand pit, then across gravel. Like that.

The official name for the place is Choeung Ek Genocide Center. A few lean-tos along the way offer cold drinks. Children ride their bicycles home from school. We soon reach a dead end. Two men, absent from the waist down, roll themselves around the dusty outer courtyard on makeshift wheeled boards, like dollies. They offer to look after the bike, but the men at the table inside the gate motion to us to ride into the compound and leave it in the designated area. We do. Several children

Killing Fields

approach and ask for money. We buy our tickets, two dollars each, hand the amputees some bills, and walk on into the compound. A couple of boys, maybe five years old, rustle in the undergrowth behind the barbed wire fence to our right. They have their hands out. We stop and give them money. If they didn't look so mischievous and happy, they could make you depressed. This is a game to them. Just as well.

The Killing Fields is where the Khmer Rouges took people for disposal. Between 1975 and 1979, something like twenty thousand people were killed and buried here. The graves have since been excavated and lie empty. Several are signposted with information about how many bodies were found in them. One reads "80

Headless Bodies Found Here." Also on the grounds is a tall modern *stupa* that was erected to memorialize the dead. It's a tower, four-sided, glassed in, maybe three meters on each side. On top it has a pagoda roof and the traditional Buddhist *ngaos*. Inside there are several "floors." They're really more like shelves. Each is completely covered with skulls. Signs on each shelf describe the ethnicity, age and gender of the victims. "Female, Khmer, 18 to 24." We're here with three other tourists. It's very quiet. A few meters from the *stupa* there is a gazebo, open-sided, containing a plaque of sorts. A one-legged man with a crutch sits under the eave. He hobbles over to us. I have a bill ready for him. He prays to us, we pray to him, and go on a stroll through the Killing Fields. It's not a very big area, about the size of a family olive orchard. As we make our way back toward the gate, a scruffy kid in filthy underwear squirts into the compound from under the fence, comes up to us, and begs for money. It takes a minute, but it dawns on us that he's one of the two we met on the way in. He's back for seconds.

■

On our last evening here, we return the bike then walk back through Phnom Penh's busy evening toward the waterfront and Sisowath Quay. Every dustbowl empty lot is now a soccer pitch. The sun's just about gone and everybody's out and about, cruising up and down the corniche, having picnics on lawns wherever those may be. We see a group of boys, all under ten years old, playing some kind of wagering game. We can't figure it out. There's a pile of small bills on the ground. One hundred, two hundred and five hundred riel. Five or ten cents apiece. The boys stand behind an imaginary line several meters away from the money. Then they take turns launching their flip-flops at the money, straight from their feet. It's something like poor boy's *pétanque*. Cyclos and Moto Taxis are everywhere. Sidewalk kiosks fry up or boil fast-food dinners. Strollers cover the waterfront, some hand-in-hand.

Kuala Lumpur, Malaysia, March 4

We're on the twenty-first floor of the Kuala Lumpur Hilton. It's high tea time in the Lounge for Supreme Invincible Omnipotent Guests. There's an arrow on the ceiling, pointing to Mecca, which reads: *Kiblat*. But for that and the call to prayer from a mosque we can't see, this could be any Hilton anywhere in the world. In here we're swaddled in five-star canapés. Out there is a bristling landscape of glass, steel, and concrete. Highrises stand tall against the misty hills on the horizon. Close enough nearly to touch, towering above everything, are the Petronas Twin Towers. They are now called the Kuala Lumpur City Center (KLCC). The world's tallest buildings are magnificent. They look like ICBMs.

The ride in from the airport is a thing of beauty, just like in Thailand. We get a nice cushy Mercedes. The expressway is perfect. What a difference the short flight has made. How can Cambodia, Vietnam, and Laos ever catch up to Thailand and Malaysia and Singapore? I think it will take enormous support from an industrialized ally. This gets us talking about colonialism. Our untested theory is that countries that allowed the colonialists of the nineteenth and twentieth centuries to stay longer, did better. Kicking out the stinking foreigners too soon seems to have had worse consequences than tolerating them. In the first group we have Singapore, Hong Kong, Malaysia, the United Arab Emirates and Thailand. In the second, Vietnam, Cambodia, Laos, and those Arab countries that gained their independence following World War Two. The first group is doing better. Could it be because they were left with a fully functional and up-to-date infrastructure on which to build a country? We think so. Is this a silly oversimplification? Of course. Nevertheless, the contrast between these neighboring countries is astonishing. It cries out for an explanation, so we made one up.

KLCC anchors a relatively recent development to the east of the city's original center at the confluence of the Kelang and Gombak rivers. This neighborhood could be an upscale business suburb outside an American city, like Vinings in Georgia, Tyson's Corner in Virginia, or Oakbrook in Illinois. Everything here is new, having been built during the past fifteen years. It's mostly hotels and office towers and condominium compounds. Very little plain old dirt remains. Kuala Lumpur is one large concrete slab. It's clean, efficient, affluent, antiseptic, and we like that. There is very little crime in Malaysia. What crime does exist is usually of the honor variety, involves slashing with machetes and jumping to certain death from great heights. It's mostly a family thing. That suits us just fine.

We've rented a Proton Perdata. That's nearly Spanish for "lost particle." It's made, or at least assembled, in Malaysia. We would have been fine having a motorbike. The roads are great and drivers generally courteous, but because of the always-high humidity and almost daily showers, motorcycle rental is not much of a business in Kuala Lumpur, so we're driving a car. Although it's comfy here in the KLCC neighborhood, we nevertheless decide to leave the city in search of something, anything, that has some local character. We head north to the hills and get lost, as usual. Instead of finding Templer Park, as we had intended, we find ourselves driving through beautiful, lush, rolling hills. The road here is narrow but in very good condition. This area seems popular with local picnic-makers. There are waterfalls and swimming holes, but we're too squeamish about water-borne death in this part of the world and just admire the ponds from a distance.

Eventually we see signs to Batu Caves. These are holes in a huge, towering limestone outcrop on the northern outskirts of Kuala Lumpur, and have become a pilgrimage site for Hindus. The principal attraction is a massive cave that has been made into a temple. It contains countless statues of countless Hindu gods. To reach the main grotto we climb nearly three hundred stairs. I don't know what the hell we're thinking. It's not as if we haven't just come from nearly a whole month of

Hindu immersion in India. We are briefly transported back to that country when the two *dalits* who are in charge of the toilet get into a fight and pummel each other with Hindi oaths and vigorous finger-wagging.

Back in town we shower and have a short rest before going out to dinner. It's a low-risk proposition. There are restaurants and bars and coffee shops everywhere. All look clean and hip and happening, but that's too easy for us, intrepid seekers of novelty. So we amble along, sweating all the time, until we find an obscure place down a quiet street. The Red House is an unassuming open-air restaurant that has the remarkable good fortune of being located on the other side of the only remaining vacant lot in KL, across from the world's tallest buildings. That's right, every table here boasts a direct view of the KLCC, top to bottom. The only thing in the way is an unfortunate chain-link fence defining the property line. Our table is next to it. Beyond that, a hundred meters of grass and dirt. Then the towers. Amazing. The menu is simple, the food great, the service warm and friendly. I try a couple of local specialties. There's a cold barley drink that is very refreshing. And we have noodles and rice. Then dessert. We're sitting al fresco. No ceiling, no air-conditioning, no walls. A lovely breeze has come up. The KLCC sparkles. This is living.

After dinner we walk through the neighborhood up the hill to the Kuala Lumpur Tower. From a distance this looks very much like the Seattle Space Needle, but it's higher and doesn't do the jitterbug twice a year. The brochure we pick up in the lobby says it's the fourth highest man-made concrete structure in the world, after the ones in Toronto, Hong Kong, and somewhere in Russia. The elevator up to the revolving restaurant clicks off meters of elevation on a digital display. By the time we stop it's gone over three hundred. If this tower falls down while we're on top of it, we'll land somewhere in Borneo. The floor is actually three concentric rings. The outer, windowed ring, revolves counter-clockwise. The central and widest ring, on which we are seated, revolves more slowly, clockwise. The core is stationary. As a result of all this opposing rotation, every table gets spectacular views of everything, as the building's superstructure drifts by. The interior view changes also, as our table moves around it, so we're not always looking at the piano player. In the distance we see the Jamek Mosque, lit up brightly.

Kuala Lumpur Tower

Because the KL Tower is on a hill, it is actually higher than the twin towers of the KLCC. It's dizzying to be up here looking down on the world's tallest buildings.

I'm still sporting two very large and irritated mosquito bites, one on my wrist, the other on my forearm. Cambodian mosquitoes got me in the departure lounge at Phnom Penh airport. The bug problem in Asia is annoying and ubiquitous. Amid the horror stories of this or that virus, we live in constant fear of being stung by a promiscuous mosquito. Even in thoroughly modern KL, we see them. Somehow we are less jumpy here. Malaysia has Islam, money, a helmet law. We just sense a higher interest in human preservation here. This assumption in a place like Hanoi could get you killed, but here it's reasonable to believe that if a whole bunch of people are walking around in short sleeves, you can too.

■

Today we're driving to Melaka, the historic coastal town about 250 kilometers south of Kuala Lumpur. Melaka is important because it was the seat of the earliest kingdom to control the Malay Peninsula. As a result, it became the vortex of subsequent invasions by the Portuguese, the Dutch, and finally the English. Nowadays Melaka is a tourist trap, replete with fajitas and burgers and Häagen Dazs and cyclos and *hello-my-friend-where-are-you-going* locals. There are a few oldish buildings to see, Dutch and Portuguese. We spend a couple of hours here, including lunch at the Bamboo Hut (please!). They've hired a young man to entertain us. He's playing a guitar and singing Neil Sedaka songs. A wireless microphone is rigged to his head, enabling him to promenade as he sings; a Malay troubadour. He spends a few minutes by the front door, facing the street, enticing passersby with his dulcet tones. Then he walks through the restaurant, threatening to drop by our table if we make eye contact. Now he disappears for a while, but we can still hear him sing. Maybe he's taking a leak. That's the beauty of technology. You can entertain and take a leak at the same time.

KL War Memorial

This is beautiful countryside; lush, green, vibrant, and incredibly clean. The roads are well maintained, the rest stops as well. We pull in to a roadside parking spot and walk up some steps to an observation point from which we can gaze at the forests and plantations in all directions. Malaysia is no small patch of country, but they somehow manage to keep it tidy. The country has a low crime rate, good climate, economic prosperity (give or take a currency melt-down), stable moderate government, and excellent infrastructure. Add to that list of pluses a reasonably stable seismic predisposition, no high-school shootings, and a mere twenty million population with a high literacy rate. I think a case can be made that this is one of the world's most attractive places to live.

■

Today, as we prepare to leave Kuala Lumpur for Indonesia, we have a serious electronic emergency to deal with. Last night the thing stopped working. I say "the thing" because it is not clear if the fault lies in the camera, the laptop computer, the cable, or what. We tried to trouble-shoot the problem, and narrowed it down to a software problem in the computer, or a faulty cable. So this morning we check out early and drive to the massive shopping mall in the KLCC. This place is like those monster malls you see in the Gulf. Like in Dubai. There are floors upon floors of shops. You can buy anything. All the latest electronics. Starbucks. The Coffee Bean. Nike. Auntie Anne's Pretzels, for heaven's sakes! So it's utterly and unabashedly Westernized, and it's devoid of Asianness. Who cares! There is a place for a mall like this in every self-respecting city. It's a safe place for kids to hang out. Old people can walk here out of the weather. Broken things can be fixed. Food can be had. The toilets are clean and require no contortionist skills. Is the American Mall a wonderful human achievement? Absolutely. We arrive at 10:00, but most shops don't open until 10:30. So we locate the floor and section where the electronics stores are clustered then go to a nearby Coffee Bean to kill some time. I get to the counter and say to Tracy, "What I really want is a Frappuccino." The gel-hair teenager behind the counter says, "Sir, that's actually a Starbucks term. We have an equivalent beverage here. We call it an Ice Cappuccino." Then we all join hands and sing "The Star Spangled Banner."

The Notebook store, specializing in these smaller computers, contains a young man who not only lends us a drive to read the CD we borrowed from the Sony Shop, but also sits with us and trouble-shoots the whole shebang. By the time he's finished, he has fixed the camera, corrected the display problem we've had in the computer for six weeks, and made the machine run faster than it ever has. He even has Palm V styluses to replace the one I lost. I looked all over Europe for these. By the time we get into our rental car to go to the airport, we are digitally sound again. How can you not love a city that does that for you?

■

The news about the bike is not so good. Lufthansa has located and referred me to a freight forwarder. He has contacted Bombay Customs. Turns out they will not hand over the bike for shipping to Australia until I pay "demurrage" fees of $4,500. That's right, *four thousand five hundred, American.* Customs charges a daily fee of fifty dollars to store the bike. Therefore, the longer they keep it, the bigger the demurrage bill. Mind you, even if I do pay up, there is no assurance that the bike will be released. I can see losing the bike *and* $4,500. No one has actually come out and said "We are emphatically liking your motorcycle and want to misappropriate it terminally if you please." Nevertheless, I think I've been taken and have begun writing a requiem for the Honda. I'd rather spend the $4,500 on a new bike. Maybe we'll buy one in Australia. Maybe we'll avoid any future customs debacles and rent a bike in each country instead. Maybe we'll fly back to Bombay and throw rotten curried eggs at Sahar Cargo Complex.

Yogyakarta, Indonesia, March 9

Indonesia's national airline is called Garuda. This is the half-bird-half-man mount of God Vishnu. Many Hindu gods had mounts. There's a little-known story in the Ramayana about Garuda's chronic tardiness. One day, while lounging on the edge of a puffy white cloud lost in contemplation of the world below, Garuda is startled by his master's voice: "Where's that damn bird? Late again? This is the last straw! He'll be in the stew tonight!" Dismayed that he has once more upset the Supreme Being, coincidentally his boss, Garuda decides it's time to take a powder, and banishes himself to the land of the suffering living, where he would serve out consecutive incarnations as an airline in Southeast Asia. That's how it comes to be that we're sitting in Jakarta Airport waiting for Garuda, already two hours late, to take us to Yogyakarta (pronounced Jogjakarta).

There is an elderly woman sitting behind us, tending the rowdiest kid in the universe. He's five or so, that magical age when children are ambulatory, raucous, and strong enough to push their grandmothers to the floor. She's exhausted. We manage a conversation of sorts. She has thirteen of these grandchildren. This one is the youngest. When she learns that Sumatra isn't on our itinerary, she makes a pout and wants us to change our plans. Her home village is in Aceh province. We think better of pointing out that there's an open revolt going on there against the government, that people are butterflying each other with machetes, and that the jungles are alive with the sound of automatic fire. She's also disappointed to hear that we are childless. We comfort her and promise to try harder. I love the bonding that goes on in airport lounges. In the meantime, the Devil's Spawn has painted his weight in spit on the window overlooking the tarmac.

Indonesia covers as much real estate as the U.S. I think that's a rough territorial boast that includes the water between the islands. There are 220 million Indonesians, making it the world's largest Muslim country, and all-round fourth most populous nation in the world. Other facts about Indonesia, culled from various guidebooks and our own intensely perspicacious observations:

- Indonesian islands named by Starbucks are: Sumatra, Java, Sulawesi.
- You can see the equator from most anywhere here.
- The country's president is Abdulrahman Wahid. He is legally blind and was once a Muslim cleric.
- Sukarno and Suharto were not the same person. They weren't even related.
- Of the 220 million people in the country, 140 million live on Java, the rest prefer tea.
- The country's official language is Bahasa Indonesia. It has no tenses, no genders, and no plurals. No kidding. It's anyone's guess what anybody else is saying.

- A Komodo dragon is a lizard that is larger than a Winnebago. It eats whole goats like we eat peanuts. It is indigenous, go figure, to the Indonesian island of Komodo, which we will never, ever see, except maybe from an airplane.

We're in Yogyakarta because we just could not face another congested "developing" Asian capital. Jakarta, on top of that, is in the throes of insurrection. Students (i.e., leftist agitators) are clamoring for Abdulrahman Wahid's resignation, claiming that he's crooked and inept. He won't leave, so there are street protests every day. If this were Europe, we might go precisely to enjoy the revolution, but we're in Asia, and revolutions here tend to be bloodier. We picked Yogyakarta because it's on Java, is considered the cultural capital of the island, perhaps the country, and has frequent in and out flights. We arrive way after sunset. It's muggy. It's dark. Our taxi is of the falling-apart variety. There are a couple of mosquitoes in here. The windows, except for the windshield, are dark-tinted against the day's sun. Through them, Yogyakarta, at night, appears like the Underworld.

Waking up in a new city is a thrill and Yogya looks much happier in daylight. Everything is adventure. We leave the hotel full of that wild mix of anticipation, caution, and adrenaline. Within minutes we've spiked that cocktail with sweat. It's hot and humid in the tropics! We immediately reach the conclusion that we must rent a bike. Motorcycle rental shops are not as numerous here as in Vientiane or Hanoi, so we have to hoof it around town for a good hour before finding one. Two actually, each of whom has exactly one bike for rent.

The first shop, really a grocery store, features a 160cc bike parked inside by the tomatoes. The dash is attached to the rest of the bike with clear Scotch tape. The man wants four dollars a day. He also wants my passport. We say we'd think about it and walk out into the street. That's when we notice the Honda 110cc across the street, and the man gesturing wildly to us to come over. We do. Nice bike, nearly new. Everything works, except the side view mirrors, of which there are one, and it floats freely in its socket. We get away for four dollars a day and just my expired Virginia

Yogyakarta

driver's license for collateral. It's good to be on the bike. The streets of Yogya (Jogja), are hot and crowded and a little stinky. If you're on foot you roast as you gag. On a scooter you get through the gamy spots relatively quicker. We do, straight out of town, in search of air and the coast. There are a couple of attractions within the city, but we're going to save these until our last day here, after we've returned the bike.

The drive out of Yogya is on a narrow road that is crowded until we get ten kilometers or so away, but it's well-paved and traffic, though heavy, is mostly motorcycles. We're used to this kind of driving by now, and just flow along with everybody else, knocking knees at the lights, eating each other's dust, smoking each other's fumes. Every once in a while, a big truck or bus plows by belching thick black plumes of diesel exhaust. We, and most everyone else, wear masks. Soon we're in rural suburbs and the road-side shanties give way to rice paddies. There are trees around: palms, bananas, banyans. Every available bit of earth has something green growing out of it, but it's mostly paddies. The complete process of raising and harvesting rice plays out in front of us as we ride. In the fields we see people ankle-high in water, tending the rice. Some has been harvested. We see threshing going on, and on the shoulder, that place we could go if we were, say, being pushed off the road by a truck, rice is spread, drying in the sharp sun on plastic sheets.

The temperature here is near thirty Celsius every day. The low is around twenty Celsius. It rains all year long, but the rain comes in concentrated downpours and does not paralyze you for a whole day of drizzling. Anything can grow in this climate. I've found little stretches of moss on the lips of Coca Cola bottles. As a result of this wonderful fertility, plants cover up most man-made ugliness. Tropical climates are esthetically forgiving. If you leave a place unattended for any length of time, the jungle will soon take it back. The overall effect is pretty much what you would expect: thick, luxuriant green foliage, a softness in the air, almost liquid humidity, and fragrance that makes you want to pull over and hug a lily. It's Friday. Noon. As we ride along this country road in the tropics, we pass a number of mosques, each of which is issuing the *Jumaa* call to prayer, the *Adaan*. It's a lovely thing. As we leave one mosque's earshot and enter another's, and for a few moments at a time, we're in the heart of a tropical Muslim fugue.

We know we've reached Parangritis because there's a ticket booth in the road. This is cute. There's a gang of five or six officials hanging out in the shade of the arch marking the entrance to the city. Somehow they can tell that we're tourists even while we're still fifty meters away. We're in helmets, wearing masks and sunglasses, on a scooter. That's why we find this remarkable. We think we look like everyone else on the road. Anyway, a couple of them jump up, straddle the road, and wave us down. If you don't live here, you have to pay 1,500 rupiahs apiece. That's about twenty cents, American. We pay and go through. There's a big map on a billboard just past the arch. After looking at it for a minute, we make a U-turn and go back through the checkpoint. The guys are all watching with interest. We stop and take a picture of the arch and, slyly, of them. As we pass through the arch again, we pull over and make like we think we have to pay again. They're tickled. We're tickled.

After lunch we ride down to the beach, very much a local affair. We stop for a look when, out of nowhere, a group of teenage girls in Muslim school uniforms attack us. They need help with their homework. Their English teacher assigned them the task of trapping and interviewing a foreigner. They make us fill out questionnaires. We each do three. There's a section of the form left open for the victim to suggest ways for the students to improve their English. Tracy and I provide the following priceless advice:

- Watch more TV.
- Go to the cinema often to see American movies.
- Read comic books.
- Eat burgers, drink Coca Cola.
- Visit America.

They're tickled. We're tickled.

Schoolgirl Ambush

Borobudur, Indonesia, March 10

Borobudur predates Angkor Wat in Cambodia and is believed to have influenced its design. A small tent city of hawkers and food stalls has sprung up around the temple compound. Our tickets are five dollars each. The guide's fee, collected by the ticket office, is two dollars. Even by Southeast Asian standards, Midi, our guide, is a mini. He's three inches shorter than Tracy. His English is good and he's from around here, so knows a lot about the temple's contemporary history. Mind you, not everything he says is fascinating or even true. Midi has Symbolism Disorder. This is the affliction, common to tour guides and literature majors, where everything is presumed to stand for something else, something heroic, meaningful, premeditated. The hills in the distance beyond Borobudur, Midi tells us, are the world's largest sleeping Buddha, carved by the elements. I look at him and smirk. He smirks back.

The temple, built in the ninth century A.D., was buried nearly up to its top in dirt. It was rediscovered in 1814 by Stamford Raffles, then-governor of Singapore and Java. The eponymous Raffles Hotel is the birthplace of the Singapore Sling. Midi is delighted to learn this from us, and will undoubtedly use it on his next tour. Then, in the seventies or so, UNESCO, with contributions from many countries, mounted a restoration. In 1985, "The Angry Ones," a group of fifteen locals who had been displaced by temple rehabilitation activities, tried to blow it up. They failed. Most went to jail. This resonates today because the Taliban have just blown up the world's largest Buddhas in Bamiyan.

The Borobudur temple is huge, built from volcanic rock, and sits all alone on a hill surrounded by tropical jungle, albeit somewhat tidied up. It has eight tiers, miles of passageways, and one famous Lucky Buddha. Like many of the other Buddhas at the temple, he is fully enclosed in a bell-shaped hollow stone *stupa*. There are holes in the stupa large enough for a human arm to get through. That's true of all the 1,500 bells arranged on all the eight terraces, and why the temple is also known as the Thousand Bells Temple. The Lucky Buddha, however, is special. Good fortune will come to a woman if she reaches inside and touches the sole of his

Borobudur

right foot. A man must touch the ring on the statue's right hand. This particular Buddha, as you might imagine, is mobbed. Trillions of young Indonesians are here on school trips, and they all want to touch him. So do the Japanese tour groups. I eventually squeeze my way through the throng and manage to get my hand into the *stupa*. I grope for a minute and grab a clammy, hairy arm. I figure that's close enough.

Our last day in Yogya starts off with a bit of a panic. We're on our way to have a look at the Kraton, the palace of the sultans of Yogya. As we walk through the parking lot I notice that the bike is gone. I'm sure of it. We parked right at the close end of the space set aside for motorcycles, and it's just not there. Guidebooks are full of warnings about rental outfits that have you followed by thieves with keys to the bike. You wind up paying for the "stolen" bike, which is not really stolen at all. So we march back into the hotel and report the disappearance to the duty manager. Everybody gets excited and we're assured that heads will roll, but when we go back outside to view the scene of the crime together, we realize that there is no crime. One of the parking attendants apparently moved the bike to another spot. They do that.

Happy to not have been robbed, we trot on out for a brief and unremarkable tour of the brief and unremarkable palace. The neighborhood surrounding it is far more interesting. Narrow alleyways form concentric squares around the palace walls. There's no room for cars, and only a few motorbikes come through. The houses are lined up against each other, sharing walls. Most are single-room one-story dwellings. The doors and windows are all open. There's always a shirtless old man inside, in the dark, napping or just sitting, watching. The women cook and clean. Washing hangs from lines strung in the street. Furniture is rudimentary: A mattress or two, a table, a couple of chairs, and of course a twenty-seven-inch ultra-woofing blast-meister Sukiyaki Trinitrink television set with Buzzarround-Sound and Colby Pixilation. A boy has his bath in a plastic tub outside the front door of their house while his mother sweeps the street.

Bali, Indonesia, March 14

I expected Bali to be junglier. We fly in from Java, in the west. It's about 5 p.m. The sun is behind us. After dodging thunderheads most of the way, we suddenly have clear sky ahead and can see all of the island. A dozen active volcanoes, some reaching three thousand meters, form a backbone across the middle of it, east to west. These are all blanketed with tropical forest, but lose their cover as they slope down to the sea and turn into farmland and settlements. Most of the southern half of the island is flat, carved up into lots of rice plantations and homes and groves. The beaches are a white, delicate, narrow apron around the island.

We're staying at the Bali Grand Beach Hotel. This is one of those resorts that gradually become towns. There is a ten-story three-wing tower, and acres upon acres of bungalows, shops, airline offices, a spa, a post office, and a bowling alley. Honest. The beach arcs away in both directions. Palms, lit by the Bali Grand and the Radisson next door, sway agreeably in the light breeze. We have dinner in the room. *Mee goreng*. That's fried noodles with vegetables, our favorite Indonesian food, if only in self-defense.

We spend most of the first day on the island getting acquainted with our neighborhood, Sanur. This is a quieter community than Bali's legendary Kuta Beach, which is west of Denpasar, the capital. We're just east. Our Internet headquarters in Bali is Krishna Internet. This is just up the street from the hotel. There's a Harley Fat Boy parked outside, gleaming. The entrance is dark under a trellis of vines. Inside it's like a temple; images of Krishna everywhere. In this long narrow room, five computer stations line the wall to our left. Telephone kiosks line the right. In the back there's a wooden hotel-style front desk. The air is thick with incense. Krishna and the milk-maidens cavort in a number of ambitious frescoes. The Bhagavad-Gita is on the front counter. They offer copies for sale. This is great. You can check email and get Hindued at the same time. Two young women are behind the counter. So is a man in his thirties, decked out in all-Harley apparel. His hair is long, black on top and sort of orange at the bottom. He looks tough enough to gnaw my arm off and beat me with it. It's dark in here and quiet, serene almost. Faint sitar music wafts in from somewhere. I strike up a conversation with the biker dude. Seems he spent a couple of years in Venezuela, mostly in prison. Something about trying to stay in the country after his visa had expired. He says the authorities threw him in criminal prison. His sister pipes in to say that he was traumatized by that. Although we don't have the experience firsthand, we are willing to believe that a South American prison is not a fun place to be.

■

To see the Bali that earned the reputation, you have to go way into the country. All the urban centers are congested and polluted. Denpasar, Sanur, Kuta, and Gyanyar are awash in traffic and tourists. So now we're on our way east and hope to reach the coast before turning back. However, we get derailed by a sign to the Bali Bird and Reptile Park. Two parks, actually, but you can buy a "combination" ticket. The reptile park interests us because Tracy is ophidiophobic. Also herpetophobic, ornithophobic, and microbiophobic. Therefore she's polyphobic, and fears anything that crawls or slithers and doesn't shower twice a day. We figure this might be an opportunity to begin a gradual desensitization treatment. After parading in front of thirty or so reptilian killers, we reach a large enclosed garden. Two keepers are in here with several iguanas and monitor lizards. The animals are all friendly, we're assured by the younger man, who happens to be missing two fingers on his right hand.

Iguanas are the ugliest animal on the planet. They're uglier than rockfish. They're uglier than possum. They're so ugly it's a wonder they have any sex at all. They must, because there is never a shortage of iguanas. Here in the "petting" enclosure, we find a half-dozen of these trolls. The first one we meet is splayed out on a tree-limb overhanging the path. It's gray-silver-blue-green, and has a tumor on each cheek that's fluorescent mother-of-pearl. Well, maybe it's not a tumor exactly, but it

Chicken Ripper

might as well be. I think I saw it puff this thing out a couple of times. Grotesque. Wayan, the young attendant, encourages me to pet it. I reach up and gingerly touch it on the butt. I figure it might enjoy that and be less likely to eat my hand. Also I figure that, like elephants, iguanas are incapable of reaching their butts with their mouths, so I'll be safe. After the iguana, I graduate to a monitor lizard. These animals are actually less ugly than iguanas. They make up for that deficiency by being carnivorous executioners. And they're big. There's one in a tree here. It takes Wayan and his quiet sidekick to drag the thing off its branch. Eventually, the keepers manage to yank the monitor down, and Wayan presents it to me much as you might hand a baby over to a non-parent. I grab it by the neck and the base of the tail. This is my

strategy for immobilizing it. The monitor just relaxes in my hands like an oversized shoulder bag. This is all relevant to us because we're in Indonesia. We want to meet the fauna of the region. We want to experience the exotic wonder of holding a chicken-ripping lizard in our arms.

■

It isn't until our third day in Bali that we finally get to the heart of this island. Again we drive out of town, this time west. The road goes past Denpasar, and that's predictably busy and smoggy. Soon we're by the coast and the crowds thin out. We stop for coffee at Mdewi Beach. Two small hotels on the beach cater to a younger crowd of tan blond surfers with scraped knees. Then we drive into the mountains. Up here it's like Germany's Romantische Strasse, without the beer and the spires. Traditional Balinese villages are strung like pearls along this narrow winding road that is completely surrounded with undergrowth. Every village marks its entrance and exit with elaborate gates. These are carved, painted, and vary in size depending on the size of the village. Bali is preparing to celebrate Nyepi, their New Year. So every house has in front of it a very tall bamboo pole, decorated with baskets and weaving. These arc over the street like an outdoor vault running all the length of the village. It's all very reverent and exotic and steamy, if such a combination can be imagined.

Driving around Bali these days, you see the young men of the villages constructing large papier-mâché creatures. They call them *ogoh-ogoh* monsters. These are paraded through the streets on Nyepi Eve, and then burned or otherwise destroyed. The demons are thus purged and Bali begins the New Year pure. These

rituals that make up Balinese Hinduism are unique to the island. They are more elegant than anything we've seen in other Hindu or Buddhist places. There is an opulence and freshness in its rituals that make this flavor of Hinduism wonderfully optimistic. Quite apart from these festivals, religion is an inseparable part of daily life in Bali. The day begins with offerings made to the spirits. These are leaf-cups filled with a little rice, fruit, some flowers, incense. It boils down to paying protection. Ancestor-worship is very much part of all this.

Bali Procession

They are believed to be in the Land Above the Mountains with the gods, or somewhere in transit. Regardless, they must be appeased with offerings of food and flowers and incense, so they don't start mucking about in people's lives. The offerings are generally placed on the ground in front of a home, or business, or even at the top of

a street. I don't know if this is a chore, like doing the dishes, over which families have spats. More likely it's done by the matriarch. We mostly see women placing the offerings. They do so with great reverence, delicately, deliberately, and say a little prayer as they do. By mid-morning, Bali is decorated everywhere with these sidewalk presents. If you're visiting, you have to be very careful not to step in someone's shrine. A lot of time is dedicated to ritual here. It's a clean, orderly and happy society, and it's isolated. This is the only place you

Bali Country Road

can find Balinese Hinduism. Maybe separation, not to say segregation, if it occurs naturally like this, is not so bad. Compared to the bloodshed going on next door in Kalimantan, with Dayaks purging the island of Madurese, Bali is truly Paradise.

Lombok, Indonesia, March 17

We've decided to extend our Indonesia visit by a week, and to make a swing through Nusa Tenggara, a chain of islands that includes Lombok, Sumbawa, and perhaps most frightfully, Komodo. The policemen guarding the entrance to Padang Bai Ferry Terminal are very happy to see us. This is the slow season in Bali, and anyway, the political situation has scared many away. So we're a rare delicacy. After buying our tickets and driving into the parking yard to wait for the boat, we are approached by an extremely friendly armed port policeman. He wants to shake our hands. He wants to know where we're from "my friends." He wants to know how we're enjoying Bali. He wants me to join him in the guard house for a chat. There, waiting for us, is another extremely friendly port policeman, whose English is quite good. The first man, having successfully delivered me, now stands by the door playing with his bullets. This one across the desk proceeds to weave a fantastical story about extraordinary regulations and missing documents and how much he loves for tourists to enjoy Indonesia. I'm tempted to remind him that the ferry leaves in fifteen minutes and to ask him for the check, but he knows exactly when the ferry leaves, and ends his story in the nick of time by offering us the choice of going back to Denpasar for an "authorization letter," or settling the unfortunate infraction right here and now. Ten dollars. He walks all the way across the port with me, back to the car, and makes sure I'm safely in there. As we drive down the ramp, I see him in the rear view mirror, smiling and waving.

We mount the Marina Primera. You must do this one day. Find yourself on a boat, in perfect weather, somewhere between Bali and Lombok, or any of the other islands that populate these seas. It is inexpressibly gorgeous. The sky is endless and streaked with cloud. The sea is immense, placid. We are at a midpoint between the ends of the earth and sky. There is vast distance in every direction from us. However, rather than feel small and insignificant, as we perhaps should, we feel somehow essential.

Apart from being Bali's neighbor, and therefore most likely to see tourist overflow, Lombok is famous for being the first island to the east of the Wallace Line. By crossing the strait from Bali to Lombok, we step across a great geographical divide. It seems that the sea between the two islands is up to three thousand meters deep. We have not personally verified this. Species of flora and fauna that managed to cross temporary Ice-Age land bridges from Southeast Asia to the rest of Indonesia never got across to Lombok. And the reverse is true. Australian and Polynesian species that reached Lombok stopped there and did not make it farther west. This was all discovered and described by Alfred Russel Wallace in 1859. Wallace was a contemporary of Charles Darwin who, coincidentally in 1859, published his *On the Origin of Species by Means of Natural Selection*. We didn't feel anything much when we crossed the Line, and most mammals we've seen so far are bipeds who look just like their cousins on Bali.

We're staying at the Sheraton Senggigi. Difficult as it is to tear ourselves away from the pool and the beach and the thatched-roof gazebos in which we recline on overstuffed cushions and gaze at the sea, we are nevertheless going sightseeing. We drive the less-traveled and scenic north coast road. To our right we get glimpses of majestic Mount Rinjani, 3,762 meters of active volcano. We see fishing villages, palms, banana plantations, horse-drawn carts, and livestock, all right up to the edge of the road. At times we wish we were on the bike. Until, that is, the sky opens up and floods the world. Now the car is a good place to be. It's raining so hard we can barely see, so we take it easy. You'd expect everyone to take cover in a downpour like this, but instead all the village mothers have undressed their young children and put them out in the rain. When your house is made of bamboo and thatch, and when the temperature never goes below twenty-five Celsius, there is not much sense in installing a shower stall. You just wait for the rain then run outside.

At one point, during a lull in the rain, we stop in the village of Amor-Amor to buy some off-the-shelf gasoline from a grocery store. Ten or so children and women are sitting under a thatch eave in front of the store, watching an Indian movie on video, masticating sugar cane shoots. There is one adult male in the group, and he's maybe twenty. One of the young women speaks English. Within minutes, we're all laughing and chatting and teasing like we've sat under these palms for years together. What a remarkably open and friendly people, these Indonesians, especially in the islands. We assume that, when they use their own language around us, they are not discussing shrinking our heads or

Amor-Amor

throwing us in the big bubbling pot with the chickens. It's Lombok for us. Bali's been "rode hard and put away wet." Lombok, on the other hand, is still fresh, but not to the point of head-shrinking.

■

There are three islands just off the northwest coast of Lombok that are scuba-diving Meccas. They are Trawangan, Meno, and Air, in descending order of size and distance from here. At 9 a.m. we walk down to the Sheraton beachfront and meet up with Sam, our dive master, and a couple of other guys. One is the skipper. He speaks no English and seems blissfully ambivalent about getting to know us. Also along for the ride to Trawangan is a chubby young woman named Su. She is one of the small army of young hawkers who prowl the streets of Senggigi. They sell beads, watches, wood carvings, and other trinkets. Most carry their inventory in attaché cases. Su's is purple. It has red stick-on letters that read "Pearls."

Soon after we hit open water, the sea gets a bit rough. We're climbing steep waves and falling off their backsides. The boat creaks painfully with every swell. It's ten minutes of this before Tracy turns green and vomits over the side. She took Anti-

Mo before we left shore, but probably not early enough. I'm barely hanging on to my own breakfast. This is a roller-coaster ride. Then a wonderful thing happens. Su, who has been quiet so far, comes and sits by Tracy and takes charge of her care. She hugs and holds her steady. When Tracy throws up again, Su cradles her head and rubs the back of her neck. Everyone on board agrees that this is the thing to do. Who knew neck-rubbing was good for motion-sickness? Now no longer burdened with anything she had eaten earlier, Tracy dozes as we continue to Trawangan. Su holds her the whole time.

We spend most of the rest of the day underwater. Each of these islands in the Bali Sea is entirely surrounded by coral reef. We are right at the point where the Trawangan reef stops its angled descent and suddenly becomes a sheer wall, disappearing into darkness. It's a little spooky to think that there are three thousand more meters below us, and that they are inhabited. I don't think of *Flipper* or *Splash*. I think of *Jaws*, and *Jaws II*. We carefully follow the edge of the reef. After a few minutes, we begin to relax. It's nice down here. And you really can breathe through these funky contraptions. You can also spit, cough, burp, and even throw up if you must. The mouthpiece is designed with a clever exhaust system so that anything you expel stays expelled. It's an engineering coup, but you don't want to imagine who else might have been sucking it before you. Visibility is better than I expected. It's easy-going underwater. The fish just cruise along, no hurry at all, picking at the coral and each other, collecting plankton, occasionally checking us out. We go deeper, eventually leveling off at about fifteen meters. We recognize sergeant-major fish like we saw in Oman, but otherwise our ignorance of marine life is compendial and thorough. What do plankton eat? Do fish have eyelashes? Do they dream? Do damselfish feel pretty? Is an eel embarrassed if it snaps out of its cave to grab unsuspecting prey and misses? Sam gets our attention and points to a sea turtle, resting below, at about twenty meters. It looks about the size of a standard television set. I've seen enough Jacques Cousteau specials to know just what to do, and dive carefully down to it. It stays there, until I touch its back, then it turns away and slowly swims off.

There is no better way to break the ice than to throw up on somebody. On the boat back to Senggigi, Tracy twice shares her bounty with Su. They are now practically family. When we arrive, I offer to give her a ride home. It's the least I can do. She, her husband Zack, her son Jodi Muhammad, and her sister Emma live in a house on the outskirts of Senggigi. There's a dirt trail off the main road that leads to their neighborhood. Another narrower and rockier path leads to their house. There is a cluster of maybe ten houses at the end of the street. Two have cows in the front yard. Chickens scatter in all directions as we drive down the path. A man in shorts squats on the edge of the path holding a white fighting cock. That's a hell of a career; every day on the job could be your last. All the neighbors turn out to snoop. It's not every day that a car comes down the lane; certainly not one that contains a tourist and the neighbor's wife.

The next day Tracy and I come back and we all go for a drive together. Su's village is on the other side of the mountain from Senggigi, in Pemenang. Her family is Sasak, an indigenous tribe that is now Muslim. Pemenang is no longer a traditional Sasak village. There are some relatively modern concrete houses. The roads are still rudimentary, but they do the job. We ease down a dirt path. People squint into the car and squeal when they realize that it's Su coming to visit. As the crowd gathers, we squeeze-park the jeep into an alley and get out to a hero's welcome. There must be fifty people here to greet us. Within a few minutes, the crowd disperses and we're left with the immediate family of fifteen or twenty, most of whom are children. Su introduces us to her brothers and sisters. Her mom's dead and her father's in the fields. One of her younger sisters goes off and comes back with tea and a coconut-pineapple dessert. We all sit in the *baruga*, a raised platform with thatched roof and open sides, where most gatherings take place. It's the family room. Zack, who is not Sasak, is still something of an outsider. He understands their language, but not perfectly. So he's circumspect. And when it's time to leave, he tries to curry favor with the youngsters by handing out small bills. The matriarch of the clan, Su's aunt, comes out to see us off. She is three thousand years old and has a mouth that's red with betel nut. Su bends at the waist, takes her aunt's hand, and gently presses her nose to it. It's a sign of respect. Yes it is.

■　oceania　■

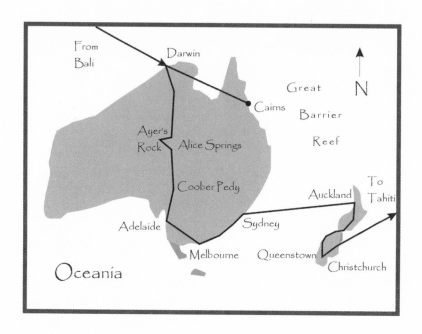

In a way Australia is like Catholicism. The company is sometimes questionable and the landscape is grotesque. But you always come back.

— Thomas Keneally (b. 1935), Australian novelist.

Darwin, Australia, April 1

Darwin is the capital of Australia's Northern Territory (NT). NT, also known as the Top End, is about the size of Texas. It contains two hundred thousand people. That's right, two hundred thousand. Half the population lives in Darwin. Let's put these numbers in perspective. India gives birth to two hundred thousand new people every four days. You could put all the citizens of Darwin in the stands of an Olympic stadium. What a change this is from Asia. With the exception of Laos, we have been in a sea of people since we left Abu Dhabi. Now it's eerily quiet. The streets of Darwin are very nearly deserted. It doesn't matter what time of day it is. There are so few people in the Top End that most of the time, they can't find each other. That's one of the NT's rewards.

The Northern Territory News is the local paper. It's a forty-page tabloid. World news takes up half of page fifteen. The rest is dedicated mostly to sports and local crime. Today's front-page headline concerns an eleven-cent reduction in the price of a glass of beer. Inside, there is a story about a man who swallowed a slug on a drunken dare and is now suffering from meningitis. If he should pass on, he will be a strong candidate for this year's Darwin Award, named after the anthropologist and bestowed posthumously on the person who, by taking themselves out of the gene pool, strengthens our species. These observations present a narrow view of the city, but not too narrow. Drinking is a central part of living in this isolated part of Australia. On our way back to the room, we share the elevator with two very large Aborigine women and a somewhat smaller, tattooed, white Australian man. They're all in shorts, flip-flops, and T-shirts. Each of the women carries a case of beer in one hand and an open bottle in the other. The man has a bottle in each hand. They're already half-pickled and give off that unforgettable bouquet of sweat, cigarettes and beer. They're lost in the hotel, looking for the fifth floor. It'll be an ugly party.

Australian English is easier to understand if you keep the following basic rules and examples in mind:

- "O" is pronounced "oy." So is "i." So is "a." Noy, moyt, Oy doyn't knoy, but Joy moight.
- "E" is pronounced "i." "Ee" is "ay." Tinnant Crayk is a toyn neely a thoysand kay Sayoth of Daahwin.
- Baby talk is popular here. Breakfast is brekky. Barbecue is barbie. Football is footy. Ticket is tickie. A deceased person could be a stiffy. Or not.
- A person who does something is a "something-roo." A soccer player is a socceroo. A conga player is a congaroo.
- Everyone's a moyt, regardless of gender. This eliminates the problem of having to remember names.

You can't make fun of Australians because they'll kick your ass. These are the biggest people, on average, we've ever seen. They're tall, broad-shouldered, muscular, big-footed, and have a look of solidity about them. And that's the ladies. We've become accustomed to Asian sizes, so this scares us. Even the food here is big. Over at Hog's Breath Café, we ordered prime rib (*ribby*) and barramundi (*barra*). They brought us enough food for a small village. Standing in line at the cinema, we were thankful to not be stranded in a mountain-top blizzard with this gang. We would surely be *brekky*.

■

The crocodiles at Crocodylus Park Research and Education Center, just outside Darwin, come in two varieties: Those that will eat you, and those that want to but can't. Keeping them straight is easy. Saltwater crocodiles, or *salties*, are big, strong, nasty, and have heads the size of Volkswagens. They can pulverize your entire skeleton with one snap of their gargantuan jaws. Their favorite hunting technique is to put the big bite on some part of your anatomy, any part, then drag you underwater, where you swallow your own tongue and call it a day. At this point, contrary to what you might expect, they don't eat you. Instead, they tow your badly mauled body away and jam it under a mangrove. This is where you will quietly decompose,

Leapin' Croc

attracting fish and other yummy tidbits that become crocodile snacks. In other words, you become bait. Evidently crocodiles, in addition to being ruthless killers who will eat anything, have a highly developed sense of irony. Freshwater crocodiles, on the other hand, are relatively small, have sissy jaws that taper to a thin needle-nose, and therefore can only eat small animals. *Freshies* fix their big buggy eyes on you, however, and you just know they're picturing you naked.

We're here in time for the noon feeding. It's a big attraction, so there are ten other people in the group. In Darwin, this constitutes a mob. We spend a good deal of time watching *salties* gnaw and crunch through big chunks of meat and bone and gristle, doled out by a man with far more courage than any of us. Brendan is about six foot two, thirty-five years old, red-headed, with matching mustache and goatee. He wears an Australian bush hat with an alligator skin sash around it. He has worked with crocodiles for seventeen years, and in that time has only lost the tip of his left index finger to one of them. From him we learn the following:

- Alcohol is known to have been involved in fifty-three percent of fatal attacks and eleven percent of non-fatal attacks. I had no idea crocodiles drank.

- Fifty-four percent of fatal attacks and seventy-nine percent of non-fatal attacks have occurred during the day. This reflects the activities of the victims at the time of the attack, rather than any preference by crocodiles. In other words, it doesn't matter when you go in the water. They will get your ass regardless.

- Eighty-six percent of fatal attacks and seventy-eight percent of non-fatal attacks have occurred during the warmer months of the year (July–March) in northern Australia. This tells us that crocodiles busy-up the time of year when sharks are out at sea.

- Crocodiles can leap out of the water. Brendan shows us how this works by suspending meat above the pond from a sort of clothes line. After a few minutes of negotiation, the elected crocodile flies out and grabs the goody. He must have been at least a whole meter above the surface. We decide then and there to pass on the harbor tour.

- Crocodiles will even eat each other if given the chance. Many here have chunks missing from their necks and snouts. This mystifies us; we tasted crocodile jerky today and very nearly puked.

The upshot of all this information is that the waters around Darwin are terribly unsafe. Not only do you run the risk of meeting a *saltie* and checking into a mangrove motel, but you also have the threat of box jellyfish to deal with. These upside-down Jell-O buckets are all over the Top End coast. They each have sixteen trailing tentacles that can stretch to three meters and contain millions of stinging cells. Vinegar will kill the venom in thirty seconds. Balsamic vinegar, on the other hand, can turn an unfortunate encounter into an impromptu meal. *Note to self: Stay out of the water.*

■

I like the way Australians do business. There is a straightforward quality about it, especially among the men. They call me *moyt*. They look me straight in the eye and tell it like it is. "G'day, moyt. Oy recken y'ken boy the boyk for less munee in Sidneee. Wee hev to paayy frayyght t'git it hyah, y'understaynd." Just like that. No bullshit, no whining, no fantastic yarns about the cost of tea in China and its impact on the production of catalytic converters in Bavaria. If you don't like the plain truth, Darwin is no place for you. This is the flip-side to the rough-and-ready, hard-cut frontier edge of the place. In that sense, Darwin is reminiscent of towns in the American West, where men are men and their word is their bond. Also, they will shoot you if they have a couple of brews and a bad mood. This is in stark contrast to Asia, where you're safe but getting a straight answer about anything is impossible. Men here are not in a state of constant competition. There's a brotherhood among them that's obvious. *Moyts* is more than just a convenient greeting. It's a commitment, a beautiful bond, a sincere anthem of solidarity. These men are held together by *footy* and beer, and the knowledge that they are a breed apart from their compatriots in other parts of the country. I can't prove this yet, but they may also have done time together.

We spent most of today trying to figure out what to do about transportation cross-country. There's a Yamaha motorcycle dealer in town who also stocks Triumphs, but even as I sit on the British racing-green Trophy 900 Sport Tourer, my mind is on the BMW R1100RT we saw yesterday. If we do buy a bike here, that'll be it. Unfortunately, a whole new set of complications will come with it. What do we do when we leave Australia? Can we bring it along? Must we sell it? If we do ship it ahead, how can we know that we will not run into the same problems in South America as we did in India? We don't want to lose another bike. These and other questions keep us occupied throughout dinner at Giusseppe's. We share a fresh and tasty Greek salad, then have pasta. There aren't many restaurants in Darwin, and those we've seen are not fancy. Most are in downtown, which consists of three streets running ten or so blocks. You can get pretty good Mexican, Italian, and Thai. Also anything barbecued. It's nice, for a change, to not worry so much about food poisoning.

Following dinner, we stroll down Mitchell Street. This is downtown's main drag. It's downtown's only drag, really. There's a Youth Hostel Association office, and it's jammed with backpackers. We stop in and look around, then ask if they have any suggestions on how we might be able to go cross-country. "Y'ken hoyre a kempah-vayn," tells us the lady behind the counter. We have no idea what that means, so she produces a brochure. It's a van, converted to an apartment-on-wheels. This would not be as ballsy as riding a motorcycle cross-country, but might present an interesting alternative if the BMW proves too complicated. Also, the *kempah-vayn* costs less than renting a car and eliminates the need to stay in hotels along the way. This last fact is especially attractive. We could sleep in the van, maybe at camping sites. We could just pull over when we get tired. We could prepare our own food. We've known and expected the Stuart Highway across this big country to be tough. On a motorbike we would be fighting the three-trailer "road trains." These create their own weather systems as they rumble down "the Track," as locals call it. We'd also definitely run over or into or very near animals that are best avoided altogether. Every account I've read about this overland crossing has included encounters with snakes and kangaroos. Only occasionally with dingoes. In a car or van, that would not be a terribly big deal. On a bike, though, it could be. I know that I'm rationalizing. Deep down inside I really want to ride the Stuart Highway across Australia. Ideally, on my own bike, which is reliable, familiar, and big enough. If that's not possible, and another bike too costly or knotty, then we'll make the most of it. We'll *kempah-vayn!*

Cairns, Australia, April 5

Cairns is to Darwin what dressage is to bronco-busting. Both sports involve horses, but the latter is meaner and more likely to break bones. These towns close to the equator have a lot in common, but there is, in Cairns, a smaller chance of trouble. We get the same small-town feeling, but without so much grit. It's more genteel. This is still tropical, but four or five degrees cooler than the Top End. There are more services. A lovely tree-shaded esplanade shoulders the harbor. Joggers and walkers come and go. Elegant restaurants, coffee houses, and bakeries can be found on every block. You can tell right away that Cairns is here to help you find your way to the Great Barrier Reef. There are dive shops and GBR tour companies everywhere. You can buy scuba gear on every block. The harbor is full of dive boats with names like Reef Divers and Reef Quest. We've booked a four-day live-aboard diving trip with Down Under Dive. Why? That's still not clear. It hasn't been two weeks since we earned our Open Water certification in Indonesia. Yet now we're preparing to spend several days diving in a real sea with real fish, some quite large.

There's an aquarium here, Underwater World, which features twice-daily shark feeding presentations. We're just in time for lunch, and watch in fascination as a young man slips into the big tank and joins the fish. He's in scuba gear, but wears no special protective clothing. No suit of armor. No cup. No Kevlar. No Saint Anything. In addition to the lone diver, the tank contains sixteen sharks, four rays, two potato cod, two giant wrasses, and several trevallies. There's not a lot of room to spare. Despite close quarters, the fishes seem to get along fine with each other and the diver. He just floats around, reaching into a small plastic bucket and hand-feeding small chunks of dead fish to the gang of carnivores nipping at his gloves. He seems wonderfully confident and at ease, even if his hand always recoils instinctively when the big fish snap at the food. After about half an hour, he leaves the tank. I notice then a sign on the wall: "G'day. You too can dive with the sharks. Please enquire at the desk." I do.

Spending forty-five minutes underwater with thirty large carnivores is an experience that teaches us much. To wit:

- Every assertion that a particular species of shark is harmless to humans is immediately qualified with the following: "Unless it is frightened, asleep, annoyed, feeding, mating, protecting its young, recently widowed, urinating, lactating, menstruating, teething, or otherwise indisposed."

- Sharks have "staring" eyes. When they circle you, they never take their gaze off you. They do not look you in the eye. They look you in the soft juicy bits, like your butt, your breasts, and your neck. Those large enough to take your whole head in their mouths often open and shut their jaws as though sizing things up.

- One reason you cannot muster up the appropriate level of fright in a shark tank is that you rarely know just how many of the creatures are stalking you, and how close they are. To do so, you would have to see everywhere around you at the same time. They, on the other hand, need only see the jugular pounding in your neck.

- All the reassurance in the world will not stop you from pissing your wetsuit when several sharks suddenly interrupt their leisurely cruising and break into a high-speed chase around the tank. The dive guide had warned us that the white-tip males might chase a female that had recently given birth, but when the water starts churning and those inscrutable eyes come at us like death on a cold night, we scream into our regulators.

- Stingrays look like flying pizza dough.

- It's true: people on the outside look like they're the ones in a tank.

Following our swim with the sharks, we are hungry as wolverines. This is a carnivorous hunger honed on the jagged edge of danger. We could eat a horse but we don't have to, because for the first time in a very long time we are in a country that is clean of mad cow, foot and mouth, head and shoulders, or any other bovine affliction. So we promenade through the shady streets of Cairns, hunting for a big, juicy steak. We find a beauty at a pub called B.J. O'Malley, or something like that. This is no fancy establishment. You go to the back and place your order. They give you a number. When the food is ready, they bring it to the table and slap it down without ceremony. We're having T-bone steaks. Big, Australian, honest-to-goodness T-bones. They come with thick slabs of sautéed vegetables and baked potatoes. There is just enough blood left in the meat to douse the fire of our lust for prey. We tear at the flesh, chew with our eyes closed, legs trembling, a light sweat breaking on our brows. The ferocity of this feral meat-eating orgy is punctuated by the screams of thousands of wild cockatoos that congregate in the trees outside and produce their nightly dinnertime racket. Maybe we belong in a tank.

Saxon Reef, Great Barrier Reef, Australia, April 7

The Great Barrier Reef is the world's largest living thing. It stretches along the west coast of Australia, two thousand or more kilometers, many hundreds of reefs. This is one of the richest marine life habitats in the world. Fish live here because it's warm and there's plenty to eat. Bigger fish eat smaller fish. Birds of prey have it good. When they're not picking their daily fresh dish from the reef waters, they can perch in any of the one thousand comfy islands that intersperse the GBR. So it goes, a beautiful cycle of nature, raw and wild.

We're exploring the GBR aboard the Atlantic Clipper, an old ketch that ran into very heavy weather back in '86 and was repaired in Portland, Oregon. It is now, following those repairs, a brigantine. The difference is about four extra meters of hull and some sail reconfiguration. I learn this from her captain. He can tell from the bare look of density on my face that I couldn't tell a brigantine from a ketch from a shrimp boat from a buoy, so the conversation dries up. The Atlantic Clipper is less elegant than in the glossy color brochure. This is a ship that earns its keep. Up on the dive deck the scene is chaotic. Forty of us are gearing up at the same time. The process involves finding a wetsuit that fits,

Atlantic Clipper, GBR

goggles that have not been stripped or hopelessly scratched, and fins that won't slip off or cut your ankle. We're scavenging in the lockers and bins like hyenas on a smelly carcass. The wind is up and the Atlantic Clipper shudders and bobs and yaws. Every few minutes one of us loses his footing and topples tank-and-all to the deck. Everything is wet. This is not going to be a picnic.

Our first dive is inauspicious. One solitary dive guide takes a dozen of us for an introduction to Saxon Reef. We descend the suspended staircase to the dive platform and fall into the water like overloaded penguins. We then fight against the waves and current to get to the bow of the ship, where we all dive and follow the anchor line toward the bottom. Well, that's the idea, anyway. Tracy and I abort the dive at five meters. She's having trouble keeping water out of her mask. Visibility is very bad and the guide is already out of sight. This is not exactly what we had in mind. In fact, we dreamt of limpid lagoons teeming with friendly and colorful tropical fish. We imagined leisurely preparation for dives, then slow easy descents into crystal clear, shimmering warm seas, maybe down to ten meters or so, and a nice weightless stay before coming up to a lunch of fresh salads and chilled lobster.

Nevertheless, by mid-morning of our second day aboard, we've slipped into a comfortable routine. All that attention at the Hilton and the Sheraton and the Radisson has become a vague and irrelevant memory. Now we're scrappers again. We're on the dive deck before anyone else to make sure we have the right size wetsuit and fins. We're among the first to get in the water, first to get out, and first in line for the simple though hearty meals. This is like boarding school, and like boarding school, it necessarily means having to be close to people you might normally avoid, and vice versa. A handful of us are working on advanced certification, so we naturally congregate. We're excited and apprehensive because tonight we do our first night dive. Following dinner, one of the dive instructors, Phil from Yorkshire, pulls us to one end of the saloon and gives us a briefing on what to expect. He has a heavy accent, like farmers on *All Creatures Great and Small*. You know right away this is a man you can trust.

Diving at night requires that you believe in the intrinsic security of the sea. You must know in your heart of hearts that nothing lurking in the darkness outside your torch beam is plotting your demise. It could be lurking just to pass the time. This is a lot to ask of humans. We're naturally suspicious of animals. Especially animals that can breathe where we can't and have three thousand fangs in multiple uneven rows lining upper and lower jaws. Still, the night dive is a requirement of the Advanced Diver certification, and I've made up my mind to get that. So, at the appointed hour, four of us and Phil go topside and strap on our dive gear. We then march down the plank with our flashlights lit, and one by one make that giant leap of faith into the black water of the Coral Sea. Phil leads the way down the anchor line, which slopes away from the ship toward the reef's edge. By the time we get to the bottom we're at fourteen meters. It's damn dark. Visibility is three meters, but only inside the torch beam. After about ten minutes, though, we reach a sandy clearing and Phil motions to us to kneel on the sea floor. We do so, gingerly, just in case something, like a stingray, is napping under there. Then we do some exercises. Phil cups his hands together and looks at us quizzically. Where's the boat? We should be able to look up and guess from a bright spot on the water. Seems pretty easy, and we all point at the same eerily lit spot behind and above us. Turns out that's the moon. The ship is in the other direction. Oops. Then Phil directs us to turn off the torches and sit still. We do. Now we're all kneeling on the bottom of the sea, at night, in the dark. I fight back the urge to scream into my regulator. The idea, as Phil pointed out before the dive, is to let our eyes become accustomed to the darkness. Remarkably, they do. Within a minute, we can see each other again, and all follow Phil as he swims off into the void, lights off. In this darkness, our movement activates the bioluminescence of certain marine organisms. They fall away from us like hyperactive sparks. Remarkable and wonderful. That's all we see. No fish, no sharks, no nothing. It's a quiet night in the GBR, and I'm torn between profound relief and even profounder relief.

Katherine Gorge, Katherine, Australia, April 13

The Track got its name because that's what it was, until World War Two. That's when the Japanese began to bomb Darwin. In order to get supplies and reinforcements to the town, the Australian government quickly upgraded the thing. Now it's a real honest-to-goodness road and carries all the traffic across the middle of Australia. One lane each way. If you must make this trip, you must make it count. So trucks pull three and four trailers, instead of the standard two we see in the U.S. They call them "road trains." On some stretches, they are allowed to be over fifty

The Track

meters long. That's a vehicle half the length of a football field. However, stories of truckers' ruthless barreling down the road are overblown. For one thing, they're restricted to 100 km/h. For another, there just aren't that many of them. This road is actually quiet, boring, uneventful. Back in Asia we had wet dreams about wide-open spaces. Now we're looking down nearly four thousand kilometers of next-to-nothingness. How can you beat that?

Most terrestrial animals we see are roadkill. We count a wild boar, a kangaroo, a mule, a dog with a collar, and a fat monitor lizard. The real action here is in the air and the trees. It's the crows and magpies and jabirus and kites. These patrol the Track, landing as soon as an unfortunate critter meets its vehicular end. We often see crowds of them hunched over in the middle of the road, pecking and tearing away at fresh carcasses. As we drive up, they flutter protestingly off, and settle in nearby trees to watch us go away. Magpies are the most numerous. We know that there are several species, but with their black and white markings, to us they all look like diminutive airborne nuns.

The thing about Australia is that you need only know it today. Almost everywhere else in the world, with the exception of North America, getting to know a country and a culture means studying its past. Or its pasts, if it's old and busy enough to have had a few. The Middle East has been making news for thousands of years. The legacy of art in Europe is staggering. Hinduism's progress in the Indian subcontinent and Asia is a fascinating and expansive chronicle. Other places have dynasties and empires. Here though, in the Land Down Under, there isn't much that predates the nineteenth century. It's true that the Dutch first fell on these shores in the seventeenth century, but not a lot happened until the British arrived in the eighteenth. It's also true that Aborigines have lived on this continent for millennia, but their art is really more a craft form, indigenous and distinctive, though not extraordinarily so. Aboriginal mythology is interesting, but too much like Hindu Lite. Anyway, the Hindus got to us first. We're left filling our heads with what we see on the road. Or rather, we're left driving. That's the essence of the Australian experience at the Top End. Moving. Just getting in your car and heading down the highway. Not a lot happens, but the endless road and elusive horizon draw you away from where you are. It's ambulatory therapy.

The Nitmiluk Campground has filled up nicely, but not too much. We're in a "powered" lot and have plugged into the 240 volt pedestal that we share with three adjacent groups. Our rent for the night is $8 Australian (AUD) per person. Power is AUD $4. So our grand total is AUD $20, or U.S. $10. It's not impossible to imagine living like this for a while, at ten bucks a day. My U.S. unemployment benefits might cover it. It's quiet; the neighbors are pleasant and keep to themselves; it's safe. Across the path there is a young couple who has pitched a pup tent in the shade of their small black Toyota. They're crouched behind their plastic cooler, taking pictures of a large wallaby grazing nonchalantly not two meters away. We'd read that it is likely to spot wallabies and kangaroos in these parts. And the trees are full of bud-gies, making an infernal music.

We've just finished dinner. Ham and cheese sandwiches on white bread. This is the first night of our trans-Australia crossing. We're "camping." Call us latter-day Bedouins. There are people who live in this caravan park full time. They're the ones with the TVs. We're happy enough with our TV-free home-on-wheels but the bugs are eating us alive. We spray. We swat. It's no use. Australian bugs are persistent. The mosquito and the fly are this continent's bane. They pester and persecute us merci-lessly. Being a Bedouin isn't all it's cracked up to be.

Elliott, Australia, April 14

Our first night camping in Australia's mid-section taught us that we are poor-ly prepared for the elements. We need a fan, since our van doesn't have A/C in the back. We need a bug zapper. We need a broom to assist the dead bugs back out of the van and into their natural habitat. Blond bugs, tan bugs, two- and three-tone bugs. Bugs that can be on you and invisible. Little yellow ants with a red sack in the back. We really need some sleep, but it's going to be a busy day. Right after break-fast, we've booked a two-hour boat tour of Katherine Gorge. As we approach the river, a loud, persistent, chilling cackle fills the air. We look up and see hundreds of bats, the biggest and ugliest we've seen, hanging like cheap black underwear from the eucalyptus trees overlooking the river. These are flying foxes. We've seen pictures in our Wild Australia book, but *Holy Outback!* in real life, they are a carnival of repulsion. They look hideous enough, but on top of that, sound like crying babies, or tortured lambs. The tour guide, Allison, tells us that they roost in these trees all day. At dusk they send out a couple of scouts to find food. They prefer the bloom of a particular species of eucalyptus. If they have to, they'll eat the fruit. Great: dis-criminating bats. To us they look like they're just waiting for an opportune moment to sink their fangs into our necks and suction a donation. We're happy to get on the boat and away from there.

The two-hour tour of Katherine Gorge takes exactly two hours. Ranger Allison would have it no other way. She is a stocky, good-looking woman of thirty or so. Crocodile Dundette. A very feminizing quirk gives her soft heart away; she ends her sentences in a plaintive high-pitched question mark. It's cute. We find ourselves talk-ing like her. Also, she prefaces any direction indicative—right, left, up, down, here, there—with the word "up." "Up down the end of the boat?" "Up left of the wild fig?" "Up below the waterline?" Katherine Gorge is a series of separate, smaller gorges connected by rapids. When the water is down, there is no way to get water-craft between them, but now at the end of the wet season, there is enough water in the river to allow kayakers and canoeists to make the trip. We, however, are in a large flat-bottom tour boat. So, after spending twenty minutes going up the first gorge, we disembark, walk across rock flats, and get in a second boat for the continuing cruise upriver. Allison manages all of this. She pilots the boat alone; she docks it and leads us across to the other boat; she provides the running commentary; she makes sure there's plenty of cold drinking water on board; she spots the freshwater crocodile for the all-important picture. The gorge is not huge like the Columbia River Gorge, or steep like the Grand Canyon, but it's dramatic on a minor scale. It's also very hot this time of year, but the trees along the banks, the clean slow river, and a breeze that whistles down the gorge all make it very pleasant. We learn that the sandstone here is the oldest in the world, having been formed fifteen million years ago. No idea what to do with this information, but it's quintessential Australia. This country is proud of its rocks.

■

"Is that a bird or a bug? I hope it isn't endangered!" Tracy says this as yet another large ripe insect meets its sudden end on the grille of the van. Listening to Paul Simon's "Kodachrome" as we plow a swathe of death and destruction through the middle of Australia, we're doing an unofficial bug census. The majority of casualties is made up of dragonflies. They thud against the metal and hang there, contorted. "Are you aiming at them?" I say no, but can see why Tracy might think that. By the time we're halfway to Elliott, the grille looks like a crazy modernist work of art. Death comes suddenly on the Track.

We're blasting along at 130 km/h. The landscape is monotonous. We see eucalyptus and red gum trees; tall grass and red dirt; and millions of termite mounds. These are the trademark of Australia so far. Once in a while I wonder if we're rushing this. Then I realize that, unless we head into the bush, strap on a backpack, and go trekking in search of the Big Quiet, we're not going to see any more than we already do. Even though we only got started in earnest at 1 p.m., we manage to do four hundred kilometers by 5 p.m., and pull into the Midland Caravan Park and Petrol Station in Elliott. It's the only place to stay and it's nearly empty. We're in much better shape tonight. We've closed up the van and have our new fan blowing nicely. All the curtains are drawn so critters are not tempted by the light. Just before turning in, we have a stroll in camp and see the blackest, brightest, clearest, most astonishing sky we have since being on the ferry crossing at night between Valencia and Palma. In the distance we hear dingoes howling in the outback.

Alice Springs, Australia, April 15

It's Tax Day. It's also Easter. The common thread is crucifixion. We start the day determined to reach Alice Springs. That's 750 kilometers, give or take, but we've had a good night's rest at the Midland Caravan Park. This morning we make friends with the resident peacocks. They're attracted to our box of Nut Feast cereal. I throw a couple of flakes out to one of the females and before you know it, the whole gang

comes over. The male, easily distinguishable by the color of his plumage and his failure to stand in line, loves this stuff. So much so, that he agrees to jump for it. Three
jumps is all I get out of him. After that he holds his head up high and struts away,
as if to say, "Screw you and your stupid Nut Feast game."

The advertised highlight of the trip between Elliott and Alice Springs is Devil's
Marbles. These are stones, boulders really, each about the size of a small bus. They

Devil's Marbles

tend to be spherical. Some lean against each
other. Some are broken, like they'd been made
of butter and had had a hot knife episode. It's
a weird landscape, and just a few hundred
meters from the Track. It would not be nearly
as popular if it were named Richard's Marbles.
There's something about involving Beelzebub
in natural wonders that renders them irre-
sistible. To prove the point, we drive right past
the turn-off to Churchill's Head.

We're going at a pretty good clip, listening to our eclectic mix of new audio cassettes.
We picked them up yesterday in Larimah (pop. 20). The Simon and the Sinatra are
great. The Little Richard makes us want to pee. The *Sixties Unforgettable Hits*
include eminently forgettable dogs like "My Old Man is a Dustman," by Lonnie
Donegan. The *Old School Classics* features an incredibly sappy "Wishin' and Hopin'"
by the Mersey Beats. That's it. Just drivin' and listenin' and wishin' and hopin'. Don't
cross Australia by land if you bore easily.

The Catch of Today on the Track is butterflies. Yesterday we collected thousands of dragonflies on our grille. Today it's butterflies. Hundreds of these beautiful,
delicate, colorful and unlucky bugs find their way into the unforgiving grille mounted on the front of the van. Blues, brilliant cheerful yellows, dappled black and white,
some unbelievably exotic looking. All Australian. All dead. Also we manage to kill
two more birds, small ones that we did not have time to identify. The first makes a
weird swooping approach and ducks under the van. When I look in the rear-view
mirror I see him falling to the asphalt like a broken badminton puck. Not much
later, a second bird flies right into the top of the van, above the windshield. I don't
see that one drop, but there is no way he survived. We see all sorts of roadkill today.
There's yet another mule and several kangaroos. We see our very first wedge-tail
eagle. It's huge, with a two-meter wingspan, and fortunately still alive. We interrupt
its lunch, but it just lumbers up unhurriedly and sits in a ghost gum by the side of
the road, waiting for our noise and fury to recede.

There are curves in the Track. Not many, but they exist. One time we have to
slow to 120 km/h. Otherwise, you can do 140 km/h all the way from Katherine to
Alice Springs, faster if you have the horses, and not often need to indicate. Traffic is
extremely light. Even lighter than we expected. We're on the road from 8 a.m. until

4 p.m., and in that whole time not once did another vehicle overtake us. I estimate that we saw about fifty cars and trucks going in the other direction, north. That works out to six per hour. Everyone makes the most of passing another car; we all do a kind of wave. Just like motorcyclists. In a car, you "wave" by holding up a palm in the windshield so the oncoming driver can see it. If you've done a lot of this sort of driving, you've probably refined your wave to an upheld finger or two, keeping your palm on the steering wheel the whole time. I find it tiring to lift my palm or finger five times an hour, so flash my headlights instead. This can be problematic. It could leave the other driver wondering if something is wrong. "Do I have a low tire?" "Is there a kangaroo hanging from my radiator?" "Could the trailer be on fire?" "Did I leave the iron on?" Maybe it's time for auto manufacturers to design a *winker*. If you are "waving" and only "waving," then you flick your *winker* and only one of your headlights flashes. It's a great way to say "G'day."

The middle of Australia is inhospitable and dangerous. Without a cassette recorder and a bed in the back, you could die of monotony, but as we approach Alice Springs, we cross the tropic of Capricorn. This has the sudden and dramatic effect of putting us in a global context. That's fine most of the time, but at the end of a long day of driving, all we can think is, "Why are all these towns named after women?" Adelaide, Alice, Augusta, Katherine, Marla, and so on. We read somewhere that the early explorers of the continent named places after the wives and daughters of their friends. Interesting…

Wish we had a winker.

Uluru, Australia, April 17

The wild animal you are most likely to meet in the outback is the fly. The scale of this problem only becomes clear as we stand in the parking lot at the Erldunda rest stop. I picked a conversation with two young men traveling on cross-country motorbikes. They're doing a Sydney-Cairns-Outback-Adelaide-Sydney loop. The whole time we're talking, fly formations buzz and swoop and annoy us relentlessly. In my Perfect World, there would be no flies. Also, there would be no mosquitoes. And no customs officials. These would be employed as hospitality clerks in remote cultural centers, like Pluto. My biker friends and I stand there, conducting.

From Erldunda we take the Lasseter Highway west, toward Uluru, or Ayer's Rock. This will be the longest detour we make away from the Track. Everyone we've met along the way has insisted that we see "the Rock," so we're going. It's 250 kilometers from Erldunda to Yulara, a community that has been erected expressly to support the visitors to Uluru. Four hotels; several restaurants; a few pools; a gas station; all in a village-like compound. This doesn't mean much to us because we're staying in the campground next door. Once we've rented our spot, we start off to the Rock, twenty kilometers down the road. When it comes into sight, we agree that

Uluru

it looks like a piece of Cadbury Chocolate Flake. It's massive, all right, and makes a particularly sharp impression because all around it is flat. There isn't a single shrub on the thing. Our plan is to climb it, and we drive around to the parking lot at the foot of the climbing path. A few people are on the red sandstone, inching upward. One section of the slope is so steep that a chain balustrade has been put up to help stop climbers from falling down and making a mess at the bottom. Several benches are placed in a semicircle behind us, and a handful of people sit contemplating the view. A few are waiting for their more intrepid halves to return. The native Anangu people do not approve of visitors climbing their sacred rock. There is a sign at the base of the rock, and it reads:

Anangu ask you not to climb Uluru. Climbing Uluru is not consistent with Tjukurpa (Anangu Traditional Law). If you insist on climbing please follow all safety advice. Please be aware that the Uluru climb is a very strenuous activity requiring considerable fitness. Numerous people have died on this climb. Anangu feel a great sadness when a person dies or is hurt on the climb.

I equate this in my mind to an Aborigine going to Rome and climbing St. Peter's Basilica. I see their point and respect their cultural imperative, so we pass on climbing. Also, I have a lot of reading to catch up on and can't afford to die just yet. Instead we get back in the car and make our way to the Cultural Center. Look, it's a rock, okay? The Anangus have a series of myths that manifest themselves in this or that crevice, this or that overhang. Here is a mark in the rock where the dishonest lizard burned to death after lying about eating the emu. Here's the rock of Kuniya, the woman python. Like that. We take it all in and remark how serpents always make it into stories of cosmology, but the flies are unbearably annoying so we abbreviate the tour and head to the Sunset Viewing Area. We pull into the lot and park alongside the fifty or so other vans and buses here to see Ayer's Rock go through its colors as the sun sinks into the outback behind us. We are not the sort of people who will applaud a sunset. Still, we find ourselves silenced by the Rock as it goes from brick red to dull gray, isolated, massive, and utterly unto itself, a rich metaphor for this continent, this country.

■

Now we're surging deeper into the great emptiness. We hope to get to Coober Pedy today. It's 750 kilometers away, so we're up at the crack and roll out of Yulara without even making coffee. Despite this initial setback, we limp the one hundred kilometers to Curtin Springs and stop for coffee and gas. The young lady who helps us is just out of bed. The gas pumps are all still padlocked. She's from Philly. Maybe twenty years old. We ask how she comes to be in Curtin Springs, pop. 7. She says she wanted to get away from people. Talk about overkill. As we drive away, the sun comes up in a clear sky and throws yellow and gold all over Ayer's Rock. Up ahead we see dark silhouettes in the road. As we get closer, I realize they're men. Aborigines. Barefoot, filthy, but mostly young and all in good enough health to dismantle us if they wished. They're walking toward us down the middle of Lasseter Highway. Some try to wave us down, but I keep going. It just doesn't seem right. A bit farther down the road there's another gang of them. Same routine; they're in the middle of the road. I slow but don't stop. These guys are not on their way to work. We don't know what they're up to. Whatever it is, it ain't cricket.

Mildred at the Erldunda coffee shop remembers us from yesterday morning. She says it's because we're the only people who order their eggs well-done. I think it's because she likes me. Her name isn't really Mildred, but it should be. She has that "Mildred" thing going on: The permanent scowl, the thin severe lips, the horn-rims, the apron. Mildred has a lot to say about the men we saw walking down the road. She makes it clear that she is not a "racialist," but doesn't try to hide her disgust. They're Anangu. The very same people who own the land, and Ayer's Rock. She feels that since they've agreed to lease the area permanently to the government, they should have no opinion about whether people climb the Rock or not. "Look moyt, y'payed $16.50 to git in. Oy saay y'should be ayble to cloymb the bladdy Rock if y'loyk." She explains that the men in the road do this every day in the hope that motorists will give them money, cigarettes, or fuel for sniffing. They have more money than "yu'n Oy" will ever see, and they live on the dole. They give the "good ones" a bad name. We don't immediately know what to make of Mildred. She seems the caring, matronly type. There must be some truth to what she says, but it's obvious she's inflamed, and painting with a broad and angry brush.

As we travel south on the Stuart between Alice Springs and Adelaide, we see the railroad run parallel. This is the famous Ghan. Someday the rest of it, up to Darwin, will be completed. For people not terribly fond of driving, it will be a great way to see the outback. This morning we have the rare pleasure of catching a classical broadcast from somewhere. Paganini. One of his many violin concerti. Paganini in the outback. Exquisite incongruity. We feel good. The road is ours. It runs away from us, shimmering in the distance like water or rippled chrome. We pull over several times and take pictures of each other goofing off in the roadway. In some places, like at the top of a crest, you can spot cars a full five minutes before they arrive. You can hear them for a couple of minutes. Tracy does cartwheels. I do push-ups. We set up our lawn chairs and pose right in the road. Here we are, in the middle of Australia, all alone. There is nothing here, not even brush. Just red dirt and stone. Desolately, silently beautiful tranquility.

Soon we'll be crossing into southern Australia. The last serious town (pop. greater than 10) in the Northern Territory is Kulgera. There is a hand-painted sign at the solitary gas station. It incorporates the following plea from the adjacent (five hundred kilometers away) outback town of Oodnadatta:

After taking all the trouble to paint and deliver this sign, you can hardly blame us (The Pink Roadhouse at Oodnadatta) for trying to sell you something when and if you visit us! We'd like to GIVE you free information, SELL you fuel, motor repairs, a swim in the pool, Oodnaburgers (famous). Also rent you a PINK push-bike to discover our village or rent you a PINK canoe to paddle on our town dam or one of our many waterholes! Look for us at the far end of Oodnadatta. Ring us anytime (there's a phone fifty meters from here!)

It's tempting, but in the nick of time we remember that five hundred kilometers gets you from Brussels to Amsterdam and back with eighty kilometers to spare. So we decide to give Oodnadatta a miss.

Coober Pedy, Australia, April 18

"Coober Pedy" sounds like something that might come out of your nose, but it's actually a town in the middle of Australia. We spent last night here at the Stuart Grange Caravan Park. The campground is a family business. A Greek family, we come to learn, that emigrated in 1970. Tracy can't understand why anyone would leave Greece for Coober Pedy. It's a good question. This town is the opal mining capital of the world. Picture a flat, parched, dusty, desert landscape. Now picture thousands of piles of sand, all over the place, some high as houses, some higher. That's how they mine for opal. Dig a hole and make a mountain of dirt near it. It's really not that ugly. If you squint from a fair distance, the outskirts can resemble a tidy tent city, like at the Hajj. Or maybe an avant-garde airport like Denver's. The town itself, however, is not so lucky. No amount of squinting will help. It is absolutely ugly, slapped together over the years to support the burgeoning opal mining industry. This is a rough place. There has been frontier violence here in the not-too-distant past. A couple of police cars were blown up. So was the post office. The guys walking the street in the afternoon sun are cut from the mines. They are not people you want to owe money to.

Our landlady is initially curt, but loosens up suddenly when she hears that we've been in Greece. We tell each other our immigrant stories, the abridged versions, and share a moment of suppressed irony. Here we are, in the middle of the outback, a couple of Olive Oils who left their countries at about the same time and ended up settling half a world away. We find our parking spot, set up the van, and go for a swim in the compound's pool. A short swim. The pool is filled with ice water and noisy Australian brats whose parents are deaf and sedated. The landlady arrives and scolds them and their children. Despite this brief desert drama, our dip is refreshing. We're dry within a minute of leaving the pool. It is drier than English humor here.

The outback is actually even drier in south Australia than in the Northern Territory. And flatter. There are places where we drive for half an hour at a time across dry, flat, still, red landscapes, and see nothing move. Nothing. No wind, not even dust. It's weird and a little spooky. We might as well be on the moon. Except for the flies. They are everywhere. You don't see them until you get out of the car. Then they're on you like you're a fresh, delicious mound of manure. So we make occasional and furtive excursions out onto the earth before ducking back into the van. Still, where else can you travel four thousand kilometers on a good road without a single traffic light and no speed limit?

Soon we start seeing indications that the outback is behind us. Juniper trees in increasing numbers dot the plains on each side of the road. Salt lakes appear as we crest hills that have welled up from the vast flats of the table-lands. Once the change starts, it comes fast. Now fields of grain stretch generously to the horizons. Flocks of sheep like fluffy, beige lint balls graze in the thousands. We stop briefly in Port Augusta, at the top of Spencer Gulf. We've gone from the Arafura Sea to the Southern Ocean, clear across Australia, and we would do it again. The outback joins the list of places in the world that we would revisit. Its aces are solitude, quiet, immensity, and in spots, the complete absence of humanity.

Glendambo

Adelaide, Australia, April 19

Adelaide is the biggest Australian city we've been to, by far. And it's very much a city, complete with traffic, shopping centers, auto dealerships, hospitals and lots of houses. We drive around looking for something extraordinary, but it's not here. This is a manufactured lower-middle to middle class working town. I'm not knocking it, not at all. Australia has reached a level of development which is able to provide for the basic needs of the disadvantaged among its citizens. Food, shelter, Nikes... You see that here. Lots of towns like this in the U.S. *Most* towns in the U.S. are like this.

So we take Adelaide for what it is: clean, uncomplicated, modern, mildly insipid. A lovely place. A tame place. Its hills are full of fancy but sensible homes built by the better-to-do. From the top of Belair Drive we get a rich sunset panorama of the city and the sea beyond. Both of us think this has the feel of suburban Salt Lake City. There's a young man in a beat-up station wagon, a local, also appreciating the view. He's working a bong as if a huge flaming meteor will collide with Earth any minute now. I accost him in mid-suck and ask if he knows of any restaurants in the neighborhood. He's caught between having to let go the precious smoke too soon, or looking like a beagle while he keeps me waiting for my answer. But he's a polite pot-head, exhales promptly, and directs us. Nice young man. I like a city in which young people feel comfortable smoking pot in public parking lots.

■

Rundle Street Mall is the pedestrian reserve in the middle of downtown Adelaide. As we walk along with the locals, we're handed a brochure by a ruffled, variously pierced young woman in black. It reads:

The world now has 800 million hungry people, 4 billion living in poverty, 250 million children who work regularly, 130 million people with no access to education, 100 million people are homeless… 60% of all shares in Australia are owned by 1% of shareholders. On May 1, for all these reasons and more, people across Australia, and throughout the world, will walk out of workplaces, campuses and schools to unite in a global protest against the greed and oppression of corporate tyranny. JOIN THE BLOCKADE!

This says a lot about and for Adelaide. Clearly the city has reached a degree of prosperity that its citizens can now turn their attention to other people's problems. Some, like this young woman, are embarrassed by its wealth and self-conscious to the point of mutiny. This encounter reincarnates a rebel streak in me so I rush into a local hair salon and get a funky buzz-cut. Immediately after that we visit a nearby trattoria and have toasted panini pastrami sandwiches. They serve us chilled rainwater out of a tall jade-colored frosted glass bottle and now we feel intensely non-activist.

Adelaide is bigger than it appears. A million people live here, but they're scattered out over four hundred square kilometers. We drive all over the place and discover cozy neighborhoods, tree-lined streets, unpolluted sandy beaches, and a generally mellow state of being. We're staying at the Adelaide Beachfront Resort Campground Caravan Park. Nice place. Clean. The plots, or perhaps I should call them lots, are flat, mowed, and include a concrete slab so we're not constantly dragging dirt and mud into the van. The place is right on the beach and we walk down for a look. A young man and his girlfriend have parked their car at the bottom of the access road and have the radio on. They're listening to heavy metal; "Massacred," by Slash and the Sutures. We wouldn't mind, except that they've chosen to lie in the sand several meters away from the car. So now all of the Southern Hemisphere gets to listen to "Massacred."

Understandably, the beach is deserted. On top of the noise, the water is cold. In fact, we're surprised at how cold we feel in Adelaide. The temperature dips to the Celsius teens at night. It's not freezing, but we don't have heating in the van, so by morning we've lost all sensation in our farther extremities. This caravan park, unlike the ones we've stayed at on the way here, accommodates a majority of permanent residents. They're not on vacation. They live here, and some of their rigs are impressive. There's an older couple across the lane from us. When we pull in, the woman is in a lawn chair in the afternoon sun, reading. Once in a while she sneaks a peek at us over the rims of her reading glasses. It's her neighborhood. We haven't minded this form of travel much. However, it gets old using public bathrooms and showers, especially when you have to go in the middle of the night and it's raining out. Also, the bed is somewhat uncomfortable. Oh yeah, it's quite cramped as well. We like each other and everything, but once in a while you want to stretch without starting an altercation. So we're looking forward to the end of this leg of the trip, when we arrive in Sydney, surrender the *kempah-vayn*, and check in at the Hilton.

We've had no trouble getting good food in Australia, and Adelaide is no exception. In fact, there are some very chic places here. One of these, Evida, is on Seaview Drive at Henley Beach, to the west of Adelaide. It's furnished in trendy blond wood and black metal. The view is of the beach and even now, after dark, we catch the play of dim lights on the water and it pleases us. Our waiter is quite gay. This is another sign that Adelaide is an inclusive, liberal, progressive town. If you live in the U.S. or most anywhere in Europe, this is no big deal. Gays are everywhere and lead open, mainstream lives, but we're just getting over Asia, and that's just not the case there. The menu at Evida is an eclectic melange of daring adventures in culinary consciousness. It utilizes many words that we have never before heard. Some are of foreign extraction, like *planchette*. Some are the scientific names for common greens, but you can never be sure, so we're full of queries. Soon we reach a compromise with our waiter. He quits gazing off at a distant constellation every time we ask a question about the menu and we stop asking questions about the menu. Tracy orders the chicken. I order the kangaroo. The food is exquisite. The waiter likes my hair.

Torquay, Victoria, Australia, April 21

Australia is so enlightened that they have annual Tidy Town contests. These occur at the federal as well as the state level. Portland was Victoria's tidiest town in 1991. We know from the sign at the entrance of town. Port Fairy has won that title twice. It is one of the quaintest little towns we've been in. Tidy houses all in a row, some with gingerbread arches on their porches. On the federal level, tidiness is a big city game. Darwin won for 1998. Can life in these cities have become so polite, so predictable, so stultifyingly easy, that their citizens have the time and inclination to worry about tidiness? What about epidemics? Natural disasters? Political upheaval? War? Corruption? Crime? Can it be that Australia has substantially dealt with the Big Questions and can now "tidy up?" The answer is "yes." I'm certain that eating beef again has made me excitable, but my affection for this country and admiration for what it's accomplished would just as easily stand on vegetarian legs.

After Portland, we're right along the sea, and spend most of the next five hours fighting high winds and driving rain, gasping occasionally at the dramatic beauty of the coastline. Huge herds of fat happy Guernseys; more Tidy Towns; a pair of yellow-beaked plovers tip-toeing across someone's front lawn; chubby fluffy sheep munching young grass; occasional Gothic-style Anglican churches. Here's a solitary white-bark gum tree twisted every which way by the side of the road and everywhere stands of pine and other evergreens. Open fields, tractors, single-line power lines, and the road, twisting along with this gorgeous coastline. We see meadows, picket fences, weeping willows along cool easy creeks under narrow stone bridges. Between hard rain we get continuous cold drizzle. There are tree limbs in the road, blown down by the wind. It's dusk in the middle of the afternoon. Low clouds and puddles and gray-beige limestone darken the day. We hydroplane on standing water by a bright white B&B and a Slow Vehicle Turnout. There's a berry farm at the end of a muddy lane. Nothing we see is astonishing in itself. But it's all, together, perfect.

By the time we get to Torquay, we're exhausted. Happy, but tired from fighting the weather all day long. At one point during the drive we saw a large group of motorcyclists out for a ride. They were on vintage bikes. We saw Nortons and Hondas and BMCs, but we were not envious. It's been a nasty wet day. We find a campground near the sea. Not a particularly good idea, given the prevailing winds, but it's the best we can do. As we set up for the night, it gets dark. Very few spaces are taken. The one right next to us has a pup tent sagging under the weight of the rain collecting in its dimples. We had a late lunch at a pizza and ribs joint in Mount Granier, so we're not hungry. Good thing, because we can't face the trouble of throwing together a meal. Traveling in a van is okay if you can open the doors once in a while and annex some of the space around you. Maybe set up a garden chair and have dinner al fresco. When the weather is like this, you just want to batten down the hatches and wait it out. We've read everything on board so try to go to sleep at nine. It's too early, and we're startled several times as the rain picks up and the wind lashes the campground. Then our neighbors the tent people return and make a small racket getting ready for the night. We pity them. Sometime near midnight, the power dies. There isn't a glimmer anywhere. It's dark as tar. Naturally, we both need to pee. Happily, we have a flashlight. As we plod through the mud to the bathroom, we see that our neighbors' tent is listing. The wind swirls between the eucalyptus trees and alternately pushes it this way and that. We briefly consider inviting them to share the van for the night, then return to our senses and lock ourselves in.

Melbourne, Australia, April 23

Our home last night was the Honey Hush Caravan Park, in the suburb of Laverton, twenty kilometers south of Melbourne. This is a mostly permanent residential caravan park. They have small cabins, each one-room big. We arrive just as the landlord is closing up for the day, but he reinforces our impression of Australians as fine friendly people and walks us down to a nice spot not far from the showers.

The next morning it's raining in Melbourne, so we decide to confine our activities to the indoors. That is how we come to be at the extensive Melbourne Museum, loitering in the Body and Mind exhibit. The story of human physiology is told with multimedia displays that begin with conception and reproduction and end in biotechnology and genetic engineering. Along the way every aspect of the body and mind is exposed and explored and explained in compelling and graphic detail. We have multimedia skeletons, a real nervous system, and an interactive circulatory system. We see an amazing video presentation about reproduction in which a man with a large tattoo on his left arm and a blond woman on his right are shown sort-of doing *it*. This is moderately interesting, but the real exciting stuff is done with those magical miniature cameras that can probe any human orifice as though it's a Disney tunnel ride. We squirm along enthusiastically with an over-achieving sperm that beats its laggardly competitors and punches into the egg. We float in the blonde's uterus and watch the embryo develop. We thrill to the appearance of fingernails and the first throbs of its heart. Then we lean way back in our seats as a real live baby is delivered by a different though vigorous woman in surround sound. The blonde and the man with the tattooed arm are gone. Now it's a couple in their thirties who seem not to mind having the arrival of their third child, as well as its vehicle, immortalized digitally.

The adjacent exhibit deals with the now-discredited discipline of phrenology. Its principles were developed by a mad Englishman, as were underground trains. It is the science of measurement and interpretation of the bumps on a person's head. That's right. Reach up right now and run your fingers lightly along your scalp. You will find some bumps. You may already be aware of these, but think, as I did, that they're tumors. There is nothing to worry about. Each of these, depending on its location, represents your endowment in several aspects of personality. For example, the bump that occurs just above and behind the ears, is representative of a person's *amativeness*. This word, taken from the definitive work on phrenology, is a polite way of saying "horniness." If your bumps are large, you're hornier than the average bear. We all know this is bunk, of course, but Tracy and I spend fifteen minutes in the curtained booth checking out each others' bumps. Seems to us unbelievable that this art fell from favor.

Yarra Yarra

Melbourne is Australia's second largest city in terms of population. It is the capital of Victoria State and contains everything you might expect such an important city to contain. There are universities here, factories, office buildings, and immigrants from all corners of the world. However, two things stand out in the city's history: It was founded by Batman and it is the birthplace of Australian Rules football, or *footy*. Batman, John Batman to be precise, negotiated a clever land-for-stuff deal with the Aborigines. Melbourne was named a town on that land in 1842, three years after Batman had gone to the big bat cave in the sky. *Footy*, on the other hand, has survived and is far more important to your average *Aussie* than anything Batman ever did. Thomas Wentworth Wills is credited with giving birth to the game when he founded the Melbourne Football Club on August 7, 1858. Since that day players in tight shorts the world over take to open fields and do their best to visit grave injury on each other. It's more a brawl than a game really, especially if you are as uninformed about its finer points as we are, and it says something about Australia. We're doing our best to stay on everyone's good side.

Honey Hush won't answer the phone so we don't know if they have room tonight, but Hobson's does and they give us good directions, so we drive down there. It's across Kororoit Road from something nasty. Could be a combination of the sea and the Mobil plant nearby. Could be a huge pride of sea lions died nearby a few days ago. We ring the doorbell of the night-man, Jim. He had just sat down to eat, and is happy to notify us of that, though not in those precise terms. We arrived just in time, it seems, to mess everything up. Jim's been in the beer, but he settles down and says that, yes, he does have a powered site we can use. It takes him three lengthy labored attempts to assemble the words required to direct us to site number ten. We set off down the lane he told us to take, make the first turn, and find it blocked by the fire department. Jim must have forgotten about tonight's fire. We back up and go around. There is a Volkswagen van in space number ten. A young man is crossing from there to the amenities building with a load of dinner dishes. It's just as well; the space is small, muddy, has no concrete slab, and jams right up to the adjacent spaces. We drive around to Jim's place, get our money back, and wish him deliverance. Then we head down the road, back to Honey Hush, hopeful that the gate will be open and that the space we had last night is still available. And hallelujah, it is! The landlords are out for the evening, so we just slink in under the cover of darkness and set up home. We do leave them a message on their recorder because we're nice people. Also because we don't want to have to vacate in the middle of the night. Having to pee is trouble enough.

■

This morning we're at the Melbourne aquarium. We're becoming experts on aquariums. It's a blast. We point at the fish we recognize and call their names out loud so everyone else in the place understands that we know fish. "Wow, that's the fiercest globefish I've every seen, hahahahahaha;" or "Is that damsel in distress?" Clever ejaculations like these amuse us and the other visitors, but mostly us. The Melbourne Aquarium is possibly the best we've ever visited, with the exception of Baltimore's. Tracy says that one is better, but I've always been too afraid of being killed in Baltimore to spend much time there as a tourist, and so I've never been actually inside the aquarium.

We leave the aquarium and walk across the river. There are several bridges across the Yarra, and the city has successfully crossed them to expand itself on the south bank. Now you can promenade along either shore, among shade trees, for several kilometers. This is not a trivial fact. There are many cities in the world that would love to have a two-bank river. Paris of course has done it. London and Prague to a lesser extent. Rome in spots. Melbourne has carefully cultivated development from its epicenter out along both sides of the Yarra. We stop for a quick snack at one of the many restaurants overlooking the river. People here continue to impress us with their easygoing hospitality. It's neither cloying nor impertinent, but a believable compromise that leaves you feeling well-served but without too much air having been blown up your skirt.

After lunch we hop on a river boat for a quiet relaxing cruise up the Yarra. The guide's commentary is mercifully succinct, so we just hang out on deck and watch the city go by. We learn that Aborigines called this river the Yarra Yarra: the river that runs and runs. That's because, unlike most Australian rivers, it never dries up. There are several rowing and boating clubs along the south bank. The governor's mansion is visible from the river as well. The most impressive things we see are the rubbish traps. The term is self-explanatory. These things float on the surface and catch any garbage going downstream to Philip Harbor. It's a beautiful thing.

We spend our last evening in Melbourne at the Cirque du Soleil. This is a Canadian company that has taken the circus concept to new heights, or lows, depending on your point of view. I'm not sure yet how I'll vote. There's a lot to consider. For starters, there are no animals. None. Not monkeys, not a horse, not even an elephant with a hat on. Circus music is altogether different in this new circus. I don't mind that it's new. Actually, it sounds pretty good, but there is something "significant" about it. It is connotative music. It suggests spirituality and insists on a deeper meaning. I hate that. Give me the old tuba and snare drum any day. The set, if you can call it that, is very sophisticated at Cirque du Soleil. Very sophisticated and very complicated. They have motors and pulleys and rappelling apparatus and centrifugal spinners that dazzle and make you wonder just how far behind the times you really are. The acts are incredible. This is what Cirque du Soleil shines at. There are gymnasts, and contortionists, and trapeze artists, and other performers who do things you can only do if you're born with the genes. There are also clowns but their acts, breaking up the breath-taking acrobatics, are heavy. Just like the music, they carry angst and a deep, disturbing melancholia. I want the clowns to step on each other's toes, to fall down, to make honking sounds with their noses. I want them to make the children giggle, and to fall on their cans. The clowns, that is. Or the children; what the hell. I don't want them to nudge me into reflecting on the ironic futility of ambition, or the rich mysticism of a simple gift. All this is counterbalanced by the undeniable wonder of seeing a woman sit on her own head.

197

The rain that's accompanied us for the past six days has created havoc in Victoria, particularly around Melbourne. It started last Friday. Now there are warnings that the deluge will cause sewers to overflow into waterways and harbors. Also, Princes Highway, which we took from Torquay up to Melbourne via Lara, is underwater and shut down.

That's Australia's news. No bombings by dissident separatists. No massive volcanic eruptions destroying villages and their people. No government scandals and no corruption debacles. Prices are reasonably stable and the Aussie dollar is under some pressure but not buckling or in danger of doing so. Industry is fine. The cows are all healthy. Nobody's burning churches and mosques. There's enough crime to keep the police employed, but not enough to stop people from going out at night. There are no monkeys taking over government administrative offices. (This actually just happened in a large Hindu Asian country whose identity we feel compelled to withhold). Everyone's not suing everyone else. The M1 intends to demonstrate in front of Australia's stock exchanges in a few days, but no one's really worried. Everything is going to be just fine. Australia will be just fine. To hell with the gloomy clowns.

Sydney, Australia, April 27

Our room is on the forty-third and top floor of the Sydney Hilton. From here we have a view of the Sydney AMP Tower and, in the distance, parts of the Port Jackson Harbor, known by everyone in the world as Sydney Harbor. One day they will stop fighting this and rename it. We find just enough energy left over to pick up the phone and make reservations for tomorrow night's performance at the Sydney Opera House Concert Hall. The luxury of sleeping in a real bed, in a real room, after two weeks of "vanning" it, is difficult to overstate.

After a very good night's sleep in snow-white Hilton sheets under a fluffy down-filled comforter, and a big eggs, bacon, and toast breakfast, we walk from the hotel, across Elizabeth Street to Hyde Park. There are statues of Queen Victoria and Prince Albert. It not only sounds like London; it feels a bit like it was well. On the east side of the park we pop into St. Mary's Cathedral for a look, then continue our walk north up McQuarrie Street to the Sydney Opera House at Bennelong Point, overlooking Sydney Harbor. It takes thirty minutes to get here from the Hilton. The downtown area is compact and the buildings are tall and modern. Maybe it's the perfect balance between strolling in NY and strolling in Paris. The streets aren't nearly as busy as the former, and neither are the sidewalks. On the other hand, you don't get the long boulevards of Paris, which though lovely, can be exhausting and uneventful. Sydney is also cleaner, but let's not hurry to give it credit for that. After all, it has only been here a couple of hundred years. Paris, on the other hand, was founded in the third century, B.C. New York more than four hundred years ago. These are cities that have had time to make a mess.

There's a commotion at the Opera House today. The wide steps leading up to the halls and the vast clearing at their base are filled with people here to protest something. There's a young man working with a tape recorder, sitting on the steps. I ask him what he knows. We find out that he's a reporter for a local radio station, here to write the story. Turns out today is the Sixth International Day of Mourning for Dead and Injured Workers. Unions New South Wales is staging a protest event. It's all very organized, but there is a wheel within the wheel. There always is. As we mill about in the middle of the throng, watch-

ing preparations underway, I am approached by a middle-aged woman in army boots. She shoves a small newspaper into my hand and asks for fifty cents. As I reach in my pocket for change, she nails me with another rag and says, "That's one dollah, moyt." Now she's gone and I realize that she's handed me the *Australasian Spartacist.* The headline reads, "Full Citizenship Rights for All Immigrants." The second paper is the *Workers Vanguard.* Its headline reads, "Defend China!" Inside the

Sydney Opera House

Spartacist I find a flyer with this headline, "Smash Imperialist Exploitation Through World Socialist Revolution!" Australia is truly a great country. Here we are at the foot of the grand opera house, seat of the well-heeled. There is a union protest going on. Young shirtless boys in baggy pants and orange-fuchsia hair are doing skateboard stunts on the stone benches by the fountain. Communists have infiltrated the gathering and are selling their papers. Fifty meters away, along the quay, well-dressed capitalists and tourists sip *lattés* and snap digital photos of the Harbor Bridge and the Opera House. There is a police car, just one, parked away from but in full view of all this, discreetly keeping an eye on things. Every race and ethnicity is represented. This is a beautiful moment of diversity and tolerance. We pick up our tickets for tonight's performance and stroll for ten minutes along Circular Quay, stopping from the exertion to have a "strong, flat, white," which is what you call a double cappuccino in Sydney. We watch the ferries slide in and out of the harbor and wave with our right hands as we sip the coffees from our left. It's gotten quite a bit warmer now and we have our sandaled feet peeking out from under the table, into the breeze.

It's a good night when we have a concert to attend. It's a great night when the concert is at a place like the Sydney Opera House. We take an easy downhill walk from the hotel. Others are on their way as well. We can tell by their mood and how they're dressed. The moon is a crescent in the western night sky, just above the Harbor Bridge span. It's an exquisite evening. This complex houses the opera house and a concert hall, as well as three small theaters, sort of like the Kennedy Center in Washington. We're in the Concert Hall tonight, in box seats. The Sydney Symphony

Orchestra is conducted by Eri Klas. The concert is terrific. I think I see the Commie lady in the army boots from earlier today. Maybe she's here in protest.

■

We expected to be the only people interested in climbing the Sydney Harbor Bridge span. Well, we're not. This is the single most popular tourist event in town, perhaps in the country. Or even, as Australians are fond of pointing out, in the entire Southern Hemisphere. The BridgeClimb office is in fancy digs at the south end of the bridge, in an area known as the Rocks. Inside, the building is decked out like a secret training facility for commando warfare. It's straight out of a Bond movie. We can see what's going on behind the reception counters, but high steel-wire fences have been erected to keep us from storming the sanctum. You half expect the old absentminded "Q," with the thick glasses and huge brain, to come right up and show us our gadgets for this mission. Groups of people preparing to do the climb have been slipped into uniforms and harnesses, and are either watching the orientation video, or undergoing a pre-climb briefing, or practicing ladder climbs on prop constructions, complete with simulated peril. This is all highly organized.

You can't just show up here, like we did, and expect to climb. The young lady at the counter, friendly as all Australia, explains that they are fully booked for the rest of daylight, but offers us a night climb today. We can't tonight, so we ask for tomorrow. It's tight, but she squeezes us in at 6:45 a.m. That's the first climb of the day. We are to be here at 6:30. She is lovely and sweet and makes it absolutely clear that the rules are stringent, enforced, and that under no circumstances are we to take them lightly. We are:

- Not to wear sandals.

- Not to carry a tissue into which we can blow our nose.

- Not to take up our camera.

- Not to wear watches.

- Not allowed to change dates and times.

- Not allowed to chew gum.

- Encouraged to go to the bathroom before we slip into the hermetically sealed suits for the three-hour event.

- Never entitled to a refund.

- Never entitled to complain in any way.

- Never, ever allowed to make "jumping" jokes.

We go along with all this because we've had an unrequited need to climb something, anything, ever since we backed out of climbing Ayer's Rock. There we were at the base of it, primed and ready, but called it off in the name of cultural sensitivity because the Anangu exhorted us to, even after they'd taken our AUD $33. Also, we see while at Climb Central that several celebrities whom we admire or despise have made the climb and found it transformational. So we're in. Or will be, come the crack of tomorrow morning.

■

The people at BridgeClimb have really turned this thing into a science. What a smooth operation! Cookie-cutter, production line, maximum efficiencies, synergistic collaboration, thinking outside the box. It's all going on here. They've thought of everything. We are invited, by a young woman who may have been Dracon in a previous incarnation, into an antechamber where we view the orientation video. She administers a Breathalyzer test on each of us, using plastic disposable whistles. We all pass, even the tall guy and the chubby short girl who have been whispering about how much beer they drank last night. We all complete and sign indemnification forms. These essentially say that: *If I fall off and die, I will not sue; If I break my leg, I will not sue; If I injure myself or anyone else, I will not sue; Under no circumstances will I sue. No way, nuh-uh.* We move through to another area of the complex, put on protective overalls, stand in a circle and introduce ourselves to each other. The first person, Johannah from Boston, tells her entire life story. The rest of us snort and state our names. Now we meet our climb leader, Harry from Dublin, complete with brogue and red hair. He is an aspiring actor. Harry instructs us in donning the safety belts. These will attach us to a sort of guide-wire for the duration of the climb and come between us and certain death if we lose our footing. We are issued caps, sunglasses lanyards, handkerchiefs, and fleece jackets. All these hook up somehow to the suit, so the only way they will fall off the bridge is if their owner is falling also.

This climb is no walk in the park. We're told that there are 1,500 steps, or something like that. Fortunately, we stop often so Harry can tell us the many myths and anecdotes that have grown up with the bridge since its birth in the 1930s. I include in what follows only the least preposterous. There are four cosmetic pylons, two at each end of the bridge. They were erected merely to reassure Sydney's populace, which was unconvinced that the steel structure could hold up under the weight. They needed to see stone. One day in the course of putting up the pylons, George, known for his clumsiness, stays behind while the *moyts* go to lunch. When they return, they find that the cement had set nicely in the pylon, and also that George is gone. They figure he's in there still. It's now called George's Pylon. There's also a story about a guy named Vincent Kelly, the only man to ever survive a fall from the bridge. He was working on the span when he lost his footing and fell forty-five meters to the river. Vincent had the presence of mind to release his tool-belt just before hitting the water. They say it got there just before him and broke the surface tension. This apparently made it possible for him to survive, even if he did sustain a number of injuries. *Note to self: Carry tool belt when falling from great heights.*

After the climb we stroll along Sydney's harbor and stop for breakfast at a café on George Street, where there is a Saturday market underway. The street is closed to traffic and there are more didgeridoos here than you can shake a stick at. These strange musical instruments produce a sound similar to the one you can make by placing your hand under your sweaty armpit and squeezing it repeatedly. Like most things Australian, the didgeridoo involves termites and eucalyptus. The insects hollow out a branch from a eucalyptus tree. I assume that they are evicted before the branch is pressed into musical service.

Sydney Bridesmaids

From here we continue our walk down to Circular Quay and take a ferry to Manly Beach, on the North Shore. It's a bit like Newport Beach, California, but with more surfers. We walk the length of the pedestrian-only Corso and stop for killer ice cream cones. Then, with the sun peeking out and heating us up between stretches of cloud, we fall asleep on the beach. Right there, on the sand. Half an hour. No one bothers us. No one. Not hawkers, not police, not children, not even bugs. We wake up only because it's getting warm. How can you not fall in love with a city where this is possible?

■

The next morning we walk the three blocks from the hotel to Darling Harbor and visit the Sydney Aquarium. It's clear from the start that this is no match to Melbourne's. Too many children, it's Sunday; the seals smell like shit and ammonia; it's too dark; the layout is tiring; and they will not take us for a dive in the shark tank. Sydney Aquarium's gravest offense, however, is having unidentified fish in the tanks. It's maddening trying to match up the fish in an aquarium tank to the illustrated signs placed there—presumably by sensitive adults for exactly that purpose—when they don't correspond. In particularly egregious cases three, four, even more mystery fish swim along with legitimate "labeled" fish, and no clue is given as to their classification. So we make it up. Hump-backed Saddle Squim. Free Range Chicken of the Sea. Tri-color Spanish Fly Swatter. Flusk. Rabbit Horned Dwillip. Schlomo Mollusk. Gerhardt Shrimp.

After a couple of sub-optimal hours at the Aquarium, we hop on the monorail and take the quick trip to Chinatown. How is it that as soon as you enter Chinatown—I first noticed this in New York's—everybody is suddenly Chinese? What happens to the Caucasians that drive in? And how is it that the Chinese disappear when they drive out? Check this out next time you find yourself in a substantial Chinatown. Look around. Everybody is Chinese. This is true in Sydney. We drop into a nice restaurant and, in a distracted moment, order the "Special Beef Noodles." "Special" is a dangerous word. It's often misapplied. Or misunderstood. Or both. Our tendency, being as we are American consumers, is to interpret "special" as something good, at least better than run-of-the-mill. Not so the case here. Based on a thorough inspection of the evidence, we learn that Special Beef is gray, gristly, gooey, gnarly and glandular.

We love Sydney and would come back in a heartbeat. That goes for all of Australia, pretty much, even with the various annoyances: flies in the Outback, mosquitoes at the Top End, and "Special Beef Noodles" in New South Wales.

Auckland, New Zealand, May 2

Exceptional places seem most strikingly so before and after a visit, not as much during. This is an optimistic axiom that I formulate in Auckland because the city appears unexceptional. Our first impression is that it's a bit like downtown Adelaide, but frumpier. It's somewhat messy, like someone forgot to tidy up after the last party. About a third of all New Zealanders live here, so this is no one-horse town. Our second impression is that it's a gambling destination. We're being absolutely unfair because we make this call too soon after we arrive. It's possible that by the time we leave we will have changed our minds. We hope so, but first impressions are what they are. Our earliest inkling that this is a gambling Mecca comes as we pass through the Sky City Casino and make our way to the ground floor reception for Orbit Restaurant. Now things start to look up. A long way up. Sky City Tower is the undisputed tallest structure in the Southern Hemisphere. The view from Orbit Restaurant on the top floor is panoramic and spectacular. This is not to say that it's especially beautiful. There's a harbor, and some hills, and off in the distance a couple of islands. From this elevation, anything looks spectacular, so we reserve judgment. It takes about an hour to complete a revolution. That's faster than the KL Tower, but we soon stop sensing the motion and focus instead on the linguini and chicken-melon salad. The food is surprisingly good. The servers, like the salad, are young and green. None of them know the points of the compass. "North" means nothing. It's "left," or "right," or "over that way, moyt." So we pull out our maps and start navigating. This is a great way to get a complete and immediate orientation when you visit a new town. Just find your way to the very highest point possible, with the best view. You'll wind up with a better sense of the place than most of the people who live there. In Adelaide, this approach also won us a brief conversation with a young local getting stoned in his station wagon.

Auckland is New Zealand's biggest city. The story of its founding involves a transaction in which the land was purchased from the resident Maori people for six British pounds. This was in 1840. I'm not sure what it amounts to in today's money, but sounds like a bargain. This is particularly the case when you consider that the area was known to the Maori as the Land of One Hundred Lovers. Today the city is a busy commercial center. There is a major shipping port, manufacturing, art and culture and all that, but you still get the immediate overwhelming sense that Auckland is not an exciting place. We have data that suggest this is false. It turns out that some of mankind's most exciting people were born here. Among these famous sons and daughters are Sir Edmund Hilary, first man to climb Mount Everest; and Lucy Lawless, better known as *Xena, Warrior Princess*. On the strength of this discovery, we rededicate ourselves to finding the spark in Auckland.

After lunch we head back to our hotel, the First Imperial, for a quick nap. That's a mighty big name to try and live up to: First Imperial. You'd expect lots of flags flapping in the breeze above the wide, gilt front doors. You might think that a doorman will snap his saber against his ample epaulettes merely at the sight of your shoe as it precedes you out of the taxi. Well, this is an okay place, but no First Imperial. Still, the room is acceptably clean and the staff is helpful. The neighborhood is close to Queen Street, which runs through town to the harbor and counts as the city's main commercial street.

■

We're back at Sky City complex tonight to see a play: *Certified Male*. It's a pop-psych self-discovery corporate parable play-musical, starring three young men and one old one, as well as an accompanist on the piano. The theater is beautiful. It's new, and that helps. Comfortable seats, unobtrusive lighting, shallow stairs, and only twenty or so rows, so every seat is a good seat. The play is also good. We worried that we might have trouble with the Kiwi accent but we don't. I just get fidgety in plays featuring several references to the prostate. It shows up for the first time ten minutes into the play. This puts me on edge until intermission, and I cross and uncross my legs compulsively. These guys between them have all of men's ills combined. One drinks, one does drugs, one's pussy-whipped, one's been married and divorced three times and has kids from each consummation. They're all insecure corporate soldiers scared to death of getting canned. Managing them is an older guy who dies at the end, but not before cleverly getting them to bond solidly. Fishing is involved, and beer, and throwing up. We're tired afterwards but stop at one of the restaurants in Sky City and have a late-night pizza. This place never closes. Like Vegas. The gamblers, mostly Japanese and Chinese men, are here round the clock. There are roulette tables and countless one-armed bandits. There's the smell of cigarettes and booze, and carpets that get no rest.

In the morning light of our second day in Auckland, we walk down (actually skip once or twice) Queen Street to the waterfront, and then along Customs Street to Beach Street. Here, in a warehouse long past a serious spring cleaning, we meet the bike we'll be riding through New Zealand during the coming two weeks. It's a

BMW R1100RT. This is the bike we thought we might buy in Australia, back before we decided on the camper-van. It's silver. It has an adjustable windscreen. It has heated grips. It has an ingenious two-part seat: The driver's section can be adjusted to slope forward more or less. If I had to point out one feature that would make me buy the BMW instead of the Honda, it's this front seat adjustability thing. That's because the single most annoying, sometimes painful side-effect of motorcycling is the constriction of blood circulation to the groin. My root chakra is occasionally isolated from the rest of my body when, leaning forward in the seat, I inadvertently bunch up my underwear and create what amounts to a vascular bottleneck. This can bring about a gradual and insidious loss of sensation in the lap region, the discovery of which at 120 km/h can cause panic. The BMW seat adjustment fixes that by allowing me to level the seat against the horizontal, eliminating the "bunching" effect. The second most annoying aspect of motorcycling is cold hands. The BMW R1100RT has heated grips. It's a wonderfully engineered bike. We can't wait to hit the open road, but there is a rain that wants to irritate far more than to irrigate. So, even as we select our helmets, our gloves, and our jackets, I decide to not take the bike today after all, but to wait until tomorrow. Hopefully the weather will have improved somewhat.

On our way back to the hotel we take Fort Street, down by the harbor, and pass a window in which a live woman sits in her underwear. She's obliviously reading something. There's a sign painted poorly on the glass that reads: "Making Dreams Come True." She's a hooker, needless to say, but this catches us somewhat by surprise. It's so un-English. There are many things about this town that surprise us. Auckland's downtown is distinctly Asian. We stop at an Internet place to check email. Most machines in the place are occupied by young Japanese men, and several are playing an online zapping game that apparently requires participants to yelp and screech as though they've been run through with sharp, hot pokers. As you might expect from the Asian proprietors, no attempt is made to quiet the ruffians down. That's just not the Asian way. If the predominant cultural influence were still English, you can bet someone would have long ago thrown a stiff "Do be quiet" at the young men.

We own a New Zealand road atlas now and have pretty much settled on the following route: Auckland, Rotorua, Napier, Wellington, Nelson, Murchison, Greymouth, Queenstown, and finally Christchurch. We'll fly back from Christchurch to Auckland rather than have to ride all the way back, and then on to Tahiti. Something will definitely change in this, but it's fun to sit at this café on Little High Street, sip our cappuccinos, and make lines on a map. After our break we head out into the rain, still here, still damn annoying. So we jump in a cab and make for the Auckland War Memorial Museum. It's an extensive facility that can keep a person busy for days but we only have a couple of hours, so spend them in the exhibits on the country's evolution from a British isle to the independent and much more Asian-influenced country of today.

Our last impression of Auckland is that it's not a place we'd excitedly look forward to seeing again. We don't have an active revulsion for it, as we do for, say, Tangier. However, despite the general friendliness of its natives, it leaves us cold. If the city ever had any charm, it's managed to give most of it up. Now it's a characterless hodge-podge of opportunists from everywhere, mostly East Asia. Some are looking for a job, some for language lessons, some for a better place than where they started out.

Rotorua, New Zealand, May 4

This morning we wait until about 11 a.m. before leaving Auckland, giving the weather as much time as possible to improve. Fortunately, it does. Yesterday the city got a third of all the rain it normally gets in May. This is not so funny anymore. Maybe we do carry a curse. We've flooded just about everywhere we've been on a motorcycle. Now the sun is out and the streets are dry and we're on our way. We start out on the South Expressway, but leave it just past Pukekohe and head east on Highway 2. When Auckland ends and the countryside begins, we see for the first time why people say New Zealand is beautiful. It is quintessentially pastoral. All

Rotorua Country

around are rolling green hills; sheep grazing drowsily; oaks and willows standing right where they ought to, shading cool clean streams. Where there are fences, they're rustic, inoffensive. The road is perfect. If God made Nepal for mountaineers, he made New Zealand for motorcyclists.

We're getting some rain, but it's okay. The good folks at New Zealand Motorcycle Rentals provided rain gear. We each have waterproof jackets, pants, and warm gloves. I can raise and lower the electrically adjustable windscreen with the push of a button. A couple of hours out of Auckland, we stop for a bite at the Halfway Café, alongside a bend in the road, just before the small town of Maramarua. The proprietor, a portly round-faced man in a white apron, is here alone. After making our sandwiches, he joins me for a nice chat about New Zealand. I'm rhapsodizing about the peace, the calm, the serenity, the fields, the sheep, the lovely weather, the hills and dales and picket fences. He says they get a lot of motorcyclists coming through here; mostly Harleys. Then, while I tell him how we lost the Honda in Bombay, he falls asleep in his chair.

■

"What the hell is that smell!?" If you arrived in Rotorua without some pre-knowledge of its claim to fame, you're going to say that. Geothermal activity is what makes it stink. The city is on the banks of Lake Rotorua. There are several other lakes in the area. It earns daily the nickname "Sulfur City." We run into a wall of the stuff. Rotorua is roughly halfway down the North Island, and its busiest tourist destination. We find a room at the Heritage Dynasty. This is a "tour group hotel" that was once the Sheraton. This time of year you pay about seventy dollars a night to stay here. We check in and go to investigate the grounds. It's a big place. They have conference facilities, a gym, and an Internet lounge. They also have thermal water coves, simulated in cement. We spend a couple of hours between the coves, the heated outdoor pool, and the Jacuzzi. By dinnertime, we're nicely pruned up.

We've reserved a table at tonight's *hangi* and concert. This is a buffet dinner followed by a traditional Maori concert. Technically speaking, *hangi* is the Maori equivalent of *tandoori*. It's a hole-in-the-ground oven where embers are used to steam food, suspended above in baskets. It's come to signify a traditional Maori feast. This is not to be confused with *hongi*, the Maori greeting, in which participants press their noses together and "share the breath of life." I have a couple of observations about this custom. First, *ick*. Second, we observed this exact same behavior in the desert of Oman. And we know that the Eskimos do it. It's a small, microbe-rife world after all.

When we walk into the large room where the dinner and concert are being held, several million people are already at the buffet table, shoulder to shoulder, hips to buttocks. We just don't see how we can get in line without becoming suddenly intimate with a perfect stranger from Taiwan, but we're hungry and can't wait to sample the *hangi*. So we bide our time, lie in wait, and shoot into the line ahead of an elderly woman who's fallen and can't get up. Then the show begins. Eight men and eight women, all ages, all sizes, are on the stage, singing and dancing. The women are in beaded skirts. The men are in loin cloths and pelts that look like the one Fred Flintstone wears. The Maori master of ceremonies looks exactly like Fred Flintstone. Come to think of it, so did the guy back at the Halfway Café. How can you not love a country that has at least two Fred Flintstones?

My greatest fear materializes when, after the first number, a few of the men step off the stage and start "volunteering" members of the audience for the traditional *haka* dance. I hate it when this happens. Tracy lifts my arm and I'm soon lined up with a few other tourist men and the Maori dancers. The best thing about the *haka* is that it's not a dance at all. This is good news for me, ambidextrously klutzy. The *haka* is what the Maori did before battle in the days when they were a battling tribe. The object is to make a series of ugly, angry faces and punctuate them with loud cries. Before automatic weapons, this apparently used to scare their enemies. I'm the last in the order. The guy just ahead of me, Japanese I think, coolly steps right up and does a reverse summersault from a standing stop, then lets out a growl that startles me. He impresses the audience so much that they scream for an encore. I follow with a predictably anti-climactic tongue out-sticking.

The Polynesia Spa Resort is heaven on earth. The receptionist welcomes and gives each of us a fresh white bathrobe, then escorts us through the large glass doors to the gardens in the back. There are four thermal pools, ranging in temperature from thirty-three to forty-three degrees Celsius. Ferns and other plants fill the area. Just beyond the pools is Lake Rotorua's Sulfur Bay. It is essential, while soaking in a natural mineral pool, to not dwell on amoebic meningitis. This is a life-threatening condition that develops when certain bugs that live in natural hot spring water find their way inside your nose or ears. They then bore a nice tunnel to your brain, where they proceed to munch on it. It's a slow, painful, hideous death. After soaking for a little while, graduating to the hotter pools as we do, we move inside to the massage center. Then we each get an Aix massage. I don't know if you can actually get one of these in Aix, or if the fine citizens of Provence are aware that there is a massage being offered in New Zealand that borrows the name of one of their towns. We were in Aix-en-Provence last summer and heard nothing about this. It ranks right up there with *pathra sweda* on our list of Massages Worth Undressing For. In the Aix massage, a specially designed shower, or showers, irrigate you continuously as the attendant massages you with warm coconut oil. You and the masseuse wear bathing suits but the continuous shower slowly messes with your mind, leading you to believe that you are naked. There is no extra charge for this feature.

After our massages, we pick up the bike at the hotel even though there's a threat of rain, and ride the few kilometers out of town to the Agrodome. That's right: *Agrodome*. It's a new word, invented in New Zealand because the fathers of English did not foresee a need for a word to describe a building whose sole function is to accommodate the Fabled Fantastic Sheep Show. We arrive just in the nick of time for the 2:30 p.m. performance. Inside, there are two million Japanese and Taiwanese folks, no doubt on the same itinerary as us. The tour buses are lined up in formation outside. We recognize Reverse Summersault Boy.

Now that we're all assembled in the large hall, a wiry man in a jumpsuit runs up on stage. He's an exact replica of Jack LaLane, but taller. Jumpsuit Man wants very badly to draw us in, to get us all just as excited as he is, but the audience is chatty. He appeals for quiet, but they're all wearing headphones, and get their information from one of two interpreters in the back of the room. Jumpsuit Man eventually succeeds, but only when he menacingly waves a pair of shears at the Taiwanese and largest section of the audience. Now, with the help of an assistant, he brings on stage nineteen rams of various breeds. I've always thought that sheep is

Star Merino

sheep. Not so the case. We see Merino, and Drysdale, and Dorset, and Black Romney, and South Suffolk, and all the rest. Some are used primarily for wool production, like the Merino, a kilo of whose wool fetches NZ $70! That's like selling hashish. Others are used for meat production. They're the jumpy ones, always fighting to get to the back of the line.

Wellington, New Zealand, May 6

It sometimes strikes us as incredible that so much of the world has existed without our knowledge. The following account will contain the names of a number of such places. Tonight we're at the Tokaanu Lodge Motel near Lake Taupo. Turangi is the "big" town at this southern end of the lake, but some guys we talked to at a café back in Taupo recommended Tokaanu for thermal baths. This little motel offers reasonably priced, clean rooms, and boasts three private thermal pools. For the first time, we're introduced to a drying room. Water is piped in from the thermal pools and used to heat a shack where clothes can be hung to dry. Perfect, because by the time we arrive we're damp through from a day of "occasional showers." It's very quiet out here. There's no food at the motel, but our host suggests we walk either to the Oasis Café in one direction, or the Tokaanu Hotel in the other. We wind up at the Oasis. It's nothing fancy, just a café with old folding metal tables and chairs. Two old folding Kiwis are at one of the tables. They're having tea and crumpets. We order burgers. Mrs. Oasis cooks and serves up the food, but doesn't crack a smile. Our neighbors, on the other hand, are very friendly. They live on South Island, and are delighted that we're on our way there, where (in hushed tones lest Mrs. Oasis overhears) "it's quieter and friendlier." Any quieter than this and we'd have to be in a morgue. We don't share this sarcastic opinion with the old folks.

The unfortunate highlight of our early evening is a combination puncture-laceration I self-inflict while wrestling with the umbrella in the doorway of the Oasis Café, following that pretty good hamburger dinner. It's a deep cut and bleeding exuberantly. We go back inside and ask Mrs. Oasis if she has any bandages. She looks at me clutching my thumb and mumbles "bad luck," or something that rhymes with that. Mr. Oasis, peeling potatoes in the kitchen, looks over his shoulder to ascertain that it's nothing serious. Just a glimpse, then he's back at his chore. Kiwis are unflappable that way, like the English.

■

We're up early at the Tokaanu Lodge, and raring to go. The weather forecast is right on. After a hundred or so kilometers of mist and light drizzle, we break out into sunny skies and dry pavement. The road south skirts the volcanoes of Tongariro National Park. There are three active volcanoes here. Beautiful. Misty. Dramatic. They're active as well. As hell, occasionally. Most active is Mt. Ruapehu, which had a real hissy fit in 1995–1996, killing the ski season and periodically belching rock, ash, and smoke into the atmosphere. There are two other major mountains, Tongariro and Ngauruhoe. I mention them here only because I find it amusing to try and pronounce these Maori names, and you might too.

The Maori ran New Zealand before the Europeans began arriving in the seventeenth century. The Dutch were here first, followed by the British, who colonized the islands and fought a series of wars with the indigenes from 1843 to 1872. The Maori's fate was sealed, however, when they forged an inter-tribal alliance under King Potatau I. I've wanted very badly to narrate this people's history without reference to the unfortunately-named monarch. Now, though, I realize that "King Potatau" are words that contain the very essence of the fight's one-sidedness. In one corner, Queen Victoria, at the helm of the British Empire and its protectorates on six continents. In the other, King Potatau and warriors who do the *haka*.

Now the sun is behind us. The three mountains are to our right, bathed in early morning sunshine. To our left it's a flat and nearly barren terrain. This section of the highway is known as the Desert Road, and lives up to the name. It's a high desert, cold and windswept, but nothing like the middle of Australia, and we're out of it in less than a quarter tank of gas. We stop for breakfast at the Gumboot Manor Café. "Gum" as in "rubber." In England they call these Wellingtons. We notice a sign on the bulletin board just inside the entrance:

World Gumboot Throwing Records

Men: 62.98 Meters	*Teppo Luoma, Finland*
Women: 40.87 Meters	*Sari Tirkkunen, Finland*

They care about gumboot throwing here. What more proof could anyone want that deception of any kind is utterly unthinkable in this place? There's a middle-aged couple at the table next to ours, having a huge breakfast. I compliment their discriminating culinary *savoir-faire* and we're immediately fast friends. That happens a lot here. Whatever we say, folks we talk to quickly jump into a conversation and display no sense of caution whatsoever. Anyway, these nice people are in the door-hanging business, and are driving to Wellington to install a couple. They live in Taupo and love the pace. They advise us on where to go on South Island, and how to get there. Among their tips is taking a helicopter tour of the glaciers and bungee jumping in Queenstown. We order what they're having.

The rest of our drive to Wellington is just pure pleasure. The road winds along without overdoing it, the hills are not too high, the sun's out now and we're in heaven. We ride past cows and sheep and occasional herds of deer, all grazing contentedly in spacious, thoughtfully fenced pastures. As though to punctuate the wonder of the moment, of the afternoon, God sends us a DC3 airplane that's now a restaurant, hoisted above the road on pillars. It's painted in a chocolate-chip cookie motif, and serves coffee and dessert. Words fail.

■

Now we're in Wellington and staying at the Novotel Hotel on Terrace Avenue. It's in the hills overlooking the city and, beyond it, the harbor. We're staying here because the manager had nothing to do when we arrived, so gave us a magnificent welcome, a good tour of the place, and a symbolic discount. He also laughed, or at least chuckled at the several clever things I said.

Wellington is built on the brief flat and the surrounding hills, in an incomplete circle, around Lambton Harbor. There is a cable car that starts downtown at Lambton Quay and climbs the hill west of town up to the Botanical Gardens and the neighborhood of Kilburn. It makes a couple of stops en route and we catch it on the way up. There's also a restaurant up here, and we drop in for a coffee and cookie. Cities on bodies of water are lucky. This is all the more true if the body of water happens to be gorgeous, like here in Wellington. The weather is perfect. The view is superb. We're here in the quieter tourist season and don't have to wait in any lines anywhere. At the bottom end of the cable car, we happen by Bond Store. Back when NZ was a colony of the Crown, this is where goods were stored after being unloaded from ships, until Her Majesty's required customs charges were paid. They've converted the building into the Museum of Wellington City and Sea.

One exhibit in particular blows us away. You walk into a dark room. A small stage of sorts is installed at one end of it, and on this stage several nautical artifacts are arranged like a still-life, under indirect lighting. Books, mirrors, candelabra, a compass, a section of rope, and so on. When the show begins, the figure of a woman materializes on this stage. She's a hologram. The woman, sized down to fit on this stage, is choreographed to appear as though she's in the midst of the objects. She disappears behind a book and reemerges on the other side. She passes behind a green glass bottle and her white dress takes on its color. As this lovely miniature spirit in white walks the small stage, she narrates the Maori myth of creation. Two other characters appear—*Papa* (Earth) and *Rangi* (Sky), holographic Maoris—and help play it out.

At the end of our visit, we chat with one of the people at the museum's reception desk. He's delighted that we're impressed, and insists that we go have a look at Te Papa, on the other side of the harbor. There's an embarrassment of cultural riches in a city where one museum recommends another. We stroll along the harbor to get there. Joggers are out for their lunch breaks. It's a lovely day in Wellington. This is the seat of New Zealand's government, so we see lots of suits and ties, but nobody really means it that way. It's just a uniform. The real Wellington is casual, relaxed, friendly, and there are more hip coffee shops per capita than anywhere we've been since France.

Westport, New Zealand, May 8

To get an accurate sense of the difference between two nations, say Indonesia and New Zealand, just try their ferries. The ones we took between the Indonesian islands threatened to disintegrate at any moment. They were arthritic hulks. By contrast, The Lynx is a brand new wave-piercing Catamaran. It was built in the year 2000 at Hobart, Australia, and registered at Wellington, New Zealand. She (nautically speaking) can carry 840 passengers and 230 vehicles, is ninety-eight meters long and twenty-six meters wide. Our on-board brochure assures us that:

> It offers not just a quick way across Cook Strait, but also the smoothest and most luxurious way! The Lynx is equipped with a Hi Tech ride control system allowing stabilizers to react to sea conditions (minimizing roll), and a wave-piercing twin hull which adds to the stability and smoothness of the vessel. Travel time across Cook Strait is just 135 minutes. Your onboard crew are here to ensure you have a great journey.

All this is absolutely true. The trip across Cook Strait is a calm, quiet, uneventful affair. The ship is steady as she goes. The Novotel hotel clerk in Wellington had warned us that it could be a nasty ride, and that The Lynx was nicknamed "Vomit Comet." Not today. Still, it's never far from our minds that in 1968, right in Wellington Harbor, fifty-one people died when the Wahine inter-island ferry went down in bad weather. That's the bad news. The good news is that seven hundred survived.

Wellington Harbor

After crossing the strait, we sail through Tory Channel. This is not more than five hundred meters across. To our left is the Picton peninsula, run through with fjords. To our right, Blumine Island. Suddenly there's a great commotion, squealing, and the stomping of clodhopper feet in unrealistically high-heeled sneakers. A school trip comprising fifty or so youngsters is on board. One of them believes she's seen a whale, so they stampede through the ship looking for it. We exit the channel into Queen Charlotte Sound. The sea is calm as we drift quietly into Picton Harbor. We have about 350 kilometers to do on the bike today, and it's already 10:30 a.m.

The very best thing about Westport is getting there and away. What a magnificent ride! This is possibly the most fun I've ever had riding a motorcycle with my clothes on. The road from Picton to Westport cuts across the northern end of South Island, coast to coast. We take it south to Blenheim then turn East on Highway 63, which runs along the Wairau River. Then, at St. Arnaud, we pick up the Buller River and Highway 6 and follow it all the way to the west coast. These are all two-lane country roads, the kind we hunt for when we're riding because they're away from traffic and crowds, and because they offer the best scenery. It's not just the road, though. Everything today works together to make it an exceptional riding experience. It's about twenty Celsius. There's no rain at all, and the pavement is dry. It's occasionally just a bit breezy, but not disturbingly so. Traffic is incredibly light. Judging by how many times we passed each other, there are only five or six of us on this road today. The very best part of the ride is the Buller Gorge, between Murchison and Westport. We stop at Murchison for a coffee and snack, and strike up a conversation with the owner of the café. I tell him how much we've enjoyed the ride so far. He says, "Wait till you get to the gorge." And how! This stretch of road is impossibly picturesque. The river cuts a breathtaking path between the mountains, and everywhere is green. In some places, the road is reduced to one narrow lane that hangs from the side of the rock. Every so often we ride underneath basaltic overhangs that extend out beyond the road. Even though it's meters above us, we find ourselves instinctively ducking.

Westport itself is a small, entirely flat, colorless place. Everything is one story high and built from particle board. All shop signs are hand-lettered by a guy named Guy. He likes to make a curlicue with the tail of the "y." The main street, Palmerston, has all the businesses on it. The Tourist Information Office is moderately helpful. Two ladies are behind the counter, and we're the only trade in town. They find us very amusing. I think they realize that we don't have the first idea how slow an evening it's going to be.

After settling in at the Westport Motor Lodge, we stroll down the street from the motel to Bailey's Bar, where they will barbecue a steak for you, or you can do it yourself. It's true. Barbecue your own: NZ $14. Have it barbecued: NZ $18. The regulars are at the bar or shooting pool. It's a quiet crowd and they all know each other. Even in the high season, I can't imagine Westport getting too many tourists. Its primary industry is coal mining. They have one or two things we could do, including a tour of the coal mine. Maybe some other lifetime.

We're going to the movies tonight at the Saint James Theatre. The owner shows up at 7:30 and sells tickets to the 8 p.m. show. We're seeing something called *Saving Grace*. Fifteen or so people are here for the film. They're all local. We know because they greet each other by name. Also because they know to jump up at the end of the first reel and run out to the foyer for the popular chocolate-dipped ice cream cones. Tracy and I hesitate, thinking that maybe the break is accidental and that the film will restart, so we miss the ice cream. The film is set in a small English fishing village. The audience, including us, is clustered in the best seats in the middle of the hall. We laugh together at the funny bits. One woman gets up to go pee and says, "Gotta pee, 'scuse."

Franz Josef, New Zealand, May 10

Westport to Franz Josef is three hundred kilometers. Three hundred kilometers of motorcycling that I would be happy to do over and over until I've memorized every last breathtaking seascape; every sweet, cambered turn; every tunnel of lush rainforest; every meadow. I think we approached having the Perfect Motorcycle Ride today.

We set out early and are alone on the road until Punakaiki. After the first seventy-five kilometers, we're ready for breakfast, so we pull in at the Wild Coast Café next door to the Tourist Information Center. We're in the kind of mood that's inspired by beauty. We're mellow. Good thing, because the young woman behind the counter has no fear of irony and uses it in every sentence. The subject of her mirth, now that she knows we come from the U.S., is the U.S. She must have spent some time studying this, because she has all our social ills in her crosshairs. We get ribbed about obesity, drug abuse, urban crime, homelessness, alcoholism, traffic congestion, Bill Clinton, George Bush (both), foreign policy, and the obscene strength of our dollar against the Kiwi. She has a galloping case of contempt for Americans' proclivity for eggs cooked to order. We can have ours sunny side up. Or poached. End of story.

The great attraction at Punakaiki is the Pancake Rocks and Blowholes. If you've managed to make life work so far without knowing about stylobedding, you'll

Pancake Rocks

care very little that it's a peculiar rock-formation process. It happens to be the way these rocks came to look like pancakes, tall stacks of them. The edges are irregular, so don't imagine round flapjacks. Rather, these look like pancakes that might have been poured into a too-hot skillet by someone with a serious case of withdrawal. Or even more like cow patties, dropped from the usual height. There's a whole bunch of these, piled up into towers reaching thirty or so meters. The New Zealand Department of Conservation (DOC) has constructed a path that takes us among the cow patties and then back to the road. The blowhole requires high tide to perform, so it's quiet now. Maybe the waitress was trying to compensate.

■

If you'd asked me three months ago where the Southern Alps were, I'd have said "Italy?" Well, they're actually here in New Zealand. From Greymouth on south, we're flanked to the east by them. This is a mountain range that runs nearly the length of South Island, on the west coast, and contains several peaks taller than three thousand meters. It's from these that the Franz Josef and Fox glaciers emerge and tumble in suspended animation down to the coast. Franz Josef village is like a modest ski resort. A handful of hotels are clustered around the three or four restaurants and the one petrol station. Several tour and helicopter operators line the main and only street. There is no bank. You can get cash against your credit card at the souvenir shop, but they charge a 5 percent service fee. The whole town would fit with room to spare in a New York City block.

Franz Josef glacier is basically a river of ice, flowing very, very slowly from the Southern Alps to the Tasman Sea. Glaciers were formed several years ago, and serve no practical purpose. Kiwis, however, never ones to let a good thing go by, have converted this one to a playground for the young and the able-to-pay. You can walk up the glacier, but only for a short distance. That's because there is a segment of every glacier called the "icefall." It's where the smooth river of ice coming down the mountain begins to crack under the weight of tourists and helicopters. If you happen to be on the icefall when it comes apart, you'll slide into one of the massive cracks that result, and the last words you'll hear will be your own. A second method for becoming familiar with a glacier is to get a ride up there on a helicopter, then walk down. They call these "helihikes." And finally, you can just take a helicopter ride up to the stable part of the glacier, the "neve," disembark for a

Franz Josef Glacier

quick snapshot, then head back down to the village for a "strong flat white." We choose this last option, partly because neither of us has ever been in a helicopter, and partly because we've seen some of the Svens and Heidis clomping around town in their climbing gear and realize that this would be work.

Our flight up to the glacier takes off at 10:30 a.m., or sometime around that. There's no great official imperative to follow a schedule. It's the slow time of year and the tour operators are happy as hell to see us. It's the two of us, a young dark-haired heavy-hipped English girl from Islington, and a local climb guide hitching a ride. At the pilot's signal, we lower our heads and walk up to the helipad. It's mildly surprising to discover that a helicopter ride is not nearly as uncomfortable as it sounds. That *thuppa-thuppa-thuppa* thing does not translate to an annoying jerkiness in flight. In fact, it's very smooth. Our pilot, Mike, is relaxed and efficient as he makes a criss-cross meandering flight path up the slope. After clearing the trees and cresting the icefall, we see the broad neve spread out in the lap of the mountain. It's white, virginal, but not a place you'd want to spend any time without a Jacuzzi. From the air we see a second helicopter, on the ice. It looks like a mosquito.

You can't go far wrong in a village like Franz. Everything you need is right here on this short main drag. Unless it's a bank, hospital, fire department, or cinema. The nearest doctor is fifty kilometers away. The people are all friendly. I've run out of descriptives for this part of New Zealand. It is inexpressibly beautiful. Every time we get on the bike and roll, we're dazzled.

Kawarau River Suspension Bridge, New Zealand, May 12

I accept that bungy jumping carries with it some degree of risk; both to the person, property and emotional trauma of friends and family spectating. Knowing of the risk I still wish to register and participate in bungy jumping and so expressly agree to assume the risk of injury, damage or trauma to loved ones while participating in this activity.

That's the first paragraph of A.J. Hackett Bungy's disclaimer. I don't read the rest because I don't want to change my mind at this late stage. The heavy-eyed, crimson-haired boy at the weigh-in counter says, "Doynt bothah; ut just sez that yu want to jump off the brudge, aynd thet we'll luk aftah yu." That is exactly the right attitude to have in the extreme sport industry. You must be relaxed, seemingly nonchalant, cool, nearly stoned. It keeps the customers calm. Like the two guys who meet me on the bridge and do all the tying up of things. They both look like they just woke up from their naps. As we stroll out to mid-span together, they take their sweet

See Ya, Moyt!

time, cracking jokes, yawning. Then, when the three of us squeeze under the bridge rail and step onto the jump platform, they perform their pre-dive activities unhurriedly. These guys, for all their apparent sloth, are professionals. They bind my ankles with an old navy blue towel for protection, then wrap that with an orange climbing rope, at the end of which there is a metal clasp. The clasp is hooked onto another clasp that's been just sitting there, waiting. The bungee rope extends from there and drips over the edge of the jump platform; the same edge I will soon drip off myself. I look to the observation deck and there's Tracy, camera in hand, preparing to memorialize my folly. Finally, I topple slowly upwards to my bound-together feet and inch up to the precipice. One of the guys says, "See ya, moyt." I dive.

Bungee jumping is scary as hell. Fortunately, there is no possibility of soiling yourself doing it, on account of gravity going in the opposite direction from where your lower parts are facing when you dive. Also, doing it in places like the Kawarau River valley brings the redeeming value of beautiful scenery. In my own distracted state, as I stand on the brink, the following thought actually crosses my mind: "Well, if I do fall to my death, at least it'll be in a nice place." This demented stunt—calling it a sport is like calling astrology a science—evolved from a tribal ritual practiced from time immemorial, or a few years later, by the people of the island-nation of Vanuatu. The young men of the island perfected a rite of passage that was a precursor to today's bungee jumping. I can vouch for all this; I've seen it on TV. They construct tall towers from bamboo. Then they climb to the top, attach a couple of vines to their ankles, and jump off. Some—the guys with flawed depth perception—crash into the ground. They're the ones who miss the sequel. We've come a long way, and now bungee jumping is nearly a science. Every jumper is weighed and the bungee cord is set up accordingly. It's so refined a process, in fact, that you can ask to touch the water with your hand, or dunk your torso. They have it down to this degree of precision. I ask that no part of me be allowed to come in contact with any part of the river at any speed. The boys tying me up find this uproariously funny. This company, A.J. Hackett Bungy, is big business. The jump I do, off the Kawarau river bridge, is the oldest in existence. They established it in 1988. There are other operators and other jumps. Soon it will be possible to jump from hot air balloons. Here in the Queenstown area, you could do the world's highest (for now): the Nevis Highwire Bungy. It's 134 meters above the Nevis River. You jump from a "pod" that is suspended above the river on cables spanning the valley like clotheslines across an alley. To reach the pod, you ride a gondola from the edge of the rock face to the center. A.J. Hackett Company operates this jump as well. In their brochure, a woman from the UK is quoted as saying that the jump is "better than sex."

There are several things about bungee jumping that you will not find in official publications and operator brochures. Here they are:

- Decline the offer to wear a crotch harness, or you might well enjoy the world's deepest wedgie.

- Make sure your dentures are solidly in place or you may lose them after the initial yank. Worse, you may swallow them on the way down.

- Don't get too comfortable after the first bounce. There are three more coming. To spectators, it seems like it's over quickly. To you, after you know that you've survived, you just want to be upright again. Unless you're the above-mentioned woman from the UK, in which case you'll be trying to work that last little shudder out of the thing.

- If you're wearing glasses, take them off, or secure them to your person. I saw a guy jump with his shades on, then struggle to recover them as they flew off his face after the first bounce. It's unseemly for a daredevil to wriggle and grope like that.

- If you're afraid of heights, what the hell are you doing up here?

- If you're overweight, plan for parts of you to stop traveling before others, and for small collisions to occur all over your person during the jump. To prevent this, wear tight clothing, but not too tight; you could herniate a zipper.

- If you're underweight, it's possible that your pointier bones will tent up your skin in places, and that you will look like you've just been taken off a metal hanger after a long period of disuse.

- Do not be alarmed when you realize that the mean age of everyone waiting to jump is twenty-two. Unless you're older than that.

- Take a deep breath before jumping; it'll be your last for a while.

At the end, when all the bouncing has stopped and you've been reeled into the recovery boat like a record tuna, do not expect any more attention from anyone. You're old news. The next jumper gets all the attention now, even from your significant other or loved ones on the observation deck. Just deal with it. This fact of life is perhaps one explanation for why people go on to do more jumps after their first. They're after the attention. As for me, once I was on my feet again at the bottom of the ravine, there was now the matter of walking all the way back up. I find, as I do so, that I am now walking with renewed machismo. It is not a great surprise when Tracy later says, as we make our way to the bike, "Well, look at you, walkin' all cool and everything." What can I say? You go jump from a bridge and see if you don't walk different.

Queenstown, New Zealand, May 13

Here in Thrill City almost every entertainment on offer involves a safety harness. The town, with not even ten thousand residents, has made itself Capital of Adrenaline Sports. Back in Rotorua, Fear of Lanolin was about the limit of personal challenge. In Queenstown, however, every fear is trotted out and exercised. Standing on a bridge or a ledge or a cliff and preparing to launch yourself into thin air you fear not just the immediate peril, but also the colossal embarrassment that would follow should you get hurt. This happened to some Dutch kid the other day. He had been taking paragliding lessons. Paragliding is where you walk off the side of a mountain and are kept afloat by a parachute shaped like a banana. These things are much more maneuverable than ordinary parachutes and allow you to change speed, direction, and aspect at will. Almost. This young man failed to change one of the above variables soon enough and found himself suspended from high-tension wires at the base of the mountain. He's lucky that he did not get electrocuted. He's lucky that Queenstown has the emergency personnel to respond. He's lucky that the citizens whose power was interrupted did not come down and lynch him.

As soon as we arrive in Queenstown and find a hotel, we head up to the highest point in town, Bob's Peak (790 m.). There's a cable-car that takes you there, and the view along the way is breathtaking. From up here we look east over Lake Wakatipu. All around it are mountains. Serious peaks, reaching three thousand meters and more. The Remarkables, every bit the name, run along the far bank of the lake, a dark and dramatic backdrop. Bob has several other places named after him around here. There's Bob's Creek, Bob's Marina, and Bob's Noodles. We don't yet know Bob's last name. Could be different Bobs. Queenstown is like that, though: a first-name-basis kind of town. It's a place where everyone is laid way back. Dress code is kamikaze casual.

New Zealand, I'm sure now, is the most beautiful country in the world. There are others with more dramatic mountains, more picturesque lakes, richer rain forests, bluer oceans and greener meadows. None, though, combine an abundance of natural beauty with a small population, a democracy, modern services, good food, and great coffee.

■

Hang-gliding, in simplest terms, is flying as nearly like a bird as you can imagine. It may be even better, because no flapping at all is required. We are picked up at our hotel by one of the flyers, John, and learn along the way to Coronet Peak that

he competes in this sport. Not only that, he currently shares the world title in a particular aspect of it, having to do with steep dives and slicing at great speed between two stone pylons. That's more than we want to know right now. We also pick up Jeff and Carl. The former is the boss. He flies as well. We drive to the ski station on Coronet Peak, just north of Queenstown. Here, in a clearing that comes to a steep slope, Jeff and John go about setting up the gliders. Hang gliders are a lot like tents. You erect them by sliding light-weight metal

Ready to Fly

alloy skeletal members into fabric sheaths. Eventually, when you've found a sheath for every rib, spoke, strut, spine, and spar, you're ready to fly. The suits we wear are like hammocks. During flight we lie in them, and a set of ropes collects us up to a ring in the frame of the glider. That's why they call them *hang*-gliders. There's a vaguely marsupial feeling about all this. Our instructions are clear:

- At the end of a reverse count from three, take two steps and then run like Medusa's on your tail.
- Do not touch the metal triangle holding the glider together. It is also the steering wheel.
- If you must throw up, look left, away from the driver.

Everything else is secondary, and we soon learn why. Once you've run down the side of the hill and taken off, there is really very little you need to do until it's time to land. The machine is easy to navigate. You use the metal bar in front of you to shift the weight of your body in the direction you want the glider to go. Shift left, go left. Shift right, go right. Shift forward, go faster. Shift backwards, stall! Shift in any direction quickly, and you will magnify these results. Jeff has been flying for twelve years. It's natural that "just gliding" would not provide him with any degree of personal satisfaction. So as soon as we're high enough off the ground to die should we crash, he undertakes a series of stalls and dives to illustrate the capabilities of the machine for me. It is absolutely thrilling to swoop. We buzz the tree-tops on the hillside. We buzz the hillside itself. We even buzz a fence no higher than a goat. This all happens in the first three minutes, after which we settle into a nice relaxed downward spiral. You lose lift quickly when you do aerobatics like we do. Tracy and John took off before us and have now landed. I can see them in a field down below; they look microscopic. Jeff says that's his backyard. Nice commute! As we come in for our landing, I realize for the first time that we will actually be using our bodies as landing gear. Sure, there are two small tires on the cross-bar up front, but these are insufficient. That's why our hammocks have leather and padding underneath. Still, consider coming in to a landing, face-first, no more than cow pie high above the ground, at 50 km/h. It's memorable. Unforgettable, even.

Christchurch, New Zealand, May 15

There's a story in the paper today about a Queenstown man who left a few years ago and settled in northern India. He did it because he had become an adrenaline addict and realized that he could only fix the problem by getting well away. That's Queenstown. The story does not have a happy end. It seems that once there, he started a hang-gliding business, and has now spawned a small industry of young local men eager to make a living from the sport. We've been helicoptering, bungee jumping, hang-gliding, luge-ing, and horseback riding, not to mention motorcycling several hundred kilometers. It's one thrill-filled pursuit after another, one death-defying stunt after the next. We've spent a great deal of time in thin air, relying on various toys to thwart gravity. That's just the way it is in Queenstown. On the one hand, we're sorry to be leaving. On the other, we're looking forward to staying close to the ground for a few days running.

Motorcycle Country

After leaving Queenstown, we ride across some very dry and desolate countryside. Still beautiful, but no longer green and lush. We're in the plains east of the Southern Alps, in their rain shadow. There are straight stretches in this road and no one around to get in the way, so we break the speed limit repeatedly and with impunity. We go as fast as 180 km/h once or twice, but pull back because it's senseless. Also because New Zealand police employ "speed cameras." These ingenious devices are installed in places where speeding happens. We know because, like the civilized country that it is, New Zealand posts signs that alert you to the fact that a speed camera is coming up. If you still go too fast, you and your motorcycle are photographed *flagrante delicto* and the evidence is delivered to you in the mail, along with a request for a fat fine payment.

We ride into Christchurch in the rain. This is never the best way to see a city for the first time. It's cold, windy, and wet. The same storm that played with us all the way from Tekapo is now sitting on top of Christchurch, so the town appears dreary and uninviting. The storm is a southerly. These come up from Antarctica. That puts into perspective just how far we are from the rest of the world. We're closer to Antarctica than we are to any other substantial landmass, with the exception of Australia. Christchurch is the official supply station for manned Antarctic stations. It's a long way to come for a pizza. We stop at the impressive and helpful Tourist Information Office at Cathedral Square, and they get us a room at Rydges Hotel, just around the corner. Apart from being central, it's the closest hotel to where we are right now, and we are desperate to get off the bike and into a hot shower.

Christchurch is New Zealand's second largest city, after Auckland. It's flat and quite sedate. We walk around the city center and find very little of note, except for Starbucks. The cathedral is interesting, mostly for the climb up to the tower, from the top of which you can confirm that Christchurch is flat and uninspiring. There are a few other things you can do here, including a punt on the Avon River, but it's no Queenstown or Wellington, having neither the range of activities of the former nor the stunning natural setting of the latter. The tourist literature suggests that Christchurch is the most "English" of New Zealand's cities. Maybe so, but not to the point where you'd notice. We do get ourselves onto a punt for a very docile and pleasant push up the river and back. We pass under weeping willows. More cities should plant weeping willows along their rivers. No other tree delivers as much pastoral ambience for the buck. Ducks and their ducklings study us from their nests in the reeds along the bank. Punt Man, the young, chubby redheaded Kiwi who is powering our boat, is a bubbly tub of information and wisdom. We learn all about New Zealand beer culture. A "couple" of beers with the "moyts" is usually about eight. Most of his friends drink lager. It seems that stout, Guinness in particular, has played a role in most of their premature divorces and other personal calamities. We also learn all about the sorry state of the New Zealand economy, why living off the "dole" isn't all bad, why he's relocating to Kuala Lumpur in a couple of months, and where to have lunch.

Roasted chestnuts have made their debut in Christchurch to a rather cold-shouldered reception. I'm beside myself with excitement when I see the forlorn-looking man near the oversized chess set in Cathedral Square. His real business is selling packaged nuts from a barrow but he's decided to diversify. The chestnut roasting division of his operation is fledgling. He has the chestnuts in a small wok with holes in the bottom, under which a few chunks of charcoal provide enough heat to cook them. His nuts, though, are small and uneven. Compared to the extravaganzas we saw in Rome and Istanbul, this is small fry indeed. When I reach him, a matronly local woman is already there, holding up a chestnut and surveying it carefully and bemusedly from all angles. This is novel fruit here. She has a few questions. The man answers patiently and courteously from behind his orange wrap-around sunglasses. She thanks him, returns the sample to the wok, and moves on. Maybe next time. His first question to me is, "Do you know what these are?" I explain that I am a chestnut connoisseur, and that I have sampled chestnuts in Paris, Rome, Istanbul, Beirut, and Athens. He sells a baker's dozen for NZ $2, but shovels up more than that into a newspaper cone, undoubtedly impressed by my résumé. He's self-taught, as is evident from the absence of any sort of slit in the skin of the chestnuts. The result, as all expert chestnut roasters will tell you, is that the nuts are charred badly by the time they're cooked at all, but every other one of these is pretty good. I thank him and wish him luck. It seems odd to me that he is not overrun with customers on a chilly day such as this. On the way back to the hotel I share my discovery with the proprietors of the photo shop that's developing our film. The two middle-aged men have no idea what I've just offered them. The thinner, older one, actually says "Chestnut," but pops the whole thing in his mouth, shell and all, before I can stop him. The other man nods agreeably, but has never been this close to a chestnut before. He's noticed the vendor selling them in the square, but admits to being a conservative Kiwi, not anxious to try something new. He holds the nut away from his face like it's liable to nip at his nose, and keeps it there for the duration of my visit. I'm guessing that he eventually tossed it or gave it to his pal.

On our last day in Christchurch, we take ourselves to the Court Theater, and see *Pussyfinger Says No to Tomorrow.* The theater is in an old colonial-style building, and that's part of the attraction. The play is a spoof on James Bond movies. We're in a polite, easy-going, casually dressed audience, like you might find at a small theater in Washington D.C. We laugh together, sometimes obligingly, as the three young stars go through the physical comedy routines that make up for the script. At the end we filter out of the theater and thread our way up Worchester Street back to the hotel. It's a pleasant, dry night in Christchurch. As we walk, a feeling of familiarity comes over us. A feeling that if we lived here, we might be making this walk every once in a while, and would recognize all the buildings that we pass. It's enough to scare the pulse out of a person.

New Zealand is right up there on our list of favorite countries, along with the U.S., Australia, Switzerland, and Oman. Its unique and unlikely attraction is that it has a good deal of good from each of these places, and little of the bad. We would not leave here to relocate in Northern India, or even Northern England.

Tahiti, French Polynesia, May 17 (Again)

We woke up tomorrow in Christchurch, but it soon becomes today, and we get to live May 17 and 18 all over again. This kind of time-warp happens when a person crosses the International Date Line (IDL), an imaginary line that runs through the Pacific Ocean, north to south, just east of New Zealand. It addresses the problem of time-travel. New Zealand is twelve hours ahead of Greenwich Mean Time, i.e., London. As we travel east, local time advances one hour for every fifteen degrees of latitude. Without the IDL, local time would continue to advance at a rate that allows indefinite avoidance of consequences. The reverse is true. We would be able to travel west, back in time, and relive all our mistakes. The IDL solves this with a back-to-the-future correction. When you cross this magical convention going east, you step back in time exactly twenty-four hours. Now you begin to travel forward in time again, and every fifteen degrees of latitude adds one hour to local time. Tahiti is twenty-two hours behind Auckland, and we get the benefit of going through parts of May 17 and May 18 all over again. Whereas yesterday we were sixteen hours ahead of Washington, today we're six hours behind it. There is no better place on earth for kiting checks.

Qantas Flight QF3343 is a Boeing 747 jumbo jet. We are in seats 1H and 1K. If you look at one of these behemoths from the outside, you'll note that the cockpit is on the second floor; up there in the cranial swelling, and that at least one row of seats on the main level is farther forward in the nose. That's us. We're in the cone. It's a good place to be for a number of reasons, chief among them that no one can recline into us. Also we're the first to arrive in Papeete, the capital of Tahiti. It's 9 p.m. and dark.

We're staying at the Royal Tahitien, just west of downtown Papeete. The hotel is between the main coast road and the sea, so our first night in this "tropical paradise" is nearly sleepless. Traffic in Papeete is heavy until the very small hours. In the morning we find our way to the side of the road and get on *Le Truck*. These are just that, trucks that have been converted to carry passengers. The back is now a wooden *salon* with equally wooden seats running the length of it. The windows are always open, and that's a good thing. Our fellow *Le Truckers* are a likely cross-section of the local citizenry, or at least that segment of the citizenry that will take *Le Truck*. Everyone, including us, is in open-toed shoes, sandals, flip-flops, and such. It makes for a happier population, we've found, when shoes are optional. Dress here follows the climate, which is warm and dry or warmer and wet. Everybody's armpits are showing. Lots of people wear tattoos and flowers. We take *Le Truck* into downtown Papeete. The fare is 120 CPF, or about a U.S.

Tahiti Panorama

dollar. You pay when you get off, because the driver is up front and you can only get to him from *Le Outside.*

Papeete stinks. And not just literally. The restaurants here—and the shops, and traffic, and everything else about it—are shabby, but in a sweaty, dirty kind of way. We stroll around the waterfront and the streets that radiate from it, looking for a *croissant.* You'd think a place like Papeete, full as it is of French people, might have an abundance of *patisseries.* Well, it hasn't. There are some cafés, but most are bars that convert to cafés in the morning, long before the must of stale beer and cigarettes has subsided. One or two have outside seating, so we go there. Don't imagine fashionable cafés where you can get a thick, creamy cappuccino in a fat cup and saucer while Charles Aznavour serenades someone on the CD player. There is nothing even faintly stylish about Papeete. It's clear that there is very little for us here, so we rent a car from Avis and hit the road.

Driving around Tahiti is a lot like driving around Hawaii and Bali and other volcanic islands. There's a road that goes all along the coast, clear around the island. There are also a few roads that go up into the hills, up the volcano, and one that actually gets you approximately across the island's middle. We decide to take the circumnavigational approach, the one that goes through all the villages. There are actually two islands: Tahiti Nui (Tahiti Big) and Tahiti Iti (Tahiti Small). From the air, Tahiti Nui looks like a turtle with its arms and legs pulled in, or off. Tahiti Iti looks like the turtle's head. There is a narrow isthmus that's the turtle's neck, connecting the Nui and the Iti. The turtle looks north, toward Bora Bora. The coast road is a good one. One lane in each direction, but traffic is light. This is important, because one of the main tourist attractions is actually in the road. About thirty kilometers west of Papeete there is a blowhole for which tourist buses beeline. It's in the base of the rock that forms a wall on the inside of a hairpin curve. The beach is on the other side. When a sufficiently large swell or wave happens, the sea forces air through a volcanic passage, and out into the street. Small bands of visitors scram and hobble across the street and hug the wall long enough to experience this rush of air. Then they cross back. You'll read about this in the papers one day.

One of the towns we go through is Hitiaa. As we approach from the direction of Papeete, we're struck by an old church tower at the edge of town. It's become overgrown with vines and makes for a good picture, so we pull over. The church is abandoned. Its large, front wooden door is rotted almost completely off its rusted hinges. There are four tall windows on each side of the single long nave. All the glass has long since been removed or knocked out. I walk in toward the altar. Tracy stays in the doorway taking pictures. Now four children, three boys and a girl, pop up in the windows on

Tahiti Church

one side of the church, shouting *bonjour* and other French things. By the time I reach the altar, they've all crawled into the church and swarmed around me, happy unkempt urchins, hair still wet, I guess from swimming. I ask if they shouldn't be in school, and they explain that it's a holiday. They're eleven or so years old. We have no trouble conversing in French. I notice that the altar is made of coral. It's actually made of cement, but inlaid with coral that has been painted over. Very funky place. The children explain that this church is abandoned, and that a new one has been built down the road. Then they ask me for money, *des sous*, a few pennies. These are not desperate, hungry, unhappy children. It's not begging, exactly, what they're doing, but rather a supplementation of their current means. I give them each fifty francs, about forty U.S. cents, and they break into a race across the street to the town store.

We go on and spend the following three hours driving along the coast or being lost in the hills of Tahiti Iti, on dirt roads. It's a peaceful, relaxing place. Better, in this way, than Bali. There isn't the mad traffic and pollution here. On the way back into town we stop at a public beach. An elderly European couple is asleep in the shade at the crest of the beach dune. A young man and his kids have taken the family horse into the surf and are bathing it. A topless young Polynesian woman sunbathes a few meters away. There's a big group barbecuing something up by the trees. Stray dogs sniff harmlessly about.

Tahiti has always stood for tropical paradise, just like Bali. It's time to fix this misconception, once and for all, and to extrapolate a more contemporary view of life. Some of these "tropical paradises" of days gone by are now only marginally paradisiacal. This may seem harsh, but is absolutely the case. The good news is that Tahiti is just one island and that there are 117 other islands that make up the rest of French Polynesia. These are clustered into four archipelagos and, if you count the water in between, cover an area the size of Europe! Some of these are undoubtedly still unspoiled tropical paradises. Our money is on Bora Bora.

Bora Bora, French Polynesia, May 24

Bora Bora from the air is unimaginably beautiful. It consists of an island completely encircled by a lagoon and outer reef. The waters of the lagoon are aqua, turquoise, sapphire, powder blue, sky blue, jade, navy, and white. All these colors are here. We're very fortunate to fly in on a clear day. The view is stunning. This is more like it! Bora Bora's airport is on a small island, a *motu* that crops up out of the encircling reef. From here there is a shuttle boat that ferries passengers across the lagoon to the main island and its capital of Vaitape. The trip takes just fifteen minutes. The pier is busy with people holding up signs welcoming arrivals. A young woman is here to meet us from TOPdive Resort. Taina picks us right out of the crowd and lassoes each of us with a garland of fragrant white flowers. They call them *tiare*. It's a very nice touch. The road to the hotel is narrow and very basic. There are a few small businesses along it, like a pharmacy and grocery store. There are also some houses, more like shacks. A few dogs stroll aimlessly, sometimes in the middle of the road. Everything is green and very primitive. To our left we see the lagoon, and occasional fishing huts and boats hanging above the water from pulleys. To our right a massive mangled rocky outcrop that was once a volcano.

■

We wake up to a sunny morning. On the lagoon, powerboats carry people out to the *motus*. After breakfast, we go diving. That's why we're here. Ten of us, including Vincent and Marcus the dive masters, are on one of the smaller dive boats. It's a bit cramped but we travel just twenty minutes before reaching Manta Point. Tracy and I join Marcus' group and we fall first into the lagoon. We're not two meters below the surface when we spot our first manta ray. It is breathtaking, magnificent, huge, graceful. This one is six meters across, and a female. We know because we can see neither penis. (It has been brought to our attention that certain fish have two penises. We have yet to verify this with an authority on fish, or penises, but consider the information plausible, and so use it here with this brief caveat.) Manta rays are also called devilfish and sea bats. None of their names inspire trust, but these monsters are utterly harmless to humans. They not only lack the poisonous spine of their relatives the stingrays, but also eat only plankton. A manta ray could kill you, but it would have to fall on your head from a third floor window.

Now we're back on the western side of the island and have gone through the only pass in the reef, then turned south into open water. Out here against the outer reef, we expect to see sharks. And we do. There are too many black-fins to count, and a handful of lemon sharks. These animals are not at all inconvenienced by our presence. They go about their customary patrols without paying us any mind at all. That's because we neither are, nor have, food. It's mildly disappointing. Before you spend much time in the inky deep with sharks, you tend to be anxious about how they might receive you, and the possibility of having a part of you removed in the process. Now the opposite is true for us. We wish they weren't so standoffish. In this sense, sharks are a lot like cats, snooty, and couldn't be bothered. On the other hand, we can't very well take our eyes off them and properly study the coral, just in case they have a seizure, undergo a sudden personality disorder and become maniacally aggressive.

If you're not diving on Bora Bora, there's very little to amuse you. On a free afternoon, we decide to rent a scooter and ride around the island. Once again, we are astonished at the price of things here. You can rent a scooter for two, four, eight, or twenty-four hours. The four-hour rate is CPF 4500, or about thirty-five dollars. In Bali, by contrast, we paid eight dollars a day. What's more, the scooters here are in terrible shape. We take them anyway, because both of us suffer from Post Indignation Trauma Syndrome (PITS). That's when it takes a while for a person to

realize that they had, but missed the preroga-
tive and opportunity to be justifiably indignant. Bora Bora is thirty kilometers around.
There is one road. Lagoon on one side, rock
mountain on the other. That's it. You can pull
over just about anywhere and go for a swim in
the lagoon. If that gets old, you can walk
across the street, into the tropical undergrowth, and look for poison arrow frogs.

Paradise

A storm is closing in from the north, and
it looks like it could blow our bungalow down
to the Southern Ocean. I can see it from here. It's a big, bad, nasty cloud that hangs
pregnant in the middle, just above the water. You can see the rain even now, in the
gray light of dusk. We skip dinner at the hotel restaurant tonight and make our own
from supplies we picked up at the market. While the storm rages, we watch a black-
and-white movie on our two-channel all-French-all-the-time television. It's a murder mystery starring Alain Delon. A sultry jazz pianist is involved, and white shooting gloves, and an empty-chambered revolver. The dialogue is Spartan. In the end,
Alain dies. For his work in this film, he deserved to.

■

Kito, the young man from the jet-ski company, picks us up at the hotel. His
name is pronounced just like the capital of Ecuador, but he finds this observation to
be uninteresting. Kito looks nineteen. He's in shorts, no shoes, no shirt. His hair is
shoulder length, and maybe he shaved a couple of weeks ago. He has achieved a state
of "laid-back" that I occasionally see in sitar musicians and very old men who feed
birds in public parks, and it drives me mad with envy. We drive halfway around the
island, very slowly, to a shack on the beach, near which are parked several jet-skis
and one French couple. They will be joining us. We say *bonjour*. The woman smiles
and *bonjours* us back. The man seems uncomfortable to be here. We get a safety
briefing in which Kito emphasizes repeatedly that we are to stay as far the hell away
from him as possible. We've heard this before. Jet-ski accidents are not as rare as all
that, and generally result from one colliding with another, or with a passing water-
craft. At the heart of these accidents is the simple fact that these machines don't have
brakes. You can only slow down by cutting the motor and/or turning. There is no
such thing as an "emergency" stop. If you've made an error in judgment, it's already
too late.

We all mount up and head out into the lagoon: Kito out front; Tracy and I
behind him; Alphonse and Antoinette behind us. There is a sticker on the dash-
board, in English, suggesting that we wear wetsuits to protect our penis and vagina.
We find this refreshingly explicit, but wish we'd known before getting this far. This

Bora Jet Ski

is one of those machines that carry two people easily, with room to spare. It seems to be in very good running order. The lagoon is a bit choppy, but beautiful, of course. Chop makes a jet-ski ride bumpy, so we cushion the wallops by standing up in the saddle as you might do on a horse. It's a beautiful day. The sun is out, there's not much wind, and we shoot along at about 40 km/h, spurting a tall rooster-tail of seawater in our wake. We feel hipper than your average jet-skier because we've also scuba dived in these waters, and know what's underneath.

Half an hour later, Kito leads us into a placid and very shallow inlet. Several men are busy shoveling white sand from the seabed onto a barge of sorts. It looks like a lot of work, standing in hip-deep water, pushing shovelfuls of wet sand up from underwater to shoulder height. It makes sense that this is where they get their building materials. We park the jet-skis and fall into the warm shallows, cavorting loudly while the French couple converse discreetly a distance away. Then we all join Kito on the *motu*. There are voodoo-like driftwood and seashell constructions up and down the beach. Another young man joins us and the two of them precede us into the tall spider-rooted yucca trees and toward the other side of the reef. Now among the trees, fifty bazillion mosquitoes ambush us. They must like it in here, and pop onto our bare backs for a little unexpected mid-morning pick-me-up. We flail wildly and break out into the open on the ocean side of the motu. They've had outbreaks of dengue fever in Bora Bora and Tahiti, and it's the last thing we want to remember this place by.

It's not immediately evident why Kito has brought us here. There's a beach, but its covered in chunks of volcanic rock and not at all hospitable. We can see a couple of neighboring islands in the distance, but that's no carnival either. Turns out that the special treat is a display of coconut cracking technique. There is a basket of the fruits at one end of the brief sand crescent beach. First Kito cuts and peels away the green outer skin. Then he demonstrates that if you strike a coconut in just the right spot, it cracks in two, right down the middle. He whacks with a machete and his coconut obligingly bifurcates. We're then offered a communal sip from the milk-filled half, and wedges of coconut pulp from the other. Antoinette gets the first drink, then Tracy, then me, then Alphonse. This is tough for him. It's too much like conversation. I think he's making an effort to enjoy himself, but wishes he could be elsewhere, having a cigarette and a nice glass of wine. On the way back to the lagoon, Tracy and I dash through the mosquito gauntlet, ahead of the rest of the group. This seems like a good idea until I trip and fall on the white volcanic gravel, scraping rich red etchings into my right shoulder, both knees, and one palm. My pride is intact because I've fallen in public often, and have become inured to this particular form of mortification. Also, they can't see us. I pick myself up and carry on, but can tell that there's blood leaving me. A limpid, warm, shallow tropical lagoon, if you're bleeding, is not the very best thing to jump into. Tracy takes the controls for the ride back and dashes us through the lagoon at a speed that ensures all my lacerations are regularly irrigated. *Note to self: Avoid future rubbing of salt in wounds.*

■ south america ■

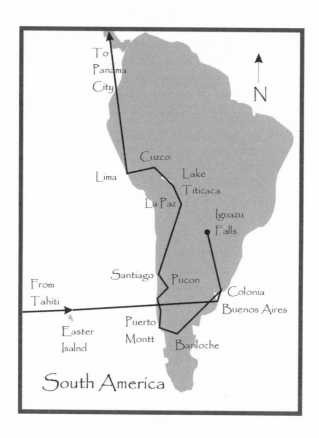

To
Panama
City

N

Cuzco

Lima

Lake
Titicaca

La Paz

Iguazu
Falls

Santiago

Pucon

From
Tahiti

Colonia

Buenos Aires

Easter
Isalnd

Puerto
Montt

Bariloche

South America

Latin America is very fond of the word "hope." We like to be called "the continent of hope." Candidates for deputy, senator, president, call themselves "candidates of hope." This hope is really something like a promise of heaven, an IOU whose payment is always being put off. It is put off until the next legislative campaign, until next year, until the next century.

— Pablo Neruda (1904–1973), Chilean poet

Buenos Aires, Argentina, May 27

It's five hours from Papeete to Easter Island. Most of us are out cold before the wheels leave the ground. It is 2:20 in the morning, after all. We're woken up for a *pankeque* breakfast an hour before landing. These doughy flapjacks have been drowned in *dulce de leche*, a thick, sweet, milk-based, caramel flavored sauce. Why anyone would want to feed this to a planeload of people at this biologically vigorous time of day is beyond me. On the ground, we find the airport to be a three-room affair. There's a café that serves soft drinks and instant coffee. The lady at the counter, Angelica, explains that there are two flights a week through here, both LAN Chile. As soon as we all re-board and fly away, everything will shut down until Sunday's flight. Then again for the duration of the week until the Friday morning flight. Angelica really wants us to come back and visit the island. She says there are great beaches, as well as the stone shrines that the island is famous for. One has been brought here and sits in the grassy enclosure between the restaurant and the tarmac. Dozens of these megaliths are strewn around the island, generally on or near burial sites, overlooking the sea. Not a lot is known about when or by whom they were created. However, you can have your very own replica, three meters tall, from Taskers Fine Arts, in Merseyside, England. It's a small, funny world after all.

Should you find yourself on Easter Island, at the airport, do not lie down on the inviting patch of lawn outside the small terminal building. This may be a long way from anywhere, but it's evidently not too far for a populous colony of little, red, hard-biting ants.

■

It's disconcerting when a big guy in a leather jacket grabs your girlfriend and gives her a kiss as you step into the Arrivals Lounge of a country you've never been to before. It's even weirder when the same guy, whom I now note has a mustache and goatee, lands a hairy peck on me. Maybe Argentines are the friendliest people on earth? Turns out he's Fernando, Gida's boyfriend. Gida is my cousin Marwan's sister-in-law. We met in Oman last January. We rode camels and slept in the desert together. We went to Musandam together and watched Iranians smuggle in livestock and smuggle out cigarettes. She has promised us at least as bracing a time in Buenos Aires.

Fernando suggests a nighttime tour of the city. It's 1:30 a.m., but he is quite serious. We explain that in our world, 1:30 a.m. is when we wake up following several hours' sleep, usually to go to the bathroom, and anyway, we have been traveling for twenty-four hours on three separate flights, the last of which, a two-hour bumpfest from Santiago to Buenos Aires, rattled us. There was a storm. We flew through it, and up it, and down it. Now all we want to do is sleep. Gida has booked us at the Sheraton Retiro and arranged for a room on one of the higher floors, a great view of the Rio de la Plata, a beautiful king-size bed, and a fruit plate. We're dehydrated from all the flying, so make the time and find the energy to shower and kill the fruit. Although we're exhausted, it takes us a couple of hours to subdue the excitement of arrival in yet another continent, especially one that is physically attached to the U.S. It was nearly 4 a.m. when I last looked at the clock.

■

Fernando and Gida pick us up at 10 a.m. They seem chipper. Maybe Argentines don't need as much sleep as we do. It's Saturday morning and traffic is light as we drive around Buenos Aires and get a windshield tour of the city. The Sheraton is on San Martín Street, overlooking the Plaza Fuerza Aerea Argentina, which contains a clock tower presented by Great Britain on the centenary of Argentina's independence. This is before Argentina decided to invade—briefly, it turns out—the Falklands in 1982. We tool around the area, criss-cross Avenida de 9 Julio a few times, and buzz every plaza and monument of note in the downtown area, including Plaza de Mayo. When England defeated Argentina in the Falklands, it brought to an end the hegemony of a military *junta* that had ruled the country with brutal efficiency since 1976. In the process, something like thirty thousand people, deemed subversive by the State, were "disappeared." *Madres de Plaza de Mayo* is a group of women, mothers of the missing, who have congregated at the plaza every Thursday afternoon for twenty-five years, protesting the kidnappings and demanding information about their loved ones. We are reminded of the Khmer Rouges in Cambodia. Argentine politics is fascinating. There hasn't been an ordinary regime here since the Spanish arrived. Despots and demigods lurk in street names, hated and loved about equally. One constituency's hero is another's villain. I want very much to crack open a can of discussion on the subject with Fernando and Gida but think better of it; we're having such a nice day.

Following the downtown tour, we take the Ruta Panamericana, Highway 9, north along the Rio Paraná out to the countryside. The roads here are excellent. This is always an indication of the state of a state. Judging by what we've seen so far, Argentina has at one time or another spent lots of money on public works. The country has gone through several cycles of borrowing and bankruptcy, although governments don't call it that. It's clear that some of the money wound up in the roads, as well as the usual pockets and boondoggles.

An hour later, we arrive at Pequeña Holanda (Little Holland). It's only a little perplexing to see a Dutch windmill by the side of this country road. Fernando swears by the place. It's a farm, or started out as one, until the owners stumbled by degrees onto a booming barbecue business. They grew a restaurant inside the big old house, stuck a few tables outside, nailed an outdoor kitchen together, and now go gangbusters, particularly on the weekends. Argentina's national dish is the *parillada*. A *parilla* is a grill. A *parillada* is a parade of beef parts, slapped over the coals and cooked to order. This one is a *libre*, or all-you-can-eat. The proprietor and a helper have three large charcoal grills going, all covered with flesh. I can't tell what's what, but there are people who can read a grill like it's a map. Fernando can. Not me. A flank, a loin, a strip; these are all familiar sounding cuts of meat, but I couldn't tell you which part of the animal they come from. That's okay if you go to barbecues occasionally in the U.S. or Canada. In Argentina, it's a problem. Who knows how creative they are with their barbecues? You could be eating cow armpit.

Country Lunch

The day has turned outright gorgeous, so we eat al fresco. Fernando orchestrates a table in the field fronting the big house. It's a peculiar scene: Here we are, just the four of us, sitting in the middle of a meadow, having a barbecue lunch in Argentina. It's not how I might have imagined our first day here, and we're tickled with the novelty and idiosyncrasy of the setting. The only company we have is a *nandu*, strolling around begging for food. This is a bird that resembles an ostrich or an emu. It eats anything and everything. The waitress said that the male went to *nandu* heaven not long ago after consuming some kid's collection of Matchbox automobiles. This whole experience is delightfully absurd, and it gets even more so when a wiry middle-aged man carrying a bow approaches and hands us his card:

Teodoro J. Aubain Balda
Presidente
Holland Archery Club

Teodoro is a man whose life can be summarized in just a few words, and most of them have to do with archery. He loves this job, this life. "Teo" can't talk fast enough to share with us all he knows about his art. We get concatenated, breathless discourses on bow hunting, on ecology and the environment, on the status of various species of Argentine game, and on the wonderful terrain of the river delta not far from here. Teodoro wears on his person and on his gear several bits of Bambi's hide. Once in a while he throws a clandestine glance at the *nandu* across the path. After we finish our lunch, he helps each of us set up and shoot the wild boar poster. This is harder than it looks, even though we're using a bow that's strung on "wimp" setting. He demonstrates his own advanced skill by shooting a target that is fifty meters away. It occurs to us that some of what we had for lunch may have been his handiwork, as well.

As spontaneous and quirky as this trip to the countryside has been, it has taken us immediately to the pulse of Argentina, and that, resoundingly, is barbecue. According to Worldwatch Institute, the average Argentine consumes nearly sixty kilograms of beef each year. The average American comes in a distant second at forty-four kilograms. In England, just so we have some point of reference, that number is sixteen. How did this happen? Well, Argentina has the perfect climate as well as the wide open pampas, ideal for cattle husbandry. Also, they have yet to reach the level of health awareness, maybe paranoia, that we have in the U.S., and therefore overlook the long-term side effects of their diet. Mind you, there's more to it than that. It turns out that the world's largest species of carnivorous dinosaurs lived in Argentina. This sounds preposterous, but it's the truth. Six skeletons of these behemoths were unearthed in Patagonia not long ago, proving beyond a doubt that meat eating in Argentina is a hundred million-year tradition.

■

Tango was meant to be. It's a thing that is so completely full of its own passion, so self-infatuated, that it defies obsolescence. Kind of like breathing, eating, and sex. Of course they tell you this in all the books, but you only really understand when you get here. You can't very well come to Buenos Aires and not see a tango show. Well, you could, but then you'd have to lie about it to your friends.

Tonight's show at La Ventana in San Telmo is magnificent. You can't watch the tango done this well without concluding that it was in God's Grand Plan from the very beginning. The first band is a quartet: *bandoneon*, violin, cello, piano. The *bandoneon* was brought here by the Germans. It had a different name back then, a German one. It has since become the national instrument of Argentina. The *bandoneon* is something like an accordion, but a little less clunky and a lot less hummy. In the right hands, like they have here, it decants Latin heat. We see several different tangos performed by three couples. There can't be a person alive who would not want to be able to dance like this. It's news to us that there are multiple forms of tango. Of course there's always the classical tango; the thing you can learn the basics of and practice for years before you figure out that you'll never be good enough to do in public. Then there's the *milonga*, a faster and more athletic version of the standard and the *canyengue*, a rougher, unpolished dance. Finally there's the unforgettable *putanesca*, often served with capers and olives.

We watch, rapt, and make the following observations:

- The women are in dresses with all the parts cut away that might otherwise conceal the crotch. That's right; if the clothing element interferes with a fulsome display of the groin area, then it's missing.

- If the man has hair, you can count on it carrying a high-gloss luster from any angle. Could be gel, could be sweat: tough to tell from here.

- Kicking between each other's legs is tango's most complicated and perilous step. Throughout the dance, as they strut and stride across the floor, dancers do a fast backward knee-down sole-up kick that brings their heel up close to their partner's hamstrings. Sometimes these kicks are high enough that the woman's ascending spike flirts with the man's butt. It's not impossible to imagine how this could lead to gluteal injury, or worse: spontaneous proctoscopies.

- The dancers, regardless of gender, are sultry, steamy, and other things that happen if you're Latin or live near the equator.

- In contrast, the music is provided exclusively by White Old Geezer (WOG) bands. The average age of a tango musician is ninety-seven.

- Tango is a lot like flamenco, but much happier. There's drama here too, but it's not of the as-soon-as-I-finish-this-dance-I'm-slashing-my-own-wrists variety.

- The "a" in tango is pronounced like the "a" in "taco." If you pronounce it like the "a" in "fancy," all the old Argentine ladies at adjoining tables will make a very disapproving hiss and suck spit through their dentures.

Tango is much more than a dance. It's a national obsession, an ethnic characteristic, like thick eyebrows. It's a declaration of Latin Americanness. At one time or another, everyone immigrated to Argentina. First it was the Spaniards. Then in the early nineteenth century the Swiss and the Germans came. On their heels, near the height of its power, the British Empire showed up. All these European powers influenced modern Argentine society and culture. The tango, however, has remained one hundred percent Argentine, and has stood in stiff-toed defense of the national spirit in the face of perversions like the foxtrot and the Morris dance.

Tango!

No question that Buenos Aires feels like a European city. As we walk around San Telmo, we're in the midst of a generally fashionable and Caucasian crowd. Something like ninety percent of the population is white, of Spanish or Italian extraction. You can tell who the tourists are because we're not quite as chic as the locals, and we're not smoking. Several blocks are closed to traffic and we're all in an easy weekend rhythm. The square itself is occupied by artisans and artists and tango dancers, naturally. The old buildings around the square have cafés and restaurants on the ground floors, and balconied apartments upstairs. It's all very charming, and nothing much happens that is unexpected or unpleasant. We could be in any European capital. The art on display runs the usual spectrum from the very, very bad to the pretty good. We stop for coffee at one of the cafés and sit inside by an unusually tall open window, watching the crowd. A young girl of five or so kneels on a

San Telmo Café

chair at the table nearest us and leans out, fiddling with a yellow balloon. She catches the eye of a passerby with a camera and the latter stops and starts snapping away. The young girl eventually tires of the spotlight and leaves to find her mother. We move on but don't get far. A cute little restaurant has tables outside on the cobblestones and serves *locro*, a local stew that looks delicious. So we take a table and share a bowl of the stuff.

From San Telmo we take a taxi to La Boca. On the way, the driver suggests that we visit the Boca Football (soccer) Club museum. We take his advice because we've found taxi drivers the world over to be the most reliable sources of this sort of information. Even if you're not a soccer fan, the Muséo Boquénse is worth a visit. The team to whose omnipotence this edifice is dedicated is Boca Juniors. There is no Boca Seniors. I never did get to the bottom of why they're called Juniors, a word that is impossible for Latinos to pronounce correctly. Entire families are here, awed and hushed as though at a shrine for war dead. There is no way to overstate the importance of soccer, actually *futbol*, in South America. Honduras and El Salvador fought a war in 1969 that was precipitated by a World Cup playoff game between the two nations. Neither is on our itinerary; they're far too hotheaded. The first World Cup was held in Uruguay in 1930 and the host country won by defeating Argentina four goals to two. People here still get all misty when they talk about it.

Boca is one of Buenos Aires' more colorful neighborhoods, both literally and figuratively. The houses on several blocks are painted in loud, bright colors, like children's blocks. This is done by the municipality as a way of setting the quarter apart. It's a working class neighborhood, and Gida tells us that the locals have complained in the past that it's the inside of the houses that needs paint. In Boca's main square, there is a tango show going on. Go figure. At the edge of the square, a tiny old man in an ancient suit and dark hat faces the wall by the side of a postcard display in front of one of the souvenir stores. We can't see his face. It's strange that the man is standing this way, facing the wall, but I realize when we get closer that he is singing along with the music. To himself, the wall, and the postcard stand. That's all. He's not taking a leak, as I first suspected. Nothing sinister at all is going on. He's just parked himself discreetly against the wall and is singing the songs he loves for his own personal audience of one.

Uptown, Teatro Colón is a grand old edifice, completed in the very early years of the twentieth century in the neo-classical style. Seven stories tall, colonnaded all around, it stands at the side of the world's widest boulevard, 9 de Julio. I prefer to listen to classical music in old concert halls like this one. The Kennedy Center, the Lincoln Center, and other relatively modern places, though technically marvelous, lack a certain mustiness, a certain authenticity. We picked up tickets earlier today and are now comfortably ensconced in our box seats. You can squeeze six meso-morphs into this box, but tonight it's just the three of us. Tracy is in her Birkenstocks and I'm in my Harley Davidson motorcycle boots. We're wearing the same jeans for the fourth day straight. However, once we get in our seats, we're half invisible and act like aristocrats from the waist up. The Orquesta Filarmonica de Buenos Aires turns in a great performance, but just to make sure we are enormously happy, the theatre *confiteria* serves ham and cheese sandwiches on white bread whose crust has been cut away.

■

Buenos Aires has neighborhoods like New York has neighborhoods. Boca is like the Village; Retiro is like Downtown; San Telmo is like Soho, and so on. Tonight we taxi up to Recoleta. This is another fashionable city neighborhood, full of restaurants and bars and parks and good-looking people in decent clothes, but we manage to blend in anyway. Recoleta developed in the late nineteenth century when wealthy *porteños* (Buenos Aires residents) moved here in droves to escape the San Telmo yellow fever epidemic. We get there past nine and join Gida and Fernando at one of the outdoor cafés that line the park blocks. There's a mass going on across the way, at Iglesia de Nuestra Señora de Pilar. The faithful have overflowed the church itself and a huge crowd fills the courtyard, al fresco, listening to the sermon that is piped out on loudspeakers. We think that's the smoking section.

We like Buenos Aires, even though it's a big grown-up city with lots of people and its share of problems. Pollution is not obscene. The city is expensive, but not ridiculously so. Most people working in tourism are bilingual; the food is great; it's clean for a city this size. What's not to like? This is pretty much how the locals feel as well. Their biggest complaints are political and economic insecurity. Folks here don't feel that they can really plan their futures as we do in the U.S. There's always the overhanging specter of a coup or another economic meltdown.

Parque Nacional Iguazú, Argentina, May 31

We can see Brazil from bed in Argentina. That's the truth, and we don't even have to stand up or anything. From right here, heads resting against the backboard, all we have to do is look across the balcony and there it is: Brazil, just off to the left. Straight ahead we see Iguazú Falls, about which we don't yet know very much. We flew in earlier today from Buenos Aires. As we approached the airport, the purser came over the PA to announce that Iguazú Falls could be seen from the right side of the aircraft. She does this not long after announcing that we should all fasten our seatbelts and place our seatbacks in their most uncomfortable positions. Nevertheless, everyone on the left side of the plane stampedes over to our side for a look, seatbelts be damned. It's worth it. The river is a red, muddy, fierce torrent that falls into clouds of mist for nearly eighty meters to the lower Iguazú River. From here we see the entire thing, all three thousand glorious meters of it, spanning the Brazil-Argentina border. This is South America's most formidable waterfall. The highest is Angel Falls, in Venezuela, but this one is widest and most powerful.

We're staying at the Sheraton again. The hotel is in the Parque Nacional Iguazú, so we don't have to journey back and forth to town, which is several kilo-

Iguazu Falls

meters away from the falls. The view from our room is truly amazing. We're on a hillside that slopes down to the Lower Iguazú River. There's rain forest all around, or *selva* as they call it here. Almost exactly at our level, across the valley, maybe five hundred meters away, is the basalt edge over which the Upper Iguazú tumbles down. We see the curtains of frothy water and hear the roar of the falls. A thick white spray fills the valley. Every few moments, flocks of colorful birds race up from the forest canopy and are thrown into stark contrast against the mist. Toucans streak behind their improbable beaks across the valley into the tall trees. All around there are busy clouds of beautiful butterflies. Some are as large as tea saucers.

To see all there is to see here, you must go the whole length of the catwalks and paths along the Lower Iguazú, as well as above the Upper Iguazú. The falls form a large arc made up of smaller semicircles, each of which is a distinct falls and has its own name. San Martín has a falls named after him, of course. He is the *libertador*, the man who liberated Argentina from the Spanish, then took his act to Chile and Peru, and later to Ecuador and Venezuela. The devil is also involved, as he tends to be where there are blowholes and waterfalls and sheer precipices and deserts. The ultimate highlight of this visit is the *Garganta del Diablo*, or the Devil's Throat. To see this falls up close, we take a boat to a dock in the middle of the Upper Iguazú, then get off and single-file along a catwalk that brings us to a *balcon* right on top of the *Garganta*. It is a powerful, exciting, yet at the same time strangely sedating sight. Millions of barrels of water come roaring down this gorge, on and on, unrelentingly violent, but if you stand here and look into the rush, you are eventually hypnotized. This would make a mind-blowing bungee jump.

■

Having just recently survived a two-hour trek on horses in Queenstown, we now consider ourselves *caballeros* and have booked a jungle ride to further familiarize ourselves with the area. So here we are, following our guide Roberto and being nibbled on by swarms of mosquitoes and other insects. He leads us single file along narrow paths through the damp, muddy, thick *selva*. Roberto keeps up a steady commentary about the plants we see around us and about the wildlife we are happy not to see. The big cats only come out at night, he says, when their prey is out and about. Fine with us. There are tigers here, and pumas and jaguars and leopards. In 1997, a park ranger's child was taken by a puma, not far from the Sheraton. Sure, the odds are slim, but they get an awful lot fatter when you tramp into the animals' own backyard. To take our minds off the rapidly approaching dusk, Roberto narrates the local legend about the creation of the falls. The Guaraní are the indigenous people who still live in these rain forests. It goes something like this:

> *Once upon a time, a big, mean serpent lived in the Iguazú River. In order to keep it from eating them all, the Guaraní annually sacrificed their most beautiful maiden by tossing her in the river, where the serpent presumably swallowed her whole. One year, the elected sacrificial beauty was seen by a visiting prince from one of the other Guaraní settlements. He fell in love with her. The village elders explained that she was spoken for, and would be taking the Big Plunge the following day. He would not stand for it, and instead kidnapped the girl. Bad move. As they tried to make their getaway down the river, the now-royally-pissed-off serpent split the river and made a big chasm into which the lovers fell. The beauty's hair became the falls, and the prince turned into a tree whose outstretched arms reach up to catch her and break her fall.*

It's a lovely story, and he finishes it just in time to dismount and show us some Guaraní animal traps. By now it's dark enough that we can't really see the path in the woods anymore. I casually ask Roberto if he's worried that we're losing the light. He smiles and reassures me that there's nothing to worry about. We mount up and head into the woods again, only to reemerge five minutes later at the stables. For all we know, this whole ride could have been within a hundred yards of the place.

Colonia, Uruguay, June 2

Maté is a beverage that consumes a great percentage of South America's population. It's not complicated to make but requires that its drinker cart around a thermos of hot water throughout. The "tea" that is the basis of the beverage is made from a South American holly, also called Paraguay tea. The leaves are ground, dried, and jammed into a hollowed-out gourd that serves as a cup. They call it a *calabasa*. You add hot water and sip the infusion through a *bombilla*, a metal straw that has tiny punctures in its swollen bottom. The *bombilla* allows the beverage to come through but not the *maté* leaves. Mostly. Trouble is, you can only get a few tiny sips out of each gourdful, since the leaves take up all the available space. So if you're a *maté* person, you must carry a thermos around at all times and refill your *calabasa* frequently. The affliction here, in Colonia, is worse than anywhere else on the continent.

We arrive in Colonia at about 9 p.m. on the ferry from Buenos Aires. Old Town is empty now and lit only by street lamps and the moon. Single-story buildings butt up one against the other on neat cobblestone streets. Some have historic plaques on them, and we learn that most date from the founding of the city by the Portuguese in the late seventeenth century. In the distance, across the river, there is a high dome of red-yellow glow in the sky above Buenos Aires. It's quite a sight. Colonia came to some importance as a corridor for smuggled goods into Buenos Aires, in defiance of the Spanish crown's dictated trade monopoly. The Spaniards eventually took the town and it lost its strategic importance. Now, all these years later, a commission has been established to study the feasibility of constructing a bridge between Buenos Aires and Colonia. If it's ever completed, it will be the longest bridge in the world. I'm not holding my breath.

■

After a leisurely breakfast the following morning, we head out to discover the town. Colonia is named for Christopher Columbus, whose name in Spanish is Cristóbal Colón. That is why this name, Colón, shows up in so many places around South America. Like San Martín. While waiting for the bus that will take us to Real de San Carlos, we purchase disposable *maté* kits. The kit includes a plastic cup full of *maté*, kind of like a Top Ramen soup thing. Also in the packet is a plastic *bombilla*. Then there's the thermos. That's right, a disposable thermos. We get our thermoses filled with hot water. You can tell that the lady at the little store does this all day long. She has three large kettles on the stove, all aboil, and charges fifty centavos for each thermos, about four cents. We're now ready to plunge into the very heart of the Uruguayan psyche and, thermoses underarm, mount the bus to the little neighborhood of Real de San Carlos. Five people live here, a horse, and a couple of stray dogs. There is also a falling-down *corrida* where matadors and bulls once gored each other. We walk past this concrete blight and down the few blocks to the beach. Rio de la Plata is about thirty kilometers wide between Argentina and Uruguay, so it might as well be a sea. That's another reason the bridge idea isn't getting a lot of support. We sit on a low wall, all that's left of an old pier, and go about assembling our *matés*. There are very important and clear instructions about leaching the leaves with cold water before adding the hot water and beginning to drink. That's because the first rinse eliminates an exceedingly strong, nauseating dose of the stuff. Unfortunately, I only see this after I've sucked down a gulletful of something wicked. The sun is out now, so we laze around the beach, sipping our *matés*, chatting. They say that there is no caffeine or any other substance that merits close attention in this drink, but I am prepared to dispute this. A young couple putters up on a scooter. They make their way to the high end of the pier, wave to us and commence some light necking in the sunshine. We will not see much more of Uruguay, but on the basis of this sighting, are prepared to endorse it as a pretty good place to sip *maté* and neck on the beach.

We spend the balance of the afternoon strolling around Colonia, looking at the old houses that we walked by last night, eventually joining the rest of the citizenry on Avenida General Flores at the municipal park. A number of wooden white park benches are lined up facing the Avenida. Across the street is police headquarters. A crumpled officer stands in the doorway, puffing on a cigarette, sipping a *maté*. He has a thermos under his arm. In a shootout, he'd have no chance. A truck comes by every once in a while, blaring out loudspeaker invitations to this or that special event. It's nearly time to get back to the boat, but Gida gets a sudden craving and leads us hurriedly down the street to El Carrito. You could come to Colonia for the relaxing ferry crossing. You could come for the charm of the authentic colonial old town. You could come to neck and sip *maté* on the beach and to get away from the hectic pace of Buenos Aires. Whatever your reason for visiting Colonia, you *must* stop at El Carrito, on Avenida Mendez just north of Avenida Flores, and eat a *chivito* sandwich. The essential ingredients of this Uruguayan national treasure are:

Chivito: Beef thinly sliced from indeterminate regions of cow.

Chimichurri: Salsa containing chili, parsley, garlic, green pepper, oil. Holy Watering Eyes!

Pebete bread, which resembles *focaccia*, but isn't as dry or as presumptuous.

Ham, cheese, bacon, lettuce and tomato.

Truth is, you can stick anything in the sandwich you want with the *chivito* and *chimichurri*. You won't really taste it, but it will provide stuff that the salsa can eat through before it gets to your stomach lining. As we stand in the fresh evening air munching on our sandwiches, we get to talking with a young Argentine couple. These kids are in their very early twenties, but outgoing and articulate. Like almost everyone else we've talked to, they think that the U.S. is the place to be, and want very much to practice their English with us. Everyone we've met here entertains the eventual dream of going to the U.S. The big draw is political and economic stability. We modestly try to talk it down, but they're immovable, and they're probably right.

San Carlos de Bariloche, Argentina, June 4

We arrived last night from Buenos Aires and caught the Avis man at Bariloche's Aeropuerto Internacional just as he was heading out the door. It seems that our online reservation didn't show up on his manifest. For that matter, we could see that there were no reservations on his manifest. This is a very quiet time of year in Bariloche. The ski season is not yet open, but the reasonably kind weather is long gone. Our LAPA flight was nearly empty; maybe twenty of us on the plane including crew. The drive into town is eerie. We're on dark, deserted mountainous roads and can't see much beyond the shrubs at the edge of our headlights. There are trees, or rather the dim shadows of trees, dancing in the night. No moon, no lights, no other cars. It's strange and a tiny bit disconcerting, but the only real excitement in the twenty-minute drive comes as we merge from the airport access road onto Ruta Nacional 237. Just past the intersection, in the pitch blackness, several policemen have a roadblock set up with nearly invisible once-orange cones. We slow, but they wave us on. No idea what they're doing here, but we manage to assume the worst in the few seconds it takes to pass the checkpoint. Kidnappers? Secret Service body-snatchers? Latter-day *junta* apparatchiks? We don't know, but it takes a moment like this to remind us that we are a long way away from home, and that this is a foreign country where even our considerable cultural fluidity would amount to zip if some-one really wanted to victimize us. The weather, wet and cold and blustery, helps very little so we pull into the best looking hotel we can find, Los Tres Reyes.

When we finally get out of bed the next morning, it's in spite of the weather. We have a bitter, soggy, windy, and exquisitely unpleasant day in Bariloche. And it's getting worse by the hour. The wind is coming in over Lago Nahuel Huapí,

Bariloche Andes

whiplashing the row of immense pines on the waterfront then slamming into our window. By the time we leave the hotel, what was mere-ly an ugly day has become violently inclement. We drive along the lakeside for a while, then up to Cerro Cathedral. During ski season, this mountain is mobbed. Today the vast parking lot is empty, except for a caretaker who is happy to see us and have a short conversation. He confirms that autumn, the present season in the Southern Hemisphere, is not the time to be here. In the winter, he assures us, some of the most famous people in the world come here to ski. Today the slopes are com-pletely engulfed in Andean fog.

The lounge of the Tres Reyes hotel is probably exactly as it was in the forties. The big room has a number of armchairs and sofas clustered into conversation groups. The newest are frumpy overstuffed round things that remind me of the so-called Upper Class Lounge at Agra Airport. The huge windows look out on the lake, but it's dim in here. You can just imagine Erich Priebke and Martin Bormann sit-ting in the dark, far corner by the fireplace, having tea and discussing extradition. We've read that a number of Nazi SS officers retired to Patagonia following World War Two. The triangle defined by Bariloche, Puerto Montt in Chile and Osorno, also in Chile, is known as the "Nazi Triangle," and it's where these guys lived, most-ly. Now that we're here, we can see why they would. For one thing, Juan Peron's ambivalent loyalties during the war encouraged immigration of people who might have been thrown in jail in most other countries. For another, this part of the world is not unlike Bavaria. Jump in your BMW and shoot along Ruta National 237, toward Llao Llao, and you'll see what I mean. Chalets with *edelweiss* nail-ons will show up regularly on both sides of the road. You might even see the odd guy in the green felt hat with the feather in it. In the eighties and nineties, several of the men who had served under Hitler and retired to Patagonia were rousted. Attempts were made to extradite them to Italy or Germany to stand trial for crimes against humanity. Some of these efforts succeeded, some failed. Martin Bormann died in the mid-seventies, right here in Bariloche. Priebke, on the other hand, ran a deli just up the street from here for many years and became the subject of intense international controversy. He was extradited in 1996, tried, convicted, and sentenced to life imprisonment in 1997. They say that the locals referred to his shop as the "Nazi Deli," more in innocuous humor than in judgment. If you didn't know this, you might go through Bariloche with nothing more than a double-take at all the German, Austrian, and Swiss restaurants.

■

We're pretty sure now that we've picked the absolute worst time to visit this strange town. Except for a brief time this afternoon there has been no let up in the rain and wind. It's also damn cold. Last night's low was two degrees centigrade, and today we might see a high of four degrees centigrade. We slept poorly last night. It was either the pork cutlets from Munich Viejo Restaurant, or the stammering of the windows all night long as the wind played them like castanets. This morning it was all we could do to drive the sixty-five kilometers to Villa la Angostura, on the north side of the lake. We're in Parque Nacional Nahuel Huapí, a vast reserve of alpine forest. Predictably, we see lots of trees and, once in a while during brief breaks in the low cloud cover, catch glimpses of the surrounding peaks. Cerro Catedral and Tronador come into view for a tantalizingly short time as we skirt the Lago Nahuel Huapí.

We find the places we visit much more enjoyable in the light of their own history, even if this history is complicated and full of dates and foreign names. We've been studying, though, and have developed our own simpler, narrower view of the past. It seems a good time, as we continue our trip through the Latin continent, to review our Layman's Summary of South American History:

- For thousands of years, Indians of various tribes lived here. They had come from Asia across the Bering Bridge, before that became the Bering Strait, frustrating early hopes for a Bering Toll Booth.

- These indigenous tribes coalesced into a half-dozen societies, including the inimitable Incas, the guileful Guaraní, and the hoochy-koochy Mapuche.

- The Spaniards and Portuguese arrived in the fifteenth century and occupied the continent, putting an end to all the senseless temple building in the jungle.

- Creollos, that is, Spaniards born in South America of Spanish parents, white folks, led the wars of independence from Spain in the early 1800s. They were led by San Martín, Bolívar, and others, like O'Higgins, whose name no one in Chile can pronounce.

- A progression of influential landed strongmen and despots has run South American countries since independence. Some were military, some civilian. A few paid for their efforts with their lives, but had the money for it. Most paid with other people's lives. One or two are believed to have been not completely crooked, just nuts. A good handful left their country and went into hiding elsewhere. Most recently, Pinochet of Chile and Fujimori of Peru have made headlines. Now Argentina's Menem is under house arrest for allegedly selling arms illegally to Ecuador and Croatia. It's a fun bunch.

Peulla, Chile, June 8

It's another sopping, gloomy day of Andean splendor in Bariloche as we mount the Tours Catedrál bus and head east along the south shore of Lago Huapí to Puerto Panuelo. Again we get fleeting views of Tronador, snow-capped, impossibly high. This is the first leg of our trans-Andean adventure. Unlikely as it may sound, we are crossing the Andes by boat. By the time we reach Puerto Montt in Chile tomorrow evening, we will have crossed three more lakes in the groins of these mountains. Tours Catedrál takes care of the whole thing, scheduling the boats, arranging overland transportation between them, and putting us up for the one night we'll spend en route.

Now we board the waiting Catamaran with our guide and a group of about a dozen tourists and cast off into the frigid mist. It's cold on the boat, and we're poorly prepared. The heaviest thing we have is a fleece pullover, so we buy hot tea from

the little concession kiosk on board and hug the cups for warmth. Traveling around the tropics for the past several months has displaced our sense of winter. I guess we figured we would work our way through the cold bits of South America quickly then be back in the warm weather before having to buy winter clothes. Silly idea. Along the way we learn that most of the passengers on board are only out for a day excursion, and will be coming back with the guide to Bariloche. For now though, we're all sailing across the Andes together.

Andes By Boat

A couple of hours later, during which we made two futile appeals to the captain for heat, we dock at Puerto Blest. There's a small hotel right on the shore, and it looks like a good place to stop and have a cup of tea into which we can dunk our toes, but the plan apparently does not include that. The whole lot of us is shepherded, shivering, straight to the waiting circa-1950 school bus for the ride up to the nameless dock on Lago Frias. The bus has been sitting here waiting for us at an altitude of a thousand meters with its engine off, so it's even colder than the boat. The ride, however, is mercifully short, and our tour guide keeps us distracted with colorful stories about this or that bit of local lore. She points out that, high as the three thousand-meter peaks around us might seem, they are stumps compared to those farther north into the Andean *cordillera*. Aconcagua, the highest, is nearly seven thousand meters high. It's even colder up there than here; a thought sufficient in its brutality to yank us back into our own chilly reality.

Now we rumble down a gravel road to a muddy dock, leave the ice-bus, and board a very small boat for the cruise across Lago Frias. It's another short trip, maybe half an hour, but this tired old tug is not far from going up in flames. You can smell gasoline and feel heat coming from all the wrong places. We seek these vents nevertheless, huddling close and trying to stop trembling. Having a boat catch fire in waters like these would be very bad news. This lake, like the others in the region, is leftover glacier. In the most recent Ice Age, you could have done figure eights in a bus right where we are now chugging. The water temperature is three degrees Celsius. Shivers run down our spines. Then up. Then down. And so on. We're in the bottom of a basin whose sides are thickly wooded mountains. Everywhere we look, sheer, beautiful, but also inhospitable peaks tower above us. As we look up into the hills, we see waterfalls every hundred or so meters. There seems no end to the amount of water that tumbles down from the Andes. Clouds sit in the nooks of these mountains, and the whole scene is unbelievably pristine. At Puerto Frias only those of us going on to Chile disembark. The others stay on the boat for the return trip, and have on their faces a forlorn expression of sympathy for us. I want to call out, "We'll be fine, don't worry," but my mouth has locked up from the cold. We're turned over to a Chilean guide, Miguél, who greets us enthusiastically and announces that he will escort us the rest of the way to Puerto Montt.

Here at this isolated outpost very nearly smack in the middle of the Andes, there is a log cabin, doors and windows flung wide open, where a lone Argentine officer checks our passports, retrieves the departure cards, and formally stamps us out of the country. We line up single file, the eight of us remaining Intrepid Voyagers, and shuffle in one door of his office and out the other. The wind comes off the sides of the mountains and cuts through this place looking for someone to kill. We're in line for one full half hour. The Argentine officer, smoking continuously, somehow manages to leaf through passports, even though he's not wearing gloves. He looks at each page of every passport, and studies us one by one as we parade in front of his exalted bureau. If you're the sort of person who worries about international intrigue, rest assured that the Argentine border at Puerto Frias is secure. By the time he's done with us, we're so cold we're practically brittle. Miguél, seemingly impervious to the elements, cheerfully rounds us up for the next and final leg of today's trip, to Peulla, Chile.

The vehicle chosen for the job looks like something you'd arrange for a crossing of Mars. It's elevated on large wheels, very moony. We get in and are secretly grateful that it's cramped. Tracy is on my left, and we're fused. The woman sitting on my right takes advantage of every bump in the road to grind her ample hip into

Mars Mobile

mine. I shamelessly grind back, shifting just slightly to make sure that as much of me comes in contact with her hip as possible. We're stealing body heat. The ride up from Puerto Frias to Peulla is a steep twenty-five-kilometer slog through mud and gravel and water and, occasionally, snow. We pass quickly through the formal Chilean border. Our driver gets down and secures permission to go through from a couple of guys huddled around a kerosene heater in the doorway of a tiny shack. These guys are far less persnickety than Officer Fastidio in Puerto Frias. The Chilean flag hangs from a makeshift wooden pole and sticks wet against the outside of the solitary window. From here it's another hour and a half to Hotel Peulla. These trails would be impassable in most vehicles. Now we're in rainforest, thick with evergreens and undergrowth and soggy with rain that hasn't stopped for weeks, and maybe never will. With Hotel Peulla in sight, we reach the real Chilean customs and passport control officials. They operate out of a small building that is marginally less decrepit than the shack we passed by earlier. We reluctantly get off the Mars-Mobile and file in one at a time. They do a cursory search of our bags, stamp our passports and send us on our way. Not much traffic comes through here this time of the year, and these men are too cold to be particular. Maybe Chileans are less fussy than Argentines.

Hotel Peulla is the only game in town. Actually, it is town. By the time we arrive, after spending most of the day freezing our butts on the unheated relay of three buses and two boats, it's a sight for sore, cold eyes. The building is a creaky old place that looks like a World War One hospital. I know this because I lived in a World War One hospital while at boarding school. It has three floors of small rooms with incredible views of Lake Todos los Santos and Monte Tronador. The mountain, at 3,500 meters, is not visible because we are socked in with clouds and fog and rain. The lake is, though, and what a creepy, wild sight it is. There is a storm blowing across it that threatens to topple the whole building. The nasty weather that has accompanied us all day is now a first-class Andean rage. It's the sort of thing you would like to watch from inside a toasty-warm sitting room, while sipping something warm or extra-proof, or both. We spend most of our first night in Chile listening to the storm outside and wondering if the lake will be at the doorstep by breakfast.

The next morning we get on Mars-Mobile again and are driven the short distance to the dock, where we board a ferry for the crossing of Lago Todos los Santos. This boat is the fastest we've had so far on this trans-Andean crossing, and the warmest. A very pleasant young woman is making tea and coffee and selling chocolates and souvenirs. We take our places alongside the radiators running along the walls of the boat, and pass the two hours gazing at the breathtaking landscape, dozing, and reading. At the port of Petrohue, we are met by a large tour bus, and mount it for the home stretch to Puerto Montt. We're exhausted from the trip and lack of sleep, so we nod off often, waking up only occasionally to look at Lago Llanquihue, along which we travel a good fifty kilometers. Crossing the Andes in this bus-boat-bus-boat-Mars-Mobile-boat-bus way, in these conditions, has been unforgettable. It's worth doing again, in summer.

Puerto Montt, Chile, June 9

Puerto Montt doesn't get enough light. Way down here in the Southern Hemisphere, the sun is always up north, at a frustrating angle, hard to catch. Even indoors, though, shops and offices in this shabby port city are severely under-illuminated. As a result, it's possible that the entire population suffers from Seasonal Affective Disorder (SAD). That's where you get so little light, natural or otherwise, that every cell in your body wants to leave you and go to Curaçao. They can't leave, of course, so they become depressed. After brief good-byes to our traveling companions and Miguél, we slosh under dark skies from one puddle to the next through the streets of Puerto Montt until God smiles upon us and delivers Hotel Gran Pacifico. It's brand new. They inaugurated it two months ago and it is spotless, modern, an oasis of light in this drab town. From our room near the top of Hotel Gran Pacifico, we have a great view of the Gulf of Ancud. It takes up all the space between Chile's mainland and the island of Chiloe. We also have a complete view of Puerto Montt. Our initial ground-level impression is accurate; there won't be much for us to see or do here. After hot showers and dinner in the room, we sleep through the night like we've been digging ditches for a week.

The highlight of our brief stay here is our lunches at Balzac. The walls of this delightful little eatery are completely covered in cartoon frescoes of diners. The tables in the frescoes look just like the real ones in the restaurant. You could cut the irony with a butter knife. This place specializes in fish, and that's what we order; Tracy the king clip, which tastes like halibut, and I the *Caldillo del Congrio segun receta de Pablo Neruda*, or "Conger Eel Stew According to a Recipe of Pablo Neruda."

Neruda is Chile's favorite native-son dead poet. He was born in Parral, Chile, in 1904. We'll be driving through there en route to Santiago. His family moved to

249

Temuco, and he eventually to Santiago. His literary prowess earned him several diplomatic assignments, including consul to Singapore and, later in life, Ambassador to France. In 1949 he crossed the Andes. This is only relevant because we have just done so as well, and wonder if he might have had the same boat we were on across Lago Frias. In 1971 he won the Nobel Prize in Literature, just in the nick of time before passing away in 1973. In any case, it is especially interesting to find that he had a recipe for delicious *caldillo*. This is like discovering that Jorge Luis Borges also embroidered. Among Neruda's memorable works is "Twenty Love Poems and One Desperate Song." He was a serious guy. Maybe he had SAD.

La Panamericana, or Ruta Nacional 5, runs the length of South America. Much of it is under construction. It's being widened here, moved there, so you can never really get going very fast. There are traffic lights and weird U-turn places and occasionally chickens in the median. We stop in Puerto Varas for a quick coffee, but find the place less attractive than we did when we came through on the big bus from Peulla a couple of days ago. It's nearly impossible to find a parking spot. Chileans drive. Puerto Montt and Puerto Varas are congested with cars. This is different from places like Cambodia and Vietnam, where developing economies have not yet made a personal car possible for many. It is here. As we leave the Puerto Varas area, we find ourselves in the countryside. This could be Sterling, Virginia, complete with rolling green hills, birches and spruces and poplars and such. A whole lot of rain has fallen here lately, and the valleys are flooded. There's fog everywhere. A few young boys are having an improvised game of tennis by the side of the Panamericana, using a construction barrier for a net.

We stay on the Panamericana until Paillaco, where we veer off toward the coast and Valdivia. We drive into Valdivia and then right out of Valdivia. There's one short stretch of pretty harbor, but it's not worth the trip. The place is a hodge-podge of poor housing and shabby shops. Towns in this part of Chile seem universally scruffy. The pervasive German influence shows up in the occasional gingerbread house and well-tended garden, but otherwise we see working-class neighborhoods that have been put together haphazardly.

Now we're going from the coast back inland, toward Villarica. At Loncoche, we leave the Panamericana again and go through town looking for the Villarica signs. A nice man pushing an old car explains that the road to Villarica through Loncoche is flooded, and that we have to go back to the highway and take a later exit. As we make our way back to the main road, we nearly turn going the wrong way into a one-way street. I compensate by making a U-turn in the confines of an intersection. It so happens that a *carabiniero* is standing at the corner, watching what amounts to four serious traffic infractions inside of three seconds. Tracy notices him and says, "Here we go again." Sure enough, he catches my eye and motions for me to pull over. I do. When he reaches the car I say "*Estamos un poco perdidos*," "We're a little lost," to which he responds with a clear "*Licensia, por favor.*" He's kind, though, and as soon as I admit my guilt and throw myself upon his mercy, returns my driver's license and issues updated directions to Villarica. Chile may be scruffy, but we have had only kindness from its people.

Once we leave the Panamericana and head northeast to Villarica, everything changes. This is a lovely country road, lined with now-naked deciduous trees and picket fences. No junk, no garbage, and no corrugated metal constructions by the side of the road. Meadows fall away from the road on both sides, and mottled white-brown cows graze in the fog. We're on this road for twenty minutes when we crest a hill, suddenly exit the fog, and find ourselves face-to-face with Volcán Villarica, covered in snow, brilliantly white, near perfectly conical. This is one of several active volcanoes in the Andes. It last erupted in 1971. We drive through the town of Villarica and keep going. It looks a little hectic. Pucón, on the other hand, twenty-five kilometers farther along Lake Villarica's southern shore, is not at all. Quite the contrary; there's hardly anyone in the streets. Most of the buildings are log constructions, reminiscent of Bariloche; very alpine.

■

Rolf is our host at the Hotel Munich. He is sixty-eight, balding, very white, and somewhat somber. He was born in Dortmund and lived in Germany until 1939, when his family left to escape the Nazis. They came to Chile. Then, in 1969, he moved back to Munich and spent several years there working in the hospitality business. Now he's retired here in Pucón, and helps his daughter and her husband with this little hotel. We learn all this and more within minutes of agreeing to take the room on the second floor. The halls of Hotel Munich are lined with pictures of Bavaria's countryside, the great church in Marienplatz, Nymphenburg Palace, and other places we recognize. There is no view, and the room is not especially nice or inexpensive, but we are happy with the welcome we get. The sign behind the door says: "Please, contact us for any douby or need during your stay, we are here to attend you!" We know what a *douby* is but might spell it differently, and doubt that it's what they have in mind.

We tell Rolf we'd like an early supper, so he walks with us to the Arabian Restaurant, just around the corner. He explains that it's owned by Palestinians who have been here for three or four generations. We order the *mezza*, Lebanon's equivalent to antipasto. Everything is fresh and tasty but only vaguely reminiscent of actual Lebanese food. We don't mind. As we eat, Rolf convinces us to change plans and not leave in the morning. Rather, he suggests, we should drive to Huife for the hot springs, and to Lago Caburgua and its nearby source: Ojos de Caburgua. We could be back in Pucón for an early steak dinner at the Arabian.

■

Road to Huife

The next morning we drive out to Huifé, a town some thirty kilometers away. This area east of Pucón has several thermal baths, a constant reminder that this neighborhood has and will again explode. This feature, exploding earth, makes Pucón the ideal playground for people who believe that the outdoors is a safe place to recreate. The road is a rutted, muddy mess. We're surrounded by thistles, evergreens, berry bushes, gravel, mud, and creeks. The smell of burning firewood is in the air. In the fields adjacent to the road we see hogs, cows, alpaca, turkeys, horses, roosters, and sheep, a couple here and a couple there. Termas de Huifé is a resort of sorts, where people come and stay the weekend and sit in thermal pools in the front yard. It's not anything as fancy or potent as the Polynesian Spa of Rotorua. There isn't that exotically therapeutic stench of sulfur in the air. Just fresh mountain air, a cold Andean river rushing by out front, and nice wholesome Chilean families enjoying their vacations. We join them in the big pool and soak silently as we gaze at the volcano.

Back at the Arabian for dinner, we order steaks. It's busy here today. The tables are full of diners, Sunday in Chile. Soon the game will be on. Today it's San Lorenzo playing Union. If they win this game, they will be Argentina's 2001 champ. Just as our dinner is served, Rolf walks in and joins us. He seems forlorn. I think he wants us to stay.

Santiago, Chile, June 12

Back when I was planning to ride the motorcycle all the way from Chile to the U.S., the fantasy included a Panamericana with long picturesque stretches of road. The Andes would soar to our right and the Pacific would stretch out to our left. They do that, certainly, but we just can't see them for the rain and fog that travel with us. Nevertheless, this is pretty country, particularly away from the universally slummy towns. It's not dramatic, mind you, just pretty and bucolic. Now on our final push north to Santiago, the roadway gets better and wider as we approach the city. It's interesting that people still hitch rides in Chile. We don't think this is a very good idea and have not stopped for anyone. The way we see it, there are too many risks involved. The obvious ones include the robbery-rape-murder scenario. There are other, less egregious but quite sufficiently annoying possibilities. In any case, as we pass hitchhikers, we wave and make sympathetic, apologetic faces. They hate that.

Santiago is best seen from within. Must be, because it is practically impossible to see through the thick porridge of pollution that squats like a lid over the huge basin in which the city sits. All around are mountains, but you can only see sickly silhouettes in the haze. Once we make our way into the center of town, though, and get jammed up in traffic with everybody else, we notice the pollution less. We do see lots of policemen on foot, on motorbikes, and in the occasional armored riot-control water-cannon vehicle. We know, however, that there's nothing to worry about. Chilean politics has been stable since the early seventies, when Augusto Pinochet came to power and Allende went to the big presidential palace in the sky. Despite the military's strong hand in the country's administration during Pinochet's seventeen-year rule, perhaps because of it, there's relative calm here. Chile is less likely to spontaneously combust than are some of its neighbors. The economy, though not winning awards at the moment, is better off than Argentina's. All this translates into bustling streets and obvious if not ostentatious consumption.

We're staying at Hotel Carreras not because we know something, but because we can no longer take driving around. It's fancy. These guys not only have a full complement of national flags fluttering from brass poles on the front of the hotel; they also have three stars and two cows. It's true. We've never seen this before, and figure it must be a Latin American thing. Instead of the traditional hotel rating system that uses stars exclusively, here they also employ cows. The elaborate brass plaques on the building show three stars and, below those, in relief profile, two cows. No bull. The hotel sits on Avenida Teatinos, in the block between Moneda and Agustinas, right on the elegant and uncluttered Plaza de la Constitución. From our room on the thirteenth floor we have a bird's eye view of the plaza and La Moneda. This dignified white building on the plaza was originally built to house the government mint, hence its name. Now it serves as

La Moneda

the seat of government. As we prepare to leave the hotel for the day, Tracy calls me to the window. There is a military parade of sorts going on, a changing of the guard. Chile's finest strut for about an hour to the drumbeat of the national brass band. There's a big crowd gathered to watch the event. We have the best seats in the house.

■

As we walk around downtown Santiago, we find that we like it. A big plus is the two long, pedestrian-only streets that intersect in the middle of the city: Huerfanos and Ahumada. Nothing strikes us as particularly chic or up-market, but it's not bad either. Chileans are hospitable, courteous people. I would not call them friendly, but they're kind and seem trustworthy. This is a better combination than friendly and slick, like some of the characters we met in Turkey and Indonesia. After dinner we walk along for a while, strolling a few blocks on Avenida Libertador Bernardo O'Higgins. This is the guy who was San Martín's Number One and later became the country's first president, or "Supreme Director," as they were fond of calling him back in those days—if they wanted to live. Every town in Chile has an avenida, a puente, a plaza, and various other civil projects named after this man, whose father was Irish. We don't sense any problem with that here. So he was Irish! Big deal. Fujimori ran Peru, and he is still Japanese. Mind you, it's not all so blasé. One local editorialist believes that there is in Latin America a resentment that has yet to be requited. It has to do with foreign influence, if not hegemony, during so much of the continent's history. Now it's economic control, or globalization, that gets people's backs up. The place to discuss all this in Santiago is one of the numerous cafés that serve *café con piernas*, literally "coffee with legs." These are places where men generally congregate and are served coffee by young or not-so-young women in wildly colorful leotards and black panty hose. The women, God love them, make every effort to be sexy, but the thing is a bizarre caffeinated caricature. Where better to talk politics?

Valparaíso is a couple of hours northwest of Santiago, on the coast. The road to it is good, despite the usual, frequent Chilean roadwork detours. We agree that this city is reminiscent of Marseilles. It has the colorful but run-down back-street neighborhoods. It also reminds us of Nice, with a waterfront corniche hugging a long crescent beach and the rest of the town climbing the steep hills into slummy and overcrowded quarters. A unique feature of Valparaíso is its *acensores*. These are cable cars that transport the citizens of this fine city from the waterfront to the hills overlooking it. Each *acensore* is named and held in varying degrees of folkloric ven-

Valparaíso Mural

eration. We take the *Concepción*, a transporter that's been operating for nearly one hundred years. It looks like a large tea can, slapped on top of a gangly metal frame. There is an operator at the bottom and one at the top. They operate electrical circuit breakers that control whether the thing moves or not. I should say that they *appear* to be operating electrical circuit breakers. For all we really know, they could just be pedaling for all they're worth. The ride is brief, but satisfyingly antique. We spend an hour walking in the cobblestone streets lined with colorful old clapboard houses and extravagant murals. Someone did Picasso's *Guernica* on the wall of a public garden. Eventually we stumble across Brighton Café and have lunch there, overlooking the city and the sea. As we drive back to Santiago, the sun sets in the Pacific behind us. Say what you will about smog; it sure can make for spectacular sunsets.

■

We're spending our last day in Santiago on foot, and begin with the changing of the guard at La Moneda, this time seen from street level. The spectacle is presented every other day. The soldiers are the best-dressed we have seen, maybe ever, except in Monaco. This is true for all of Chile's military. So are the police. Accessories such as holsters and clubs are color-coordinated to match the rest of the outfits. We see a number of female police, some on foot, a number on new Honda scooters. They are dressed to the nines and, surprisingly, wear obvious make-up, like lipstick and eye shadow. They could slip into an evening gown and be immediately ready for a night at the opera.

After the changing of the guard, we walk into La Moneda, and loiter a while in the inner courtyards. The fact that we can do this speaks volumes for the country. After all, this is the presidential palace. For all we know, President Lagos could be in his office right now, doing what presidents do. Several officers and guards are in here as well, presumably the guys who just came on duty. It's all very relaxed. There was a time, not all that long ago, when this beautiful building and this courtyard were the scene of the bloody coup d'etat that has shaped Chile's history since. In 1973, General Pinochet launched an attack on La Moneda and overthrew president Salvador Allende. Some say Allende was killed. Others say that he committed suicide in his office on the second floor. It's like this in South America. You can safely bet that every major plaza in every major city has been the scene of political violence.

This passage through La Moneda exits on Avenida Bernardo O'Higgins, or the Alameda, as it is known here. This tree-lined boulevard has become the main motor thoroughfare in Santiago, and it is often clogged with buses that belch diesel as they go through, making the street sometimes intolerable for walkers. We duck into the National Library for a quick break and discover that we can check email here, free of charge. More good news in Santiago.

Cerro de Santa Lucia is a hill, one of three or four in Santiago, which rises up in the middle of the city. This one is historically significant because it marks the spot at which Pedro Valdivia founded the city on February 12, 1541. Back then city-founding was not such a big deal. The *conquistadores* were busy invading the Americas and assigning new names—usually their own—to communities that may have existed there for millennia. In this particular case, Pedro fought and defeated the Mapuche who lived here and undoubtedly had a different name altogether for the place. He went on to found Valdivia and Concepción farther south before the Indians killed him in 1554. We are jolted from this historical reverie by a deafening explosion. A passing local explains that it is merely a ritual noon firing from a historic cannon in the fort. The hill is now a metropolitan park, small enough that it has been completely built up with a church, a faux castle, and a system of walks and stairs and balconies, from which you can look out over the city. Young couples are on benches here and there. There's graffiti on many of the walls, especially up toward the higher observation points. This is stuff along the lines of "*José y Juan, Junio 2000.*" Or, "*Marika, te amo. Rubén.*" A furtive young man is already at the highest turret when we reach it. He's contemplating his own sentimental vandalism, but we break it up.

Now we continue the big loop around Santiago and visit Cerro San Cristóbal, an Andes outlier that pokes into the city. At the very top of this pine-covered hill there is a thirty-five meter tall statue of the Virgin Mary. Pope John Paul II held mass up here in 1987. Pinochet was still in power at the time and the pope was criticized for coming. We could use a prayer when we lose our way walking off the mountain and wind up following dirt paths with nothing to navigate by except for the sun. Eventually, after dodging a ferocious, salivating guard-dog on a very long leash, we run into a group of workmen who point us to the exit. When we finally reach the bottom, we set off in search of Pablo Neruda's house in the nearby neighborhood of Bellavista. However, we've had enough of being lost for one day and are now hungry, so we substitute a *parillada* for the Neruda and call it a day.

■

We're leaving Chile now. On the drive out to the airport this morning, and despite the fact that it's 6 a.m., we have a lengthy chat with the taxi driver. This was not a conversation at which the devil's advocate was welcome. This man is proud to be Chilean. You get this sense from everyone you meet in this country. People here have a very strong sense of their own nationality. They're proud to be only fifteen million and regard that as an achievement of sorts. They consider their peculiarly shaped country to be unique in the world, and they're right. Not even in Australia do you get the extreme range of climate that you have in Chile, going from the world's driest desert in the north all the way practically to Antarctica. I can also report that, based on a thin but compelling census, Chileans like General Pinochet, and wish the world would leave him alone. The reason they feel so loyal to the man is that they hold him primarily responsible for the country's apparent success in keeping up with its powerful neighbors while not suffering comparable economic woes. He's also "Dad," in the nationalistic sense. They know he did bad things, but consider that to have been the necessary price for the stability they enjoy now.

La Paz, Bolivia, June 17

La Paz is making our heads hurt. We're both in bed suffering, asphyxiating. Breathing here is a chore. Technically speaking, we are enjoying what's known as Acute Mountain Sickness (AMS), or colloquially as altitude sickness. It comes in two more serious flavors: moderate and severe. In all cases the symptoms are headache, lethargy, fatigue, dizziness, shortness of breath, disturbed sleep, and a general sense of malaise, to say nothing of an overwhelming urge to leave the country.

Our symptoms started not long after we arrived. Even at the airport, as we passed the special clinic set up to assist incoming travelers who are struck on arrival, we were breathless. That's because La Paz is the highest capital city in the world; 3,600 meters above sea level. You could climb to Denver twice and have six hundred meters left to climb before you get this high. Earlier, before we were sidelined by AMS, we took a brief walk in the city, stopped at a pharmacy and bought altitude sickness medicine, which is really just a mix of analgesic and caffeine, the first to ease the headache, the second to encourage the heart to work harder and get more oxygen to the body. Two very young women are behind the counter. A cocker spaniel is at the door. They're all very friendly, the dog perhaps somewhat more demonstrably. Patricia and Ineka are sisters, have visited the U.S., and speak good English. They excitedly advise us on where to go and what to see around La Paz. These girls are of Amerindian extraction, it's clear, but act cosmopolitan and hip and show no sign of their heritage. They present a very different picture of La Paz from the one we've acquired in the first couple of hours here. In particular, they seem cultures away from the bowler-hatted ladies—they call them *cholas*—out in force throughout the city's dry, dusty streets.

Bolivia has the same effect on us, early in this visit, as a lost puppy might. It's a forlorn place and has been bullied by the bigger dogs on the block for more than 150 years. First it lost its Pacific littoral to Chile. This happened over a hundred years ago but has left a large scab, often picked at by leaders anxious to rouse a nationalistic rabble. Then Brazil grabbed a strip of Bolivia's eastern Amazonian frontier, where rubber is produced. The territory had become a bone of contention. Then, in a dispute over potentially oil-rich territory, the country lost a chunk of its south to Paraguay. It seems to us unfair and unkind to pick on Bolivians. These are a kind and unassuming people. If we could, we'd ask Chile to give back Arica and the 350 kilometers south of there that they took from Bolivia in the War of the Pacific.

Bolivians, certainly Amerindian Bolivians who make up about half the population, are small people. They remind us of South Asians except that here they tend to be fat, especially the women. They emphasize this by wearing flowing skirts under thick sweaters and woolen capes, and on their heads, incredibly, bowler hats. At the end they approximate the shape of an eggplant, or lampshade. We don't know enough about this culture to say why this is the case. The bowler hats are a vestige of European influence; this much we have read. The rest of the ensemble must serve a practical function or else, why? The men, also small, are in Western dress. Everyone is friendly and has a great tan. The older folks look much older than they might in a place with a kinder climate. In Chile we were impressed by how polite people were, but not so much with their friendliness. Here we find that they are always happy to engage in conversation, smile easily, and do not hold against us the fact that we're relatively tall.

The streets of La Paz are dry, dusty, reminiscent of Damascus or Amman, perhaps more the latter for all the hills. The sun is out and feels good, but the fourteen degrees Celsius are as warm as it will get today. Come nighttime, it will be very cold, probably below zero. This morning we start out from the Radisson, a bit gingerly, concerned that the only direction we can take is uphill. That's the way it is. The hotel is on the main thoroughfare that traverses La Paz. It changes names many times, but is always at the lowest point in the valley. Rio Choqueyapu once ran through here, but it has long since been driven underground. A few blocks from the hotel,

Chola in La Paz

the street becomes El Prado, and today there is a festival in full swing. We see booths selling everything from cell phone service to birth control classes. We see food stalls and artisans and wool ponchos and lots of other things, but mostly we see soldiers. La Policía Militar (PM) is headlining this event. It sounds weird, but let's not forget that this is South America. We figure it's a *get-to-know-your-military* kind of thing. Here the soldiers and civilians mix easily. You don't get the sense of unease and strict separation that exists in Vietnam and Cambodia. There are a few Westerners around, mostly younger backpackers. Some are selling stuff, like hand-made jewelry. These are ex- or neo-hippies. They have the wardrobe, the hair, the works. It gives me a good feeling to see this rich tradition sustained.

Then, with no intent whatsoever, we find ourselves in the middle of a folkloric dance festival. A thick crowd is at the entrance of a pink and white neo-classical building past El Prado. We join the stampede into a courtyard that leads to a passageway and on to another much larger courtyard. Turns out we're at Colegio Corazones Sagrados, and today is their annual Festival de la Danza. Dance troupes from communities all over Bolivia are here to show off their regional dances and costumes. We climb the stairs to the second level and are now on a balcony overlooking what normally serves as the sports yard. There are balconies on all four sides of the yard and spectators are four-deep along the railings. Down below the bleachers are thick with the families of the performers. It's a fascinating melting pot of the traditional and the up-to-the-minute. Kids in high-heeled sneakers and Nike apparel hang on their mothers, who are resplendent in their colorful indigenous dress. Today and yesterday, scrunchies and bowler hats.

Back outside we continue our walk around town, huffing up and down hills, dodging microbuses from whose windows designated callers shout out completely unintelligible itineraries. Everywhere shoeshine boys huddle against walls, hoping to ambush dusty shoes. Shoeshine boys in La Paz wear masks, like bank robbers. We learn that many are university students, druggies, or both, and want to keep their identities secret while they earn a few bolivianos in this unglamorous profession. It's just another little thing, like the bowler hats, that makes walking around this city so very different from anyplace else in the world.

For lunch we stop at Cocina de Katy. They advertise an *almuerzo*, or set lunch, for fifteen bolivianos, about three dollars. The restaurant is on the ground floor of a colonial style building that has not been much maintained. It overlooks Plaza Murillo, a lovely square surrounded by the city's cathedral, the Congresso, and the Museo Nacional del Arte. So we march in and ask for the *almuerzo*, expecting a Bolivian lunch. The soup's Bolivian, but the main courses are sweet and sour chicken and spaghetti with tomato sauce. They're playing Beatles songs. After lunch we join the crowd in the square. This is a tolerant city. You can wear your hair in dreadlocks, throw on a bowler hat, pierce your nose, even kiss in public. No one much cares. We like La Paz. It doesn't surprise us one bit to learn that we're sitting at the site where Pedro Domingo Murillo, one of the heroes of the country's independence revolution of 1809, was hanged.

■

We've rented a four-wheel-drive truck and are headed to Valle de la Luna. This is a weird and fascinating natural landscape that has been created by a combination of erosion and aridity. We start out of La Paz but don't get far. There is a protest march coming down the city's only main road. We've heard from many people that demonstrations here are commonplace and a colossal inconvenience, and now we see just how true this is. Take one million people, put them in a city that has one and only one through street, and an inadequate one at that. Now block this street and see what happens. *Carnaval!*

After an hour of wandering, we land in the obviously affluent Zona Sur (Southern Zone) of La Paz. There's a McDonalds so we stop to pee, but are defeated by the cheeseburger medium-fries medium-drink combo, beautifully depicted in four-color Spanish posters, and so pull up a chair. All the rich kids are here. There are no Indians on this side of the counter, and not a single bowler hat in sight. The table immediately adjoining ours is occupied by a fair-haired, tallish woman in her thirties, her mother, and three children. They're in DKNY, GAP, Tommy Hilfiger, and Adidas. This is the face of Bolivia you don't see in the streets of La Paz. We move on and get lost in the prosperous neighborhood of San Miguél. It's not difficult to understand why the disadvantaged feel compelled to march. There is a huge disparity between the rich and poor here. In contrast to the walled mansions you see in San Miguél, there is an entire city, El Alto, which covers most of the high plateau overlooking La Paz. The hundreds of thousands living there can barely manage basic subsistence. We saw this sprawling ghetto from the air as we came in to land a few days ago and consider it remarkable that there isn't even more social upheaval here than we've seen.

Eventually we arrive at Valle de la Luna, and it's very strange, like a landscape of super-sized anthills. You can get around among these, but only if you're agile and strong and can afford to fall down often. There are no paths as such, just tight crannies between the crowded earth cones and spikes. A gang of men is digging a foundation ditch on the edge of the *valle*. They could care less about Valle de la Luna, and examine us briefly with eyes that say, "Silly, isn't it?"

Copacabana, Lake Titicaca, Bolivia, June 20

The road to Lago Titicaca is an unremarkable two-lane artery, used mostly by *micros* taking people back and forth to the capital. These converted vans miraculously manage twenty or so people into a space designed to suffocate no more than nine. Modest villages show up every once in a while along the sides of the road. We see a few houses, mud-made, and the occasional brick two-story with windows and everything.

Valle de la Luna

We suppose that's the school. There's nowhere to go from the main road, and nothing much to see. That's okay. We're really after one thing, and that is to set eyes on the world's highest navigable lake, Titicaca. For the time being we're accepting assertions that Titicaca means "Rock of the Puma." The lake, like La Paz, is nearly four thousand meters in altitude. The terrain around it is rugged, barren, capable of supporting very little life. From Puerto Perez on, we drive through rolling *altiplano* hills, a sort of high rolling desert. It's only when we look closely that we realize people are up here cultivating. We think they're raising potatoes and maybe *quinoa*, the local grain that's used in everything from soup to nuts. A few animals roam the hills. Llamas, donkeys, pigs, and dogs. All domesticated, all busy working for the indigenes. The people that live here, predominantly Aymara, are very poor. They farm to produce enough of something to keep food on the table and to barter for other essentials. Their poverty, however, is considerably more dignified than that of their urban cousins. Here they have the mountains and the lake and wide open space. There, in La Paz, they're shoehorned into dismal tiny kiosks selling whatever they can, or huddled by the side of the road panhandling.

As we round a broad curve, a man appears in the road ahead of us. He's walking toward us, in the middle of the road, waving a red flag. I figure: We're dead. This guy is either a crazed communist agitator or worse: a *cocalero*. This area, as well as the Yungas east of La Paz, has been a center for political upheaval recently. At issue is the eradication of coca plantations. The Bolivian government, under pressure from the U.S., has undertaken a program to stop coca growing, because of the obvious connection to cocaine production and smuggling. The farmers who have made their living from this plant argue that coca is not a drug. They resent U.S. interference in their livelihood and often stage protests to amplify their grievance. The Bolivian government is stuck between a rock and the good ol' U.S. of A. On the one hand it risks losing U.S. aid if it doesn't halt coca production. On the other, it must deal with widespread unrest among *cocaleros*, peasants who depend on the plant for their meager revenue. There is a compromise and it appears to have been reached, but folks on either side of the argument are not confident enough in the outcome to stop their activism. In particular, there is a fringe group led by a man named Quispe, which intends to continue closing rural roads in order to keep the government on its toes. We've been reading about this, and know that Quispe has planned road-closures in the Huarina area, right where we happen to be. All this crosses my mind as the man with the red flag draws closer. I slow down, then stop. He comes up to my side of the truck and I lower the window. This menace turns out to be the forward flagger for a village race. He smiles and shows off a mouthful of white teeth framed in gold caps. They do that here. He explains that children from the schools in the area are having a road race up ahead, and he's out to make sure people don't come barreling through at dangerous speeds. We thank him and move on carefully, grateful that we're not hostages. A few minutes later we reach the kids. Hundreds of them, in green shorts and white T-shirts racing in both directions, on both sides of the road. We are winded just looking and drive on with renewed admiration for Bolivian aerobic capacity. The sun is out, and it's sharp. Up here near the upper limit of the troposphere, there is a crisp clarity in the air. Edges are sharp. It's as though we're looking at everything through freshly sluiced eyeballs.

We're a little surprised when we get to the center of San Pablo de Tiquina and discover that the road disappears into the lake. My planning for this drive is so poor that I didn't even realize we have to cross a strait en route to Copacabana. Twin villages, San Pablo here, and San Pedro on the other side, both "de Tiquina," are the points of passage for people crossing the Estrecho de Tiquina. It's not more than two kilometers across, maybe three. We're told by amused and incredulous locals that the road picks up on the other side, and that we can drive on to Copacabana. There are small passenger ferries at one pier, and you can cross for about fifty cents, American. There are also several flat-bottom boats waiting at the dock. Funny looking things. They have three low sides and an open fourth. The skipper uses a long punt to maneuver the open side against the pier, ties the boat down, and invites you to drive aboard. One vehicle per boat. You drive on and down the sloping deck to the other end of the boat, where a greasy and oil-covered outboard engine lives out its advanced years. We take our time deciding whether or not to chance it. Three or four of these craft are already in the strait, so we watch their progress and assess the risk. They look like larger versions of those betel-nut-leaf offerings we floated in the Ganges not long ago, bobbing tenuously along, hoping that Krishna is feeling magnanimous. Finally, disgusted by our own tentativeness, we take the plunge. A lone soldier managing the process motions to one of the guys, and the latter brings his barge alongside. Our captain today is a young man, maybe twenty, who says he's

Estrecho de Tiquina

been piloting these barges across the strait since his childhood. He charges twenty-six bolivianos, about four dollars at today's exchange rate. There is a fair amount of traffic in the strait. A group of twenty or so tourists is making the crossing on a tour-boat, while their bus is squeezed onto a vehicle barge like ours. The trip is surprisingly long, close to half an hour. That's because the motors on these boats are barely powerful enough to overcome the strong current that would otherwise take us to Peru. At the other end of the *estrecho*,

San Pedro's square is lined with stalls. Aymara *cholas*, decked out in the skirts and bowler-hats, stand in wait. There are a couple of restaurants. We pick the one with the unbelievably massive woman in the doorway. There is no empirical proof that a fat cook is better than a thin one, but it's intuitively reassuring.

After lunch we drive on into the hills. Eventually, as we crest another rise in the road, the plain falls away from us and we see Copacabana on the shores of Lake Titicaca. We start downhill but come to a fat chain blocking the road at a *Carabiniero* checkpoint. A man inside the open doorway of the small one-story adobe building motions to me to approach. I do. He asks for my driver's license and the toll receipt from when we left La Paz. Fortunately, we've kept it, and he stamps *Copacabana* on one side and asks for five bolivianos. Then he asks where I was born. I say, "Syria." He likes that and wonders if I know any Arabic female names. I write down the first three that come to mind: *Najwa, Dana, Ameera*, and ask him why he wants to know. He says that he has a two-month-old baby girl and wants to give her an Arabic name. I ask why, and he says that he likes the sound of them. I'm in no position to debate this, since he has the gun. In any case, he lets us through and we continue downhill to Copacabana.

This lakeside town has become an important hub for travelers between Bolivia and Peru. The Peruvian border is just four kilometers on, or so. It's also the port from which boats leave for the nearby Isla del Sol, supposedly the birthplace of the sun. As a result, a rash of hostels, restaurants, tour operators, and Internet cafés has sprung up to serve the tourist trade. We decide against taking the boat to the island. As important as it is to Inca tradition, we figure we've already spent enough time today on iffy watercraft. Instead we join a large gathering of young backpackers in an open-air restaurant attached to a hostel. We bask together in the hot sun, drinking Cokes and munching hamburgers. Almost everyone here is under thirty. Outside, in the dirt road leading down to the lake, a young couple is juggling bowling pins, tossing them to each other. They're barefoot. You can tell that it's been a while since they've had a shower. These guys are at the rugged end of the tourist demographic, but Copacabana does not attract high-end visitors like its Brazilian namesake might.

Before leaving Copacabana, we stop at the central square to visit the cathedral. It's a lovely place that reminds us of the churches of Andalusia with their broad expanses of white walls, inlaid domes, Moorish arches, and great big carved wooden doors. The stairs leading up through the arched entryway to the courtyard are a gallery of vendors selling snacks, souvenirs, and candles. The candles are supervised by a boy no more than five years old. He's there alone when we arrive and also when we depart, so we assume he runs the spread. Once past the front arch, there is a huge courtyard bisected by a tiled path to the church. On each side of this path, Aymara women sit under their frocks, begging. We make a wide detour around the courtyard because we have no change. The Virgen de Candelaria is here. She is Bolivia's patron saint and attracts the faithful from all around the country. Back outside the church, a priest is consecrating a *micro* while its owner stands reverently beside him. We learn that this happens regularly; it's ecclesiastical collision insurance, so to speak. We head up the bumpy dirt road back to La Paz. When we reach the top of the hill, our young friend the *carabiniero* comes out to undo the chain. I jokingly ask if he's decided on a name for his daughter. He smiles big and says, "Ameera." Hey, stranger things have happened.

Copacabana Cathedral

Tiwanaku, Bolivia, June 22

After our Copacabana trip, we are rewarding ourselves with a day of indolence in La Paz. It's nice that we have a few days here. This way we can rest between excursions. Also, now that we've been here a few days, we are very nearly acclimatized to the altitude and can sneeze without passing out. Our big discovery today is the Museo del Arte Moderno. It's right on El Prado, up the street from our hotel, housed in one of a pair of fascinatingly decaying late nineteenth century buildings with intricate wrought-iron facades, almost filigreed. The contents are an eclectic mix of the kind of art you might expect to find in a country such as Bolivia. Everything here is loaded with the angst of a people still in the grips of overwhelming political, economic, and social issues. You can't produce and present art in Bolivia that skirts these concerns; it would be utterly irrelevant. So the works on display cry "Revolution," "Poverty," "Hegemony," "Freedom," "Loss," and "Pride." All this in the awkwardly elegant Art Nouveau building. We are completely won over by the place, even before we see this sign:

Dear Art Lover

We apologize for the deficiencies you may find in your visit. This is a new insti-
tution in the process of development. Although it has been in the planning and
"dreaming" stage for more than twenty years, we need more time to make it fully
operational. This is the first museum of its type in Bolivia privately run by a
family. No moneys from governmental, state, cities, nor any other national or
foreign institutions were received.

Please bear with us. We want the improvements as much as you do.
Thank you for visiting.

■

The Aymara New Year corresponds with the Southern Hemisphere winter solstice. Aymara from all over the region gather here once a year to witness this singular dawn, of the sun and the year, and to celebrate. We're here as well, freezing cold.
The bus that brought us to the site has a broken heater. By the time we finish the
long drive from La Paz, we're nearly catatonic. When the time comes, we fall off the
bus and file behind our guide to the "special" group entrance. This is a great thing.
Without the "special" arrangement, we would have to stand in the long queue and
would probably die on our feet. We walk through the site to what at one time was
the central temple courtyard. A few thousand people are here already. Mostly
natives, but with a substantial smattering of white folks. There is Aymara pan flute
music, drums, fires, Andean flags, and groups of locals huddled around big pots of
maté. This is all in the open air, of course. At the head of the crowd, standing on top
of the eastern temple stone gate, is a solitary Aymara man, under colorful poncho

Tiwanaku Solstice

and hat, waving the Andean rainbow flag. A
handful of drunks are happily dancing around
and through the crowd, troublesome only
because they stop and piss wherever they happen to be when the call comes. We're all waiting for the sunrise. It's dawn now and we see
more of the crowd. It's all over the place, not
just in the temple. There are people on all the
surrounding low hills. And then, when the
first sliver of bright sunlight winks over the
horizon, all hell breaks loose. People chant and
scream and applaud. Most hold up their bare
palms to the sun. They say that you channel the "positive power" of the sun into
yourself if you do this. They say that for it to really work, however, you must take
off your gloves. Tracy and I gamble that enough "positive power" will make it
through the woolen gloves, and hold our hairy palms up with everyone else. I say
that'll have to do.

When the crowd thins around the ceremonial fire, we make our way there and drop offerings of confetti and coca leaves into it. Like all such ceremonies, the faithful are offered the opportunity to gain a wish by throwing something into the conflagration. At the Trevi, we threw money into the pond. In Thailand we rubbed several Buddha's feet. On the Ganges we launched little betel-nut-leaf boats of stuff, and a candle, to appease the gods. And here we are, ten months into our trip and still in one piece. You can't argue with success, so we close our eyes and wish for a portable space heater.

The Tiwanaku people organized a very successful community on the banks of Lake Titicaca starting in 1,500 B.C. They were great sailors. The Kontiki expedition some years ago set out to prove that these people, or at least their relatives, made reed ships that could cross oceans. Thor Heyerdahl, the leader of the Kontiki, wanted to prove that Polynesia had been settled and colonized by South Americans, and not Indonesians. We've been to Indonesia, Polynesia, and South America. It's easier to believe that Pacific Islanders are related to Indonesians. Some of the symbols on the statues in the temple represent crabs, thus strengthening the hypothesis that the Tiwanaku reached the sea. Then something happened, something apocalyptic that put an end to Tiwanaku society. Some speculate that Titicaca dropped several meters, changing the community's environment radically, land-locking it. Others think the Tiwanaku were subjugated by raiding tribes from the neighborhood. We believe, and now have compelling proof, that they all got tired of the cold and moved to Costa Rica.

Cuzco, Peru, June 24

It's a clear, beautiful day high up in the Andes and the flight from La Paz to Cuzco is about as dramatic as a flight can get without those oxygen contraptions falling out of the ceiling. We spend the first half of the one-hour flight over Lake Titicaca and spot Copacabana from the air. The second half of the trip we meander among the mountains surrounding Cuzco, now above the peaks, now below. This is an imposing, magnificent country. These mountains, the altiplano, the vast expanse of the lake, and the unending emptiness between the few population centers combine to pack a powerful visual wallop. It builds a rising sense of elation, not just because it's stunning, but also because it is for the most part beyond man's reach.

At first glance, Cuzco is a jumbled, dusty, not particularly attractive place. There isn't much color here. The hills are brown and beige, and so are the houses and the people and the animals. Grey stone occasionally breaks that monotony, but only just. It's a little like Santa Fe, away from the malls. We are staying at the Colonial Palace Inn, which is none of these three things. Cuzco is jammed, so options are limited. That's because our trip happens to coincide with the city's most important annual event, Inti Raymi. This is a reenactment of what used to be the greatest and most opulent feast of the year, devoted to the most important of Incan gods, the sun. It is a great fluke that we'll be here, and further evidence that life is what happens when you're busy making other plans.

Since it's Inti Raymi time in Cuzco, we run into parades pretty much everywhere we turn. The big one has completely blocked the central Avenida El Sol. Band after band makes its way north to Plaza de Armas, orbits it once, then disperses into the side streets and adjacent squares. Dancers in traditional, amazingly colorful costumes dance along. It's tubas and trumpets and glitter and those rich mixes of color that we've seen up and down South America. Everything is even more brilliant in contrast to the drab surroundings. Most of the bands are made up of a brass section, a pan flute or two, and one big drum whose sweet spot is invariably patched with duct tape. Nobody hurries here. We're on South American time. Thirty minutes is an hour and a half. 10 a.m. is anytime before noon. The bands shuffle along unhurriedly, blowing for all they're worth. We're enjoying this almost total immersion in South America. It's the eve of the Big Day, and we're here for it.

We have lunch in one of the many restaurants near Plaza de Armas. The house specializes in *ceviché*, made from raw fish, often sole; diced and marinated in lemon and vinegar; smothered in onions and other spices; and served up as an appetizer or main course all over Peru. It's this country's equivalent of antipasto. I want very much to try it, but will wait until we're someplace where hygiene standards are a little higher, like in Connecticut.

■

There was an earthquake in Arequipa overnight. That's about five hundred kilometers from Cuzco, and it's far too close for comfort. Peru gets big quakes routinely. The last big one in 1970 killed seventy thousand people. This one was comparatively minor, but as we sit in the stands during Inti Raymi, the possibility of a good shake here is never far from our minds. Inti Raymi is a huge spectacle. We're at Sacsayhuaman, an ancient, fortified Incan site. The center of the big clearing now contains a raised stage, built and painted to resemble the original rampart boulders. The show opens with hundreds of flagbearers coming over the crest of the hills overlooking the ramparts. Hundreds of men in Incan dress, that is to say, draughty tunics, all waving large Andean rainbow flags, stream up from behind the hill. Big drums and horns and flutes fill the air with an eerie warlike music, an unholy din. When the flagbearers have taken their positions, hundreds of dancers and actors begin to enter the clearing from both sides. By the time they have all come down from the hills, the field is full. The ceremony is elaborate, like opening ceremonies at the Olympics. Behind us at ground level near the main path a toothless woman sells candied apples. She calls out, "*Manzana, manzana, manzana, manzana!*" in a musical and painstakingly annoying way, resting between calls only long enough to take air. She wipes the red apples down with a damp cloth. We see her reach into a dusty bundle on the ground and pull out a small plastic bottle of water from which she liberates just enough to dampen the cloth. She's doing such a brisk business that the cotton candy man relocates near her, hoping to pick up some of the crowd. A neo-hippie attempts to sneak up into the bleachers by scaling the scaffolding. He is busted immediately by a uniformed policeman. A band of young urchins go around begging for whatever they can see. These distractions help to pass the time but the celebration takes too long and we tire of the Inca's communion with the Sun God, who is frying us where we sit. People start sneaking out. The candied apple lady has abbreviated her call by one *manzana*. It's clear that everyone wants to go home. The flag bearers in the hills are all sitting down now. The llama's been sacrificed, the

Inti Raymi

dancers have all danced, but the King Inca is still on stage, delivering with all his might a long *Quechua* monologue into the sun. We could use a small quake right about now.

Machu Picchu, Peru, June 25

The tour company picks us up at the Colonial Palace Inn at 5:30 in the morning, and transports us, with one other young woman, to the Cuzco train station. Several trains leave for Machu Picchu this time of day. The local train is cheapest, but slowest and least comfortable. We're on the fastest and most comfortable, the 6:20 Inka Class train, and are immediately impressed as we walk up into the carriage and see white table cloths and silverware and china and wood paneling and attendants in crisp navy blue jackets and slacks. We soon realize that we have a two-fold problem. The first is that the train is unheated. It's several degrees below zero outside, and only marginally warmer than that in here. The second is that there is a Brazilian woman across the aisle from us who feels compelled to leave her window open. Facing us is a couple in their thirties. She's Peruvian and he's French. They're getting cold, annoyed as well, and huff frequently in French.

We cast off, or whatever trains do, and begin the slow chug up the hill. It's still dark and we can see inside mud-brick houses that stand alongside the track. Single naked bulbs hang from a wire in the middle of nearly empty rooms. To get up the mountain, this narrow-gauge train has to do a stair-climbing sort of thing. We go east, uphill, the locomotive pulling us along. Then we stop where the track ends and go west, this time the locomotive pushing. Chutes and Ladders. Back and forth like this a half-dozen times until we finally make it to the top of the mountain and start the journey in earnest, northwest bound. Three young attendants, one female, begin the breakfast service. Things go slowly because there is only just enough of everything to exactly serve those present. When one of the attendants accidentally pours pineapple juice for a customer who wanted orange juice, the remedy is to return the unauthorized pineapple juice to its carton, send the glass to the galley with the third attendant to be washed, and then refill it with orange juice. One passenger, one glass. It's only when we reach Ollantaytambo that the train warms up sufficiently for us to peek out from under our Bolivian ponchos and to start drawing normal breaths. The cold, the abysmally slow service, the absence of spare anything, the inefficiency, might at first frustrate the inexperienced traveler, but we see past all that to the good news. The train left on time; the cars are clean; there are no bugs here; no smoking of any sort is allowed; the other passengers are polite and quiet. Peru has not had political and economic stability long enough to be held to standards common in Europe and the U.S., but they're getting there. Now if they can just keep their politicians from robbing the country.

In the meantime, Vladimiro Montesinos was busted in Venezuela and returned to Peru to stand trial for ripping the country off during the Fujimori regime. The latter is still in Japan, but Peru argues that his extradition is subject to international, not Japanese law. Montesinos, known by the populace as Vladi, was Fujimori's spy chief, and had a reputation for tough, omnipotent invincibility. Then, scandal. Fujimori fled to Japan, of which country he is a national, while Vladi disappeared somewhere in South America. The FBI helped nab him by monitoring communications among his known associates. Now every channel shows footage of him, emaciated, downcast, shell-shocked I think. It's a hell of a fall.

Our train threads the valleys among the Andes and we are often in the shadow of sheer rock-faces. From Ollantaytambo to Machu Picchu, the track runs along the bank of the Rio Urubamba. Families live by the river, tending to small plots of grain, raising a few head of livestock. Few take notice as the train goes by. We arrive at the station and disembark, then get on buses for the ascent to the sanctuary. It's a very steep dirt road that must switch back often to minimize the angle of ascent. If you happen to be on the precipice side of the bus and look out, you can quickly figure out why the Incas thought they'd be safe up here.

Our guide, and the star of this tour, is Darwin Camacho Paredes. Darwin is a ball of fire. He is in his early forties, a student of all things Inca. He taught for a while at Cuzco University. Darwin's most endearing quality is his fervent zeal as champion of Machu Picchu and Inca civilization in general, his own ancestors. On top of all that, he cultivates a healthy ambivalence for the modern-day discoverer of the site, Hiram Bingham, now long departed. As we stomp around this unbelievably beauti-

Machu Picchu

ful place, he goes on about what Bingham said and what is actually the case. Darwin has published his views on all this in "*The True* [sic] *of Machu Picchu.*" Throughout the tour, he methodically takes the meat off the bones of Bingham's work. He accuses him of having been a brutal taskmaster; of obfuscating the identity of the true discoverer of Machu Picchu—an Indian named Lizarraga—and of stealing many artifacts found at the sanctuary. It's tough to argue with Darwin. The facts he presents are compelling and, where that's not the case, his enthusiasm prevails.

On the train ride back we see cactus, yucca, glaciers and rivers, subsistence farming lots, a boy hanging wet laundry on a tree by the side of a mud house, cows grazing, field fires burning. In the hills to our west is the Inca Trail, a trek that passes a dozen Inca ruins, and that has become a tourist favorite. Tour operators can organize the thing so that all you have to do is walk. They provide the tents, the food, and any other equipment needed. Once in a while the rock face strikes out from just past the rails, straight up, like a wall. We pass protrusions in these walls and you'd swear we would scrape against them. Down here, quite a few hundred meters below Cuzco, there are flowers and berries all along the route. Shocks of yellow speed past as we pass forsythia bushes. Arriving at Cuzco after dark, we reverse the zigzag we did on our way out of town, this time making descending cuts down the side of the hill. The air is so clear up here that lights barely twinkle.

Lima, Peru, June 28

Andean babies don't cry. Tracy first makes this observation in La Paz, and we confirm it repeatedly as we travel through Bolivia and Peru. They can be slung on their mothers' backs in the heat and cold, with diesel and noise and dust all around, but they don't complain. They sleep a lot. Or they observe silently. It's as though they understand that it will do very little good to grumble. There is an exception, and she is of course on our flight from Cuzco to Lima, up ahead somewhere, far enough from us to be odorless, but we hear her. This child, we assume it's a girl just to be egalitarian, may have Infantile Tourette's. Every few moments, she screeches. Short, jagged, penetrating shrieks that breach the body at each and every pore and orifice, not needing ears at all. From the air Lima is under a famous bank of thick coastal fog that makes its winters gloomy and damp. They call this fog *garúa*. When we drop through it, we see a flat, sprawling city. It's notable for the dearth of tall buildings. Good thinking. They get earthquakes here often, and these are sometimes disastrous. Last week's bad one in the country's south is still on the front page of every newspaper. At last count there were 150,000 homeless in and near Arequipa.

Taxis in Lima are like the stray dogs of San Marcos de Bariloche. They are numerous, come in all sizes and colors, will not leave you alone, are always in the streets, and emit an impressive trail of pollution. It seems that all you need to operate a taxi here is a plastic sticker that reads "TAXI." Could be red, yellow, white, any color sticker, any shape. The single consistent condition is having this sticker on the windshield. There are no meters in these cars. You negotiate the price and you go. On arrival at the airport, there is a *Taxi Oficiál* kiosk just inside Arrivals. They want seventy nuevo soles to Miraflores. You get three and a half soles to the dollar. We skip them and go outside. Here a large man in a see-through white shirt offers us the same ride for fifty soles. We take it. If we had gotten past this nice goon on the sidewalk, we might have paid twenty, but there's no telling what kind of a rattler we'd have found ourselves in. Taxi drivers are a city's ambassadors. As has been the case throughout South America, we find Lima's to be engaging, chatty, and willing to discuss anything, from the innocuous, like weather and the view from here or there, to the explosive, like politics or sports. This one is no exception, and what's more, he only drives like a maniac in short bursts, following which he quickly regains his equanimity and slows down. He has just one important fault: He's lost.

We intend to relax in Lima. These past couple of weeks in La Paz and Cuzco and Machu Picchu have worn us out. The travel, the altitude sickness, the unbelievable range of temperature in the course of a given day, have beaten us up. So we're staying at the Double Tree Pardo hotel in Miraflores, an American hotel in the city's up-scaliest suburb. They issue us their trademark, complimentary chocolate chip cookies at check-in. We couldn't be happier.

Miraflores is clean, convenient, and very cosmopolitan, but there is also an intense focus on security. Houses and apartment buildings and businesses all have big, tall, nasty fences around them. Barbed wire and bougainvillea. Armed guards stand in front of commercial doorways. Smaller businesses are locked up behind iron bars and will only buzz customers in after they've eyeballed them. As we drive through the area, the taxi driver explains that this is all merely a vestige of the days when the *Sendero Luminoso* (Shining Path) and the *Movimiento Revolucionario Túpac Amaru* were alive and active throughout the country. He says this is all in the past, since these groups were pretty much dismantled by the government in the early nineties. He insists that the only explosive thing left in Lima is the *ceviché*. We hope he's right about that.

Still, certainly in this neighborhood, you feel safe as you walk in the street. Away from the main thoroughfares, we see a wonderful assortment of Art Deco houses, pillboxes with clean lines and funky colors like pistachio and mauve. Buildings that have been reinforced to withstand earthquakes plant a green placard in their front yard with a big letter *S*, for *sismo*. The newest and shiniest hangout in Miraflores is Larco Mar. This is an American-style shopping mall that is built into the cliffs, for lack of a better word, overlooking the Pacific. These are a hundred or so meters high and are composed of a mix of soil and pebbles. To us they look very precarious and likely to fall down in a good rain or a brisk shake. Everyone we ask, including the usually reliable taxi drivers, seems unconcerned. We become unconcerned also, and spend a lovely couple of hours at a pizzeria perched right on the edge of these mounds. The people hanging out here are thoroughly First World.

Larco Mar is a community that has adopted the trappings and aspect of a uniform world. Shoppers Without Borders. You can find a place just like this one, minus the precarious cliffs, in nearly every country we've visited.

We've hired a guide to show us Lima. Her name is Antonia. She is a mile-a-minute firecracker tour guide, is scared to death of earthquakes, and sleeps with her purse and coat and shoes right by the bed. Her father was in government but is now eighty-six and retired. He is leaving his family only two things: a love for the country and his good name. She says that were it not for the family's impoverishment due to her father's scrupulous incorruptibility, she would now be a choreographer instead of a tour guide. We don't know for sure, but suspect that Antonia tells us this about her father because of the recent corruption scandal that brought down president Fujimori and his chief of security. She may be trying to distance herself from these guys. It's understandable, but strikes us as paradoxical. When Fujimori came to power in 1990, he took on and defeated the *Sendero Luminoso* and *Movimiento Revolucionario Túpac Amaru.* He's discredited now but you could argue that were it not for him, Lima would not be attracting tourists and Antonia would not have a job at all.

Downtown Lima is interesting and hospitable, even if everyone thinks you'll get mugged if you wear anything shiny. The city was founded in 1535 by Francisco Pizarro. Incidentally, Pedro Valdivia, the man who founded Santiago, worked for Pizarro. It's astonishing how few the men who shaped world history. This is the same Pizarro who had played the two Inca sides against the middle, taking advantage of the quarrel between the brother kings Atahualpa and Huascar. After helping the former defeat his brother, Pizarro eventually killed Atahualpa as well. This Spaniard's progress in South America was perhaps even bloodier than his countrymen's.

No doubt thanks to Pizarro and his countrymen, the population of Lima is today predominantly mestizo. We don't see Indians here like we did in La Paz and Cuzco. The historical center of the city is at Plaza Mayor, previously Plaza de Armas. It is surrounded by a number of restored colonial buildings, including the government palace, the cathedral, and the Franciscan monastery. We pull up to the palace for a look at the changing of the guard. It takes place here daily but, unlike the ceremony in Santiago where the soldiers are out in the open, these guys are behind an obnoxiously high fence that surrounds the building. The few people who jam up to the iron bars can see the show. The rest of us get a vague sense of the thing from the moving blue and crimson uniforms. Antonia says that she spent seven years as a Presidential Palace guide. She can vouch for the fact that the president's representative, who shows up at the palace door and is informed

Plaza Mayor

by the Master of the Guard that everything is fine, actually hoofs back to the president's office to deliver this news every day! Now we pop into the city's cathedral for a look. We're jumpy anyway, but Antonia confirms our jitters when she says that if there were the slightest tremor, she would run outside of this big church immediately. It's already had a couple of tower reconstructions.

From here we walk on to visit Casa de Aliaga. This colonial treasure has been in the same family for seventeen generations, four hundred years, give or take fifty. Regardless, it is considered to be the oldest continuously inhabited house in the Western Hemisphere. It's wonderfully graceful on the outside. Inside it's understandably dusty and old and full of dusty old things. There are portraits of the family on the walls. Some are quite recent, photographs of weddings. The family still lives here, but in sections of the big place that are not open to the public. Living in the same house that your family occupied when Pizarro was chasing Mapuche in the hillsides must be a peculiar experience. Also, it occurs to me, seventeen generations of photo albums could pose a logistical problem.

At the end of our organized tour with Antonia, we stop at the Archeological Museum for a quick visit. She recommended it, saying that it is well organized, didactic, and not too big. And it is all of these things. There are exhibits spanning the long history of indigenous South American cultures including the Chavín, the

The Simpsons of Lima

Tiwanaku, and the Inca. There are wonderfully preserved mummies, displayed in pairs, sitting in the fetal position. This is how they were buried, in convenient pouches. From a distance these pouches look like burlap eggs. There are also several examples of skulls that had undergone trepination, the ancient science of drilling holes in people's skulls to relieve pain, then plugging the holes back up. We wonder what they had for anesthesia, and how they might react if they were to come back today and meet aspirin. Some skulls have been "customized." Back then, the Indians figured out how to gradually reshape the skull of a child (kind of like foot-binding in Japan) in order to illustrate the bearer's social status. The specimens on display look like The Simpsons.

■ central america ■

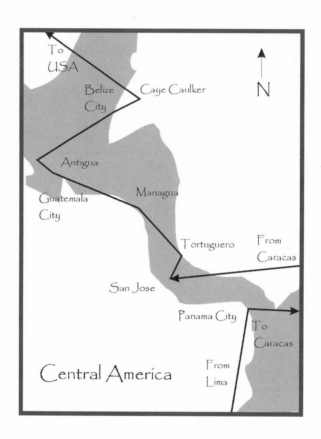

To
USA

Belize
City

Caye Caulker

N

Antigua

Managua

Guatemala
City

Tortuguero

From
Caracas

San Jose

Panama City

To
Caracas

Central America

From
Lima

"...the America that shudders in hurricanes and
survives on love.
She lives, you of Saxon eyes and barbarian spirit.
And she dreams and she worships and she throbs, and
she is
the daughter of the Sun.
Beware. Viva Latin America!"

— Rubén Darío (1867–1916), Nicaraguan poet

Panama City, Panama, July 2

"*Un Canal Para El Nuevo Milenio*": A Canal for the New Millennium. This is painted in large letters on the Canal administration building at Miraflores Locks. The Panama Canal is not just a big ditch that cuts across Central America between the Caribbean Sea and Pacific Ocean. It is the defining event in this country's history, and probably its future. Without the Panama Canal, there would be no Panama. Literally. The French won first whack at building the canal in the late 1800s. It didn't work. They ran out of money, lost thousands of workers to yellow fever, and discovered numerous other exotic jungle diseases. So the United States offered to buy the con-

Panama City

cession and carry on the work. The French agreed, but back then, in 1903, Panama was part of Colombia. Colombia considered the deal and said "*No, gracias.*" Not long after this resounding but polite rejection, Panama unilaterally declared its independence from Colombia. This was no coincidence; U.S. interests, represented by a few enthusiastic businessmen, breathed life into the secession. Bogotá sent a fleet to quell the upstart nation-to-be, but ran into the U.S. Navy on the way. So Panama happened, and the many agreements signed then or shortly thereafter gave the U.S. a concession to build the canal, the right to deploy troops in the area, and the option to use military force if need be to defend it. In other words, Panama came to be a country because of the Canal. The first ship sailed through here in 1914, on August 15. The other big news of the month was the start of World War One.

Now we're here, with about thirty other people, overlooking Miraflores Locks from a platform erected alongside the canal. This is the southernmost of three such locks that help ships climb mountains that would otherwise get in the way of crossing the Panamanian Isthmus. The Canal is not, as I had imagined, a channel that's been dug through the middle of Panama. It's really more like a staircase, rising from both sides of the country, from both seas, thirty or so meters up to Gatun Lake in the middle of the isthmus. Ships are raised up to and lowered down from this lake by the locks. Without this system, the canal would still have been possible, but only after three thousand years of excavation. An announcer delivers a blow-by-blow narrative in English and Spanish. We learn that the massive *Heijin* is paying more than $130,000 to get through here today. She's a huge cargo ship hauling automobiles. The average ship pays $30,000. The *Heijin* inches into the lock under its own power, being guided by locomotives on tracks that run on each side of the canal. The gate closes behind it. Twenty minutes later, now lower in the lock, she emerges into the Pacific and we abandon the platform and head for the small exhibition room, where we spend fifteen minutes watching a film about the canal. It was interesting, but steered clear of anything controversial. Our own interest lies in the scandalous, though, so we did some digging. Turns out that the man in charge of the project when the French had it was none other than Ferdinand Lesseps. This is the same *monsieur* who built the Suez Canal. When the French withdrew from the Panama Canal project, Monsieur Lesseps was found guilty of helping himself to some of the project funds. Corruption is not a new thing in this part of the world.

From Miraflores Locks we drive northbound, along the canal. The road winds through thick tropical rainforest. You can see just how difficult it must have been cutting through here back in the days before air-conditioned 4x4s and heavy machinery and Jungle Jim mosquito repellent. Panama is a poor country, or at least a poorly administered one. As soon as we reach population centers, the place goes to hell. There's garbage and debris and a seemingly endless supply of broken-down buses with which to fill clearings by the side of the road.

We reach Portobelo in just under two hours. There was a time when this Caribbean port was one of the wealthiest outposts in the Americas. The Spanish protected it with four fortresses. The town still got sacked often, especially by the English, pirates and lords alike. Representing the latter group, Sir Francis Drake completely destroyed the city in 1572. He got his comeuppance in 1596, when dysentery got him not far from here. A procession of invaders and marauders, including Sir Henry Morgan—famous these days for the eponymous rum— attacked the city repeatedly in the ensuing two hundred years. That was then. Now the town is a dusty, rusty, forgotten and somewhat scary place. There's a church, San Felipe, in the square. We pull up and park the car. Four women in faded once-colorful dresses hang out alongside a wooden cart from which hang necklaces and charms. Tracy and I are the only visitors in town. A big boy in his late teens, in torn khaki trousers and a brown, soiled T-shirt, walks past us and into the church, where he slides into the last pew. He's watching us the whole time. There's no one else in the church. The huge front doors are flung open. So are the side doors at the other end of the church. As we walk in he mutters something about keeping an eye on the car. I notice that the stick he leaned against the bench has a big nail through the end of it and enthusiastically give him a dollar. There is the famous "Black Jesus" statue here, carved three centuries ago. It's behind glass near the altar and is dressed in a flowing purple robe. They take this statue out for an elaborate annual procession in October, and thousands come for the celebration. I ask the boy about this and he says he has a purple robe also. I ask him what people in Portobelo do for work. He says they don't. It's a conversation that begs for a merciful end, so we leave and drive through a couple of the narrow back streets for a look. Nothing much happens here. We see folks lazing about. It's hot and cloyingly humid. The urge to do something does not come often in this weather. It takes a certain resilience and boundless sluggishness to exist here.

■

We spend our last morning in Panama touring Casco Viejo, the city's old quarter. There is a Caribbean feel to this place. The people are black, mostly, and not Indian. It's a ramshackle but very colorful place where most of life is lived in the open, in the street or on balconies or just inside window shutters. Laundry hangs over wrought iron balustrades. Old people watch from every other dark doorway. One couple leans out of the cut-out in the bright green wood wall that separates their living room from the street. These two are ancient. We see him from the waist up, her from the chest up. He's in white shirt and straw hat. She's in a black dress with white embroidery on the shoulders, and she has a pipe in her mouth. We stop for a picture on a quiet street along the waterfront. There's a constabulary so we figure it's safe. One police officer is at the door and he studies us for a moment before coming over. We just carry on taking pictures. He joins us and asks that we be very careful in the plaza one block over, because there are some miscreants who will apparently come down from their house and take our camera away, even if it means hurting us in the process. To animate his mean-

Casco Viejo

ing, he points to a man sleeping menacingly in a ditch not far from where we stand. It's not clear whether our new friend the police officer expects payment for this information. If he does, he is not explicit about it, and I'm not about to risk being thrown in a Panamanian jail for paying off a representative of the law. We get in the car and move on. Judging by the look on his face as we do this, he would not have minded some sort of consideration.

The highlight of our visit to the Casco Viejo is the Teatro Nacional. We had read that this is a lovely old concert hall, so when it appears we stop for a visit. It costs one dollar apiece to get in and we have the run of the place. It so happens that El Insituto Nacional De Cultura and the Ballet Nacional de Panama are here rehearsing for this coming Thursday's performance. We snoop around for a while, then find the VIP box and settle in for a half hour of spectating. We tried the door to the Presidential Box, but it's locked. As we sit watching the dancers, it occurs to us that Manuel Noriega probably enjoyed a few performances here before taking the Extended Penitentiary Tour in the U.S.

Caracas, Venezuela, July 5, 2001

"Venezuela" means "Little Venice." "Caracas" means "Hand over your car keys and bolívares and jewelry or I will Uzi you right here on the plush leather interior of this fancy car at this busy intersection, *pronto!*" There is a pathological crime problem here. The capital especially, this modern, rambling metropolis of ten million people, has won a reputation for rampant, violent crime. Eighty-five people were killed in Caracas this weekend. Most of these deaths were apparently the result of ongoing gang wars, mostly over turf and drugs. We hear all kinds of horror stories: "They'll kill you for the change in your pockets; they'll take you hostage and keep you until your family gives up every dime you're worth; they'll carry you to the jungle and make you their plaything."

Although Venezuela won independence from Spain in 1821, it didn't have democratic elections until 1947. No rush. Nowadays President Hugo Chávez seems strong and very much in control. He's been in power since 1998. This reflects well on the country, since this same man led a failed coup in 1992 and spent two years cooling his jets in jail for it. In most other nearby nations, he'd be pushing up coca plants. That's all behind us. It's the Fifth of July, Venezuelan Independence Day, and Chávez has presided over the celebrations all day long. We're watching on TV. Our own participation began involuntarily at 7:30 a.m., when thirty-four thousand Air Force helicopters took off from the nearby military airfield and provided a thundering wake-up call.

Recreational travel is not all fun and games. We've done better in some countries than we have in others. In terms of sheer coverage, we did well in New Zealand, Australia, Europe, and India. We saw a lot of Oman, Argentina and Chile. We did okay in Thailand and not quite as well in Malaysia. Venezuela will remain, for now, a mystery. We spent our two days in Caracas eating sumptuous home-cooked meals with friends, enjoying their company and the comfort of their apartment, and watching TV. We strolled and shopped around the upscale neighborhood of Las Mercedes on the western fringes of town, but we did not venture far because we're scared to death of this city. You can tell, just driving around, that there is something very wrong in Caracas. It does not invite you to walk and explore, or to sample public transport. It's not a city that opens its arms to you, like Buenos Aires or Santiago. In a sense it's very much a city at war. People come and go and work and shop because they have to, but the possibility of trouble is never far off.

On the drive back out to Maiquetia Airport, I chat with the driver about life in Caracas. He confirms what we've heard about crime and says that it's been like this for years. Everyone he knows has been robbed. He avoids stopping at intersections because he once was robbed while idling at a light. He points out the shantytowns on the hillsides flanking both sides of the road. These are called *ranchos*. He chuckles at my misunderstanding of the word. They're not ranches, but slums, built from whatever can be found; discarded wood, adobe, whatever. I can almost hear the time-bomb tick.

Edwin and Fernando are shoeshine boys at Caracas airport. Tracy and I had finally found a cleanish table in the second-floor cafeteria when Edwin comes by and asks if I want my boots shined. He drops easily into a crouch and gets to work. Soon Fernando comes along, carrying not just his shoeshine box, but also a large, empty coffee tin which he slings under Edwin, who nonchalantly sets his butt on it. We are impressed by this cooperation and invite Fernando to shine Tracy's boots. He's six or so. Edwin is a couple of years older. These boys have had haircuts recently; they're clean and speak good Spanish and a smattering of tourist-useful English. Two other, bigger boys carrying their kits shuffle up and join us, also polite and presentable. They all go to the same school, but shine shoes to supplement family incomes. Their homes are in the *ranchos* in the hills by the airport. These guys seem not in the least unhappy with their lives. All are fascinated by our digital camera so we shoot a few and show them. They laugh out loud at each other's pictures. We're laughing and kidding around as the two kids shine our shoes, but of course it's a shame that they couldn't be doing something else at this time of their lives. On the other hand, they don't live in the street and burn garbage for warmth.

San José, Costa Rica, July 14

All hell has broken loose in San José. The national soccer team just scored the first goal of their match against Honduras. From our hotel room we can hear shouting and jubilation and a whole lot of car horn honking in the streets. They're playing in Medellín, Colombia. Police are on every corner down San José's main Avenida Central. While strolling through downtown earlier, and before we knew about the event, we stop and ask one pair of officers if this is normal. The two are young men, in their twenties, and easy to smile. They explain that Costa Rica is playing Honduras in the Copa America tonight. If we (Costa Rica) win, there will certainly be a party in the streets. "What if we lose?" we have the audacity to ask. "There'll be a party anyway." Regardless, we will hear about it, because we're staying at the Gran Hotel Costa Rica in the very heart of San José.

The story of this soccer championship is emblematic of Latin America. It's the world's oldest international soccer championship, first staged in 1916. This year Colombia is host. In May deadly bombings in Medellín raised concerns that the country's forty-year-old guerilla war would spill over and disrupt the event. Then in June, as participating countries were preparing to send their teams to the competition, the vice president of the Colombia Soccer Federation was kidnapped by rebels. He was released a few days later, but the tournament was suspended by the South American Soccer Federation. A couple of weeks later, the group reversed itself, but it was too late for Canada and Argentina, who pulled out of the games. Honduras and Costa Rica are filling in. So far the tournament has gone on without incident and we've watched a couple of matches on TV. Security is tight. Fans are frisked as they enter the stands. Colombia's president, Andres Pastrana, has named the games "The Peace Cup." It's all very strange.

In my book, Costa Rica's singular achievement since its independence in 1821 is the abolishment of the military. This came on the heels of the 1948 civil war, an

Museo Nacional

affair that lasted several weeks and did away with a couple of thousand people. So they banned the military. Simple enlightenment. A beautiful thing in a universe of despots and idiots, crooks and incompetents. The largest remaining vestige of that era is Bellavista Fortress, which used to be Army headquarters but now contains the Museo Nacional. What sweet irony, taking a thing that epitomizes force and making it the serene house of the country's culture and art and anthropology. Another remarkable and unusual thing about Costa Rica is that prostitution here is legal. Without passing judgment on the moral rectitude of this action, it at least tells us that this is an eminently pragmatic country. There's big common sense in this little isthmus.

San José is a busy, bustling city, especially here in the center. People mill about in the pedestrian mall that runs the length of the compact downtown. It feels safe. The sidewalk café attached to the Gran Hotel Costa Rica is open twenty-four hours. So is the casino on the ground floor. It's nice to be in a place where such a thing is possible. From our window on the fourth floor we look down on the Plaza de la Cultura, an open space with concrete benches and an especially ugly seventies fountain. Notwithstanding its unattractiveness, the square is a great gathering place and people swarm around all day and night. Photographers with Polaroid cameras make their living by scattering birdseed on their customers' heads and snapping away when the pigeons land. The fixture pan flute ensemble has worked out a deal with McDonalds and performs to big crowds in the restaurant's spacious entryway. We see no drug deals or violence. The young people who gather here want to see and be seen. They dress as much like teen idols as they can, and bear the burden of young people all over South and Central America: They want to be from Miami.

There is a tiny butterfly reserve in San José, not far from downtown, called Spirogyra, Jardín de Mariposas. After spending the morning walking around the city's several small, cozy parks, we make our way across the Rio Torres to this place. It's tiny all right. Our host is Luis, a delicate man in his sixties. He greets us at the gate and hands us a plastic-wrapped instruction board before releasing us into the wire-mesh enclosure. A sign on the door reads:

Butterflies and Frogs in Your Path.
Watch Your Step!

It's a miniature jungle in here. We learn that most butterflies live for somewhere between four and six weeks. Their primary contribution to the world is as pollinators. They're also on the menu for various predators. We take a slow amble through the enclosure and observe that, just as Luis said, butterfly species live in particular plants to the exclusion of others. A visible exception is the largest in the compound, a gray thing when its wings are folded that hides a brilliant velvety blue when they're open. These relative behemoths will sit anywhere including on the ground. A couple must have dozed off in that position because now they're tiny prayer rugs: flat, velour, motionless. Soon we find ourselves feeling very much at home. Various butterflies come to check us out. They land on us. They get startled and flutter away, but they come back. We pose with these delicate visitors. We give them pet names. Then we start hearing voices in our heads, so we move for the exit. Luis is right there waiting for us. He shepherds us, daintily, to the two chairs in front of the TV in the "auditorium." Here we sit for twenty minutes and watch a well-made video, with English voice-over, that rounds out our first serious poke into the world of the butterfly. Until this moment, they were to us just worms with wings.

Costa Rica is a seriously religious country. We have a group of singing evangelists in Plaza de la Cultura. Three young women with very long black hair and one bearded, much older man. They have an electric keyboard, a couple of tambourines, and a guitar. The man does the speechifying. In between his passions, the women entertain the crowd with pop rockin' hallelujahs. You can feel the healing as the colónes drop into the guitar case. The show starts at 6:00 or so and goes for a couple of hours. Tonight they're hitting all the high notes and the crowd is on fire. We can see that the people know this group. They sing along. One guy, a few meters back from the throng, is up on a cement bench, doing an animated parting-of-the-waters sort of dance. We're in our room on the fourth floor of the Gran Hotel and can survey the scene in its entirety from here.

Also in this plaza you can see young Western missionaries chatting up the locals, making the case for Jesus. They are unmistakable in their sixties frocks, Birkenstocks, beaming wholesome smiles and wild manes of born-again hair. Back in the U.S., where evangelism has kept up with fashion and technology, this mud-and-patchouli approach is dead, but here they get a sympathetic ear. Up and down Avenida Central this Sunday morning, we hear the sound of sermons and other zeal coming from doorways and windows of places that don't resemble churches. So we conclude that there's a lot of worship going on. We support all this, and believe that it promotes a more peaceful society, especially in crowded urban centers. Nevertheless, despite the great and joyous gatherings that happen at our doorstep, we have reason to suspect that San José is not without its own crime problem.

The city's central cathedral has two burly, white-shirted, revolver-hipped guards who continually stroll up the nave and down the aisles. Can a church be robbed? From where we sit, in the very back pew, we see nothing that you can walk away with. In the streets of San José we see lots of barbed wire and iron bars on businesses and homes. Just last weekend, in one of the city's suburbs, a prominent journalist was shot dead in front of his home. Parmenio Medina was the host of the highly popular, satirical radio show called "*La Patada*," or "The Kick." People here and the press speculate that this crime, the first-ever killing of a journalist in Costa Rica, may mark the beginning of the end of the country's relative peace and stability. We hope they're wrong, but won't deny that the country's reputation rang too good to be true.

The good news is that we beat Honduras 1–0, and now downtown is jammed with celebrating fans, waving the country's red, white and blue from car windows. We watch from our room and are overwhelmed with Latin Americanness.

Tortuguero, Costa Rica, July 18

Now we're driving from San José to the Caribbean coast. The ultimate attraction there is the turtles of Tortuguero, but everybody says we must also go south to Puerto Viejo and spend a couple of days relaxing in its Caribbean climate and atmosphere. All around us is tropical rain forest. The road climbs through the Cordillera Central. This chain of volcanoes runs north-south through the middle of the country. From here we descend to the lowlands, and the thick forest gives way to banana plantations. An hour later we're on the outskirts of Limón and now both sides of the road are covered with rough slapdash houses. Limón is built around its port and features the typical architectural abuses. The population here is predominantly black. We can tell as we drive around that there is a greater Afro-Caribbean influence than a Latino one. The drive from Limón to Puerto Viejo takes another hour. The Caribbean is to our left and swamps are to our right.

Puerto Viejo is like Key West might be immediately after a very big party, followed by a disorderly evacuation. The very fanciest place along the strip of road that goes through here is Villas Caribes, and it's not much. We stop for a look. They're asking for sixty-eight dollars a night, plus the usual Costa Rican sixteen percent sales tax. That's twenty dollars a night more than the Gran Hotel Costa Rica in San José, and about forty dollars more than we'll pay for what they have to offer. We carry on, and stop at the Yaré Hotel. This one is more reasonable, thirty-five dollars a night plus tax, but there is a small problem: It's built on the swamp. There is a catwalk that leads from the reception desk near the road to the two-story wooden cabins. As we make our way back there to have a look, we see millions of mosquitoes splashing around in the muck, shaking off their afternoon naps, helping their youngsters hatch. We can't get out fast enough, and sustain a few nibbles in the process.

Back in the heart of Puerto Viejo, things are very laid back. If you happen to be here someday, you'll see several people wearing "Listen to Bob Marley" T-shirts. It's that kind of place. Rastafarians hang out along the sides of the all-dirt-all-the-time paths, selling handicrafts or just "being." Puerto Viejo is a messy little place. Public services are minimal, so if a plastic bag full of garbage or a pop bottle finds its way to the beach, it will probably reside there until the next tsunami. The beach is okay, but just okay. Most "hotels" are really flophouses. The one we finally settle on, the Maritza, offers rooms, double-occupancy, for twenty-five dollars. For that we get the Puerto Viejo Caribbean, just across the gravel road; three single beds with thin mattresses and threadbare linens; one yellow light bulb in the room; and one ceiling-mounted fan. As we lie in bed listening to the four Scandinavian girls giggle uncontrollably in the room below ours, it occurs to us that maybe we're missing entirely the point of coming here.

■

By 6 a.m. we're in the car and driving away from Puerto Viejo. We're hoping to get to Tortuguero today for the sole purpose of seeing turtles wash up in the surf, shuffle across the black sand beaches, and lay their eggs. I've seen this a hundred times on TV, but am assured that it's an experience not to be missed in real time. So we drive back halfway to San José and take the Cariari turn-off, northbound. We've heard that you can catch a bus from here that will eventually get you to a boat that in turn will get you to Tortuguero. We've heard there's no overland route to the village but we're not convinced, so follow the paved road for a half hour past Cariari until it ends. Then we spend another half hour bumping along unpaved paths through remote farmland until we can't take the jolting any more. We turn back and go to the bus depot in town, where we meet Rubén, the *bananero*. He runs a bus-boat-turtle-trek tour for twenty dollars per person and says he'll get us to Tortuguero today and back tomorrow. In a fit of boundless faith, we leave our rental 4x4 at the adjacent gas station and join the group.

There are only five of us who get on the bus at the main terminus in Cariari: Tracy, me, and three Spanish women. We're a little concerned about how *Bananero* will make money on a nearly-empty bus, but we worry needlessly. Moments later, the driver pulls into the "other" bus station, where a mob of locals is waiting for our bus. They pile in. A young man with arms the size of hams brings two machetes on the bus. We hope he is emotionally stable. Several women are going back home from the shopping and bring aboard bags of food and other things. A very pregnant young woman makes it on board but only long after the bus is packed even past standing room only. The man in the single seat in front of us rises and gives it to her. Everybody on the bus congratulates him. It's nice to see that common kindnesses happen here on *Bananero*'s bus. Tracy and I are exhausted, so we doze off occasionally during the long and bumpy ride on gravel and boulder roads. We stop often. Among the people we pick up later is another pregnant woman, this one holding a very young baby in her arms as well. I get up and offer her my seat. It's only then that I realize she is nursing the baby in her arms. She must have been in mid-feed when the bus rolled up. What incredible balance. Anyway, she asks for my hand because she can't move. I help her sit down. The baby's working like there's no tomorrow. Tracy has been asleep, but now wakes up face-to-face with a generous Costa Rican breast to which a child is attached. She's startled, of course, but only long enough to close her eyes and pretend she never woke up in the first place.

The bus stops at the gates of a banana plantation. These are everywhere here. We're asked to disembark and walk through an inch-deep disinfectant pond. It's to keep certain pests off the plantation. Everyone gets back on the bus and we drive another ten minutes through the banana orchards to *Rio la Suerte.* River Luck. The dock is a slippery muddy slope, at the bottom of which is a large flat-bottom fiberglass boat with an outboard motor. Twenty-five of us are going on to Tortuguero and we board the boat. This is five more people than it's designed to carry, but the genius of these tours is that the customer is never in a position to complain. The alternative is to stay here with the bananas and the pests that made it past the disinfectant moat. *Bananero* and his crew load the baggage in the front. Along with the passengers' bags and backpacks, there is a large armoire. We cast off and along the way see two two-toed sloths hanging from a tall tree. We see weird trees misshapen by the elements. One or two have been maimed by lightning. Most are overgrown with moss and bromeliads. We see crocodiles and iguanas and different birds and just one Jesus Christ lizard, known as such for its ability to scamper on the surface of the water. Of course we also see a great deal of the armoire.

Rio Suerte eventually joins the Penitencia Canal. Tortuguero village lies on the strip of land between the Caribbean and the canal. It's a swamp, really. On the boat we meet a young Dutch woman who says she used to work here for the organization that manages the national park. She turns back in her seat and wins our instant loyalty by guessing that we are not "serious backpackers," then recommends Morena's Cabinas. We pay twenty dollars. Our neighbors are out on the common porch. Some are reading. This reminds us a lot of Indonesia; there's mud, and mosquitoes, and rudimentary housing. A formidable dogfight breaks out nearby. There's a soccer match going on in the village pitch. Life in Tortuguero is very basic, simple, barefoot.

Tortuguero Arrivals Lounge

Gene comes by at 8 p.m., as promised. He's *Bananero's* sidekick and speaks pretty good English. It's pitch black. We can't see a thing. Gene is here to escort us to the beach so we can observe the famous turtles that gave the village its name. It's a good thing we hired him to do this. No lights are allowed on the beach after dark, to avoid spooking the turtles. We have to take their word on this. If I were a turtle in the throes of labor, and I've swum all the way back here to Tortuguero from wherever I've been, just to lay my eggs, it would take much more than a flashlight to turn me back into the surf. So we march behind Gene, absolutely blind. He is in dark clothing, and happens to be a black person. If we let him get more than three meters away, he disappears. We expect to tread on a frog or something else that can explode. Now down on the beach, we walk in the direction of the huge garbage fire. We had seen it earlier, in daylight, when it had not yet been set aflame. Half a dozen vultures were holding hands around it. Let us prey.

In the quivering light of this fire we see fifteen thousand other tourists, skulking in each other's shadows, waiting for a turtle to happen. Two hours later, the solitary mom who has decided to deliver tonight does so to a huge audience of awed spectators. Each group of us, led by their guide, takes a turn at the turtle's backside. The guide shines his red flashlight at the animal's tail and the hole it has dug beneath itself. Then, for a few moments, we watch as she squeezes out her hard-boiled cargo. Mostly they come two-at-a-squeeze. Sometimes just one. Regardless, there's plenty here for all of us. She'll shoot 160 of these before she's done. Then she'll cover up the ditch and head back out sea, where she will hunt down the boy turtle who made her go through this and poke his eyes out.

Volcán Arenál, Costa Rica, July 20

If you must fall ill in Central America, plan to be at Tabacón Resort just west of La Fortuna. By the time we arrive here, I can barely stand and Tracy is becoming just as sick. Still, we pluck up the energy to go to the thermal pools and soak for a while, thinking that might help our conditions. Tabacón is the premier resort in the Volcán Arenál neighborhood. Here's what they say about themselves in the elaborate four-color origami folded brochure and map:

Our 73 rooms and 9 junior suites are equipped with air conditioning, color television with satellite programming and private patios or balconies. Rooms are equipped with ice coolers, coffee makers and water. Ice machines are located on each building. All of these must be returned to the front desk at checkout time.

We consider pointing out the humor in this paragraph to the young ladies at the reception desk, but don't want to interrupt the gum-smacking. We're here and socked in. It hasn't stopped raining since we arrived. Folks tell us it's been this way for weeks. This is not much of a surprise. It's the height of the country's "green" season. In Australia they call it the "wet," but Costa Rica has dubbed it the "green" season in order not to scare away the tourists. And it works. We are here in force. The place is full. The thermal baths are especially busy, since the whole area is under clouds and fog and the highlight attraction, Volcán Arenál, is hidden.

By the morning of our second day at Tabacón, we realize that something is not right with our bodies, so ask for a doctor and they send us Teddy. Tracy thinks his name is Eric. I heard Teddy. In any case, this young man shows up at our room in a baseball cap and sneakers and a T-shirt that reads "Imperial." That's Costa Rica's most popular beer. He explains that he is a paramedic and that the actual doctor won't be on the property until 4 p.m. We don't mind, and invite him to bring in his toolkit and check us out. Turns out we're both running high fevers. Teddy prescribes immediate injections of Sodium Somethingorother in the butt. Injections in the butt are no longer fashionable in the U.S., unless they contain collagen, so we're a bit reticent but he promises that they will lower our temperatures and ease the crippling body aches. We spend the ensuing hours passed out, or watching TV, or on our knees thanking our gods that we are not in Puerto Viejo in this condition.

Costa Rica is a spectacularly beautiful country. We get another opportunity to appreciate this during the drive back to San José from Arenál. This road splits the Cordillera Central and the Cordillera Tillarán. It's a side-winding roller coaster through and up and over eternally green hills and down into misty river-run valleys. We much prefer this part of the country to the Caribbean coast. It's cleaner.

■

Back in San José, the folks at Gran Hotel Costa Rica are happy to see us. We're regulars now. As we settle back into the same room we had before leaving for the coast, the fourth floor under our feet ripples menacingly for a few extra-long seconds. We grab our irreplaceables and make for the stairs. Two nuns blast past us on the second floor, on their way down. This confirms our analysis, conducted throughout this world tour, of crowd behavior under stress. We have concluded that people fall into one of three categories:

- **Pushers**: These have one gear, fast forward, and can always be counted on to shove the others in front of them in order to get to the front of the line. Many Pushers are nuns. We first made this observation in Venice, but have since corroborated it a number of times. Most recently, we spotted three sisters squirreling through the queue at the Avianca desk in Caracas. And now the flying nuns in the stairwell. Also, with very few exceptions, all Latin and Mediterranean people are Pushers.

- **Blockers:** Parents and bulky people are the culprits here. We have nothing against either condition, but see the game and tell it like it is. The tactic is simple: Acquire and protect as much space as possible at all times. It works very well in narrow jetways and sky-bridges. French Polynesians are Blockers. So are Australians.

- **The English**: Undisputed exemplars of civilized crowd behavior, the English for centuries have set the standard for orderly queuing and embarking and disembarking and anything else having to do with buses, boats, planes and trains. The English are neither Blockers nor Pushers. They proceed at a moderate pace, unhurried yet jaunty, even when departing their colonies under fire.

We spend the entire evening and most of our first night back in San José coughing, taking each other's temperatures, and trying to ignore the hooker mooing next door in room 404. We both flirt with forty Celsius a couple of times, but manage the fever down with water, alcohol-soaked hand towels, and enough acetaminophen to julienne our stomach linings.

Managua, Nicaragua, July 25

Managua needs help. Maybe the entire country does. Nicaragua's ills are chronicled in the daily paper, and they're humdingers. The failure of this year's coffee crop has led to farmers around the country experiencing a famine. They can't sell coffee, they can't make money; so they can't eat. Many have descended on the capital looking for food. They want the government to declare a national emergency. We would declare a national emergency even without the famine.

There's a gang war going on in Managua. All we know is that these gangs have taken the streets of the old part of the capital, and that one of their members introduced himself to us by urinating on the wall of the food kiosk where he and his girlfriend would immediately thereafter order lunch. We were merely walking by. These are nasty people. None of this is aided by the weather. It's hotter than hell here, and as humid as the inside of a cow. During the day, every day, the temperature in Managua reaches the mid-thirties, Celsius. There aren't enough malls here for that kind of weather. The earth itself gives Nicaragua trouble. They get earthquakes here regularly, and they're always devastating. The 1972 shake destroyed all of downtown, and they haven't rebuilt because the area sits on a major fault. If you go to downtown Managua these days, you see wide open spaces, a few trees, a few squatters, and a lot of thugs.

How do I say this nicely? Managua may be one of the least hospitable places in the world, but we really didn't know that when we arrived from San José. We're met at the airport by the Hotel Intercontinental representative. It's hot and humid outside, and someone has thoughtfully made a giant tire fire in the distance. We see the billowing black smoke and smell the acrid gas. While we stand on the curb waiting for the shuttle to arrive, a girl of ten or so approaches us begging. She has only one eyeball. The other eye-socket is empty. Are we back in Bombay?

On the shuttle bus it's just the two of us and the driver. There's been an accident on the road leading to the airport, so the army has blocked off a half-kilometer of it, and all traffic is forced to squeeze through two lanes. It's a mess. Along the way our bus is attacked by beggars and window-washers at every traffic light. Shoeless children scamper up to the bus and bang on its sides for as long as we're stopped. One of the taller people manages to wash the entire windshield, but the driver gives him no money and the boy whacks the bus as we drive off. Lovely. Maybe this was a big mistake. Fortunately, the hotel is top-notch, one of the few buildings in the city to survive the 1972 quake. It was built in the sixties, we're told. Nice hotel, five stars, pool, gym, a couple of restaurants and a casino. Despite the heat, we decide to stroll from the hotel to the old city center. We want to see the ruins of the cathedral and some of the other buildings, but we don't get far. In the ten minutes that we're out there, we come to the conclusion that we must not only avoid walking at all, but that we must also leave this God-forsaken country and fast! So we start back in the direction of the hotel, but come across a cab along the way and board it. The taxi driver, as usual, is a nice man. He is wondering what the hell we're doing walking around. We ask him to drive us to the Plaza de la Republica. The taxi man knows what's good for us, however, so he goes right past the plaza and drives us to the strip of restaurants that line the Lake Managua corniche. They call this Malécon. It is utterly uninspiring, all the more so for the polluted backdrop of the lake. We ask the driver to take us back to the hotel. This is no place for us. It may be no place for anyone else, either, if they had the choice. As soon as we get back to the room we call Copa Airlines and move up our departure date to the twenty-seventh.

■

Pierre Gédéon picks us up at the Intercontinental in a shiny clean white van with Nicaragua Adventures painted on the sides. He's a young Frenchman, somewhere in his thirties. We get acquainted as he drives us out of town, southbound. We feel compelled to share with him our unpleasant impression of Managua. He listens patiently then asks if we really tried to walk to Plaza de la Republica. "And you survived?" These are his words, and he's lived here for nearly two years operating a tour company, so we figure he ought to know. Pierre assures us that what we see today will change our opinion of this country.

The first stop is at Masaya Volcano National Park. The park was established in 1979, the same year as the Sandinista revolution, in which Marxists came to power in the country. You may remember the Oliver North trials. He was skewered for leading a covert effort in the U.S. to support the Sandinistas' enemies, the rebel Contras. The civil war lasted throughout the eighties. Then the Contras came to power in elections. It's been liberals and moderates in power ever since, but many analysts feel that the Sandinistas, under Daniel Ortega, are poised to win the upcoming elections in November.

The volcano, like the revolution, often burned up sacrifices tossed to it by ignorant and superstitious residents of the area. The indigenous people believed that eruptions were a sign of the anger of the gods. Even the Spaniards, when they took over, believed that the devil resided in the volcano, so they erected a large cross at its mouth. The last "serious" eruption was in 1852. A "serious" eruption, we come to understand, is one during which several thousand people are killed or a new crater is formed, or both. So the thing that happened in April of this year, when van-sized boulders of fire were propelled into the air and came crashing down on actual vans, well, that was not serious. We mull this over as we walk up to the very lip of the Santiago Crater and peer over the edge. At first the bowl is filled with sulfur fumes,

288

but the smoke soon clears, and we get a clear view of the thing. Here's what the park brochure has to say about it:

> *An active crater could present some phenomena without advisement such as: emition of smokes, expulsions of rocks, sand and others. We advise you that gases irritate the eyes, the respiratory tract, affect people with asthma and diminish the visibility of the area. We recommend to keep away from the area.*

Well, we're already here, so we walk around the craters a while. We might as well be a million miles away from Managua. The air is fresh and clean, the hills are covered in green, and the distance is filled with Lake Nicaragua. They have a modest Visitor Information Center that makes up for the quality of its displays with an astonishingly peculiar bat room. Pierre explains that the bats just sort of moved in and took up residence one day. They like this room because it contains a replica of a cave. Pierre is amused to hear about the National Museum in Phnom Penh, where rabid bats have invaded and taken the attic. It's a small, bats-in-the-belfry world after all.

From Volcán Masaya we drive to La Catarina. This lovely village is perched on the rim of old and dormant Volcán Apoyo, whose crater is now a crystal clear lake. After taking in the view, we drive down and around the hill to Norome Resort. This place has a few cabins and a restaurant hidden in the woods on the lakeshore. Tracy and I put on our bathing suits and join some people who are already in the water. Turns out they're all Americans, here with a group called El Porvenir. They pay their own way to Nicaragua; they get put up in an old schoolhouse; and they spend their days building

Lago Nicaragua Retreat

latrines for local communities. We salute them and affirm that the world needs more of them and fewer of us. Then we cut out and rejoin Pierre for a lunch of grilled fish as we look over this spectacular place. He is right; there is some gorgeous, pristine country out here. We're glad we didn't immediately run screaming from Nicaragua.

After lunch we drive to Granada, the country's premier tourist town. A thunderstorm breaks over our heads just as we crest the top of the hill coming up from the lake. The road to Granada quickly turns into a river. This place was not affected by the devastating 1972 earthquake that flattened Managua, so there are many colonial buildings to see and the town has a much friendlier air. It's a little reminiscent of Colonia, in Uruguay. There are a few tourists here, practically the first we've seen all day. Beyond Granada is Lake Nicaragua. This body of water is 165 kilometers long and sixty across, so it's big enough to be a country.

Lake Nicaragua contains 350 or so islets. A few are large. One's even a volcano, but most are a few acres, just right for a house, swimming pool, and a few mango trees. It seems that there is a brisk business going on buying and selling these islands. Pierre says you can buy one of these for something between $10,000 and $50,000 then build a house on it for $30,000. Now you've got your very own private island getaway in Lake Nicaragua. When we get back to the dock and start the walk back up to the car, Pierre calls out to a woman in the small food kiosk, "Hey, where's your husband?" She answers that he's already left for Costa Rica. Pierre says, "What, escaping the next revolution?" Everybody chuckles, but like they're sitting on hot nails. It's understood that the lid could get blown off any stability that this country is enjoying now, and that it would take very little for that to happen. Maybe we'll wait a while for that private getaway.

We spend the whole day with Pierre. He does a great job of educating, feeding, and driving us safely around Nicaragua. Nice young man, and brave. He is one of a handful of expatriates who feel much more at home in faraway places like Nicaragua than they do at home. Do not come to Nicaragua if you don't have a Pierre here.

Guatemala City, Guatemala, July 28

Guatemala is the heart of the Maya world. This means a lot of interesting things, none of which include good food. And since we're one country away from being back in the U.S., we both have a paralyzing hunger for a good steak and a clean, fresh, cool salad. A salad that contains no bugs of any sort, no matter how microscopic; no hair; no rot; nothing but salad. Our hankering is a good sign because we've had no appetite since the Costa Rican flu nailed us two weeks ago. Truth is, getting good meals in Central America is not easy. They can be had, but you need to have done your homework, and to know where to go. In the meantime it's been hit or miss, mostly miss. Just to be sure, Tracy has emailed her sister Robin in L.A. and planted the idea of a steak dinner when we arrive. We are very happy to be here, nonetheless, and willing to wait for good food. That's because Guatemala has the incredibly attractive attribute of not being Nicaragua.

This trip around the world has taken us through a wonderful spectrum of cultures and societies. Some have been familiar, like the Romans and the Greeks and the Arabs, all societies which still exist and retain much of their original character. Others, like the indigenous Indian cultures of South and Central America, are surprises. From the Guaraní of Argentina, to the Aymara of Bolivia and the Quéchua of Peru, we've spent time among people whose impact on the world has been subtle if not trivial.

Now we're among the Maya. Half the population of Guatemala is indigenous Maya. A few archeological monuments remain a testament to their early success. Pyramids in the jungle. I personally know very little else about them. I know they weave. I also know that their most sacred text is something called the Popol Vuh. It chronicles the history of the Maya people during the heady days of their dominion over Mesoamerica. Then, right around 900 A.D. the Maya stopped being and were replaced by the Quiché, who took charge until the Spaniards came and spoiled everything. Some consider the Popol Vuh an exquisite pinnacle of native American literary achievement. I can see how that might happen. It's weird enough. Take only the Maya's view of the origin of man. Two gods, Gucumatz and Tepue, are the Creators. Being new to the business of making humans, they experimented a little. They made the first few men from mud, but these failed to hold on to their heads, which fell off. They also left unattractive footprints when they walked in the house. The gods then carved a couple of guys out of wood, but these were stiff and stupid, and had trouble smiling convincingly. Finally, during lab period, Gucumatz and Tepue stumbled across the perfect material: corn dough. No kidding. That is what the Popol Vuh puts forth as the theory of human creation. Okay, so it's cute. Really, though, can a people prosper if they still believe that they were made from maize? Of course not. That is why the majority of the Guatemalan population has transcended the Maize Man Theory. Now they're Catholic and believe that they come from a handful of dirt, except for women, who started life as a male rib.

The country's modern history reads like a tragicomedy of dictatorial failures. Idiot after idiot, despot after despot, men came to power in Guatemala, robbed the people blind, decimated every institution worth preserving, and laid the foundation for more future anguish. It's only in 1996 that the various combatants in a thirty-five-year civil war came to agreement on a peace that has so far held up. Read the newspaper, though, and you can't help but wonder if there isn't serious trouble on the horizon.

This is a restless time in Guatemala. The government just approved legislation that raises the Value Added Tax from ten percent to twelve percent. They've also introduced new excise on cigarettes and alcohol. Everyone's royally ticked. Tomorrow there is a national strike. All over the country people are staging protests and putting up roadblocks and burning things. This current political crisis, and it's a whopper, could spiral out of control. An assault here, a car bomb there, and before you know it no one will want to come and visit. That would be a shame. Even though we haven't been here very long, we have a good feeling about this place. It's stuck somewhere between what Bolivia is and what Venezuela has become. Not quite as naïve as the former, yet not nearly as tough and jaded as the latter. If the country can hold this spot for a while, gather up some of the guns that proliferate among the less desirable elements of society, and grow its tourism sector, it could easily become a gem.

We're staying at the Marriott in Zona 9. This neighborhood and the adjacent Zona 10 are the city's hippest. The ride from the airport is brief, but we can already tell that there is much more money here than in Nicaragua, or even Costa Rica. We check in and head out for a walk. Every American brand-name restaurant is in this neighborhood. We have a Champions in the hotel lobby, a McDonalds at the corner, a Schlotzky's Deli, a Chili's, and so on. There's a Gap store, and a Citibank, and a Häagen-Dazs ice cream parlor. There is also an army of guards, standing watch at the entrances of most of these establishments, prepared to blow away anyone making trouble. Every other Guatemalan male is a security guard. We've heard the parallel drawn before and agree: This is a lot like Mexico City. A few years ago I was having dinner at a fancy restaurant in the Zona Rosa of that city when an armored truck rolled up and disgorged a half a dozen men with sawed-off shotguns. These guys spread throughout the place, between the tables, while one of them retrieved and escorted to the truck a large bag of what I assumed was money. The whole operation took under two minutes. I might have been less alarmed had I known that the men were hired to do this by the restaurant, in order to avoid having large amounts of cash on the premises. Here in Zonas 9 and 10, Guatemala City is a relatively safe, pleasant place, but you can't miss the goons.

Elsewhere in the city, violence is not uncommon. A couple of days ago, on Saturday, a gang of robbers stopped traffic on one of the city's busy avenues then proceeded to shoot their way into a bank. They quickly killed two guards and two innocent bystanders. This is not to say that the guards were not also innocent. The poor bastards probably made five dollars a day to stand around brandishing their sawed-off shotguns, hoping like hell they'd never need to use them. In spite of this sort of thing, we feel safer here than we did in Managua. Maybe we're missing something.

Depending on whose guide you read, you might completely misunderstand a place like Guatemala City. We find it lovely here. For one thing, the weather is mild and pleasant. During the day it warms up enough that you can lie by the pool and sunbathe without being cold. At night it can be chilly, but just a bit. Pollution is surprisingly manageable. They still have fleets of big ugly buses and trucks that puke a trail of thick, black diesel fumes, and you can hate being in that, but there isn't the nasty smog of Santiago. Walking around Guatemala City is nice, particularly in Zonas 9 and 10, so we do a lot of that. In particular, we head out in search of the Popol Vuh Museum, anxious to diminish our deficiency in the area of Mayan history.

This excellent museum is actually in one of the buildings on the campus of the Universidad Francisco Marroquín. The exhibits are organized into the three main chronological periods of Mayan history, starting around 1000 B.C. and ending in the tenth century. They include pottery, burial urns, sculptures and maps. We stroll through the well-lit rooms chatting about how similar all this is to the other indigenous cultures of the Americas. We snap a few pictures but are soon busted by the matron who sold us the tickets. It seems there is a charge for using a camera. We didn't know, but are impressed that she magically knew we were doing so. It's calm and scholarly in here, and that precipitates a freak philosophical moment in which we chuckle at the inevitability of decline. Every culture we've met this past year has had its heyday. Each and every one has decayed. Some left important legacies, good or bad. Some are barely remembered and likely to become foggier still as time passes. We predict thick fog for the Maya.

The center of downtown Guatemala City, in Zona 1, is the Plaza Mayor. All around this central square are busy streets full of cars and shoppers and sidewalk food stalls. Like most other downtowns, this one supports an army of homeless, maimed, or otherwise disadvantaged folks. Every street corner has its panhandler. Every entrance and exit to the cathedral has its urchins, and everywhere you look go armies of armed men, in doorways, in driveways, in trucks. It's especially tense here today because of the debacle over the tax

Guatemala City Cathedral

increase. As we exit the taxi in front of the Palacio Nacional, a protest demonstration comes around the corner into the square. They're carrying large sheets that read "*No Mas Impuestos!*" "No More Taxes!" They're chanting those same words. The guards clustered at the entrance of the Palacio Nacional tense up and tighten their grips on their nightsticks. Interestingly, these guys are not armed. It makes sense that they wouldn't be. After all, the Palacio Nacional is now a museum, and unlikely to attract any serious violence.

The man responsible for erecting this colonnaded marble and wood edifice is General Jorge Ubico, the country's president between 1931 and 1944. It's arguable that he was the sole bright spot in the country's contemporary history until the nineties. You can imagine, as you walk through the halls of this beautiful building, how it must have represented to Ubico and the country a dream of progress. Now there are other buildings, especially in Zonas 9 and 10, which represent a new but familiar promise. These are tall glass and steel houses of banking and commerce. It's where tomorrow's Guatemala will grow up. The country is at a crossroads. Its future could be grand, or it could be terrible. One thing we can bank on: The earth will certainly shake again.

Antigua, Guatemala, August 1

Finally, a decent cup of coffee. We happen across Tostaduria Antigua as we walk from our hotel on the fringes of town toward its center. First we smell a sweet malty aroma that fills Calle 6. We wonder if someone's cooking something, but soon we're close enough and here it is. The place is a tiny storefront on the corner of Calle 6 and Avenida 7. It has one small but tall wooden door on each street. Both are open, and the smoke from the roaster exits into Calle 6 and floats back in on Avenida 7, luring in addicts as it does. We walk inside. It's a bit dark. There are three rough, small wooden tables and a few chairs. The roaster is in the corner, and it looks like it could blow any minute. The counter has several wood-frame glass boxes that contain coffee beans. A large mural of Guatemala covers one of the walls. The floor is littered with large burlap bags of coffee. There is one man in the place. He's reading the paper, drinking a cup of coffee, and eating Dunkin Donuts. He's Antonio, the owner, and makes me the best cup of coffee I've had in a very, very long time. Antonio is from California and has been in Antigua for ten years. He says that the place has changed a lot in that time. More people, more cars, a few Mercedes' even. He can't figure it out. There can't be that much money in coffee cultivation.

This village is our favorite spot in Central America. It's an oasis of calm in an otherwise berserk isthmus, but you don't have to live in a hammock and suffer the absence of all services in order to be here. In this sense, it's a lot like Cuzco, where there are banks and Internet cafés and hip grocery stores and restaurants. More good news: It's a lot cleaner than Cuzco. We think that the majority of tourists here are Guatemala City folks or Americans, but there are also visitors from all over the world. We catch French, German, Dutch and a Scandinavian language that we can't be more specific about. There are no tall buildings in Antigua. The highest have two floors. As we stroll around town, we always have a big sky overhead, and can see the three volcanoes that guard the city: *Fuego* (fire), *Agua* (water) and *Acatenango* (no idea). The streets are all cobbled and the houses are painted dusty colors like rose and rust and sea green. The whole city is like this, ten square blocks of rustic seren-ity. The Plaza de Armas is the central gathering place for locals and visitors alike. At each corner of the square there are hand-painted yet very official signs declaring the rules of the place, in Spanish and English:

> *No use of bicycles*
> *No topless or bottomless*
> *No public games*
> *No putting of feet on benches*
> *No lying on the grass*
> *No climbing of trees*
> *No washing in fountain*
> *No spitting or pissing*
> *No erecting of kiosks*
> *No picnics*

We find a bench in the sun and watch the public. It looks like there is general agreement that this place, unlike its analogs nearly everywhere else we've been, will stay clean and pleasant. All the rules are observed.

Young adorable children in native Mayan dress peddle trinkets and handicrafts to the tourists. Two men, the older of whom looks like he could have been planted here by the Antigua Tourism Association, are engaged in an animated conversation. Flocks of students going home from school pass in front of us, all polite, all clean, all in uniforms. Catholic school. The tourists are easily recognizable and unusually circumspect. We watch a young blond woman start to put her feet up on the bench she occupies. She quickly realizes her potential offense and sits up straight. At the other end of the square an orange-haired Japanese boy and a barefoot American girl are standing ten meters apart, tossing beanbags back and forth to each other. So far they're being tolerated, but we can see one of the local policemen scratching his chin, formulating a rebuke.

Plaza de Armas is surrounded on three sides by two-story colonial-style buildings that house the town hall, a few shops, and a tourist information office. On the fourth side is the Catedral de Santiago. Like all structures dating from colonial times, this building has often been destroyed by earthquakes and then rebuilt, but there comes a time when people figure out that there is no point in rebuilding. That point was reached here in 1773. Today you can worship in what was once the narthex of the original cathedral. The rest of it is in ruins, converted to a museum of sorts. For three quetzales, or eighty cents, you can walk around the vast place. There's no roof, and it seems that someone started then stopped a reconstruction project. New brickwork rises from the old walls but doesn't get very far. In some corners there are cracked remains of angels in niches. We walk down to the dank crypt to investigate the advertised remains of nameless *conquistadores*, but see nothing and get spooked at the thought of getting buried down here by a sudden quake.

We're happy to be here for a couple of reasons. First, it's such a lovely place. Second, today is a national general strike. This has been organized by the country's various labor organizations in protest over the recently approved tax increase. It's likely there will be trouble, and we'd rather be in bucolic Antigua than in Guatemala City, where angry protesters were already burning the U.S. ambassador in effigy even before we left to come here. Still, as we stroll around town this morning, we see posters all over declaring this "National Dignity Day." Guatemalan flags and black banners are draped across the shut front doors of businesses. The Bagel Barn, at which we were hoping to get breakfast, is closed. We

Volcan Aguas, Antigua

figure Antonio's roastery will be as well and head back to the hotel, where we spend the day at poolside.

As the day wears on we decide to go out for a stroll and see what, if anything, has happened in town. Turns out, nothing. People are out and about, local artisans are selling their work in the squares, and several restaurants are open for business. We wind up having a delicious late lunch at La Posada de Don Rodrigo. Whole grilled fish, filet mignon, and fresh-baked corn tortillas that are being clapped out just as fast as possible by a diminutive young woman in the garden adjacent to the patio where we're eating.

■

Our hunch that Antigua would be a better place to pass the day of the strike was a good one. Today's paper lists the various protests and other disturbances that swept the country. There was a march in Antigua as well, but it was peaceful and dispersed in time for lunch. In Guatemala City, however, the Plaza Mayor was the scene of violent confrontations. Hundreds were arrested. Other cities around the country also saw their share of trouble. In the evening, President Portillo interrupted all broadcasting to deliver an impassioned ten-minute speech to the people of Guatemala. He's a good speaker, emotional, articulate, and appears sincere. His point is that the increase in the Value Added Tax is needed to avert a budget deficit, the results of which would be catastrophic for the country. As for the excise on cigarettes and booze, he says that the people who use the two products and get sick and rely on the government to pay for their treatment should be the ones to pay for it. He wags his finger at the camera a lot and threatens to imprison people who do not pay. He acknowledges his opponents' concern about state corruption but says his is not the first government to have corrupt officials, and promises to jail anyone caught messing around. I'm convinced. He makes sense. Unfortunately, the great majority of Guatemalans don't buy it. We'll never know who's right and who's wrong, but it looks like the tax increase is here to stay. It also looks like there is a large affiliation of powers that wants to make this Portillo's Waterloo. We just want to get out of the country before anyone does anything rash.

Belize City, Belize, August 5

We're flying Grupo Taca again, on our way to Belize with a planeload of folks who truly represent the country's wonderful ethnic mix. We have Rastafarians, Creoles, Garifunas, Mestizos, and Mayas. The only significant group not represented on the plane is the Mennonites, but I don't think they're allowed to fly in anything but horse-drawn wagons.

Belize Creoles are a mix of Africans and English. Mestizos are a mix of Spanish and Indians. Garifunas are black Carib Indians, but to us, the most interesting component of Belize's ethnic mix is the Rastafarians. Here's what you believe if you happen to be *Rasta*:

- Haile Selassie, now-dead once-Emperor of Ethiopia, is God. They call him "*Jah*." The emperor himself, back when he was alive, was not aware of his most divine status. A group of Rastas went to Addis Ababa to honor him, but they were turned away at the palace gates. Haile, it turns out, was a devout Christian. This did not discourage the faithful Rastas, but actually strengthened their commitment. After all, God isn't supposed to know he's God, is he?

- The Christian Bible is used for "guidance" in much the same way as it is by TV evangelists, that is to say, hilariously.

- Ganja, grass, marijuana, is a blessed weed that can and must be consumed on the road to enlightenment. To validate this belief, Rastas have scoured the Bible for any phrase that contains the word "herb" in a flattering context.

- Whites as a group are oppressors and the enemy. Rastas call them the Empire of Babylon.

- Heaven is in Ethiopia. On *Jah*'s signal (by then we assume that *Jah* will know that he is *Jah* and will indeed give the awaited signal), blacks around the world will begin a final exodus there, from wherever they happen to be at the time.

- Hair must be worn in dreadlocks, which grow to represent and resemble blacks' roots in Africa. This is a badly misunderstood hairstyle. Although at first glance it looks like something that can be cultivated by anyone with frizzy hair and an aversion to water, it is in fact a much more complex undertaking. You can acquire "dreads" through specialized techniques including Back-Combing, Wool Hat Rubbing, Neglect, Perming and Twisting. I'm not making this up.

We're nearly all out of cash. So as soon as we arrive at the Radisson Fort George in Belize City, we ask if there is an ATM nearby. There isn't. For that, we're informed by the languid front desk clerk, you have to walk to downtown. So we do. This should not be encouraged. Belize's Tourism Association ought to advise any and all visitors to the country against visiting downtown Belize City. It's an unbridled mess. The streets are lined with a startling array of strange and dangerous characters. And on top of that, there seems to be stagnant standing water along every sidewalk. Drunks fold over in doorways. The concrete obelisk at Regent and Albert streets reads ninety-seven degrees, Fahrenheit. It's hot and sweaty and smelly and ugly. Every Belizean with an infirmity or deformity is here. The sun is hot and bright, so shops look even darker and danker inside than they really are. We do find a money machine and make a withdrawal, then immediately start back to the hotel. In a moment of innocent optimism we walk into a supermarket to buy a couple of bottles of water, but last a couple of minutes before turning tail and bolting out of there. There is no air-conditioning and the stench from the butcher in the back of the building is crushing. As we make our way back to the Radisson, we seriously discuss the possibility of just grabbing our bags, taking a taxi to the airport, and flying to Los Angeles.

■

This morning we're on a bus with two other Americans, men from San Francisco, on our way to the ancient city of Lamanai. This is one of many Maya ruins that dot Central America from El Salvador to Mexico. We head north to Orange Walk on the New Northern Highway. It's "New" because the old one got washed away by a hurricane, not sure which. Anyone you meet in Belize will mention at least three hurricanes: Hattie, Mitch, and Keith, in order of chronological occurrence. Mario, our guide, spends a couple of minutes discussing each. Keith is the most recent. Mario says those were the scariest three days of his life. The storm just sat on top of the Cayes and blew and rained. He saw palm trees lean all the way down to the ground, then straighten up again. Some were uprooted. Many buildings were destroyed. People took shelter in the few concrete buildings and the churches. Belizeans by and large want to stay in Belize. They like it here, even if they're not doing well economically and even if the next killer hurricane is a matter of time. Hattie, Mitch, and Keith all happened in October. If I were living here, I'd spend my Octobers in Norway.

Now that we're out of Belize City, the countryside is predictably lovely. The homes along the road are shanties, really, but that's the style here. You don't need much protection from the elements; it's warm all the time. An hour and a half later we arrive in the community of Orange Walk. Here we leave the bus and get on a small powerboat, also piloted by Mario, for another hour and a half on the New River to the Lamanai site. Every few minutes Mario cuts the motor and points out a bird or a monkey or a lizard that he has managed to spot. We see cormorants and swallows and heron. We also see Jesus Christ birds, as they are known for their ability to walk on water. Actually they walk on water-lily leaves, unlike Jesus Christ lizards that in fact walk on actual water, but only at high speed and for short distances.

Lamanai is a Mayan city that was built and occupied over a period of three thousand years, starting all the way back in 1500 B.C. It still had residents as late as the 1800s A.D. What's left is a number of pyramids. Some are now just mounds, buried in jungle and soil. We stroll along the well-maintained path in the jungle, fighting off mosquitoes and other bugs that do not recognize insect repellent. Along these walks, between the ruins, it's thick jungle. Enough so that two pairs of black howler monkeys are sprawled out in the branches of the tall trees right where we can see them. Most of the time there's no one here but them. At the largest of the pyramids, I climb up to the very top. There are broad steps at the bottom, but these disintegrate halfway up and you have to pull yourself by a rope the rest of the way. It's well worth it. From up here you get a spectacular view of the world above the jungle canopy. Maya society collapsed, inexplicably, around 900 A.D. You could hypothesize that they spent all their money on pyramids.

Caye Caulker, Belize, August 8

The Longest Barrier Reef in the Western Hemisphere runs for three hundred or so kilometers along the Belize, Guatemala and Honduras east coasts. Some people call it the Maya Reef. Caye Caulker is one of three major islands that emerge from the reef. To get here we make our way to the Belize Marine Terminal at the north end of the Swing Bridge. We buy our tickets, $12.50 each roundtrip, and then scuffle with the other passengers for a seat on the powerboat. These are operated several times a day and make the run between Belize City and the Cayes. Other boats go to Guatemala or north to the Yucatan peninsula in Mexico. This morning's boatful is a cross-section of Belizean society. Half the forty or so passengers are tourists from all over: A couple of Italian women, three older American men, one Spanish-speaking family, complete with suckling child, and one albino young man from France. We know he's French because he's carrying a copy of *Le Guide Vert de Belize*. He is cooked to a bright, nearly florescent pink, and his eyelids are painfully ripe.

We all look our best. That happens when you're on a speedboat. The wind forces heroic expressions on our faces: eyes slit; chins out, slightly elevated; mouths fixed resolutely; hair carried on the breeze. We're moving, crossing the waters. There's no canopy on the boat, so the sun blinds as it bakes us further. Albino Boy is pain personified. It's good to see young people from around the world go to this much trouble to see the rest of the planet. In sharp contrast is a wrinkled old Caribbean buzzard sitting across from us. You can't tell how old this guy is. His slight patchy beard is white, but his thin straggly hair, blowing around like a weather-beaten flag, is dishwater blond. His skin is leathery, brown, wrinkled like an iguana's. He has made this trip many times and yawns wide as we cast off, his head down, in his own world. The flip-flops, the old shorts, the tank top, and the solitary shark's tooth earring all say "tax evasion." Next to him is a very black Belizean youth with gang insignia tattoos and a red headscarf. This man's wife is traveling with him, and she's pregnant. They're being very tender, kissing and cuddling and chuckling. Our captain could be a high school math

Front Street

teacher, originally from India or its vicinity. Very proper and businesslike, he delivers a welcome speech in which he informs this assorted gathering that anyone sticking a finger off the side of the boat is likely to lose it. Six crates of bananas sit in the middle of the boat.

We immediately fall for Caye Caulker. There are two north-south thoroughfares: Front Street by the water and Back Street one block away. Folks stroll in the middle of these "streets" that are really sandy paths. In sandals, shorts and T-shirt, you'd be two items of clothing heavier than most. We grab our bags and walk the five minutes from the dock to the Tropical Paradise Hotel. Fifty dollars a night gets us a cabana right on the beach, air conditioning, private bath, cable TV, a fridge in the room, and ants, lots of tiny little red ants. We check in and go for a stroll around the neighborhood, such as it is. The houses here are mostly made from wood, up on stilts. Nothing looks permanent. We come back to the hotel and walk down the finger pier in front of it. A young man and woman are in deck chairs on the dock, looking out on the Caribbean. We say hi and they hi back. They're English, and teachers, here for a couple of weeks from Cambridge. They're staying at the less expensive hotel next door but like this dock and the chairs. We promise not to give them away, so they tell us that the lobster burritos at the Tropical Paradise restaurant are the best in town. Then they tell us that there's a guy who docks his sailboat here every evening, and offers sailing trips to fabulous snorkeling spots along the barrier reef. It's like that here. Everyone is friendly, helpful. It's stereotypically Caribbean in attitude and temperament, but not swampy like the Costa Rican coast. Just right. As we stroll along Front Street, a raccoon, someone's pet, pops out from behind a low fence and accompanies us for a couple of blocks.

Some very young children in shorts are in the alley, playing in a tiny mud puddle. The boys in the group grab handfuls of the sandy white mud and paint their bellies with it. The girls stand to the side being delicate, but think about joining in. Soon the mud painting turns to mud slinging and then fisticuffs. They don't want to hurt each other, but there are girls here after all, and territory to mark. The blows land exclusively on air. After a few moments someone's mother responds to the commotion and hoses the boys down. Each retrieves his toy and moves on. One boy walks toward the beach with his fishing rod. Another, hair in cornrows, mounts his too-small Kenton bicycle and rides away as if he's expected at a very important meeting. The girls must live here because they stay put, still unmuddied. That's the news from Caye Caulker.

■

This morning we're going snorkeling. Harry is our tour guide and boatman. He's Garifuna, an African-Indian mix that happens along Central America's Caribbean coast. He seems perfectly content. When he's not talking, he sings reggae songs to himself. Nothing is urgent. Life is simple, good. Our companions on this trip include a Dutch couple, an English couple, and a single skinny fellow who says not one word. Our first stop is at Hol Chan Marine Reserve. *Hol chan* is Mayan for "small channel," we are told. We all strap on our snorkels and jump in the perfectly calm, clear, warm water. Harry leads us on a breathtaking tour of the reef. He carries a baton of sorts, and uses it to point out the marine life. Stick a couple of gills on this guy and he could live down here. There is a tradition of free diving on Belize. The young men who do it grow up picking lobsters off the reef. It's illegal to do so in scuba gear, so they free dive. Harry goes below and stays under water for a couple of minutes at a time, socializing with the morays and the angels and the barracudas. We see everything but sharks. Then, as we drift along the northern side of the channel by the reef slope, a large manatee comes walking on the sandy seabed across the channel in our direction. He is literally walking, using his front fins like feet, one in front of the other. As he approaches us he speeds up to a silly run and launches himself a few inches above the sandy bottom, then swims right under Tracy and me before pulling a U-turn and going back across the channel. Manatees are much more graceful swimmers than they are walkers. Also interesting about them is that the female's nipples are in her armpits. She nurses her young in a headlock.

After lunch we head back out to the reef and stop at Shark and Ray Alley. We pull up to the buoy that marks the spot and Harry starts tossing bits of dead fish overboard. Ours is the only boat in the vicinity and within seconds there's a cloud of sharks and stingrays under it. We fall—yes, with some trepidation—in with them. This may sound nuts, but these are nurse sharks, a harmless species that we've been around before. Soon three other boats pull up and we wind up with a colossal underwater traffic jam. There must be forty snorkelers here, twenty sharks, and ten rays. As promised, Harry ambushes a ray and holds him while we all give the animal a pat. It feels like you might expect, smooth, slippery, like wet leather. Then he buttonholes a shark, and we feel it up. Its skin is rougher

Caye Caulker

than we expect, like sandpaper. Even its belly is like that. This particular specimen is more like a child than a shark. It lays there in Harry's arms, happy to be fondled by the gang. Pet shark. That's Belize.

As soon as we figure out how to do it, we're moving to Caye Caulker and opening a place offering lobster barbecue, classical music, fresh roast coffee, snorkeling tours, and *pathra sweda* massage. We'll make a mint. We'll buy a boat. We'll save the manatees.

Los Angeles, California, August 12

It's good to be back.

The U.S. is different when you've been overseas for a whole year. Immediately on arriving in Dallas airport, we notice the abundance. We notice that people are bigger and healthier than we've seen in a while. Taller, heftier, stronger. We notice a hundred things that happen only when there is an excess of prosperity. Like dental braces and forty kinds of turkey sandwiches and designer clothes and ubiquitous laptop computers and enough luggage carts for everybody. Everything is cleaner and newer and shinier and people leave each other alone. As we wait for our connecting flight to LA, we drift into a sort of mild, dizzy shock. The contrast between this and most of the rest of the world is startling, almost unbelievable.

Tracy's sister Robin, her husband John, and their baby girl Elena live in Hermosa Beach, one of several seaside communities in LA's South Bay. They are quintessentially American. They come of European origin, varying generations ago. They're handsome and smart. They're hospitable and generous and welcoming. The house they live in is impeccable, comfortable, bright, spacious. The newspaper is delivered to the back door every morning. There's a trash compactor and "Insinkerator" and Krups coffee maker and grinder in the kitchen. The fridge contains a bag of Guatemalan coffee beans and dispenses cool, clean drinking water with which to make delicious, strong coffee. They have cathedral ceilings and blond wood dining room furniture and TVs and stereos and computers. Everything looks and smells great. They have two cars, either of which could be considered luxurious. The weather here is temperate. There are no bugs. Certainly no mosquitoes and that is such a nice change. From the patio off the second floor of their house, we have a panoramic view of the Pacific. The sense that we are in one of the world's largest cities is completely absent. It feels more like a small, familiar coastal community. The houses are cute, the streets are clean and quiet, and become pedestrian-only walks for the one or two blocks nearest the beach. Nicely tanned walkers and joggers and inline skaters and mothers pushing fancy strollers come and go on the paved promenade along the waterfront. You can take your pick from any number of restaurants. You can surf, swim, or just sit and contemplate the waves as they caress the clean sandy beach. There are no crocodiles here. No snakes, no snake-charmers, and no Iranian smugglers.

Nine out of ten people brought here from anywhere else in the world would consider this heaven. We do. For our first lunch back in the U.S., John barbecues enormous porterhouse steaks while Robin makes a fresh salad.

■

Epilogue

It took us almost exactly one year to circumnavigate the globe. The scale of the undertaking can boggle the mind, so here's a breakdown by the numbers:

Continents:	6 (Antarctica was closed for repairs)
Oceans:	4 (there are no Hiltons in the Arctic)
Seas:	25
Countries:	45
Capitals:	35
Hotels:	101
Stays with Friends/Family:	11 (not once evicted)
Food Poisonings:	1 (but it was a whopper)
Bad Cases of the Flu:	1
Mosquito Bites:	356,000,000
Flights:	30
Ferries:	14
Trains:	8
Motorcycles Ridden:	11
Motorcycles Lost:	1 (still at Bombay Sahar Cargo Complex)
Cars Rented:	12
Camper Vans Rented:	1
Elephant Rides:	1
Camel Rides:	2
Horseback Rides:	3
Air Miles:	34,000 (lots of zigzagging)
Land Miles:	18,000 (ditto)
Sea Miles:	1,400
Scuba Dives:	38
Sharks Petted Intentionally:	1
Unintentionally:	1
Speeding Tickets:	5
Officials Bribed:	12,590
Bungee Jumps:	1
Hang Glides:	1
Helicopter Trips:	1
Words Written:	280,000
Photos Taken:	18,000

We're ready to go again.

■

The road is life.

— Jack Kerouac (1922–1969), U.S. author

■

about the author

Rif Haffar is an American telecom executive, businessman, traveler, author and humorist. He received his early education in the Middle East and England before immigrating to the US in 1978 and earning an MBA from Portland State University. Mr. Haffar has lived in Beirut, Damascus, London, Singapore, New York, Washington, DC, Portland, OR, and Seattle. He speaks four languages. His professional life has included careers in construction, restaurants, horticulture, video production, and telecommunications. Most recently, he was Executive Vice President of Marketing and Business Development at a New York telecommunications company. Whatever else he happened to be doing, he has always traveled widely. These travels have taken him to nearly 100 countries on six continents. He has twice circumnavigated the globe and crossed three continents entirely by motorcycle. This is his first book.

■ bibliography ■

Bosrock, Mary Murray. *South America: A Fearless Guide To International Communication And Behavior*. St. Paul, Minn.: International Education Systems, 1997.

Bowker, John Westerdale. *World Religions*. New York: DK Pub., 1997.

Bryson, Bill. *A Walk In The Woods: Rediscovering America On The Appalachian Trail*. New York: Broadway Books, 1998.

Buckles, Guy. *The Dive Sites Of Indonesia: Comprehensive Coverage Of Diving And Snorkeling*. Lincolnwood, IL: National Textbook Company, 1998.

Calvert, Peter. *Revolution And Counter-Revolution*. Milton Keynes: Open University Press, 1990.

Cohen, David Elliot. *One Year Off: Leaving It All Behind For A Round-The-World Journey With Our Children*. New York: Simon and Schuster, 1999.

Coleman, Neville. *The Dive Sites of the Great Barrier Reef and the Coral Sea*. McGraw Hill–NTC, 1997.

———. *A Look at Wildlife of the Great Barrier Reef*. Rushcutters Bay, N.S.W.: Bay Books, 1978.

Cronin, Lynda. *Midlife Runaway: A Grown Ups' Guide To Taking A Year Off*. Toronto: Macmillan Canada, 2000.

Halstead, Bruce W. *Dangerous Marine Animals: That Bite, Sting, Shock, or Are Non-Edible*, 3rd ed. Centreville, Md.: Cornell Maritime Press, 1995.

Hasbrouck, Edward. *The Practical Nomad: How To Travel Around The World*, 2nd ed. Emeryville, CA: Avalon Travel Pub. Distributed in the U.S. and Canada by Publishers Group West, 2000.

Heat Moon, William Least. *Blue Highways: A Journey into America*. Boston: Back Bay Books, 1999.

Hough, David L. *Proficient Motorcycling: The Ultimate Guide To Riding Well*. Irvine, Calif.: Bow Tie Press, 2000.

Hughes, Robert. *The Fatal Shore*. New York: Vintage Books, 1988.

Ibn Batuta, 1304–1377. *The travels of Ibn Battuta, A.D. 1325–1354 / translated with revisions and notes from the Arabic text edited by C. Defrémery and B.R. Sanguinetti ; C.F. Beckingham. Tuhfat al-nuzzar f'i ghar-a'ib al-ams-ar wa-`aj-a'ib al-asf-ar.* English. Selections. London: Hakluyt Society, 1994.

Kadodwala, Dilip. *Hinduism*. New York: Thomson Learning, 1995.

Kristal, Efraín. *The Andes Viewed From The City: Literary And Political Discourse On The Indian In Peru, 1848–1930*. New York: P. Lang, 1987.

Lansky, Doug, ed. *Travelers' Tales Guides: Best of Travel Humor and Misadventure*. Travelers' Tales Inc.: San Francisco, 1998.

Lawson, Wendy, ed. *Great Highways of the World*. Skokie, IL: Rand McNally, 1995

Libbon, Robert P. *Instant European History: From The French Revolution To The Cold War*. New York: Fawcett Columbine, 1996.

Lyon, James, Andrew Draffen, Krzysztof Dydynski, Conner Gorry, and Mark Plotkin. *Lonely Planet South America on a Shoestring*, 7th ed. Oakland: Lonely Planet, 2000.

Marx, Karl. *The Communist Manifesto*. New York: Oxford University Press, 1998.

McAleavy, Tony. *Modern World History: International Relations From The First World War To The Present*. New York: Cambridge University Press, 1996.

Microsoft Encarta Encyclopedia Deluxe 2001. Seattle, WA: Microsoft.

Morris, Arthur Stephen. *South America: A Changing Continent*, 4th ed. London: Hodder and Stoughton Educational, 1995.

Murphey, Rhoads. *A History of Asia*, 3rd ed. New York: Longman, 1999.

O'Byrne, Denis, Jon Murray, and Paul Harding. *Lonely Planet Australia*, 10th ed. Oakland: Lonely Planet, 2000.

O'Rourke, P. J. *Holidays In Hell*. New York: Vintage Books, 1989.

Pelton, Robert Young. *Robert Young Pelton's The World's Most Dangerous Places*, 4th ed. New York: Harper Resource, 2000.

Pirsig, Robert M. *Zen and the Art of Motorcycle Maintenance: An Inquiry into Values*, Quill ed. New York: W. Morrow, 1999.

Robinson Mark, ed. *Corruption And Development*. Portland, OR: F. Cass, 1998.

Rogers, Jim. *Investment Biker: Around the World with Jim Rogers.* Holbrook, Mass.: Adams Pub., 1995.

Stevens, Thomas. *Around The World on a Bicycle: From San Francisco to Yokohama.* London: Century, 1988.

Symmes, Patrick. *Chasing Che: A Motorcycle Journey In Search Of The Guevara Legend.* New York: Vintage Books, 2000.

Twain, Mark. *The Innocents Abroad, Or, the New Pilgrims' Progress; Being Some Account of the Steamship Quaker City's Pleasure Excursion to Europe and the Holy Land.* Pleasantville, N.Y.: Reader's Digest Association, c1990.

Williams, Jeff, Christine Niven, and Peter Turner. *Lonely Planet New Zealand,* 10th ed. Oakland: Lonely Planet, 2000.

index